A CULTURAL HISTORY OF SEXUALITY

VOLUME 1

A Cultural History of Sexuality

General Editor: Julie Peakman

Volume 1

A Cultural History of Sexuality in the Classical World
Edited by Mark Golden and Peter Toohey

Volume 2

A Cultural History of Sexuality in the Middle Ages
Edited by Ruth Evans

Volume 3

A Cultural History of Sexuality in the Renaissance
Edited by Bette Talvacchia

Volume 4

A Cultural History of Sexuality in the Enlightenment
Edited by Julie Peakman

Volume 5

A Cultural History of Sexuality in the Age of Empire
Edited by Chiara Beccalossi and Ivan Crozier

Volume 6

A Cultural History of Sexuality in the Modern Age
Edited by Gert Hekma

A CULTURAL HISTORY

OF SEXUALITY

IN THE CLASSICAL WORLD

Edited by Mark Golden and Peter Toohey

Oxford • New York

English edition
First published in 2011 by
Berg

Editorial offices:
First Floor, Angel Court, 81 St Clements Street, Oxford OX4 1AW, UK
175 Fifth Avenue, New York, NY 10010, USA

Berg is the imprint of Oxford International Publishers Ltd.

Library of Congress Cataloging-in-Publication Data

A catalogue record for this book is available from the Library of Congress.

British Library Cataloging-in-Publication Data

A catalogue record for this book is available from the British Library.

ISBN 978-1-84788-800-6 (volume 1)
      978-1-84520-702-1 (set)

Typeset by Apex CoVantage, LLC, Madison, WI, USA.

Printed in the UK by the MPG Books Group.

www.bergpublishers.com

CONTENTS

PREFACE

A *Cultural History of Sexuality* is a six-volume series reviewing changes in sexual attitudes and behavior throughout history. Each volume follows the same basic structure and begins with an outline account of sexuality in the period under consideration. Academic experts examine major aspects of sex and sexuality under seven key headings: heterosexuality, homosexuality, sexual variations, religion and the law, medicine and disease, popular beliefs and culture, prostitution, and erotica. Readers can choose a synchronic or a diachronic approach to the material—a single volume can be read to obtain a thorough knowledge of the body in a given period, or one of the seven themes can be followed through time by reading the relevant chapters of all six volumes, providing a thematic understanding of changes and developments over the long term. The six volumes divide the history of sexuality as follows:

> Volume 1: A Cultural History of Sexuality in the Classical World (800 B.C.E. to 350 C.E.)
>
> Volume 2: A Cultural History of Sexuality in the Middle Ages (350 C.E. to 1450)
>
> Volume 3: A Cultural History of Sexuality in the Renaissance (1450 to 1650)
>
> Volume 4: A Cultural History of Sexuality in the Enlightenment (1650 to 1820)
>
> Volume 5: A Cultural History of Sexuality in the Age of Empire (1820 to 1920)
>
> Volume 6: A Cultural History of Sexuality in the Modern Age (1920 to 2000)

Julie Peakman, General Editor

SERIES ACKNOWLEDGMENTS

This series has been a long time in the making, mainly because it is not an easy task to bring together fifty-four international scholars, even when they are all willing and eager. Every one of us had other commitments—to our universities, to other books, to our families. I therefore appreciate those who came together to create this special project. I want to thank the editors of all the volumes—Peter Toohey and Mark Golden, Ruth Evans, Bette Talvacchia, Ivan Crozier and Chiara Beccalossi, and Gert Hekma—for their sterling efforts in the face of my continual demands, and for helping to keep their contributors on track, especially when the occasional one dropped out with little warning. Huge thanks also go to all the contributors who freely contributed their time and efforts. I also want to thank Tristan Palmer at Berg for all his support, and Catherine Draycott from the Wellcome Trust Picture Library for making available the Wellcome images.

Julie Peakman, General Editor

ACKNOWLEDGMENTS

Mark Golden and Peter Toohey would like to thank Julie Peakman for all of her assistance. Mark Golden would particularly like to acknowledge Peter Golden and Charlotte Bell for always making their homes his own; and Peter Toohey acknowledges the Killam Trust for a resident fellowship at the University of Calgary during which his part of the work was completed.

Saying good-bye to sex was like waking up from a delirium, a tropical fever, into a world of cool, Canadian breezes. Good riddance.

—Richard Russo, *Empire Falls* (New York 2001), 127

ILLUSTRATIONS

CHAPTER 4

CHAPTER 8

CHAPTER ONE

Introduction

MARK GOLDEN AND PETER TOOHEY

HOMER, SUMMING IT ALL UP

In the fourteenth book of Homer's *Iliad*, the goddess Hera gazes down from Olympus to the battlefield far below. Things are not going well for her beloved Greeks; the Trojans have forced them back from the walls of Troy to the ships drawn up along the seashore. Poseidon, taking on human form, spurs the Greeks to resist, but his efforts are limited by Zeus's commands: the gods are to take no part in the fighting. It is time for Hera to take matters—as well as the master of the gods—into her own hands. She resolves to seduce her husband, and so leave the field clear for Poseidon and the Greeks. In her private chamber, Hera prepares herself: she washes, anoints her body with olive oil, combs and arranges her hair, puts on an embroidered robe and sandals, and adds accessories (a golden brooch, a belt with one hundred tassels, earrings, a veil). She then borrows from Aphrodite a *kestos himas*, a magic strip of leather the sex goddess wears around her breasts (or her waist) that is furnished with all enchantments—"love, desire, the whispered endearment that steals the good judgment from even the sensible" (*Il.* 14.197–8).[1] Though she pretends it will be used to reconcile Oceanus and Tethys, older divinities in need of marriage counseling, Hera has actually secured the strip to enhance her own allure. After obtaining further assistance from Sleep, whose reluctance she overcomes with the promise of marriage to the Grace he has long desired, Hera travels to Mount Ida, where Zeus catches sight of her.

And when he saw her, desire enveloped his strong understanding
Just as when they first joined in lovemaking
And went to bed together, escaping their parents' notice. (*Il.* 14.294–6)

Shrugging off that his wife's mission to Oceanus and Tethys has turned out to be a ruse, Zeus professes his need to enjoy her without delay. His desire, he says, is greater than any he has felt for a goddess or mortal woman before. (To make his point, he spends fourteen lines listing seven other sexual partners who inflamed him less, detailing in some cases the sons they bore.) Zeus and Hera make love then and there, hidden from sight by a golden cloud he gathers around them, and the earth beneath breaks out with fresh, young grass, clover, crocuses, and hyacinth. Afterward, Zeus does indeed take a nap, and Sleep tells Poseidon to take advantage of the occasion to do what he can for the Greeks.

Already in this, our earliest extant literary evidence for the Greeks and Romans, we find elements emblematic of ancient sexual attitudes. The first is that sex is clearly a powerful force, and one that works on both humans and gods, whether minor deities such as Sleep (won over as he is by the promise of his dream girl) or Zeus, most powerful of all. Second, sex is one of the good things in life; here, it serves to distinguish the gods from the Greek and Trojan humans, who suffer and die as Zeus and Hera while away the afternoon. Third, sex is a tricky thing. Hera is *dolophroneousa*—"scheming" or "troublesome" (*Il.* 14.197, 300, 329)—and her playfulness is part of a program of deceit designed to promote yet more hardship below. The episode is often called the Deception of Zeus, but others are betrayed through and for sex, from Aphrodite herself (lied to for the loan of her seductive strap) to the parents Zeus and Hera hid from when they were young. (And the struggling mortals are not so different after all, since they fight in a war over another female figure who deceived her husband through sex.) Fourth, despite all the dark overtones of force and falsehood, sex also produces beauty—the flowering earth that cushions the divine lovers—and is a lot of fun. Fifth, sex can be a source of humor. The delay that intervenes as Zeus recounts and dismisses escapades of his past is meant to be amusing—and to raise doubts about just who the joke is on. Is Zeus really as fooled as Hera thinks, or is his time-consuming catalog of slips a way to suggest he could thwart her plot if he were so inclined?[2]

A sixth point should also be made: sex can be a profoundly dangerous activity. We derive this point not specifically from *Iliad* 14, but from the very name and nurture of Zeus's daughter Aphrodite. This goddess is sometimes said to be the daughter of Zeus and Dione, one of the most insubstantial of the god's many dalliances, her name a mere doublet of his (the genitive and other oblique cases of Zeus are formed from the root Di-). In this genealogy, she is a part—if an unruly one—of the Olympian world over which her father reigns. But, as early as Homer, or nearly so, Hesiod's *Theogony* tells a grimmer tale (Hes. *Th.* 126–206): long before Zeus established the present order, Ge (earth) lay penetrated and clasped in the embrace of Uranus (sky). Their offspring remained painfully trapped within her until one, Cronus, used a sickle-shaped knife his mother provided to sever his father's penis. It was thrown into the sea, and from the foam arose Aphrodite. This origin (like that from Zeus and Dione) has an etymological underpinning—the Greek word *aphros* means "foam"—but it also sounds clear and terrible overtones, especially for men engaged in *ta aphrodisia* (the things of Aphrodite), the usual way Greeks referred to sexuality. And while Zeus's liaisons with goddesses and mortal women are invariably productive, Aphrodite's partners often lose their potency. Her lover Adonis is fatally gored when a boar thrusts upward at his groin; her lover Anchises is left unmanned after a casual encounter on Mount Ida; her husband, Hephaestus, alone among the gods in his physical imperfection, a lower-body disability, is cuckolded by the warrior god Ares.

The passage from the *Iliad* with which we began our discussion does not tell the whole of the story. No text, no piece of evidence—no matter how rich and fecund—can fully illuminate any aspect of ancient life. Some individual items may mislead. Did ancient Greeks marry within the immediate family? In the case at hand, Zeus and Hera are brother and sister; so (in some traditions, at least) are Oceanus and Tethys. Half-siblings with the same father could marry in Athens; those with the same mother could do so in Sparta; and marriages of full brothers and sisters were known and even encouraged in Greco-Roman Egypt during the first three centuries of our era.[3] But, in general, sex between close relatives was taboo. The Greeks and Romans regularly invoked incest with a sister in political invective (against Cimon in Athens, against Publius Clodius in Rome). So the Ptolemies, the Hellenistic rulers of Egypt, took their siblings as consorts to proclaim their uniqueness and disdain for the limitations that fettered their subjects,[4] and the poet Catullus used accusations of incest to suggest that his enemies among the Roman elite were no better than barbarian perverts.[5]

Moreover, the passage of the *Iliad* we have chosen to highlight is concerned only with heterosexual desire and fulfillment. This is a puzzling characteristic of Homeric poetry as a whole. Though later Greeks, familiar with carefully articulated and culturally resonant codes of male homoeroticism, often regarded Achilles and his close companion Patroclus as a romantic couple—albeit an unusual one—neither the *Iliad* nor the *Odyssey* makes any explicit references to sexuality between men. (See Daniel Ogden's survey in Chapter 3.) This may be a result of the conventions of the epic genre. It is more likely, however, that institutionalized pederasty—the accepted link between an older and a younger male that informed so much of ancient literature, philosophy, and art—was an innovation of the late seventh or early sixth century B.C., along with athletic nudity and the rise or reorganization of Panhellenic festival competition.[6]

More generally, indications for some sexual feelings and phenomena may be lacking altogether, and not just in Homer. For example, as Hans van Wees notes, "Presumably there is simply not enough evidence to reconstruct the size and shape of Galatian genitals."[7] And ancient texts rarely discuss or depict romantic love—Greek novels are exceptions. An equally perplexing problem is posed by the interface between our outlook and the evidence that does remain. Here, for instance, is a modern, biochemical account of falling in love:

> The initial feelings of attraction are heavily associated with the b-phenylethylamine (PEA) norepinephrine. Norepinephrine triggers the breakdown of glycogen and triacylglycerols, which provides the body a boost of energy. The stimulant functions by binding the surface of liver cells, signaling them to produce cyclic AMP (cAMP). This molecule then breaks the active parts of protein kinase A (PKA) away, enabling them to alter certain proteins.[8]

All this, the account goes on to say, helps us understand the diverging sexual habits of two species of voles, the monogamous prairie variety and its promiscuous montane cousin. But it is hard to imagine medical writers such as Hippocrates or Galen responding to it, let alone Sappho. Is this her take on falling in love? "Once again Eros the limb-loosener shakes me, the bittersweet irresistible creature."[9]

WHAT SEEMS FAMILIAR CAN EASILY FOOL US

Of course, it is our response to the ancient evidence that is more pertinent here. The history of scholarship on ancient sexuality is replete with failures to communicate of this kind, from the interpretation of the Greek word *olisbos* (often used to indicate a dildo) as a pessary or vaginal suppository to the casting of Sappho herself as an asexual schoolmistress.[10] Naturally, our contemporary cultural blinkers are less easy to spot.

As John Younger remarks in Chapter 4, "Most of the sexual practices and attitudes of the ancient Greeks and Romans have parallels in modern life." But, paradoxically perhaps, seeming similarities may prove more difficult to deal with than what seems utterly strange. Some examples follow of how what seems familiar may fool us.[11]

1. Minoan figurines are often interpreted as images of a mother goddess, a reassuringly maternal and monotheistic concept for modern Europeans, at least. Yet the goddesses of the contemporary Near East and Egypt were both versatile and sexual. Mother-child duos are strikingly absent from Minoan art—female breasts are prominent, but for their own sake, it seems. The figurines are found in too many contexts for one explanation to fit them all.[12]

2. A number of Athenian vases show the goddess of the dawn carrying off young mortal men. Dawn is best known for asking Zeus to grant her mortal lover Tithonus everlasting life without remembering to add youth to the gift. He aged endlessly, dried out and chirping like an insect. Rather than being intended as warnings about female sexuality, these images highlight the arbitrary and unexpected impact of the gods on human life.[13]

3. The comic poet Terence, esteemed in antiquity and after for the refinement of his language and his care in characterization—especially in contrast to Plautus, his broad and bawdy predecessor, is now treated as a serial sexual offender, unfit for today's theaters. "It is hard," says a recent critic, "to imagine a modern staging of Terence ... three of whose six plays turn on sexual violence."[14] So, too, is it unlikely that schoolboys in a society much keener to buy oil made from canola than from rapeseed (the plant's original name) would be exposed to tales of adultery, rape, and incest—staples of rhetorical training in Rome.

4. In an act of sexual violence, Jupiter takes the form of a bull to abduct Europa. For the ancients, as for us, this animal was a model of male potency. Yet his horns, which stand in for his penis, are small (Ovid, *Met.* 2.854–6): a small, well-formed penis was more desirable than an oversize one, an attribute of the ithyphallic rural deity Priapus.[15] Similarly, in scenes of sexual pursuit, randy satyrs and other theriomorphic creatures have erections—gods don't.

5. Some of Martial's epigrams celebrate the sexuality of the Roman matron. She should be a Lucretia, or paradigm of chastity, by day but

a wanton Lais for her husband at night, using all that courtesan's tricks—sexy movements, erotic language, fingering.[16] This has a very modern sound, more in tune with contemporary therapy for couples than, say, with Aphrodite's *kestos himas*. But Martial's Rome, of the late first century A.D., also featured mixed nude bathing, phallic images, scenes of sexual congress as part of domestic decor (discussed by John Clarke in Chapter 9) and portrait statues that had the heads of elite women perched atop scantily clad torsos of Venus (much as if we populated our public buildings today with amalgams of Queen Victoria and Pamela Anderson).

6. Finally, though Plato has Pausanias opine that there ought to be a minimum age for the *erōmenos* (the youthful, passive partner) in a homosexual pair, and Strato sets the lower limit at twelve, the ideal age was in the mid-teens, well before the age of majority in most Greek cities. Existing texts display much more anxiety about *erōmenoi* who are sprouting hair and otherwise growing out of their roles. The contrast with our own complicated legal strictures and their different minimum ages for sex with other minors or with adults, their push to criminalize depictions of those who are of legal age but appear to be underage, and their utter indifference to the behaviors of those no longer in need of protection could not be clearer. As Christian Laes remarks, "The famous Warren Cup ... would be enough nowadays to put the artist in jail for indecent pornographic art with minors."[17]

With these caveats and complexities in mind, let us return to some of our initial themes.[18]

POWER (AND PAIN)

The Greeks and Romans viewed sex as a force of nature—and nature was more than crocuses and clover. It was powerful and fearsome, all the more so because they were much closer and more vulnerable to nature than we are today.[19] Sex was therefore regularly associated with the imagery of fire, war, madness, disease, and death: in other words, with dire consequences. (In both Greek and Latin, for instance, the words for death and dying can also refer to orgasm.[20]) Its personifications, Aphrodite/Venus and her son Eros/Cupid, are as dangerous as they are delightful. We have already touched on Aphrodite and *ta aphrodisia*. No less troublesome is Eros, "the most unconquerable god, the tyrant of gods and men" (Eur. *Hipp.* 1274–80). He shares his name with the Greek word for sexual passion, a strong term implying the usual restraints of reason have been overthrown. As Prodicus put it, "Desire (*epithymian*) doubled is sexual passion (*erōta*), passion doubled is madness" (Prodicus DK 84 B 7). In antiquity, Eros/Cupid carried a bow and quiver. But these were more than cute trappings on a Valentine's Day card. Greeks and Romans knew the pain that arrows could cause in battle, how they struck brave men and cowards alike, how their wounds, delivered from a distance, brought little honor to the warriors they hit. We may compare our phrase "falling in love." It, too, implies an accident, essentially out of our control, that causes a decline from our previous position. When we fall, we say we wish to right ourselves; ancient philosophical writers regarded desire as an illness demanding treatment.[21] Sexual desire often entered through the eyes, an emanation penetrating its victim (according to one common ancient theory of vision) much like arrows themselves. Arrows, *erōs*, eyesore: the first two words make a pun, the second two a palindrome.[22] Invasive as it was, sight could even lead to conception or change the appearance of the embryo *in utero*—pregnant women were advised to gaze at attractive statues or paintings in order to produce handsome babies (and chance looks could explain a child who didn't resemble the husband).[23]

The GAZE?

SEXUAL HIERARCHIES

Politics

Force of nature though it was, sexuality was mediated and molded by culture, especially hierarchies of various kinds. To have her way with her brother Zeus, Hera must trick him. He is a dangerous and powerful creature, used to getting his own way. Asymmetry was indeed one of the defining qualities of ancient sexual thought and practice.[24] Reciprocal relationships, especially if they weren't clearly structured by penetration, might not be categorized as sexual at all. This offers one possible explanation for our sources' almost complete silence on female homosexuality between the sixth-century B.C. poems of Sappho and Alcman and the Roman writers of the first century A.D.—as well as for their tendency to treat the subject as a species of signs and wonders.[25] Let us begin our discussion of ancient sexual hierarchies with political power. Rulers took sexual privileges as their due. The troglodytes of what is now the Sudan—or so we are informed—held their wives and children in common; only the wife of the tyrant was beyond the reach of others.[26] Among the Greeks and Romans themselves, the link between sexuality and political power was usually demonstrated more actively. It was often stressed in the rhetoric used to

portray tyrants and other oppressors. Aristotle devotes a passage of *Politics* to
rulers' lusts for the wives, daughters, and sons of their subjects and the trouble
these could cause (Arist. *Pol.* 5.1311a31–b30). Athens's famous tyrannicides,
Harmodius and Aristogeiton, were driven to overthrow the sons of Peisistratus
after the younger ruler, Hipparchus, sought sexual favors from Harmodius and
was rebuffed. The lesson despots took from this, says Plato's Pausanias, was
that pederasty ought to be suppressed (Pl. *Symp.* 182c, cf. Ath. 13.602ad).
Other rulers were unwilling to take no for an answer. Polybius's account of the
Hellenistic dynasties contains numerous examples. Assuming absolute power,
Philip V of Macedon no longer confined himself to the seduction of widows or
married women, but ordered any woman he chose to come to him, insulting
those who did not do so at once (10.26.1–2). Agathocles of Syracuse drank day
and night and was so debauched that he spared no woman who was of age,
married or not—and made a display of his conquests to boot (15.25.22 [15]).
In aristocratic communities, the sins of the fathers were repeated by their children, who abandoned themselves to vice—greed, graft, partying, the rape of
women and boys (6.8.4). In such circumstances, the idea that citizens should be
erastai (older, dominant members of a homosexual couple) is especially striking (Thuc. 2.43.7–8).[27] Valerius Maximus, writing for the emperor Tiberius,
devotes a long chapter (6.1) to sexual crimes, many committed by officeholders
of the republic.[28] Still more lurid rumors abounded about the most mighty
rulers of all, Tiberius and his successors; these are as familiar from contemporary films as from Suetonius's equally sensational scripts. Even Augustus is
alleged to have required the warmth of young girls as a comfort in his old age
(a perk he supposedly shared with King David and Gandhi).

   In both Athens and Rome, the role of sexuality in political discourse
extended far beyond individual abuses of power. The tyrannicides' plot, which
we've just mentioned, did not succeed. But although Hippias retained control for several years after the assassination of his brother and was in the
end overthrown by Spartan intervention, popular belief credited Harmodius
and Aristogeiton with restoring the democracy Solon had founded. (See Holt
Parker's discussion of popular culture in chapter 7.) So the sexual union of two
men—one older, one younger; one from the elite, the other of more modest
origins—was represented as both a building block of the democratic political order and a model of sexual relations.[29] Fifty years later, citizen women
entered the story of Athenian democracy when the assembly passed Pericles'
citizenship law (451/0 B.C.) and stipulated that Athenians needed citizen
mothers as well as fathers (see Susan Lape, chapter 2). But this time it is reproduction that is at issue, not sexuality. (Among its other resonances, the

identification of citizens with *erastai* effectively excludes women's sexuality from public life.) Sexual violence against women does take on a political color, but only in the sense of colonization: the forcible seizure, that is, of others' territory.[30]

The Romans, by way of contrast, granted sex with women a central role in the political development of their community. Rome's rise to greatness was supposed to have begun with the abduction and impregnation, orchestrated by Romulus, the city's first king, of the wives and daughters of the neighboring Sabines, and with the subsequent incorporation of their menfolk on equal terms. The end of the monarchy in Rome and the establishment of the republic was a consequence of Lucretia's rape by Sextus Tarquinius, son of the last king. (See the discussion by Esther Eidinow, who surveys the regulation of sexual activity, especially adultery and rape, in chapter 5.) These stories, told and retold by the leading writers of the day, were surely in Augustus's mind when he first introduced his laws imposing new restrictions on the sexual behavior of the Roman elite—and on the capacity of fathers and husbands to police it. This leading role for Roman women reflects their greater public presence. Only in Rome was there a group of celibate women, the vestal virgins, whose chastity helped to ensure the safety and survival of the state. Only in Rome were there a cult and shrine of Pudicitia, coins bearing her image, and competitions among women for a publicly awarded crown.[31]

Gender

Even those members of the elite who held no formal political position or exercised no influence in the state might wield class power over their sexual partners. When Phrynion took Neaera to parties and had sex with her before other guests, he did so, as Apollodorus tells an Athenian jury, to flaunt his control over her ([Dem.] 59.33–4). Of course, gender must inform sexuality in any patriarchal society, and Greece and Rome were no exceptions. Phrynion's use of Neaera to demonstrate this was merely an unusually naked instance. More subtly, but no less telling, Martial's wish for a wife who becomes her husband's whore has only his pleasure in mind. Males were normally figured as active and females as passive; in this instance, the wife's own satisfaction is clearly subordinate despite her initiative.

This double standard in relation to sexuality was expressed by ancient understandings of physiology.[32] Both men and women were thought to have reproductive organs with minds of their own. In the case of men, this belief was represented by the winged phallus-bird in Greek art and the free-flowing phallus in Roman decor. In the case of women, whose genitals are more hidden, it was symbolized by the wandering womb, "a thing living inside that desires to create a child" (Pl. *Tim.* 91bc). But while the male desire for sexual satisfaction was spurred on by an external stimulus—the sight of an attractive object, regardless of gender—female desire was rooted in an internal drive, the need to be filled by pregnancy. This is one of the reasons why sex between women was difficult for men to imagine, and why the concept of homosexuality, defining both gay male and lesbian desires and acts, did not arise. Men could therefore control their sexual urges; women could not. Here, too, were implications, with women's intentions and emotions playing little part in public Greek responses to sexual violence. Herodotus therefore treats Helen, Paris's willing accomplice, much like he does the nymph Io, though the latter was forcibly abducted by Zeus (Hdt. 1.1–3). And because it was the male *kyrios*'s consent that counted in Athenian law, the heroines of New Comedy found happy endings by marrying their rapists.[33] Varyingly inspired as it was, sexual intercourse likewise led to diverse outcomes, since women had no sperm to ejaculate. Colder and wetter than men, they could not concoct or condense blood to form it.[34] Elements of this picture were called into question or modified at times. Aristotle believed that female bodies were much like those of males—except they were imperfect. Thus, he regarded women as moral agents, if less effective and self-controlled than men. Soranus, of the early second century A.D., did not believe in wandering wombs or in sex as a cure-all for female complaints. For Galen, writing perhaps fifty years later, the uterus was analogous to the scrotum, and the vagina compared to the penis—though he, too, invoked heat to explain why the female organs were hidden. It is unlikely that such views made much difference in the power dynamics of heterosexual relations. But there was a theory that a female seed was also required for conception and that this necessitated female orgasm. Though the attractive suggestion that this belief was formulated and spread abroad by women is most likely unfounded, its existence might nonetheless have influenced husbands to pay more attention to the sexual needs of their wives.[35]

Age

Priority in age generally merited respect in antiquity. Though primogeniture was unknown in Athens, the first-born son rated *presbeia* (an acknowledgement of seniority) in inheritance. The *gerousia* (council of elders, men older than sixty) was an important organ of the Spartan state—a nod to the role of experience and seasoned judgment that was reflected in the name of the Roman senate, which was derived from the Latin *senex* (old man). Sobriety and self-control, including a reduced liability to sexual passion, were also thought to mark maturity. The Athenians of the fourth century B.C. required those who sponsored a boys' chorus to be more than forty years of age—a means of preventing sexual scandal. (This was not a community in which men were expected to undergo midlife crises.) Adultery, Hyperides claimed, is a crime no man can begin in middle age—perhaps not after fifty, though the text is unclear at this point (Hyper. 1.15). This is not to say that elderly men were assumed to be celibate; Sophocles welcomed release from sexual desire toward the end of a life of ninety years. Older women were a different matter: past the age of reproduction, their sexuality was ridiculous, repugnant.

Greek and Roman husbands were typically much older than their wives, by as much as fifteen years. Men married at about thirty, women in their mid- to late teens; elite husbands of Rome were younger, Spartan wives were older. This must have contributed to the imbalance between the sexes. But the role of age is nowhere more evident than in male couples, free as they were of the complications of gender. In both Greece and Rome, homosexual *erōs* was strongly marked for age. The older partner (as the Greek term *erastēs*, or "lover," implies) was dominant. He was by convention older than the *erōmenos*, the "beloved," or passive partner of the pair. The *erōmenos* was not driven by a reciprocal sexual drive for sexual satisfaction; he was to benefit from the guidance of his lover and to grow into the same role with another young protégé. This pattern prevailed until late antiquity; any other arrangement was shocking at best (Xen. *An.* 2.6.28). Only in the fourth century A.D. is Hadrian's passion for the young Antinous represented as a sign of weakness unfitting for an emperor. But, even then, it might be excused by Antinous's depiction as soft and fleshy, womanly rather than macho—as well as by the fact that he was, after all, a god.[36]

It should go without saying that we do not know what *erōmenoi* really wanted, and that irrefutable indications of individuals who were as aggressive in seeking sexual pleasure as their older partners would not, in any case, controvert the conventions. Scientific writers refer to boys who have become acclimatized to being penetrated anally and who have even learned to enjoy it—a pathological condition, however, and one explained by their having the physiology of women ([Arist.] *Probl.* 4.26; Caelius Aurelianus, *On Chronic Diseases* 4.9). Similarly, it may be that the Latin word *exoleti* refers to sex slaves who have grown up to enjoy passive intercourse as well as penetration. But these individuals were not Roman citizens, and, by definition, they lay beyond the pale.[37] There are traces of a less restricted code on Athenian vases from the archaic and classical periods. Courtship scenes sometimes show the younger man in pursuit of the older[38]; in general, the depiction of the *erōmenos* as hunted is a characteristic of sixth-century black-figure, whereas later red-figure vases portray the younger man as more partner than prey.[39] Some *erōmenoi* make eye contact with their lovers—not just a sign of intimacy but also, it may be, an indication that their gaze at times can penetrate.[40] The touch of the beloved's hand on his lover's arm or wrist may be another symbol of closeness and affection, much like our taking someone's hand.[41] *Erōmenoi* on black-figure vases are occasionally sexually aroused.[42] In general, the vases seem to reflect a concern to de-emphasize subordination of the *erōmenos*; it is noteworthy, for example, that it is the senior partner who bends his knees, lowering himself to his beloved's level while the *erōmenos* stands straight.[43] Status was another guiding principle in the organization of Greek and Roman sexuality, and so, in all of this, we may sense a concern that the younger man—a free citizen, after all—is not assimilated to a slave.

Status

Hetairai we have for the sake of pleasure, *pallakai* for the day-to-day care of our bodies, wives to bear legitimate children and guard our homes faithfully. ([Dem.] 59.122)

Shamelessness [buggery] is a crime in freeborn men, a necessity for slaves, an obligation in a freedman. (Sen. *Controv.* 4.10)

Above are two well-known passages, one Greek, the other Latin. Each is as rhetorical in its original context as in its present one; both are less straightforward than they may seem. For example, the exact status of *pallakai* (concubines) is uncertain. Are they slaves, poor citizens, or even, at times, women in an entirely different sphere of service: priestesses of the gods?[44] And Seneca's passage, a quotation from the Augustan orator Quintus Haterius, likely cannot be taken to show that freed slaves in Rome still owed sexual services to their former masters.[45] It is clear nonetheless that questions of status complicate any discussion of ancient sexuality.

This is truest of slavery. It has been fifty years since M. I. Finley's dictum, "There is no problem or practice in any branch of Greek life which was not affected, in some fashion, by the fact that many people in that society … were (or had been) slaves."[46] So for Rome as well. It amuses Valerius Maximus that two men died while engaged in sex with two children (Val. Max. 9.12.8). No Roman, let alone a stern moralist such as Valerius, would find sex with freeborn boys a laughing matter. These boys, however, were likely slaves, so the usual outrage is inappropriate. Similarly, rabbinical sources approve the use of slave girls for sexual purposes as long as they have reached the age of three—long before even the youngest citizen girl would marry.[47]

Obviously, slaves were readily available for sexual exploitation by their masters, or by anyone to whom their masters loaned them.[48] It is a mark of the respect Laertes, Odysseus's father, bore for his wife—and of the uxoriousness his son also exhibits—that he did not have sex with the slave girl who became Odysseus's nurse (Hom. *Od.* 1.429–33). Horace's attitude was more prevalent: "When you're horny, don't wait until someone high-class or sexy comes along—just jump a slave girl or boy" (Hor. *Sat.* 1.2.114–19). This advice seems to conform to the normal ancient notion that sex is an appetite like any other. So Plutarch can equate the pleasure of quenching hunger and thirst with that of going to bed with a beautiful woman; he can compare sacrificing in thanks for sex to praying for a rich meal (Plut. *Mor.* 1093c, 1094b). It also betokens the ready availability of sexual release in societies where human bodies were not merely for rent but for sale.[49] This form of trade was not only for those rich enough to buy or rent their own slaves: tradition credits Solon, the father of Athenian democracy, with the introduction of cheap brothels, staffed by slaves, which gave even poorer citizens access to women's bodies (Philemon fr. 3 K-A; Nicander, *FGH* 271/2 F 9 = Ath. 13.569df).[50] Women, too, could take advantage of such opportunities. Herondas—a male poet, to be sure—presents a woman who rebukes a slave partner for his infidelity (Herod. 5), while Spartan stories about the founding of Tarentum by helots who slept with Spartan women, and by their offspring, may reflect concern about what went on during citizens' frequent absences.[51] Such sex was not always satisfactory for those who sought it. The sex strike in Aristophanes' comedy *Lysistrata* will succeed (or so its leader explains) because men enjoy women's willing pleasure (Ar. *Lys.* 163–6, cf. Xen. *Oec.* 10.11–12).

Slave boys on Roman Arretine ware show more animation than we are accustomed to seeing in pederastic scenes involving citizens, and their penetration is not obscured or elided. In this respect their status may have allowed the artists more freedom to play with iconographic convention.[52] The slaves themselves are silent. Trimalchio regales his guests with stories of his sexual services in his days as a slave—"What the master orders is not shameful" (Petr. *Sat.* 75.11)—but this is a work of fiction, and its creator, the

Roman courtier and ex-consul Petronius, means to mock his character. Even for a slave, to be used for others' gratification was degrading. For instance, Romans writing about estate management recommend against giving a slave who has played the passive partner the responsibilities of a bailiff (Columella, *Rust.* 1.8.1; Pall. *Agr.* 1.6.18). Such realities pack the image of *servitium amoris* (love slavery) with more punch than we might otherwise feel from our vantage point. It is one thing for pop star Britney Spears to sing "I'm a slave for you" and quite another for Greek and (especially) Roman poets from among the elite to either lament or celebrate this form of servitude.[53] These role reversals had ringing resonance in a world where even prosperous citizens could indeed find themselves on the slave market through the vagaries of war or piracy—as well as testifying to the force of sexual passion. (The potential power of the slave bailiff over a master who was also a sexual partner was another reason he was unsuitable.) As Tibullus introduces himself in his first poem, he is not a man to go soldiering in search of wealth—which is often, his readers would know, to be found in the form of slave booty. No, he is a stay-at-home, chained to his mistress: a *ianitor* (a doorman) sitting—a most inglorious posture—before her door (Tib. 1.55–6). But nowhere is the statement of this theme stronger than in Catullus's epigram (85).

> I hate and I love. Perhaps you ask me why I do this.
> I don't know, but I feel it happening, and I'm torn apart.

Excrucior, the poem's last word, refers to crucifixion. For us this may bear overtones of suffering for a noble cause. But Catullus's passion has nothing to do with Christ's. Sexual desire has been his undoing (note his disavowal of any agency of his own), and it has come about in a fashion as debased as it is painful: in Rome, crucifixion was a punishment for slaves.

LAUGHTER-LOVING APHRODITE

This is not the image to end with. Homer did not hesitate to show us the humorous elements of the encounter between Zeus and Hera. This an almost constant theme in ancient depictions of sex. Hesiod calls Aphrodite *philommeidēs* (member-loving), deriving the term from the word *mēdea* (sex organs) in reference to her birth (Hes. *Th.* 200). But this is a play on words. The moniker is more likely derived from *meidaō* (smile); indeed, Hesiod goes on to list the goddess's allotment as "girls' whispers and smiles and deceit, sweet joy and love and gentleness" (*Th.* 205–6).[54] A *Homeric Hymn* describes her as "always smiling" (*Hom. Hymn.* 10.3), and Greek and Roman literature and images abound with the joy of sex. Artists and writers often play with and against convention to great effect. A red-figure cup attributed to the Pedieus Painter displays members of an orgy.[55] One participant, a young man, is being fellated by a woman; like others on this piece of pottery, she is fat and middle-aged and seems to be having trouble fitting him into her mouth. The scene appears to illustrate many of our hierarchies—men over women, free over slave (or hireling), young and attractive (in this instance) over old and unsightly—with a kind of "brutal humor."[56] But does the young man escape unscathed? His penis is depicted with its glans exposed, generally an attribute of barbarians rather than Greeks, and he is otherwise vaguely ridiculous as he tries to balance a drinking horn, itself erect, so as not to lose a drop. Perhaps, we may imagine, he will spill both wine and himself when the time comes. To turn to a literary example: Catullus uses the hyperphallic deity Priapus to lampoon the masculine obsession with penetrating others; such single-mindedness, like the god, is laughably rustic and crude.[57]

Sexual humor has other targets, too. The core of Plato's *Symposium* is a series of speeches on *erōs*, one by the comic poet Aristophanes (Pl. *Symp.* 189d-93d). It amounts to nothing less than an origin myth for human sexual behavior. Once upon a time, our ancestors were round and eight-limbed and boasted two faces and two sets of genitals, each facing in opposite directions. Ungainly creatures—they moved by cartwheeling—they were of three sexes, male, female, and a mixture of the two. But Zeus feared their power and pride, and had them sliced in half vertically, with their heads rotated to the front. Divided as they were, they strove unsuccessfully to reunite themselves, so persistently in some cases that they went without food and drink and died. Out of pity, Zeus moved their genitals also to the front so they could join temporarily through intercourse and, satisfied (at least for a moment), go about their business. This fairy tale is funny on a number of levels. There is something absurd in making Aristophanes, famous for the bawdiness and crudity of his comedies, responsible for such whimsical fantasy—and the situation is all the more absurd in that his speech is given out of turn due to a bout of hiccups. These spasms were as ridiculous in classical Athens as they are today, and this case is made even less dignified by the doctor who cures it, named, appropriately enough, Eryximachus, or "Belch-fighter." Plato may be paying Aristophanes back for his own parodic portrayal of Socrates in *Clouds*. The punch line arrives later, when Alcibiades, coming late to the party, tells how he once tried to seduce Socrates—by putting his cloak over and his arms around him—but failed. Zeus's plastic surgery on our ancestors has not cured every case of sexual frustration.

Finally, we have Ovid, whose wit finished off the classical Latin love elegy as a genre of poetry. No one could take the form seriously after him—so why should he not end this introduction too? *Amores* 3.2 recounts a day at the chariot races, where the narrator tries to pick up a neighbor he finds desirable. Shamelessly on the make, he uses every opening afforded by the design of the circus and the action on the track to achieve his goal. Does the girl try to avoid his advances at first? The assigned seats keep her in reach. Does her dress trail on the ground? He picks it up—and cops a look at her legs. They're like Atalanta's, another girl who was won through a race, and they promise more and better to come—the Latin *sustinuisse* alludes to her suitor Milanion holding them up in bed. Dust on the dress provides a chance to check out the goods manually. Then they're off! The narrator urges the girl's chosen charioteer to take the most direct route to the finish line, as he does himself. After a false start—an echo of the missteps that had put the girl off earlier—the charioteer obliges. And the narrator? The girl smiles winningly, but is she won? The last line of the poem—unpunctuated in our manuscripts—is ambiguous. The joke may be on the pushy narrator after all. Recall that the episode termed the Deception of Zeus turned out to be less straightforward than it first seemed. Is he a fast runner, like the horses and Milanion, or just a creep doomed to rejection? Perhaps the joke is on us, forced as we are to use such finely fashioned publications when what we really want to see are private feelings and facts.

CHAPTER TWO

Heterosexuality

SUSAN LAPE

Heterosexuality did not operate as an autonomous category of self-identity in the classical Greek and Roman worlds.[1] Although the sources attest to keen interest and investment in heterosexuality, this sphere did not designate an independent identity category but rather served to aid in the constitution of social identities based on kinship, gender, morality, polis affiliation, and political ideology. In this study I investigate the embeddedness of heterosexuality in other social categories—or, to put it another way, the factors that blocked or inhibited its emergence as an identity category in its own right. I elaborate on the work of heterosexuality in creating and reproducing classical social identities, and, conversely, on the role of ideologies in shaping the perceived meaning of heterosexual experience, bearing in mind that the sources most heavily reflect the attitudes of elite men.

ATHENS AND GREECE: MONOGAMY AND EQUALITY

Without doubt, marriage was the most important institution organizing heterosexual conduct in the Greco-Roman world. Every free person of citizen status in classical Athens and Rome was expected to marry for the sake of having children; for this reason, we can say that heterosexual conduct and kinship were built into the marriage system in both cultures.[2] In addition, monogamous marriage was the only form of that institution allowable in most of Greece and in Rome.[3] Although Greek and Roman men were able to have multiple sex partners, they could only have one wife at a time, and hence only one legitimate reproductive partner.[4] Since polygamy rather than monogamy has been the ideologically preferred marriage system in 83 percent of recorded human societies, we might consider how and why the historical anomaly of monogamous marriage acquired such traction in the classical world.[5]

The Greeks certainly had knowledge of real and reported polygamous societies. The case of King Priam of Troy and his many childbearing consorts in Homer's *Iliad* was well-known (e.g., *Il.* 21.100). But the Greek leaders at Troy appear similarly polygynous (albeit not polygamous), taking captured women as concubines.[6] By the classical period, however, having a wife and a concubine at the same time and in the same household was implicitly ruled out in Athens and, presumably, throughout most of the Greek city-states.[7] Fifth- and fourth-century Athenian sources identify polygamy and polygyny (in the form of keeping wives and concubines in the same household) as a barbaric and despotic practice characteristic of the Persians, Thracians, and Macedonians.[8]

Although it is unclear when monogamy emerged as the uncontested Greek norm, we can form a hypothesis regarding the ideological attractions of monogamy as a cultural practice. Anthropologists have detected a correlation between monogamy and egalitarianism between men and, conversely, between polygamy and male inequality and hierarchy.[9] This correlation is perhaps most easily seen in the case of Rome. As the Roman government transitioned from oligarchy to monarchy, we find new evidence for polygamous practices.[10] For example, according to the biographer Suetonius, Julius Caesar ordered the tribune of the plebs to propose a bill making it lawful for him to marry as many wives as he wished, "for the purpose of begetting children" (Suet. *Iul.* 52). However true the anecdote is, it illustrates the conceptual connection between male political hierarchies and the uneven distribution of fertile women.

Returning to the Greek world, we know that an egalitarian ethos took hold in Athens and in many cities during the archaic period (roughly 800–490 B.C.).[11] Yet, we do not know exactly why this happened; that is, what prompted the emergence of egalitarian thinking in the first place?[12] Anthropologist Christopher Boehm argues that egalitarian ideologies do not usually spring from idealistic commitments to human equality but rather emerge as a byproduct of resentment and resistance to hierarchy. When enough people come to resent a given hierarchy, the weak or disaffected often band together to subordinate the strong, forming a special kind of hierarchy based on anti-hierarchical feelings, or what now traffics as egalitarianism.[13] In the ancient Greek context, it is entirely plausible that resentment at the unequal distribution of power and wealth in the archaic city-states stood behind the appearance of a widespread egalitarian ethos.[14] Similarly, resentment at the ability of powerful men to monopolize more than their share of fertile females may have been a driving force behind the triumph of monogamy, an institution that guarantees and creates a domain of male equality by limiting every man to having one wife at a time.[15] We need not, of course, imagine that Greek men actually banded together to prevent more powerful men from taking more than their share of resources. Rather, envy may have simply worked to block the emergence of intolerable levels of inequality with respect to women and wealth.[16]

Although this story is admittedly speculative, it seems to be replayed in the curtailing of concubinage in sixth-century Athens. The triumph of monogamy as the only acceptable matrimonial form did not prevent elites from using relations between men and women to forge and assert hierarchical relations between men. It was possible for elite men to father freeborn children with wives and concubines, thereby converting reproductive power into additional social capital.[17] The reforms of Solon (around 594 B.C.) effectively brought this practice to an end. Solon's laws removed bastard children (i.e., children born outside the marriage context) from both the family and state, thereby eliminating their usefulness to their fathers.[18] With this exclusion, the laws simultaneously privileged the conjugal family and legitimacy, its characteristic kinship status, effectively putting every Athenian on exactly the same reproductive footing. After Solon's legislation, every Athenian could father legitimate children and heirs with only one woman at a time: his current wife. The new importance attached to legitimacy and legitimate wives led to a corresponding bias against bastards and concubines. Because any offspring produced with a concubine would be severely disadvantaged by its exclusion from family and city, Solon's laws had the practical effect of discouraging men from keeping concubines at all.[19] Although we hear of concubines kept for the purpose of producing free children in the Athens of Draco's day, Solon's reforms made such women obsolete, relics of aristocratic and pre-democratic social structures. In the classical period, citizens never cohabit with a wife and a concubine at the same time, and only rarely do they choose to live with a concubine in place of a wife.[20]

SEX WORKERS AND SEXUAL OFFENSES

Although Solon's laws inhibited men from monopolizing multiple fertile females in their households, they did not prevent relations between men and women from being used to index relations between men. There was nothing to stop men (who had the resources and the time) from finding occasional and long-term, nonmarital sexual partners. During the archaic and classical periods, elite men often formed intimate associations with *hetairai* (high-class prostitutes or courtesans). It is important to note, however, that these labels do not entirely capture the historical specificity of the *hetaira*. Indeed, the precise definition of what a *hetaira* was, and the services she may or may not have performed, is difficult to pin down in the sources.[21] According to recent critics, this is no accident: they argue that the construction of ancient sex workers offers a snapshot of larger processes of ideological contestation taking place in Greek communities. In general, the *hetaira* can be differentiated from the *pornē* (common prostitute) on the basis of the exchange ideologies within which they operate. Whereas the *hetaira* is defined in terms of unspecified gift exchange with one or more friends or clients in relatively enduring relationships, the *pornē* is cast as a creature of commodity exchange, hiring her body out for cash to anonymous customers.[22]

For our purposes, the distinction between the *hetaira* and the *pornē* underlines the work of heterosexuality in constructing other social identities—that is, those based on class and status rather than sexuality per se. For although the *hetaira* might be presumed to be a sex worker, neither she nor her elite customers were viewed primarily in sexual terms.[23] To put it another way, we might say that the *hetaira* was a variety of sex worker without a sexual identity. This is not to deny that we often find *hetairai* in frank sexual situations: being used or abused by drunken symposiasts on late sixth- and fifth-century vase paintings, or being forced to perform sexual services in public contexts.[24] But the sexual element of these less-than-glamorous, sometimes violent encounters is embedded in a larger dynamic of masculine self-fashioning. As the Athenian orator Apollodorus puts it, the ability to have sex openly with a slave-courtesan could be seen as a mark of honor (*philotimia*).[25]

For free men in the Greek world, heterosexual relations in and out of marriage were critical to achieving and maintaining status distinctions among their gender. Although the sexual conduct of respectable women was also key to status distinctions between men, it was strictly limited to the conjugal relationship—at least, according to the official ideology. This expectation is reflected in the language and laws pertaining to sexual offenses in Athens. For instance, there is no specific word or category of offense corresponding to adultery, an injury to the marriage bond. Although *moicheia* could and did mean adultery in certain contexts, the term could be wider than that in scope and application, covering premarital as well as extramarital sexual activity with respectable women.[26]

The history of female sexual control in Athens (or, perhaps better, the ideology thereof) tells us a great deal about the work of heterosexuality in constructing classical social identities. For instance, the effective ban on non-marital sex for respectable women appears to date back to Draco's time, when, we are told, a father was able to entomb a daughter discovered to have pre-marital sexual experience. Solon, however, took away a father's ability to punish an unchaste daughter with death and instead allowed Athenian men to sell unchaste female relatives into slavery. This likely meant that unchaste women could be installed in brothels or forced to work as prostitutes.[27] Solon also seems to have passed the first law effectively regulating sexual access to respectable women both before and during marriage, the law against *moicheia*.[28]

Solon's efforts to formalize the laws pertaining to sexual conduct with re-spectable women can be correlated to his reforms of family structure and heir-ship. Most significant, Solon's laws excluded bastards or a man's nonmarital children from full family and civic membership. By making a man's wife the privileged and sole bearer of his heirs, Solon's laws implicitly attached new salience to the sexual respectability of wives and potential wives. Accordingly, female fidelity and the perception thereof became crucial to the standing of a man's children and the very continuity of his household.

The Periclean citizenship law, passed in 451/0 B.C., added to this dynamic and the culture of female sexual control it fostered.[29] Although the language of the law as we have it does not mention marriage, the majority of scholars agree that marriage stands behind the legal provisions.[30] Although there is by now a very large literature on this law and its possible aims, for present purposes I mention only its consequences for women and their sexual con-duct.[31] While reinforcing the idea that women served as guardians of male legitimacy and civic boundaries, the law also recast women as coproducers of "Athenianness"—the package of political and national qualities and charac-teristics citizens of Athens came to see as hereditary.[32] To put it another way, the law made the transmission of democratic culture dependent on the sexual integrity of female bodies.[33]

Given the new importance attached to women's bodies and the new, more narrow definition of marriage, we might have expected Athenians to pass ad-ditional legislation specifically criminalizing—and defining—adultery. Rather than doing so, however, they continued to make use of the *moicheia* statute. Accordingly, we might ask why the Athenians failed to draw a distinction be-tween a woman's premarital and extramarital sexual conduct—one that David Cohen argues is common to many, if not most, Mediterranean societies.[34]

There are probably several answers to this question, but we need to bear in mind that the law aimed to punish the behavior of an offending man rather than a woman.[35] As the law failed to distinguish seduction from adultery, it also failed to provide any category of offense under which women could be prosecuted for illicit sexual conduct.[36] Athenian law does not formally recognize female consent.[37]

There was no category of offense to prosecute women for consensual but non-licit sexual conduct, and no law to draw an explicit distinction among rape, seduction, and adultery on the basis of female consent.[38] The recognition of female consent would have raised uncomfortable questions about female agency, implying that women were able to control their sexual destinies. In turn, this would have pushed against the conventional view of women as incontinent—controlled by both sexual and alimentary appetites—one that served to justify the gender asymmetries structuring Athenian law and culture.[39] While the categorization of women as incapable of self-restraint was no doubt an ideology contributing to their subordination in Athenian culture, there are many references to married women having lovers in our sources—a fact perhaps suggestive of a discrepancy between the official ideology of female sexual control and actual sexual mores.[40]

Respectable women were defined first as wives, mothers, sisters, daughters, and only secondarily—if at all—by considerations of polis identity, ethnicity, or class position.[41] To put it another way, gender and kinship were prime coordinates of female social identity. For an Athenian female, insertion into, and perpetuation of, heterosexual kinship relations was the very reason for her existence. Athenian girls married young, perhaps as early as age fourteen, and began childbearing as soon as possible.[42] Both men and women regarded a woman's failure to marry and/or bear children as the greatest of tragedies. Whereas bearing children ensured happiness and the fulfillment of a woman's purpose, childlessness signaled unhappiness and, likely, disease. The Hippocratic medical writers constructed a model of female nature in which good health depended on regular sexual intercourse and the bearing of children.[43] As Nancy Demand points out, their theories of female physiology "did much to bolster traditional Greek (Athenian) practices of early marriage."[44]

FROM ATHENS TO ROME

Toward the end of the fourth century B.C., large-scale political changes rocked Athens and the Greek world generally. The rise of the Macedonian empire, the conquests of Alexander the Great, and the division of the empire into regional kingdoms upon his death brought the era of the independent polis firmly to a close. The shifting plates of the international landscape had significant consequences for the organization and ideology of heterosexual practices in the Greek and Mediterranean worlds. For instance, polygamy appears at the highest levels of the politico-military leadership as a means of asserting dominance and as a vehicle of international relations.[45] By contrast, at the level of the subordinated Greek city-states, there is increased attention brought to bear on the male-female couple. This emphasis can be detected earlier in the fourth century, in vase paintings: images of a man and woman engaged in sexual activity come to replace the scenes of group sex that are common in the fifth century. "This new conception," according to John Clarke, "may reflect a change in attitudes toward sex that finds parallels in the waning of the collective democratic city-state; the couple replaces the group orgy just as the cult of the individual overtakes that of the community."[46] Similarly, scholars contend that this tendency continues during the Hellenistic period, with an increased emphasis on the individual, exemplified especially by the new priority given to romantic love between men and women.[47]

For our purposes, it is important to clarify that, whether these narratives are wholly or partially correct, the evidence does not suggest that heterosexual behavior was in any way unmoored from traditional social identities. I supply this caveat to emphasize that there is no evolutionary story to be found here regarding the emergence of the "heterosexual" or its counterpart, the "individual." In turning to Rome, we find both similarities and striking differences in the way heterosexuality was recruited in the making of identities and ideologies. To illustrate these differences, it will be useful to begin with two stories of rape and political foundation, one Athenian and the other Roman.

READING RAPE IN ATHENS AND ROME: FROM RACIAL TO MORAL PURITY

The Athenians had multiple foundation tales for their polis and political institutions. Euripides' *Ion* provides one such account, grafting the contemporary norms of endogamous citizen marriage onto the myth of autochthony.[48] According to the traditional story, the Athenian princess Creusa, daughter of Erechtheus—an autochthonous city founder—was given in marriage to Xuthus, a foreigner, because he gave her father crucial military assistance in a war against the Chalcedonians.[49] Although Xuthus's pedigree was certainly distinguished—he was the grandson of Zeus—this does not compensate for his fundamental lack of Athenianness. From the standpoint of fifth-century ideology, this mixed marriage threatened to compromise and contaminate the autochthonous bloodline almost from its inception. Accordingly, to maintain autochthonous purity, Euripides writes Xuthus out of the bloodline. To this end, he tells a story in which the god Apollo rapes and impregnates Creusa prior to her marriage. This divine rape serves mainly prophylactic purposes, enabling Creusa to give birth to a child with an unadulterated bloodline. It also marks the transition from the time of myth and single autochthonous ancestors to the time of the city in which the autochthonous bloodline is encased in and transmitted through processes of sexual reproduction.[50] For present purposes, the significant issue centers on the rape. Although it is portrayed as causing great suffering to Creusa and as deplorable behavior on the god's part, it nevertheless secures an undeniably positive outcome.[51] The rape of an Athenian princess turns out to be a small price to pay to secure the intergenerational transmission of autochthonous purity.

Euripides' story of Creusa's rape clarifies the role of sexual relations in bounding the citizen body, as well as in protecting and transmitting the distinctive characteristics of that body (autochthonous lineage, patriotism, even democratic proclivities).[52] The foundation of the Roman Republic also begins with a rape—at least, as Livy tells the story.[53] In contrast to the Athenian story, this rape has a human perpetrator and is problematic in ways that shed light on the interface between heterosexual conduct and distinctively Roman ideologies.[54] While the Romans were waiting out a lengthy siege under the reign of Tarquin the Proud (509 B.C.), the king's sons and some other Roman soldiers began arguing about whose wife excelled in womanly virtue. To settle the matter, they decide to spy on the women. Lucretia wins the contest hands down, prompting her husband, Collatinus, to invite his fellow soldiers into his home for hospitality. But Lucretia's beauty and chastity incite the passion of Sextus Tarquinius, one of the king's sons. In consequence, he secretly returns several days later, forcing himself on Lucretia during the night and coercing her acquiescence. After the assault, Lucretia summons her husband, her father, and two of their closest companions. She reveals Tarquinius's offense and extracts their promise to avenge the wrong. Although the men seek to console her, she stabs herself with a knife concealed in her robe. Her reason, as she explains it, is to avoid serving as an example for unchaste women in the future. While the others are absorbed in grief, Brutus (her husband's companion) extracts the knife and vows on Lucretia's blood not only to take vengeance against the perpetrator and his family, but also to permanently abolish the kingship at Rome.

Livy's narrative correlates unjust monarchy with adultery—Lucretia specifically calls Tarquin an "adulterer"—making the adulterer-rapist symbol and symptom of despotic rule. Although this association is hardly novel in either Greek or Roman political thought, Livy's narrative puts a unique spin on the connection.[55] By rendering Lucretia's rape the driving force behind the elimination of kingship, the narrative links the abolition of kingship with the abolition of polygyny in one of its most onerous forms—or, to put it more positively, to the triumph of monogamous marriage. In other words, Livy's narrative roots the foundation of the Republic—and the limited political egalitarianism it brought—with equality in the domain of gender. That is, a group of Roman subordinates band together to prevent the strong from violating or taking their wives, with the result that a reverse-dominance hierarchy (equality, egalitarianism) emerges to protect and structure men's rights as husbands.[56] At the same time, however, the male resentment and energy needed to ignite this transformation requires a female catalyst, specifically a woman who values chastity more than life. In this way, the narrative recruits a woman—albeit a fictitious one—to embody and enforce the double standard limiting women to one legitimate sexual partner, namely their husband, and to embed this principle in the very foundation of the republic.

These stories spotlight some core differences in the ways sexual relations between men and women were involved in the articulation of symbolic boundaries and identities in Athens and Rome. Whereas Athenian civic ideology recruits female sexuality to construct such things as male status, legitimacy, and bloodline/racial purity, Roman ideology deploys female sexuality to generate male status and nationalized moral norms. We might say that, in Rome, an ideal of moral purity replaces the Athenian concern for bloodline/racial purity. Several factors probably help account for this key difference. Perhaps most significant, the early Romans were thought to have been immigrants rather than children of the earth. In one popular myth of early Rome, the problem is not writing women out of the city's origins (a service performed by the Athenian myth of autochthony), but, rather, finding women there at all. According to Livy, the deficit of women compelled Romulus and his followers to kidnap and rape the Sabine women, forcing and cajoling them into becoming their wives.[57] In this way, marriage is founded by an act of force that inaugurates and validates the gender hierarchy structuring relations between the sexes in Rome, no less than in Athens.[58] At the same time, the myth links Roman expansion to the intermarriage of peoples and customs, with the gender hierarchy of marriage serving to model Rome's pride of place in such acts of expansion and incorporation.

IDEOLOGIES OF ROMAN MARRIAGE

As in the Greek world, the institution of Roman marriage affirmed a normative heterosexuality and employed heterosexual conduct and mores to assist in the creation of other social identities (kinship, gender, class). But Roman marriage also had a distinctly political character: according to Cicero, it was the seedbed of the state.[59] And while the story of the Sabine women emphasizes the role of marriage in bringing together disparate peoples in a new union, marriage also had an exclusionary role in bounding and delineating the citizen body. Lawful marriage was the prerogative of Roman citizens and Latins, as well as of foreigners who possessed the right to intermarry with Roman citizens (*conubium*).[60] Although grants of *conubium* usually went hand in hand with enfranchisement, it was clearly possible to have *conubium* without citizenship, given the legal provision that children issuing from the marriage of a Roman citizen to a spouse with *conubium* (but not citizenship) follow the status of their fathers.[61] Slaves had no rights of marriage, and freed slaves could only marry if they became Roman citizens.[62]

Although there is some debate as to when an ideal of conjugal warmth and affection arose in Rome, it is clearly articulated for the period most abundantly attested to by our sources (the late Republic through the first two centuries A.D.).[63] Still, the Romans do not seem to have regarded love as a valid single motive for making a marriage. According to Susan Treggiari, the Romans based their marriages on considerations of birth, rank, wealth, personal qualities, family connections, and friendship.[64] Nevertheless, although they may not have initially forged marriages on the basis of physical or romantic attraction, Roman material culture attests that an ideal of conjugal *erōs* was current in some circles. Some elite Romans decorated their bedrooms and other household items with paintings depicting sexual positions and/or the preliminaries to intercourse.[65]

The sources present Roman marriage as a partnership based on the mutual consent of the spouses.[66] There were two necessary conditions for a Roman marriage to be valid: the partners needed the requisite status (*conubium*) and the intention to be married to each other.[67] If they remained in their fathers' power (*potestas*), however, each partner would have also needed the consent of their father in his role as *pater familias*—a factor that may have diminished the significance of consent for both men and women.[68] The institution of *patria potestas* (paternal power) can be viewed as the cultural correlate of Athenian autochthony in that it served to distinguish the Romans from all other peoples.[69] In theory, the *pater familias* had the power of life and death over his descendants, lifelong ownership rights, and enormous influence in making and dissolving his children's marriages.[70] Although the *pater familias* probably did not autocratically dictate his children's marriage choices, and although many Romans would have been released from *potestas* at the time of their marriage, the very existence of *patria potestas* provides a caution against assimilating marriage and the Roman family to modern constructs of the companionate and affectionate nuclear family.[71]

The double standard was alive and well in Rome. A female slave in Plautus' *Mercator* rails against the unfairness, that, as she puts it, husbands can freely introduce low-class mistresses into their homes while wives can be divorced for simply stepping outside without a husband's knowledge. This is something of an overstatement. A husband who brought a mistress/concubine into his home was clearly regarded as crossing a line, in Rome as in Athens. Men who try to do this, or who seem to be so endeavoring, are regularly made fools of or otherwise disciplined in Roman comedy (the *Mercator* is no exception). That said, sexual fidelity was certainly not required of Roman husbands. Roman men had ready access to female sex workers and unlimited sexual entitlement to their slaves. By contrast, the only socially sanctioned sexual partner for a married woman was her husband. Although this constraint is very similar to what we find in Athens, the Romans idealized and required female chastity for culturally specific reasons.[72]

SEX, MEDICINE, AND NATIONAL HEALTH: THE POLITICS OF FEMALE SEXUALITY

Most conspicuously, a link between female chastity and the health of the Roman state was institutionalized in the service of the vestal virgins, six priestesses assigned the duty of preventing Vesta's sacred fire from being extinguished. As the name implies, virginity was a requirement of service. Their "perpetual chastity," according to Beth Severy, "was part of their religious caretakership of the state, and their unchastity was often diagnosed as the cause of national disasters."[73] Similarly, the sexual integrity of Roman *matronae* was also believed to be necessary for the well-being of both men's households and the larger sociopolitical order.[74] This is evident in Livy's stories of early Rome, in which sexual assaults on chaste Roman women catalyze political reform.[75] By contrast, Tacitus's narratives of early imperial

Rome express both sides of the moral equation: bad wives (i.e., hypersexual, adulterous ones) signify corrupt imperial power and autocracy, whereas good wives (the nondesirous, sexually faithful ones) symbolize "good empire."[76]

Despite the importance of female chastity to Rome's national and imperial ideologies, some genres intimate that good wives were hard to find. Depictions of women's sexual insatiability recur throughout Roman satire, but are hardly limited to that genre.[77] Today, however, most scholars doubt the accuracy of the portrait of widespread sexual immorality we find in satire and various first-century A.D. works of literature.[78] Still, it appears that the Romans took steps to guard against the possibility of women's sexual license. Some writers argued that women should marry very soon after menarche to ensure their virginity.[79] It seems that the Romans attached more weight to a woman's physical virginity at first marriage than did the Greeks.[80] Although a woman's premarital sexual experience was frowned on (and, indeed, was illegal) in Athens and in Rome, Giulia Sissa argues that the sexual activity of a *parthenos* (an unmarried woman) was imperceptible if it was not publicly known in the classical Greek world.[81] Similarly, David Konstan maintains that women with premarital sexual experience were not viewed as "damaged goods" in Athenian culture, and that such experience was not a barrier to marriage.[82]

As in Greek culture, medicine in Rome tended to support the ideological imperative that women marry and reproduce. Yet, Roman medicine, although certainly influenced by its Greek counterpart, lacks the sexualized model of female health that we find in the Hippocratic writings. For example, Soranus, a physician working in Rome during the reigns of Trajan and Hadrian, argues that permanent virginity was healthy for females and males (although he concedes that sexual intercourse is necessary to perpetuate the species).[83] In his *Gynecology*, in part a training manual for physicians and midwives, he also argues that it is dangerous for young girls to bear children, recommending abortion in cases of early pregnancy.[84] While Soranus certainly views women as reproductive beings (a view that precludes the separation of female sexuality from kinship), he rejects the Hippocratic correlation of female health with sex and childbearing.[85]

THE AUGUSTAN MARRIAGE LAWS

Augustus's legislation on marriage and adultery, enacted in 18 B.C. and strengthened by subsequent legislation in 9 A.D., had profound effects on the interface between heterosexual behavior and social identity—for both men and women in Rome, and especially for members of the upper classes.[86] The marriage law seems to have been designed to encourage Roman citizens—particularly those belonging to the senatorial and equestrian classes—to marry and have children.[87] To this end, it established penalties for men and women who failed to reproduce and rewards for those who did.[88] In so doing, the law inextricably linked citizenship to the reproductive body. On the one hand, the marriage law supported and strengthened the existing gender regime by enhancing the political status of "respectable" women precisely on the basis of their traditional position in the heterosexual kinship system as *matres familias*.[89] But, at the same time, by rewarding women who had produced their quota of children with freedom from guardianship (*tutela*), the legislation pushed against the conventional gender ideology that deemed women too light-minded to act in the legal sphere without male supervision.[90] Thus, for women, the legislation had the effect of both emphasizing the traditional construct of female social identity in terms of body-specific functions and providing a release from their traditional gender-specific "disabilities" (i.e., feeblemindedness).[91] Similarly, although the moral legislation (Augustus's laws pertaining to marriage and adultery) effectively enshrined the double standard legally, emphasizing that a woman was either a *matrona* or a *meretrix* (a courtesan or common prostitute), it also gave a new and highly privileged status to the *mater familias*. While *matrona* and *mater familias* are basically synonymous terms for "mistress of the household" or, in some contexts for "respectable woman," *mater familias* seems to have had more moral weight simply because it served as a social counterpart to *pater familias*.[92]

While the marriage law inadvertently paved the way for remodeling, if not jettisoning, the very gender regime it sought to instantiate for women, it placed new emphasis on male gender identity understood in terms of conjugal kinship and sexual reproduction. Gender was, of course, a long-standing component of Roman male identity. According to historians of Roman society and sexuality, the Roman male was condemned to a life of maleness—a hypermasculine/macho identity demonstrated through aggression, penetration, and status-seeking behavior.[93] But, in contrast to the conventions of macho/maleness, the marriage legislation articulated an ideal of social identity for men directly tied to family and fathering: a domain of gendered kinship traditionally associated with women rather than men.[94] Similarly, the adultery legislation, discussed in more detail below, restricted a man's ability to cultivate a hyper-masculine identity by making it a state crime to seduce respectable women (i.e., the daughters, sisters, wives, and mothers of Roman men).

While Augustus's legislation had the effect of investing gender with new forms of political salience, it more deliberately aimed to produce a people with a particular moral and class structure. By formally articulating who could marry whom, and, hence, who could bear legitimate children with whom, the legislation endowed the Roman people with new (or newly explicit) moral character.[95] I emphasize that the law characterized the Roman people rather than the citizenry per se because one provision of the marriage legislation blurred the line between citizens and former slaves to give salience to the moral makeup of the populace, both the freeborn and the freed. No citizen or former slave was allowed to marry a so-called infamous person (a category including prostitutes, pimps, and women convicted of adultery).[96] The impact of the provision was to underscore the moral character of respectable Romans by contrasting it with that of the socially despised infamous. The law also fortified the class division between elites and nonelites by forbidding senators, their children, and all other descendants in the male line to the third degree from marrying former slaves, actors and actresses, or anyone whose father or mother was an actor or actress.[97] In so doing, the law did not make the senatorial class an endogamous elite because it was possible for freeborn Romans lacking a senator in the family tree to intermarry with those not so impoverished. Again, the provision seems intended less to restrict actual marriage practices than to reinforce the elite status of the senatorial order by publicly identifying those with whom its members were not to marry and reproduce.[98]

ADULTERY IN ROME

Several months after the passage of the marriage legislation, Augustus put through a second law covering adultery and criminal fornication (*stuprum*) that attached additional political significance to sexual behavior.[99] This "adultery" law actually criminalized all sexual activity with women who did not fall into one of the exempted categories (i.e., prostitutes, procuresses, slaves, or foreigners not married to Roman citizens), along with homosexual rape.[100] On one level, this prohibition was nothing new. Already, in the early second century B.C., in Plautus' *Curculio*, a young man explains to his friend that nothing prevents him from loving prostitutes, provided he can pay, but that he must keep away from the "wife, widow, virgin, youth, and freeborn boys." These are the same prohibited categories found in Augustus's law. Nevertheless, the passage of a formal law recast the significance and consequences of the forbidden behavior. This was particularly true in the case of women's adultery, the primary offense the law was designed to punish.[101]

Prior to the passage of this law, adultery was primarily a private matter.[102] Though, in theory, Augustus still allowed families recourse to self-help, the associated conditions were now so limited they virtually ensured that trials would take place.[103] Hence, a new permanent court (*quaestio perpetua*) was created specifically to deal with adultery.[104] An aggrieved husband was required to divorce his wife within sixty days of discovering her infidelity and to prosecute her and the lover for adultery. If he failed to do so, the law allowed a third party to prosecute the adulteress and charge the lenient husband with *lenocinium* (acting as a panderer for his wife).[105] If convicted, the adulteress lost half her dowry, and she and the adulterer were relegated to separate islands. Finally, the adulteress was required to wear the toga, the dress of Roman men and prostitutes, advertising the irretrievable loss of her respectability.[106]

The punishments imposed on the adulteress may have been calculated not only to deter marital infidelity but also, more pointedly, to pressure respectable men and women into marrying. For it was now legally impossible for respectable women—widows, divorcées, and so on—to enter into any sexual relationship without marrying their partner. Similarly, men seeking casual sexual relationships with respectable women ran the risk of being brought before the new public tribunal. Men, however, found a way of negotiating and ultimately bypassing the laws restricting nonmarital sex: they took concubines.[107] Men too young for marriage, or men who had children and heirs from a prior marriage, were the most likely to opt for this strategy.[108] Respectable women, however, were largely barred from taking this route because concubinage, although often functioning as a de facto marriage, was regarded as distinctly less reputable than marriage.

In contrast to the Athenians, the Romans defined adultery as a specific category of offense. According to the third-century A.D. jurist Papinian, adultery is an offense "committed with a married woman, the name being derived from children conceived by another (*alter*)."[109] Yet, though the term itself may derive from the issue of confused paternity, the Romans generally did not base the problem of adultery on either legitimacy or bloodlines. Although satire contains its share of paternity jokes, sneering comments about duped husbands raising other men's children, the trope is not as common or developed as we would expect.[110] For instance, we do not find Roman elites maligning their rivals with taunts of illegitimacy or tainted bloodlines, as we find throughout Attic Old Comedy and oratory.[111] As a matter of fact, in some respects, the Roman characterization of adultery reverses what we find in Athens. Whereas Athenian sources generally downplay female adultery but express bastardy fears, Roman sources harp on female infidelity but mostly elide its consequences for legitimacy.

I suspect the reason for this difference can be traced back to Athenian and Roman notions of national particularism. The autochthonous Athenians emphasized the integrity of their bloodlines on the national and individual levels, leading them to worry about the female role in the reproductive process as the guarantor of male legitimacy and identity. The Romans did not center their identity around a mystified concept of blood kinship—a factor that seems to have given them some release from anxieties about a woman's control over purity. However, they did employ a mystified construct of legal kinship in the form of *patria potestas*. Roman law gave fathers an extraordinary ability to create their descendents as well as to control their behavior. The emphasis on the *pater familias*'s control over kinship is emblematized in the Roman formula for filiation: marriage shows the father (*is est pater quem nuptiae demonstrant*).[112] With this principle, Roman men privileged law and husband-right as the determinants of kinship, effectively denying women's roles in guaranteeing male legitimacy and identity. In the context of this kinship ideology, unrestrained female sexuality challenged not bloodlines but paternal power, including the moral authority of Roman fathers to regulate the behavior of their household members.

Roman ideology frequently likens political authority to a brand of paternal authority.[113] Accordingly, just as a promiscuous wife or daughter could jeopardize a husband's or father's authority, so, too, could an adulterous woman undermine the state's paternalist moral authority. It is hardly accidental that adulterous women loom large in Roman accounts of political crisis, particularly in narratives dealing with the civil wars.[114] Similarly, the adulteress's transgression posed a special threat to Roman social boundaries. The social structure in Rome was anchored and perpetuated by a gendered form of class endogamy that allowed downward sexual and marital mobility for men but forbade downward movement for women.[115] This is probably why the thought of an elite woman committing adultery with a slave or social inferior strikes terror in the Roman imagination.[116] Such fears appear to be more than mere projections of anxious male minds. According to Sarah Pomeroy, downward sexual mobility was a persistent possibility, "since unlike Athens, where women lived in separate quarters, in Rome wealthy women were attended by numerous male slaves, often chosen for their attractive appearance."[117] Liaisons between elite women and slaves jeopardized social boundaries not because of fears about interclass mixing or the possibility that tainted offspring might be produced. Rather, the problem was that a woman's selection of a low-class lover upended the status distinctions that the conventional social hierarchy required, undermining not only "the good of the state as a whole," but also "those who had the greatest interest in the state, whose identities were most closely bound up in its political fabric, men of the senatorial and equestrian elite."[118]

Although the adulteress seems to be wholly despised, adulterers meet with a mixed reception in the sources. On the one hand, the adulterer's close association with women could leave him vulnerable to slurs on his manhood, specifically to accusations of effeminacy—being, or becoming, like the women he sought.[119] But since the adulterer also demonstrated his own power and attractiveness, albeit at the expense of other men, he could be depicted as hypermasculine, powerful, and desirous of a dangerous dominance.[120] It is no accident that Antony and Octavian (soon to be Augustus) constantly accused each other of adultery during their power struggle prior to the battle of Actium.[121] In such contexts, adultery operates as a conceptual stand-in for polygamy, linking the perpetrator's sexual excess with tyrannical power and aspiration.

PROTESTING THE AUGUSTAN LAWS

Tales of adultery are common in Roman sources from the first century B.C. to about the second century A.D.[122] The multiple symbolic associations attached to adultery, however, make it difficult to discern whether these stories index actual behavior.[123] Similarly, it is not known if the passage of Augustus's law was a response to perceived behavioral changes. Nevertheless, though we cannot be certain how prevalent adultery actually was in Roman society, we can say something about one key effect of this legislation on traditional social identities. By making female adultery a state crime rather than a private matter to be handled or hushed up at a family's discretion, the law brought new attention to women as legal agents—as beings capable of choosing their sexual partners, either in accordance or at variance with the law. In so doing, the law may have had the paradoxical effect of detaching sexual conduct from the very social identities and familial contexts in which Augustus sought to root and contain it. One scholar contends that the law separated "sexual behavior from its traditional familial context, where it had been regulated by forces of honor and shame, and instead described it as a freely chosen activity between legal persons, one subject to scrutiny and regulation in the public sphere."[124]

According to this claim, Augustus's moral legislation carved out the conceptual space in which a sexual identity detached from conventional social articulations could emerge. The actions of Vistilia in 19 A.D. offer perhaps the best evidence for this process. Though married, she put her name on the aedile's list of prostitutes in order to engage in extramarital affairs with immunity from prosecution as an adulteress.[125] This attempt to legalize extramarital sexual activity seems to indicate that Vistilia jettisoned her identity as a *matrona* (limited as it was to heterosexual kinship) and attempted to define herself on her own terms, to the extent that was possible. Once this ploy was brought to light, however, the Roman state quickly moved to remedy the situation: Vistilia was punished as an adulteress and relegated to the island of Seriphos. That the state was moved to pass new legislation expressly forbidding her dodge suggests that Vistilia was not alone in seeking to escape the confines of *dignitas matronalis* (a woman's traditional social identity).[126]

Still, if Vistilia's behavior does suggest an attempt to express a self-concept free from conventional social constraints, there is no reason to think that it corresponds to, or prefigures, the modern heterosexual identity category. These days, the heterosexual is understood as a type of person based on enduring sexual orientation implicitly defined against the homosexual as its other and opposite. Evidence that Vistilia's sense of sexual identity depended on object choice (and so was defined against beings who selected other objects) is simply lacking. Rather, her apparent construction of an identity oriented around what we would call heterosexual conduct must be seen in its historically specific context as a rejection of traditional social identities and/or Augustus's new political freighting of those identities. Even without passage of additional legislation criminalizing her behavior, it is doubtful whether Vistilia's choice was a realistic possibility for most women. In an era before safe contraception and/or abortion, women's heterosexual conduct could not be easily and reliably detached from its reproductive consequences, and hence from kinship of one sort or another.[127] (While recent studies suggest that the Greeks and Romans had knowledge of effective herbal contraceptives, we do not know whether these remedies were widely available.)[128] Accordingly, the most we can say is that the uncoupling of sexual behaviors and attitudes from traditional social identities was an uneven process, varying in accordance with gender, class position, and individual temperament.

While Vistilia ultimately failed in her attempt to bypass the double standard, it was soon to come under attack from other sources. Paradoxically, the Augustan adultery legislation played a role in enabling and encouraging these attacks. The public prosecution of women for adultery brought into high relief the glaring asymmetry of a social and legal system that failed to classify a husband's affairs with slaves and prostitutes as adultery. The Roman Stoic philosopher Musonius Rufus (around 30–100 A.D.) came out strongly against this hypocrisy, arguing that "no man with self-control would think of having relations with a courtesan or free woman apart from marriage, no, nor even with his own maidservant."[129] He advised those who claimed that a man's sexual use of his female slaves harmed no one to consider how they would feel were their wives to have sex with male slaves.[130]

CHANGE AND CONTINUITY: SEXUAL ETHICS AND CHRISTIAN IDENTITIES

Early Christian writers appropriated and developed the Roman Stoic critique, advising a similar single sexual standard: virginity for men and women before marriage, and chastity within marriage.[131] In seeking to defend the behavior of a female friend who divorced a dissolute husband, Jerome (a fourth-century Christian apologist) explains that Christianity mandated this form of sexual equality because men and women were subordinated to the same god.

> It must not be the case that, while an adulterous wife could be divorced, a dissolute husband had to be kept ... indeed the laws of Caesar are different from those of Christ; Papinian commands one thing, our own Paul commands another. Secular laws allow men to be unchaste, condemning only seduction and adultery, while lust gets its free range in the brothels and with servant girls—as if what made the act a sinful one was the rank of the person assaulted, not the intention of the assaulter. With us Christians, however, what is unlawful for women is just as unlawful for men, since both serve the same god, both are bound by the same ties.[132]

Scholars point out that this and the numerous Christian polemics against the double standard were ultimately ineffectual. Long after the Christianization of the Roman Empire, extramarital sex for men continued to be acceptable—particularly with female slaves.[133] By calling attention to this continuity, I do not wish to imply that the organization of heterosexuality remained basically the same from 500 B.C. to 300 A.D. Rather, we see real change in the meanings attached to heterosexuality in some early Christian communities scattered throughout the empire. By way of conclusion, I will mention one such change because it clarifies the central argument of this study, that heterosexual acts and attitudes were deeply embedded in traditional social identities—identities that were, in turn, shaped by dominant political ideologies.

In seeking to explain the turn to asceticism in early Christianity, scholars have argued that the elaboration of a new sexual ethics was a key way Christian communities carved out an identity distinguished from both Pagans and

Jews.[134] Some early Christians went so far as to renounce sex and marriage entirely. In so doing, these groups and individuals were not reacting to the sexual debauchery of the Roman Empire.[135] Rather, they were protesting and opting out of a political society that depended on sex and marriage for its existence and continuity.[136] According to Peter Brown, some early Christians treated married intercourse "as the linchpin of the towering structure of the 'present age.' To break the spell of the bed was to break the spell [of a] ... world whose social structures stood condemned."[137] By renouncing all sexual activity, early Christians were taking a stand against the state, offering eloquent testimony to the continuing role of tradition, whether set forth by the Greek polis or the Roman emperor, in endowing heterosexual conduct with meaning and significance. Needless to say, with Christian asceticism we remain a world away from the emergence of the heterosexual as a person who is defined by their attraction to members of the opposite sex.

CHAPTER THREE

Homosexuality

DANIEL OGDEN

GREEK WORLD

Men

Homosexuality in the ancient world has received much attention from scholars over the last three decades, but the bulk of this attention has been focused more narrowly. Most of it has been focused upon what is commonly referred to as "Greek homosexuality,"[1] but this in practice is almost always taken to mean little more than the male pederastic culture of classical Athens. The evidence for this, textual and iconographic, is rich and complex, and its interpretation remains challenging and highly controversial. But Athens was by no means the only city in the ancient Greek world. Indeed, it is sometimes claimed that there were a thousand.[2] While we do not have evidence from any other of the cities to match the sort provided by classical Athens, we do have significant evidence bearing upon quite a few of them. This is substantial enough to indicate that the structuring of homosexual culture in Athens was by no means typical of the Greek world as a whole. Accordingly, we will begin our review with a brief consideration of male homosexual culture in classical Athens, and the modern debates to which it has given rise, before casting our eyes more widely over the Greek world.

The model of classical Athenian homosexual culture that continues to be the most influential is firmly based on that put forward by Sir Kenneth Dover in his 1978 book, *Greek Homosexuality*.[3] The views he developed

there reached an audience beyond that of classical scholarship when they
were taken up (in somewhat misunderstood form) by Michel Foucault in his
1984 book, *L'usage des plaisirs* (translated in 1985 as *The Use of Pleasure*).
The model might be summarized in the following terms.[4] Male homosexual
acts normally took place between an *erastēs* (lover), a young man, ideally a
bachelor, and an *erōmenos* (beloved), a beardless, adolescent boy between
the ages of twelve and eighteen. Both would belong to the elite. The *erastēs*
would court the *erōmenos* with such things as hunting gifts and, if success-
ful, consummate his desire through anal sex. As the boy turned to manhood
in the period between the ages of eighteen and twenty—the transitional period of life associated with service as an ephebe (a border-guard)—he would
himself cease to be a passive partner and pursue other boys in turn. Later
on, by around the age of thirty, he would give up homosexual activity altogether in favor of marriage. The role of the *erastēs* was one of dominance,
the role of the *erōmenos* one of subjection, and they participated in a zero-
sum game of social advantage and disadvantage. As a result, the pursued
boy was in a morally precarious situation, but he could retain his honor so
long as he was extremely discriminating in his acceptance of a lover, took
extravagant gifts for his favors but money on no account, and did not make
any show of enjoying the anal sex. The lover would use his dominant position to give the boy valuable help, material or ethical, in becoming a full
adult member of the community, as is reflected in Plato's *Symposium*. So
far as the Athenians were concerned, only an extremely deviant grown man
would put himself in the role of the *erōmenos*, and those who did, whether
as prostitutes (as Timarchus was alleged to have been in a well-known
speech of Aeschines) or as *kinaidoi* (men who simply enjoyed and sought to
receive anal sex, were conceptualized as effeminate and reviled, and at Athens the former group was deprived of at least some citizen rights.[5]

Even within the most familiar documents of classical Athenian life it
is easy to find examples of relationships in conflict with this ideal model.
The age boundaries, for example, seem to have been particularly porous.
The pots of the black-figure painter known as the Affecter portray bearded
erōmenoi receiving anal sex.[6] And we know of *erastēs-erōmenos* relationships that endured into much later life for both partners. The eighteen-year-
old Agathon was the *erōmenos* of Pausanias in Plato's *Protagoras*, set in 428
B.C. Plato's *Symposium* is set twelve years later, in 416 B.C., and yet in this
Agathon remains Pausanias's *erōmenos*. Furthermore, Plutarch tells us that,
at the age of forty, the bearded Agathon was *erōmenos* to the seventy-two-
year-old Euripides.[7]

Occasional exceptions need not undermine completely the general integrity of the model. But a more serious challenge to it has been mounted by James Davidson in an article first published in 2001. Davidson endorses from the Doverian-Foucauldian consensus the notion that a loss of honor on the part of an *erōmenos* or, for that matter, on the part of anyone engaged in homosexual activities could ensue from a perceived failure of self-mastery (*enkrateia, sōphrosynē*) in initially yielding to a relationship or in the conduct of it thereafter. A boy or man could demonstrate such a failure of self-mastery by yielding too readily or too eagerly, by yielding to many lovers at once or at random, or, most damagingly, by accepting money to yield—in other words, by becoming a prostitute. But Davidson decries what he sees as the fallacy of the "polarity of penetration" upon which the Dover-Foucault model otherwise depends. The notion that the anal penetrator was a "winner" and the anally penetrated was, to an equal and complementary degree, a "loser" in a zero-sum game of social advantage and disadvantage is to Davidson anachronistic and without warrant in the evidence for classical Athens. And, he maintains, there is insufficient evidence for the contention that the normal mode of sex between *erastēs* and *erōmenos* was the anal penetration of the latter by the former.[8]

There is certainly a strong case to answer here. On the one hand, it is far from clear that anal penetration of the *erōmenos* by the *erastēs* was the usual mode of homosexual encounter. Of course, we cannot aspire to know what went on between couples behind closed doors—but neither could the people of classical Athens. The most we could hope to discover would be what was popularly believed to take place between *erastēs* and *erōmenos*. Contradictory projections have been bequeathed to us. The pots of the Affecter aside, Athenian vase paintings of pederastic couples depict only intercrural (between the thighs) copulation, whereas the comic poet Aristophanes exclusively talks of anal penetration as the mode of homosexual gratification.[9] On the other hand, few would now oppose Davidson's own understanding of the importance of the ethics of self-mastery (i.e., the avoidance of uncontrolled excess; the key terms are *akrasia* and *akolasia*) in sexual relations, which he has done much to establish in other work.[10]

But it has yet to be proven that we can afford to abandon thinking about penetration completely when looking at the classical Athenian evidence. Let us leave the controversial Eurymedon vase out of the debate as too problematic. This ostensibly shows a Greek, accompanied by the phrase "I am Eurymedon," running, erect penis in hand, toward the exposed anus of a bending Persian (or other Oriental) figure, who, in turn, is accompanied by the phrase "I stand bent over." The vase is traditionally read as a celebration of Cimon's naval victory over the Persians at the battle of the river Eurymedon in around 466 B.C. Less controversial might be an engaging fragment of the comic poet Eubulus, who was active in the mid-fourth century B.C. He speaks of the deprivations supposedly endured by the Greek army during the protracted siege of Troy:

> Nor did any of them see a courtesan, but they kneaded (*edephon*; i.e., "masturbated") themselves for ten years. Bitter was the military service they saw, who, having taken but one city, came away far wider-arsed (*euryprōktoteroi*) than the city that they took at that time. (Eubulus F118 K-A)[11]

The logic of this seems to be that the Greek soldiers passed the time not only by masturbating but also by having a lot of anal sex with each other—and, as a result, when they finally left Troy, they had all been more thoroughly buggered than the city they had completely devastated. In other words, it seems that the quip does indeed depend upon a strong identification between the notions of buggery and defeat or subjection. For Davidson, the familiar comic term *euryprōktos* (wide-arsed) is abusive not because of its implication that the person so designated has been the recipient of anal sex—and thus demeaned—but because of its implication that he has been engaged in an excess of sex in general, and is therefore incapable of self-mastery. With such a reading, Eubulus's joke comes to seem somewhat less pointed: we would have, I suppose, to understand that Troy was metaphorically *euryprōktos* in the sense that, as enslaved, it was no longer in a position to exercise mastery over itself.

And what of the *kinaidos*? He is a figure who plays a rather more substantial role in the scholarship of ancient homosexuality than he seems to have done in the Greeks' own thinking about it. The pseudo-Aristotelian *Physiognomonica* winningly describes him thus:

> The signs of a *kinaidos* are as follows. He has drooping eyelids. He is knock-kneed. He inclines his head to the right side. He makes effete gestures with open hands. He has two varieties of gait, one in which he wiggles his bottom, and one in which he keeps it still. He rolls his eyes around a great deal, like Dionysius the Sophist. ([Arist.] *Phgn.* 808a12–6)

The same text elsewhere takes the drooping eyelid as a sign of cowardice and notes that all female animals have knock-knees.[12] But Davidson contends that nothing is said of him in our classical Greek sources to suggest that he specialized in receiving anal sex: he was womanish because he was uncontrolled in his sexual desires: a quality the Greeks regarded as belonging more naturally to women, whose desires could never find satisfaction in a conclusive ejaculation.[13] For similar reasons, seducers (*moichoi:* the term is commonly but misleadingly translated as "adulterers"), whose transgressive desires impelled them to attempt sex with other men's women, were also regarded as effeminate, despite the vigorously heterosexual nature of their desires.[14]

In the other Greek societies of which we are able to say anything, the culture of homosexuality often seems to have been strongly entwined (at the ideological level, at any rate) with that of warfare and military organization.[15] The evidence is clearest in the case of Thebes, in Boeotia. Plutarch gives us a detailed account of the city's elite infantry force of 300 picked men—its so-called Sacred Band (*hieros lochos*). This was founded by Gorgidas, perhaps in 378 B.C., and subsequently came to greatness under Pelopidas. It had its barracks in the heart of the city on the Theban acropolis, the Cadmeia. The band was made up of 150 pairs of *erastai* and *erōmenoi,* and these stood beside each other in the battle line. The underlying principle was that the bond between the two was the strongest of all human bonds, thus encouraging bravery in defending a partner: the *erastai* were induced to fight bravely by love; the *erōmenoi* by shame. The band was unbeaten until it was annihilated by Philip of Macedon at the battle of Chaeronea in 338 B.C. Thereupon the King, impressed by its steadfast bravery during the fight, is supposed to have said, "May those that suppose that these men do or suffer something shameful perish!"[16] The culture of the Band is enshrined in Phaedimus's Boeotian epigram of the mid-third century B.C., which refers to "the arrows that love sends against the Bachelors, whenever they defend their fatherland, made bold by the love of lads. Love has the strength of fire, and is the chief of the gods in helping those that fight in the forward line …"[17] It is likely that the band had a similar precursor in the fifth century. Diodorus speaks of a Theban elite infantry force of 300 in 424 B.C., known as *hēniochoi kai parabatai* (chariot-drivers and chariot-fighters). The metaphor by which they were known clearly indicates as a minimum that the men were divided up into cooperative pairs, and so strongly suggests that the force already consisted of *erastēs-erōmenos* couples.[18] Here it is worth noting that, because only adults could serve in Greek armies (maturity sufficient for service in the army was, in a sense, the definition of adulthood for men), both the *erastai and* the *erōmenoi* of the Sacred Band must have been adult.

Xenophon and Plato alike bracket Elis with Boeotia as places where it is in no way shameful to gratify an *erastēs.*[19] The Eleans probably had an elite force organized according to principles similar to those of the Sacred Band. Xenophon tells that it was the custom of the Eleans to place *erastai* and *erōmenoi* side by side in the battle line, and he speaks elsewhere of an elite Elean force of either 300 or 400 men in 366 B.C. Compatibly with this, we hear that Elis held beauty competitions for boys, with the prize being a set of arms, which the winner would at once dedicate to the warrior-goddess Athena. The combination of the celebration of boys' desirability with their symbolic acceptance into the warrior community coincides suggestively with what we hear of Cretan practices.[20]

Our principal evidence for Cretan customs comes by way of a fragment of the fourth-century historian Ephorus, preserved by Strabo. He tells how an *erastēs* who conceives a desire for a boy first approaches the boy's group of friends and asks them to help him set up an ambush in which he can seize him in a ritual capture. If they think the *erastēs* worthy, they agree to help. After such a seizure, the *erastēs* takes his *erōmenos*, known in Crete as a *parastatheis* (stander-beside: cf. *parabatai*?), to the *andreion* (men's house, or mess). The *erastēs* gives the boy gifts before taking him, along with the friends who participated in the capture, off to the country. There, they hunt together and are feasted by the *erastēs* for two months. The *erastēs* then releases the boy back to the city laden with statutory gifts: a military cloak, an ox for sacrifice, and a drinking cup. As he feasts on the ox, the boy recounts his adventures and declares whether or not he is pleased with his *erastēs*: if he is, the relationship will continue. It is held to be disgraceful for handsome and well-born boys to fail to acquire an *erastēs*. This is a text of obvious importance for those who wish to see Greek pederasty as initiatory: the rite served as an introduction for the boy and his friends to the warrior community (the mess and the military cloak), and to the communal drinking that formed the heart of adult male society (the cup).[21]

Under the so-called Lycurgan system, the male population of Sparta between the ages of seven and thirty lived within the military mess, segregated from the city's womenfolk. Such a system was obviously favorable to the development of a culture of homosexuality, and the context of this culture was, by definition, military. Given their life in training, the entire citizen army of Sparta constituted an elite force—and was famously recognized as such. We should not, then, be surprised by Xenophon's strong implication that it was normal practice in the Spartan army for loving couples to be drawn up side by side in the battle line. Further, he tells us that when the Spartan leader Anaxibius sought death in battle, his *erōmenos* stayed by his side until the end. Athenaeus subsequently makes the point more explicitly: before battle, he tells us, the Spartans used to sacrifice to Eros on the ground that safety resided in the love of those drawn up alongside each other.[22] Plutarch tells us that boys in their training "herds" (*agelai*) became of interest to *erastai* once they turned twelve.[23] The Spartans described their institutions of homosexuality with a vocabulary that remains partly obscure, but that may suggest they believed an *erastēs* transmitted military prowess and vigor to his *erōmenos* by means of his semen. Key here is their application to the *erastēs* of the term *eispnēlas*, which means either "one who blows in'" or "one who is blown into." The ancient lexicographical sources lean in favor of the latter. For Bethe, who took the former reading, the Spartan *erastēs* inseminated his *erōmenos* with his prowess anally, an institution for which he finds anthropological parallels among the Keraki Indians and the Marind-Anim of New Guinea.[24] Plato noted that anal sex was widely practiced in Sparta (and, indeed, Crete), and that the Spartan fondness for anal sex was common knowledge among Athenian comic poets, who, it seems, were responsible for coining the term *kysolakōn* (arse-Spartan).[25] But on the latter reading, "one who is blown into," we might wonder whether the Spartan *erastai* inseminated their *erōmenoi* by means of fellatio, an anthropological parallel found in the "flute players" of another people of New Guinea, the Sambia. (The homosexual culture of the Sambia seemingly exhibits a remarkable range of similarities to that attested for Sparta in the ancient sources, and thus invests the sources with a degree of credibility for which they might otherwise want.)[26]

Women

The evidence for female homosexual culture in the Greek world is much more limited than that for male. Mentions of female homosexuality are rare enough in the literary texts, while no sex acts between women are preserved in the iconographic record. The literary evidence, such as it is, seems to suggest that it was calqued on male homosexual culture and that its typical context was (while not, of course, military) nonetheless similarly institutional and educational.[27] It is in the evidence for Sparta that this comes across most clearly. Plutarch draws an explicit parallel between the role of a Spartan *erastēs* in educating his *erōmenos* in martial valor and ethics and that of women in educating girls. Respectable women, he tells us, would have sexual relationships with unmarried girls, and such relationships were highly valued. Idealism may get the better of Plutarch when he goes on to affirm that if two women found themselves competing for the same girl, they would put aside rivalry and make their common affection the basis for friendship, combining their efforts to protect the character of the beloved they shared.[28] A parallelism with male homosexual culture at Sparta may be implied also by the existence of the word *aïtis*, a feminine version of *aïtas,* which was applied to Spartan *erōmenoi.*[29] It is hardly surprising that Spartan women should have occupied themselves in this fashion, seeing as little as they did of their menfolk. An open culture of homosexuality between women at Sparta seems to have gone back at least as far as the time of the poet Alcman, whose floruit coincided with the twenty-seventh Olympiad (672–68 B.C.).[30] He composed lyric songs for choruses of young girls to sing, and the surviving fragments of these seem to give expression to erotic desire between the females. The fragmentary *Louvre Partheneion (Maiden Song)* speaks in a female voice and addresses a female subject. It tells her that she will not, as she might have been expected to, go to the house of Aenesimbrota, presumably a woman who trains girls in their choruses, and say, "I wish I had Astaphis," or "I wish Philylla would look at me, and so, too, Damareta, and lovely Vianthemis," before the speaker affirms that she herself is lovelorn for Hagesichora.[31] In another fragmentary *partheneion,* what we may assume to be a female voice again speaks of its desire for the sweet and glossy-haired Astymeloisa. When Astymeloisa looks at the speaker, she instills in her a desire that slackens her limbs, and which is more melting than sleep or death. But Astymeloisa gives the speaker no answer. The speaker longs to see if Astymeloisa could love her and dreams of the girl taking her by the hand, whereupon she would become her suppliant.[32] In the performance of these songs, young girls in choruses would seemingly have expressed desire for their peers, other young girls no doubt also in choruses. But whether we should conclude from this that sexual relationships were actually conducted between girl-peers, as opposed to girls and older women, remains unclear.

Our richest evidence for female homosexuality in the ancient world derives, of course, from the fragments of Sappho, the poetess of Lesbos whose floruit was the forty-second Olympiad (612–608 B.C.) and who gave the English language the word *lesbian.*[33] (She knew herself, incidentally, in her distinctive local dialect, as Psap-phō.) Sappho's world was perhaps not so far removed from the one hinted at in the fragments of Alcman. She presides over what is sometimes seen as a "finishing school" for girls, whom she trains in choruses but also prepares for marriage, and she is evidently one amongst a number of such "schoolmistresses."[34]

The most economical introduction to the world portrayed—or constructed—in Sappho's poems is to be found in an imaginary scene described by Philostratus in the third century A.D. The setting is a myrtle grove in which delicate maidens are singing a hymn to Aphrodite, goddess of love, who is present in the form of an ivory statue. The hymn tells of the goddess's birth from the sea. The grove is redolent with frankincense, cinnamon, and myrrh, which have been offered to the goddess on her altar, and the spices give out "a fragrance as of Sappho." A skilled woman chorister, whom we are to understand to be Sappho (or, at any rate, a figure closely akin to her), conducts the girls. She is beautiful still, and not yet past her prime. She claps her hands and frowns at those who are singing out of key, to bring them back in line. The girls are dressed in simple floral tunics with tight-fitting belts, and they dance on the dewy grass with bare feet. Eros, the god of sex, is also in attendance, and he accompanies their song on his bow, as if it is a lyre.[35] The implication of Eros's presence may be that Sappho and her girls will turn to sex-play when their song is done.

Several of Sappho's fragments seem to speak of sexual encounters with her girls, often in the context of an idealized meadow. In the one complete poem of Sappho's to survive, the "Hymn to Aphrodite," the goddess, summoned again by Sappho as on so many previous occasions, asks Sappho which girl she is to compel to love her this time. The language used is the familiar one of erotic pursuit.[36] In a substantial fragment, which begins, "I just want to be dead," a girl forced to leave Sappho against her will, no doubt for a marriage, laments her lot. Sappho consoles her with memories of the good times they have shared. The broken lines seem to have gone on to speak of the two dressing in garlands of violets, roses, and crocuses and satisfying their longing on soft beds. References to a grove, a chorus, and sound follow, perhaps bringing us close to the scene described by Philostratus.[37] In another fragment, Sappho compares a girl to golden-haired Helen, before, it seems, imagining that she would be freed from all her cares if she could spend the night awake with the girl on dewy banks.[38] A further brief fragment speaks of one (female) person sleeping on the breasts of a soft (female) companion.[39] And yet another fragment suggests that pairings between females might be recognized by them with a degree of formality. Archeanassa is referred to as the *syndygos* (yoke-mate, or partner) of Gorgo; such a term is expressive of a strong union, though not necessarily of equality within it.[40]

Some of Sappho's songs celebrate the state of marriage (with men) for which the girls are being trained—and perhaps, in a sense, even sexually trained, albeit in a fashion that conveniently preserves them from unhelpful impregnation. Sometimes these songs can be quite ribald.[41] But they also celebrate virginity, which is not, for Sappho, a condition of sexlessness, deprivation, or anticipation, but rather the opposite: the highly sexualized condition of the not-yet-married girls with whom she enjoys her affairs.[42]

It is possible that Sappho sometimes plays with accepted ideas about sexuality. The poem that is perhaps her most famous opens with the line "That man seems to me the equal of a god." But, as the poem unfolds, it is revealed that the man is not godlike in his desirability, but rather in his good fortune: he happens to be sitting opposite the girl Sappho desperately desires. The poem continues with a description of the overwhelming physical effects of this desire on Sappho's body: she is rendered speechless, she cannot focus her eyes, her ears buzz, she has a hot flush, she sweats, she turns pale, and she feels as if she is about to die.[43] And some may wish to see Sappho advocating a self-consciously female aesthetic over a male one when she declares that, while some may find armies of cavalry, infantry, or ships the most beautiful things on earth, for her, that thing is whomever a person loves.[44]

Of the conventional mode of sexual gratification amongst Sappho and her girls we hear little. The tantalizing word *olisbodokois,* which would normally mean "dildo-receiving," appears in one particularly obscure fragment of Lesbian-dialect poetry, but, alas, it is not clear whether the poem belongs to Sappho or to Alcaeus, her fellow poet of Lesbos. Nor does it seem that Sappho, if the poem is hers, is defining herself and her group with the term. Nor, indeed, is it completely certain that the word does, after all, carry a sexual reference in its context.[45]

Sappho's contemporary Alcaeus speaks of beauty contests on Lesbos "where the Lesbian women/girls go in their trailing dresses, being judged for their beauty."[46] These contests were also mentioned by Theophrastus, who noted that they were also to be found on Tenedos.[47] We hear nothing of the judges: it is probable that they were female, and it may well be that these were homoerotic exercises, just as the beauty contests for boys were in Elis.

How typical was Sappho's world in archaic Greece? Its seeming comparability with the world of Alcman may lead us to think it was widespread, but that is not necessarily so. Writing just half a century later, Anacreon, who was active at the court of Polycrates of Samos (traditionally dated to the 530s–520s B.C.), wrote a gently humorous poem in which he tells that Eros has struck him once again with his purple ball and filled him with a desire to frolic with a girl in multicolored sandals. But, he says, because she comes from Lesbos, she is dissatisfied with his head of white hair and yearns after "another." The word for "another," a feminine adjective, is deliberately ambiguous: does the girl yearn for another, i.e. a younger (man's), head of hair, a feminine noun in the Greek, or does she yearn for another—female—person? It is clear that, already in the mid-sixth century B.C., Lesbos had come to be regarded as a place distinctive and iconic for female homosexuality, and this was due in no small part to the fame of Sappho's poetry.[48]

Our evidence for female homosexuality elsewhere in the Greek world is thin, and this thinness is perhaps most noticeable in the case of classical Athens itself, given the relative profusion of our evidence for life in the city. The most noteworthy reference to the phenomenon is perhaps Plato's in his *Symposium,* where an absurd myth is put into the mouth of the comic poet Aristophanes to explain the origin of human sexual attraction. According to this, humans were originally eight-limbed creatures that came in three varieties: male, female, and male-female. But Zeus split them down the middle for conspiring against the gods. Thereafter, the two halves ever longed to be reunited with themselves, and sexual desire was the manifestation of this longing. The creatures who were originally male-female and then divided into their two constituent parts gave rise to people with heterosexual desires. Those who were originally purely male gave rise to men with homosexual desires. And those who were originally purely female gave rise to women with homosexual desires. One has a feeling that this last category is specified primarily to fill out the logical grid rather than because it is one of great significance for Plato, but the philosopher does nonetheless have a previously unattested word to apply to such women. It is *hetairistriai,* which seems, somewhat curiously, to be built on the term *hetaira* (courtesan), perhaps borrowing its suffix from *laikastria* (female fellator).[49]

We also hear briefly of female homosexuality from the Hellenistic poet Asclepiades. He makes a mock complaint about a pair of Samian women (Anacreon worked on Samos) who refuse to pursue the practices of Aphrodite in accordance with her rules, instead doing things that are not *kalos* (good, beautiful), and he purports to ask the goddess to punish them. Seemingly, this is a complaint about these women's homosexual preferences. Here we may note that Asclepiades elsewhere proclaims his own homosexual desires with vigor.[50]

ROMAN WORLD

Men

The Romans[51] often considered pederasty an alien implantation in their culture, a vice—or an affectation—taken over from the Greeks.[52] It is, of course, highly unlikely that this was so, but it was certainly true that much of the elite Latin literature that idealized or celebrated pederasty self-consciously saluted Greek models.[53]

The Romans had an ideology of male homosexuality that was rather more simplistic than the Greeks'. In accordance with this, the following polarities were strongly aligned:[54]

active (penetrating) — passive (penetrated)
masculine — feminine
free — slave
victor — victim
buyer (or stealer) — seller

In other words, the Romans tended to equate the active or penetrating role with masculinity, freedom, and victory (in short, with winning), and the passive or penetrated role with femininity, slavery, and victimhood (in short, with losing). It was a commonplace that Roman masters routinely penetrated their slave boys.[55] The exchange of gender roles by the penetrated male is encapsulated by Epictetus, who affirms that a man surrenders his manhood when he takes on the role of a catamite.[56] There was also a notion that the practice of homosexuality between men weakened society as a whole. When the Romans measured themselves against the sorts of northern barbarians they feared, pederasty became a token and indeed cause of their own comparative decadence and weakness. So it is by pederasty that Dio Cassius's Bodicea is made to distinguish the decadent Romans from her own tough Britons.[57]

It was at the points where the neat alignment of categories laid out above became confused that the Romans became particularly anxious about homosexual sex. This was particularly true when men attempted to have sex with freeborn, as opposed to slave, youths. According to Livy, the 326 B.C. riot that ended the Roman Republic's practice of debt slavery (a temporary form of slavery to which the free and, indeed, the citizens could be subjected), erupted when a creditor, Papirius, attempted to force himself upon his debt-slave youth, Publilius, who resisted his advances while protesting that he was freeborn. Papirius had the boy whipped, and his pleas to the crowd that gathered set in motion the repeal of this ambivalent variety of bondage.[58] It is possible that sex between freeborn men was actually banned under the terms of an obscure (and admittedly rarely invoked) law, the Lex Scantinia of 149 B.C.[59] Plutarch offers as one possible explanation of the origin of the *bulla* (the amulet worn by freeborn boys) that it was a symbol to enable men to distinguish between free and slave youths—between, that is, unavailable and available ones.[60]

Desire, inevitably, followed the sanctions. First, because freeborn boys were morally out of bounds, they accordingly seem to have been found all the more desirable. The notorious late-republican demagogue Clodius supposedly bribed the judges at his trial by contriving to buy them nights of passion with freeborn noble youths and married women, the variety of woman supposedly the most unobtainable.[61] Secondly, the passive, penetrated role evidently appealed to at least some free men. Along with the prostitutes who sold themselves to be penetrated, we hear of ones who offered penetration. According to Plautus, writing in the early second century B.C., both varieties peddled their wares on the Tuscan road.[62]

The Romans envisaged the penetration that was central to their ideology in two forms: anal and oral, applying to the latter the distinctive term *irrumatio*. Our English use of the word "fellatio" and its cognates is not a very satisfactory translation of this term, because it tends to imply that the fellat-*or* does something to the fellat-*ed*. The Romans, however, were clear that it was the fellated man who did something—and often something highly aggressive—to his fellator.[63]

A function of the power dynamic the Romans associated with penetration was that verbal aggression between men derived its imagery from the penetration of the abused by the abuser, a notion amply illustrated in the poetry of Catullus, who threatens his enemies with buggery and *irrumatio* alike.[64] When Octavian besieged Lucius Antonius and Marc Antony's wife Fulvia in the city of Perusinum (Perugia) in 41–40 B.C., both sides exchanged slingshots inscribed with messages not dissimilar to those the modern U.S. army paints on its bombs. One slingshot affirms that it is heading for Octavian's arse, another for his mouth. From the other side, a slingshot asks both Lucius Antonius (described as bald) and Fulvia to open up their arses to receive it.[65]

Political abuse similarly made much of the notion that its victims had been penetrated. We repeatedly hear the allegation that Julius Caesar had in his youth allowed himself to be penetrated by Nicomedes of Bithynia.[66] Cicero asserts that his great enemy, Clodius, admitted men to the most intimate parts of his body in his youth.[67] When he abuses Catiline in similar terms, he speaks of him making himself a slave to the passions of others.[68] When he abuses Antony as having in his youth allowed himself to be penetrated by Curio, he speaks of him having sold himself to the older man, as if a slave. Antony in his turn abused his rival Octavian as having secured his adoption by Caesar by allowing himself to be penetrated by him, and then as having sold himself to Aulus Hirtius.[69] The emperor Nero, it was said, had himself penetrated by his freedman Doryphorus, whose name, appropriately enough, means "spear-carrier."[70] The emperor Elagabalus, it was said, prostituted himself in his own brothel, and had himself given away in marriage as a woman, and—as it were cementing the inversion—to a Carian slave, to whom he accordingly became enslaved in turn.[71]

The iconic figure of Roman male homosexuality is Priapus. Priapus was originally a minor Greek deity, but the Romans took him to their hearts and made him their own. He was permanently ithyphallic, and that too to a prodigious degree, and he has accordingly given us the word "Priapic." His small pedestaled statues, often made of wood, served the Romans' gardens, vineyards, and orchards as watchmen. He warded off the birds in the manner of a scarecrow, but he warded off human thieves with threats of vicious and violent buggery or *irrumatio* via his punishing member. Priapus's guardian role—and the threats he would issue in pursuit of his duty—are celebrated in the rich body of poetry that has come down to us, some 141 poems or "Priapea." Most of these are in the voice of Priapus himself, who, despite his role and savage threats, contrives to project himself as a strangely engaging personality. A recurring theme in this poetry seems to be that to be subject to *irrumatio* constitutes a stage of degradation beyond that of buggery.[72] In one poem, he threatens that he will rape girl thieves in the usual way and bugger boy thieves, but subject bearded men thieves to *irrumatio*. In another, he suggests that those he has failed to deter already with buggery will be subject to *irrumatio*. In a third, he tells thieves that they will be buggered for a first offense, subject to *irrumatio* for a second, and subject first to buggery, then (presumably, without benefit of intervening ablution) to *irrumatio* for a third.[73]

Women

Our evidence for female homosexuality (and attitudes thereto) in the Roman world is again modest in quantity—but it is strongly consistent and dominated by the simple, indeed simplistic, notion that women who desire other women thereby resemble men.[74] The point is crisply made by our earliest Latin witness, Horace, in his passing reference in the late first century B.C. to *mascula Sappho* (masculine Sappho).[75] Even the most casual perusal of Sappho's fragments reveals the force of the local paradigm upon him: to our eyes, there is nothing more feminine.

Phaedrus composed a book of Aesopic fables in Latin in the early first century A.D. One of these is true to the Greek inheritance of the Aesopic tradition in that it is broadly reminiscent of the Aristophanic tale of mankind's creation in the *Symposium*, but, in other respects, it seems to express a distinctly Roman notion of the nature of female homosexuality. When Prometheus was molding mankind from clay, he got drunk one night with Dionysus, and so accidentally fixed male parts to women and female parts to men. In telling this tale, Phaedrus is the first to preserve for us an originally Greek word, *tribas*, that thrived in both languages. It defines a woman who has sex with other women. This word, which gives us "tribade" (lesbian), means "rubber," or "one who rubs," and may imply a view of the means by which women typically found sexual gratification with each other. It is interesting that the ancient world has given us a specialized term for a habitual practitioner of female homosexuality but not one for the male equivalent.[76]

The most elaborate statement of the notion that women with homosexual desires were men trapped in women's bodies is to be found in the Greek satirical writer of the High Roman Empire Lucian, who wrote in the late second century A.D. In his *Dialogues of the Courtesans* we meet the rich Megilla, from Lesbos, who has been hiring the services of the courtesan Leaena. Leaena explains in conversation with a friend that Megilla is very much like a man. Beneath her wig she has a shaved head, in a fashion that resembles male athletes. She asks Leaena to call her by the masculine version of her name, Megillus. Megilla claims that she was born in the body of a woman but has the mind and desires of a man. Leaena is too shy to disclose the method by which Megilla achieves satisfaction with her: use of a dildo or rubbing may be implied. Lucian's attitude, insofar as one can be divined, seems to be one of curiosity rather than of any significant hostility.[77]

A similar notion may have informed, in part, Ovid's version of the story of Iphis in his *Metamorphoses,* completed around 8 A.D. Ligdus and his wife, Telethusa, are to have a child, but Ligdus rules that, in view of their poverty, the baby should be exposed if a girl. In a dream Isis tells Telethusa to rear the child regardless, and that she will protect it. A girl is duly born, and her mother secretly raises her as a boy, with the conveniently unisex name of Iphis. At thirteen she is accordingly betrothed to another girl, Ianthe, and they fall in love with each other. Iphis rails against her own desires, insisting to herself it is a natural law that females do not lust after females, cows for cows, or ewes for ewes. As the wedding approaches, Telethusa brings Iphis to Isis's temple and prays for help. As they leave the temple, the goddess transforms Iphis into a boy.[78] This is a quirky story, and it is difficult to know what sort of evidence, if any, it might provide for Ovid's or wider Roman attitudes towards female homosexuality. Iphis's protestations about the unnaturalness of her desires are probably to be read in the first instances as projections of the simple, pastoral, innocent life she has led rather than as any essentialist, moralist crusade on the part of the poet or the civilization in which he lives.

Women characteristically fulfill their homosexual desires in Roman thought, accordingly, by taking on the sexual role of men. The more bitter

Roman satirist Martial, writing at the end of the first century A.D., makes emphatic use of the notion that women with homosexual desires are manlike, and contends that they do all they can to play the male role in their sexual encounters. In a pair of poems he tells us in excoriating terms of the virago Philaenis, a hard-eating, hard-drinking, hard-vomiting lady wrestler. She has sex with eleven girls a day, and also buggers boys (presumably, with a dildo). Her chosen mode of gratification with the women, apparently, is cunnilingus, but she refuses to give oral sex to the boys because that is insufficiently manly. Interestingly, he also defines her as a "rubber" (tribas) of women who are themselves rubbers. This may imply a notion that rubbers more usually rubbed women who did not themselves rub, and so actively performed a sex act on passive recipients, in alignment with penetrating and penetrated males. In this case, we are told that Philaenis is so masculine she dominates even women who themselves usually dominate, and this therefore forms a sort of parallel to her penetration of male partners.[79] Martial speaks in similarly contemptuous fashion of one Bassa, who scorns the company of men in favor of a host of women. He suggests she finds her gratification by rubbing her vulva, which she pretends to be a penis, against those of her lovers. He also projects her as a female "adulterer," moechus, a term usually applied to a man who seduces the wife (or daughter) of another.[80] He was not the first to make this connection. In the early Augustan period, Hybreas composed an imaginary forensic speech (controversia) in defense of a man who had found his wife in bed with another woman and killed them both, as he might normally have done had he found her in bed with a male "adulterer". After the killing, the husband supposedly discovered that his wife's lover had been wearing a dildo on a harness. The paradoxical nature of this genre frustrates any temptation to infer that such circumstances were common.[81] In the later second century A.D., the physician Soranus, writing in Greek, spoke of "rubbers" (the word tribas is used again) who exhibit greater lust for women than for men and pursue them with the sort of jealousy expected of men. He tells us that they are supposedly driven to corrupt other women in order to mitigate the shame of their desires.[82]

The pseudo-Lucianic Loves, composed in the fourth century A.D., suggests, only with light irony, that homosexual activity between women is nobler than that between men because at least it does not involve effeminacy: clearly, if any excess is involved, it is one of masculinity.[83]

Can we do anything to recover the voices of women with homosexual desires from the Roman world? We might turn to two of the erotic curse texts made and used in Roman Egypt.[84] One is a second-century A.D. papyrus curse

C's pursuit of N
Oliver - "demon of the Dead" [53]

text made by Heraeis in her pursuit of Sarapias. The curse, as often, invokes a ghost, or "demon of the dead," to carry out its magic.

> I adjure you, Euangelos, by Anubis, Hermes and the remaining powers of the underworld, to bring and bind Sarapias, to whom Helen gave birth, to Heraeis, to whom Thermoutharin gave birth, now, now, quickly, quickly. Draw her by her soul and heart to Sarapias, to whom Helen gave birth with her own womb, MAEI OTE ELBOSATOK ALAOUBETO OEIO AEN. Bring and bind the soul and heart of Sarapias, to whom Helen gave birth, to Heraeis, to whom Thermoutharin gave birth with her womb, now, now, quickly, quickly. (*PGM* XXXII)

The second is an extensive and seemingly insistently repetitive double-sided lead curse tablet from Hermoupolis, dated to the third or fourth century A.D. Here we find Sophia in pursuit of Gorgonia. The tablet opens with an iambic trimeter hymn that makes appeals to Cerberus and the Erinyes and asks the former to transform a ghost into a fire-breathing demon to heat up the beloved with desire. Amidst many magic words, the curse text then makes the following petitions:

> ... Through this demon of the dead set fire to the heart, liver, and spirit of Gorgonia, to whom Nilogenia gave birth, so that she feels sexual desire and love for Sophia, to whom Isara gave birth. Compel Gorgonia, to whom Nilogenia gave birth, to be cast into the bathhouse for Sophia, to whom Isara gave birth, and yourself become a woman bath attendant. Burn, fire, inflame her soul, heart, liver, and spirit with sexual desire for Sophia, to whom Isara gave birth. Drive Gorgonia, to whom Nilogenia gave birth, drive her, torture her body night and day, compel her to come bounding out of every place and every house for love of Sophia, to whom Isara gave birth, giving herself up entirely to her as a slave, along with all her property, because the great god wishes and commands this ... Compel Gorgonia, to whom Nilogenia gave birth, to be cast into the bathhouse for Sophia, to whom Isara gave birth, for her, compel her to love her, as if through a love potion, passionately and with unstoppable sexual desire ... Drive Gorgonia, to whom Nilogenia gave birth, so that she feels sexual desire for Sophia, to whom Isara gave birth. Burn, set fire to the soul, heart, liver, and spirit of Gorgonia, to whom Nilogenia gave birth, as she is burned, fired, and tortured, until she is cast into the bathhouse for Sophia, to whom Isara gave birth, and you yourself become a woman bath attendant. (*Supplementum Magicum* no. 42, side A)[85]

The burning imagery is emphatic throughout, and continues with the request that the demon become a bath attendant. Such attendants stoked up the heat in the *caldarium*, or "hot room," of Roman bathhouses.

Such texts are to be treasured, no doubt, as rare documents of actual erotic passions between women in the ancient world. There may be a sense in which curse texts such as these allow us to see directly into an ancient heart, for the voices that speak through these texts need not have been limited or qualified by any self-consciousness on the writers' parts. They would not have expected their curses to be read by any other living person, only by the ghosts to whose graves they were entrusted. But, it must be admitted, we may not find in these texts traces of any structuring or coloring unique to ancient lesbian sexuality. Their elements are highly formulaic and can be found in countless parallel curse texts made by men against women, women against men, and men against men. Even the curious maternal-lineage formula, which might initially seem to suggest that the curses were made in the context of a microsociety structured in accordance with female relationships, is common across all four permutations of erotic curse texts in the imperial period. Nor, sadly, can we tell very much about the profile of lesbianism in the imperial period from curse-text statistics. In Winkler's survey of extant imperial-period erotic curse texts in which the sexes of both curser and victim can be identified, he found twenty-five in which men pursued women, six in which women pursued men, three in which men pursued men, and then these two in which women pursued women.[86] The fact that far fewer women seem to have made erotic curse tablets than men may be an indication of restraint in matters of sexual and religious transgression on their part, but it is more likely to be a function of their more restricted access to literacy or to the literate. They may, accordingly, have favored varieties of erotic magic that left no trace in our record. Potentially the most interesting statistic here lies in the numbers of homosexual texts in relation to the numbers of heterosexual texts produced by the two sexes respectively. Amongst men moved to make erotic curse tablets, one in nine sought a victim of the same sex, whereas amongst women moved to make them, one in four sought a victim of the same sex. However, the sample in question is doubtless too small to yield results worthy of full faith.[87]

CHAPTER FOUR

Sexual Variations: Sexual Peculiarities of the Ancient Greeks and Romans

JOHN YOUNGER

Most of the sexual practices and attitudes of the ancient Greeks and Romans have parallels in modern life. There are differences, of course, but it is difficult to categorize them, mainly because what seems normal to one person may seem perverted to another. The U.S. Supreme Court, after all, leaves the definition of pornography to the local community. What follows here is a broad discussion arranged around eight major sexual themes—I leave it to the reader to identify the peculiar.

SEX AND STATUS

Both societies were slave-owning, which, coupled with the general attitude that women were second-class citizens, meant that men had sexual access to those who were lesser in status: unchaperoned proper women, as well as slave, foreign, resident-alien, and noncitizen women and men. The Augustan orator Haterius may have been exaggerating when he stated, "Debasement" [i.e., being raped] is a crime [*stuprum*] for the freeborn, a necessity for the slave, and a duty for the freedman." ("Inpudicitia in ingenuo crimen est, in servo necessitas, in liberto officium"; Sen. *Controv.* 4 pr 10.)[1]

As with status, age difference was eroticized: it seemed natural for adult men to desire boys and youths as much as they did nubile women. Having sex with both was considered natural in both societies. There was, however, a long-running discussion about whether it was possible for men to love women (cf. Plut. *Eroticus*); a man's love for a youth was a given. A man could grow to respect his wife, but love between a man and a woman was unusual and rarely was the basis for marriage. Among Romans, however, heterosexual love was possible—though it occurred primarily within the lower classes.

It seemed natural for men to desire youths, their social and generational inferiors, though we hear of a few instances where a homoerotic relationship continued beyond the boy's youth. A certain Pausanias of Athens and the playwright Agathon (floruit 430 B.C.) were such a couple (Pl. *Symp.* 177c, cf. Plut. *Mor.* 770c). It was thus noteworthy that the emperor Galba, who briefly ruled from October 68 to January 69 A.D., preferred not youths, but "men, adult and strong," after his wife died (Suet. *Galba* 12, 22).

While love between men was not a problem, sex between citizen men was—both societies were concerned that there would be anal penetration, which would jeopardize the penetrated man's citizenship. Penetration inverted a man's proper gender role, turning him into a woman—that is, a noncitizen (the common Latin expression associated with this was *muliebre patitur,* or "he behaves sexually like a woman"). Many classical Greek societies had institutionalized *paiderastia,* in which adult citizen men indoctrinated proper youths (citizens in the making) into proper male society (see Daniel Ogden, Chapter 3): it was assumed this relationship would be eroticized. There was, therefore, concern that anal intercourse not take place; intercrural intercourse (two males stand, facing each other in embrace, the adult ejaculating between the youth's thighs) was apparently an acceptable substitute.

The time it took for Roman men to become citizens (to assume the *toga virilis,* the plain, white toga worn on formal occasions) was far shorter than the twenty or so years it took an Athenian to become a full citizen, and because Roman citizenship did not require a long-term, adult-male sponsorship, there was no Roman equivalent of *paiderastia.* There was, however, *paidomania*—an adult man's desire for a noncitizen youth (e.g., Catullus and Juventius in Cat. 48 and 99).

Sexualizing inequalities ("otherness") implies that foreigners, as "others," are also characterized sexually (for instance, our "French kissing" or "Greek love"). Herodotus reports that the people of Libya and Scythia copulate promiscuously: if a man wants a woman, the Nasamone places a pole in front of her house or the Massagetan hangs his quiver before her wagon; Machlyes and Auses men meet every three months to determine who fathered which child; and Gindane women wear leather anklets corresponding to the number of their lovers. Hippocrates attributes the female characteristics of Scythian men—their large, fleshy, feminine bodies—to Scythia's wet and chilly climate (*Aer.* 15.17).

Black Africans were sexually exciting. Certain Athenian drinking mugs associate a negro male head with a white female head (*ARV²* 1529–52 *passim*),[2] and a Cnidian jug depicts a negro head with three heterosexual couples in frontal intercourse.[3] The large erections of negro men appear in Roman mosaics.[4] But negroes could also be problematic. A Pompeian woman writes a graffito that probably reproduces a popular song: "White women have taught me to hate black women; but I am able (and not unwillingly) to love them" (*CIL* 4.1520, cf. 1523, 1528, 1536; Ovid, *Am.* 3.11.35; Verg. *Ecl.* 2.56). Similarly, if a man wants to fall out of love with a dark woman, Ovid recommends that he imagine she is a negro (*Rem. Am.* 327).

THE UBIQUITY OF SEX

We tend to think that sex is everywhere nowadays, but in antiquity it was even more pervasive. The sexual behavior of the gods forms the basis of many myths, and while modern retellings have the male gods "fall in love" with mortal women and boys, it is really rape that these stories recount. In addition to the major male gods, there are minor divinities whose main trait is their sexuality. The goat-god Pan is always randy. Bearded, erect satyrs follow Dionysus and accost women. Priapus, also bearded, protects Italian gardens by threatening thieves with rape, especially anal. The Roman Faunus protects fields and livestock and induces strong erotic desire—he turns himself into a snake and has intercourse with his daughter (Macr. *Sat.*1.12.24, cf. Lactant. 1.22.9 ff.; Servius 7.47 and 8.314). The sanctuary of Mutinus/Tutinus had a statue of a seated, erect Mutinus on which new brides sat to ensure fertility (Festus s.v. Mutini, Tutini, Sacellum; Lactant. 1.22.9 ff.).

In Greece, herms (short pillars with the head of Hermes on top and erect male genitalia halfway down the front side) stood at crossroads and in front of important buildings; a hall in the marketplace of Athens displayed a famous series of them. Their "mutilation" on the eve of the Sicilian Expedition (mid June 415 B.C.) was a scandal that contributed to the downfall of the expedition's most famous general, Alcibiades. Romans also had herms with phalli, but theirs had a greater variety of heads that included portraits of real people.

In Athens, the festival Theogamia celebrated the sacred marriage (*hieros gamos*) of Zeus and Hera in mid February, and many real weddings took place

FIGURE 4.1: Herm
from Siphnos (late
sixth c. B.C.); Athens
National Museum
(photo, author).

around this time. On the festival's second day, the wife of the *archōn basileus*
(the magistrate in charge of religion) had sex with the god Dionysus in the
archon's office (the Boukoleion). Presumably, "Dionysus" was the archon himself. In the late fourth century B.C., the daughter of the prostitute Neaera had
passed herself off as a proper Athenian woman who had married a man selected
to be the *archōn basileus*; she thus profaned the mystery of her "marriage" to
Dionysus ([Dem.] 59).

   One activity, temple prostitution, is often assumed. In Herodotus's description of the cult of "Aphrodite" (Mylitta) at Babylon, he says, "[all] women were
required at least once to have intercourse with a stranger within the temple pre-
cinct" (Ht. 1.199). He mentions "similar rituals in Cyprus," where Aphrodite's
most famous temple was at Paleopaphos. There, the faithful consulted an oracle
(Suet. *Titus* 5), bathed, visited the sanctuary of Adonis and Apollo, and practiced
temple prostitution. The *Acts of Saint Barnabas* (first century A.D.)[5] refers to the

religious procession and to "lewd" doings near the sanctuary. Justin (third or fourth century A.D.) quotes Pompeius Trogus (first century B.C.): "the Cypriots send their young women before marriage to the seashore to get money by prostitution" (*Epit. Hist.* 18.5, cf. Ennius, *Euhemerus* 134–8; Ovid, *Met.* 10.238–46). Strabo (around 64 B.C.—20 A.D.) also claims temple prostitution for the Paleopaphos sanctuary (his text closely mirrors Herodotus's) and cites similar practices in Corinth, Locri Epizephyrii, and in Eryx, Sicily (6.26, cf. Diod. Sic. 4.83).

In Corinth, there were "more than a 1,000 sacred prostitutes, whom both men and women dedicated" to Aphrodite, the patron divinity (Strabo 8.6.20, cf. 12.3.36; Ath. 13.573f-574c). Presumably, these prostitutes practiced all over the city, and not just at the small temple at the top of Corinth's acropolis. Hiking the 1,900 feet to its summit would not have added to the enjoyment of sex.

Several scholars have taken these ancient references at face value.[6] But Herodotus is vague and may be attributing odd sexual practices to "other" peoples (Babylonians and Cypriots); the other references were written long after the period they claim for temple prostitution. As for temple prostitution in Corinth, Herodotus does not mention it, nor does Pausanias (mid-second century A.D.; 2.4.7). This last point seems telling, since Pausanias is greatly interested in peculiar religious practices.

Prostitutes, female and male, were, however, common everywhere (see Allison Glazebrook, Chapter 8): there were streetwalkers (*pornai*), who had small cells, prostitutes (*meretrices*) in brothels, and high-priced *hetairai*, who could own bordellos. "Flute-girls" (*aulētriai*) performed at all-male Greek parties, mimes performed at Roman parties, and bath attendants gave more than baths in both Greece and Rome.

Prostitutes may have been thought dirty (Anacreon, *PMG* 346; Ar. *Eq.* 1397–1401; Men. *Samia* 390 ff.), but they were considered better than wives because they "must get and keep a man by being amenable."[7] They were deemed essential to military expeditions, accompanying Pericles to Samos and dedicating a famous statue to Aphrodite there (Ath. 13.572f). They also joined the Ten Thousand on their march through Persian Anatolia (Xen. *An.* 4.3, 19).

It has been estimated that there was one prostitute for every 50 men in Pompeii.[8] In the early second century B.C., Rome was introduced to Greek symposia that included prostitutes as entertainers (Livy 39.6.7–9). In the city, prostitutes hung out at the walls, in the arches of the Colosseum, and especially in the Subura on the lower slopes of the Esquiline (Livy 3.13.2; Propertius 4.7.15; Mart. 2.17.1, 6.66.2, 11.61.2, 11.78.11; Pers. 5.32ff.; *Priap.* 40; Dio Chrys. 8.5). The city also had thousands of young male prostitutes who acted effeminate, wore the woman's *stola* (long, pleated dress), and offered

FIGURE 4.2: Building Z, a brothel in the fourth c. B.C., tucked into a corner of the fortification walls in northwest Athens, with the Pompeion of the Ceramicus beyond (photo, author).

themselves in the same regions the female prostitutes did. They also hung out at the latrines, for which they were known as *sellarii*—"stoolmen" (Cic. *Phil.* 2.44; Petr. *Sat.* 81.5).

There were so many male prostitutes in Rome, they were a nuisance. Caligula first wanted to ban them—even to drown them at sea—but he eventually saw their value and taxed them. His tax was rescinded only much later, in 498 A.D. (Suet. *Cal.* 16.40; Justin Martyr, 1 *Apology* 27) The emperor Alexander Severus (222–35 A.D.) had also contemplated banishing male prostitutes from Rome, and Philip the Arab (244–49) apparently actually did so (SHA, *Alex. Sev.* 24.4; *Elagab.* 32.6)—though not for long.

Caracalla's extension of citizenship to all freeborn men and freedmen in the Roman Empire (212 A.D.) had an unexpected consequence. Unless he was a slave, the man a citizen man penetrated was now also a citizen. Penetrating a freedman thus became a capital offense. An edict of Constantius and Constans (342 A.D.) declares that, "when a man marries (*nubere*) in the manner of a woman (*muliebre*), or a woman is about to renounce men," the appropriate laws are to take effect (cf. the later Theodosian Code, 438). Valentinian, Arcadius, and Theodosius (390 A.D.) ordered Orientius, the vicar of Rome, to publicly burn all male prostitutes; he instead gave them two months to leave the city.[9] In Gaius's *Institutes* (published 533; restated in 544), the *lex Julia de adulteriis coercendis* makes any sex between men punishable by the death of both (4.18.4; *Digest Novel* 141). And, in 538 A.D., homosex becomes sacrilege: Justinian decreed that those who commit "crimes against nature" answer both to God and the law (Justinian, *Novel.* 77; Procop. *An.* 11.34–6).

A common ancient practice we moderns rarely indulge in is to use sexual innuendo against important people, especially one's political rivals (Sen. *Controv.* 1.2.23). This, however, was so routine in antiquity, there must have been the assumption that powerful men were so powerful that they automatically trespassed all moral boundaries. Typical accusations included sexual profligacy, incest, fellatio, cunnilingus, prostitution, masturbation, effeminacy for men, and masculine behavior for women. Stock charges included "unspeakable" crimes (that is, fellatio and cunnilingus), using one's "entire body" for sex, and performing cunnilingus on menstruating women.

The writings of the moral Cicero, for example, are rife with such charges: Publius Clodius used all parts of his body for sex, prostituted himself, and had incest with his sisters; Sextus Clodius performed cunnilingus on menstruating women; and Quintus Apronius, Gaius Verres' henchman, had bad breath—a sure sign of a fellator or cunnilictor (*Har. resp.* 59; *Dom.* 25; *Verr.* 2. 3. 9, 23, respectively).

Even the famous Julius Caesar was not immune to reproach. At nineteen he was sent on a military mission to the court of Nicomedes IV Philopator of Bithynia (ruled from around 94 to 75 B.C.); it was rumored that the two became lovers (Plut. *Caes.* 1; Cass. Dio 43.20.2 ff.). Suetonius reports that he seduced many women—including queen Eunoë, the Moor wife of Bogudes—and quotes Curio that he was "every woman's man and every man's woman" (*Iul.* 50); Suetonius also castigates Caesar for being "overnice," carefully trimmed, shaved, his superfluous hair plucked, bald spot combed over and covered by his laurel wreath. Suetonius charges Nero with similar crimes (*Nero* 29), and the *Historia Augusta* casts similar aspersions on Commodus (SHA, *Comm.* 5.11) and Elagabalus (SHA, *Elagab.* 26.3–5, 31.7–8).

THE BODY

Greeks and Romans shared a holistic concept of the body as a balance of "humors" (blood, phlegm, yellow and black biles) and of pairs of opposites (dry/wet, hot/cool). (See Helen King, Chapter 6.) The pairs of opposites connoted gender: men were dry and hot, women were wet and cool. Thus, it was natural for men to exercise in the nude (to be both hot and dry) and for women to stay indoors. Since women contained a lot of wetness, their bodies were thought spongy. To keep the liquids circulating inside women's bodies, it was necessary for women to be "opened up," sexually penetrated. It was also natural for men to expel their (wet) semen, since this was accomplished by hot air coursing down the body ([Arist.] *Probl.* 30.1), and for women to take in the semen, since they needed more wetness. As we have seen, men who lived in wet and cool zones (e.g., Scythia) were thought to be feminine with soft, spongy bodies. Similarly, women who lived in hot, dry areas conversely were masculine (like the Amazons in Libya).

Because all Greek citizens were in the military from the ages of eighteen to sixty, one of the purposes of exercising nude in the gymnasium would have been for men to check out each other's bodies—and, by this, to put social pressure on each other to keep physically fit. It was preferable, however, for a man to avoid getting aroused there. Consequently, he might double his penis back up onto itself and tie it in place using a leather thong (the "dog knot"); we see this in some vase paintings of men at the gymnasium and in many sculptural depictions of the (otherwise) always randy goat god Pan.

FIGURE 4.3: Hellenistic statue of Pan with his penis tied with the "dog knot"; Athens National Museum (photo, author).

In the Roman period, there were other methods for preventing an erection. Closing the foreskin (infibulation) with a fibula (like a large modern safety pin), ring, or thread would prevent full erection (Oribasius, *Peri krikōseōs*). Male singers, entertainers, gladiators, and athletes were often infibulated to ensure the abstinence that benefited their performances. The fibula was also used to keep slaves chaste (Mart. 7.85, 9.27, 14.215; Galen 9.12 Kühn, cf. Arist. *Gen. An.* 7.1); Juvenal satirizes women who paid to have to have fibulae removed from the entertainers they desired (6.379 and schol.). Other Roman devices for preventing erections included the *theca* (a metal pouch) and the *aluta* (a leather bag), both of which enclosed the genitals (Mart. 7.35, 7.82). Of course, all these devices could also function as chastity belts for men; chastity belts for women are unknown in classical antiquity.

It might be thought that the scrutiny in the Greek gymnasium would extend to appreciating penis size. Kenneth Dover, analyzing Greek vase paintings and erotic poetry, came to the conclusion that desirable youths were depicted with small penises and tight, young bodies; their adult lovers, however, when erect, have larger penises.[10] "I think this should mean, not that Greek men in general thought small penises more desirable, but rather that it is not the youth who should be doing the desiring (his true feelings to the contrary)";[11] for example, we never see a depiction of intercrural sex where the youth is ejaculating between the thighs of the adult man. As with many modern S&M and intergenerational relationships, the sexual pleasure of the passive, younger partner is not the central issue.

The power of the phallus is made clear, however, by its large size: women in Greek vase paintings carry huge phalli in procession; perverted Roman emperors such as Commodus and Elagabalus desired *vassati*, or "hung men," endowed like donkeys (*onobeli*) (SHA, *Comm.* 10.8–9; *Elagab.* 8.1). When erect, for example, the Greek god Pan and the Roman god Priapus have large penises, as do satyrs. In Greek comedy, especially the satyr plays, it was common to have the actors strap on long leather phalli and go up into the audience to accost and threaten the spectators, sometimes even hitting them.

One would think that exercising nude in the gymnasium would also lead to bodybuilding, but this is not directly known. Bronze cuirasses from the archaic through the Roman imperial periods are shaped to display taut pectoral muscles and a defined abdomen, regardless of the age or physical shape of the soldier—they were, in effect, a sham to arouse fear in the enemy.[12] Archaic sculptures of *kouroi* (youths) are often thickly built with powerful thighs, but they are not muscle-bound. There are, however, examples of known "strong men"[13]: Bubon (sixth century B.C.) lifted a 315-pound stone with one hand and threw it over his head. The stone, now in the Olympia Museum, carries an inscription commemorating this event (*IvO* 5.717, *SIG*³ 1071). Overblown Hellenistic sculpture in the baroque style (second century B.C.), such as the Laocoön and the Polyphemus group at Sperlonga, shows figures that certainly resemble bodybuilders.

Another consequence of Greek men exercising in the nude might have been the decorative trimming of pubic hair. Most male statues are nude or only partially clothed; several from the sixth and fifth centuries B.C. show the pubic hair trimmed, mostly in a pointed ogive arch (e.g., the Anavyssos kouros), but occasionally in rows of curls (e.g., the Striding God from Artemisium and the Omphalos Apollo). The Romans had specialists, girl *picatrices,* who could arrange the pubic hair thus.[14]

After exercising, Greek men would pour oil on their bodies and scrape off the mixture of oil, dust, and sweat with a curved metal strigil; this "goo" (*konisalos*) had erotic, pharmaceutical, and magical qualities. Scrapings from famed athletes and gladiators were often sold at high prices (Ar. *Lys.* 918; Galen 12.283 Kühn).[15]

Body care was clearly an important part of a man's grooming; some cities even conducted men's beauty contests. Tanagra judged ephebes in honor of Hermes Kriophoros; the winner was declared "most beautiful in form" and carried a ram on his shoulders around the city walls (Paus. 9.22.1). Elis held a beauty contest in honor of Athena, and the winner, beribboned by his friends, received weapons as prizes (Ath. 13.609f-610a). In Athens, old men, chosen for their beauty, bore olive branches in the Panathenaic procession (Xen. *Symp.* 4.17; *Etym. Magn.* s.v. *thallophoroi*). There were women's beauty contests, too—at Olympia, Tenedos, and possibly on Lesbos (Ath. 13.609e-610a; *Odyssey* 6.292 scholiasts A and D, cf. *Iliad* 9.129; Alcaeus fr. 130.32 LP).

The perfect body was defined by sculptors: the 'Doryphoros' by Polycleitus (mid-fifth century B.C.) for men, and the Aphrodite of Cnidus by Praxiteles (mid-fourth century B.C.) for women.[16] Romans, especially, substituted these idealized bodies for their own in portrait statues. Men of high rank, such as Gaius Ofellius of Delos and Nero, and high-ranking women, such as those at the Flavian court, are examples. While the bodies would be in the style of the classical period, the heads would be realistic portraits, making for a jarring contrast.

In Athens, bathhouses and barbershops were popular places to hang out—as they are today—where attendants, barbers, and perfumers spruced up customers. These establishments could, of course, double as brothels or cruising areas (like those in the Ceramicus).

Too much grooming, however, could render a man effeminate. Julius Caesar, as we have seen, was deemed "overnice," and Augustus was said to have singed his leg hair (Suet. *Aug.* 68). Oddly enough, too much hair also feminized a man. The hypermasculine, hirsute man was thought hypersexual and thus unrestrained in sexual activity—including, therefore, being penetrated (Juv. 2.41).

BODY MODIFICATION

With so much interest in the body, it is curious how little interest there was in body modification. Proper Greek and Roman citizens certainly did not go in for tattooing, body-piercing or circumcision. In the Greco-Roman world, such body modifications identified those who were not Greek or Roman, as well as slaves and criminals (the last could also have their ears or noses cut off).

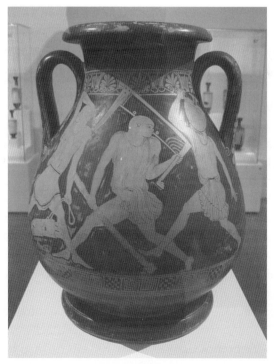

FIGURE 4.4: Athenian red-figure pelike, depicting circumcized Egyptian priests, by the Pan Painter (ca. 470 B.C.); Athens National Museum (photo, author).

Voluntary self-castration was practiced by the priests of Cybele (Pliny, *NH* 35.165, cf. Lucilius 306–7). Castration was performed on slave and noncitizen boys, and sometimes on men, to turn them into eunuchs, loyal servants, entertainers, sexual passives. Castration could also be a punishment: Periander, the tyrant of Corinth, who ruled from 627 to 585 B.C., shipped 300 sons of the Corcyraeans, who had revolted, to Lydia to be castrated (Hdt. 3.48). The Roman emperors Domitian and Nerva outlawed castration (Cass. Dio 67.2.3, 68.2.4).

Egypt had a long history of tattooing, branding, piercing, and male and female circumcision.[17] Ptolemaic mummies of women provide evidence for clitoridectomy and infibulation of the vaginal opening.[18] These procedures were done when the girl was fourteen, prior to marriage (Strabo 17.2.5; Philo, *Quest. Gen.* 3.47).

Male circumcision was common in the Near East, from as early as pharaonic Egypt.[19] In Israel, it originated with God's covenant with Abraham, requiring him to circumcise himself and his descendants and slaves (*Genesis* 17); Jews, Christians, and Muslims who abide by Abraham's covenant circumcise their boys a week after birth. In classical antiquity, circumcision was practiced by Jews and Egyptians (by Roman times, only by priests; Josephus, *In Ap.* 2.141), as well as by Arabs, Ethiopians, Phoenicians, among others. Converts to Judaism were also circumcised (Tac. *Hist.* 5.5; Juv. 14), but the first Christians debated whether circumcision should be required of their new converts (*Acts* 10–11, 15; *Galatians* 2.3).

Since circumcision physically marked Jews out from most other members of the empire, it became a matter of imperial concern. On the basis of circumcision, Domitian could identify Jews for taxation (Suet. *Dom.* 7.1, 12). Hadrian forbade the practice (SHA *Had.* 14.2; *Digest* 48.8.3.5), while Antoninus Pius restored the right of circumcision to Jews but not to converts (*Digest* 48.8.11.1).[20]

Men who had been circumcised and then wanted their foreskin restored went through one of two complex processes.[21] The one known as epispasm (from the Greek for "stretched") restored the foreskin by attaching a heavy weight on the skin of the penis, slowly lengthening it (Soranus 2.34, cf. Mart. 7.85, 9.27; Cels. 4.25.3). The other procedure, called recutitio (from the Latin for "re-cut"), cut the skin around the penis and pulled it forward to cover the glans as a new foreskin (Cels. 7.25.1–2). Jews who hellenized, participated in Greek-style nude events, or went to the Roman baths either covered their penises to hide their circumcision or underwent restoration (1 *Corinthians* 7.18; 1 *Maccabees* 1.15; Joseph. A. 12.241; *Talmud, Sanhedrin* 44.1, *Shabbath* 19.2, *Yebamoth* 72.1).

Ear-piercing was practiced throughout antiquity by women (as surviving earrings attest), and sometimes by men, but there is little evidence for the piercing of other body parts.

Tattooing, temporary or permanent, may have been practiced from the earliest times[22]; one thinks of Ötzi, the Neolithic mummy found in the Alps, who has simple marks tattooed on his wrist and ankles.[23] In the classical period, however, we have little evidence for tattooing; the Pistoxenos Painter (around 460 B.C.) produced thirty-eight vases with tattooed Thracian women, twenty-seven of which portray the death of Orpheus.[24]

Waist-compression constricts the waist to wasp-thinness using a laced corset or a tall belt. The effect on the body is startling: the organs are pushed up into the lower chest cavity, producing a pronounced chest and shelflike hips; walking is difficult, sitting in a chair is uncomfortable, and breathing is replaced by panting. The practice, for both women and men, began in Greece's Late Bronze Age. The tall belt can be seen in Late Geometric vase paintings (eighth century B.C.) and in Daedalic sculpture (seventh century B.C.), again for both genders. Waist-cinching apparently died out by the archaic period.[25]

In both the Greek and Roman periods, a *strophium* (tight breastband) was used to bind or compress a woman's breasts and restrict her chest. Greek vase paintings show the female athlete Atalanta wearing the strophium when she wrestles Peleus (e.g., *ARV*[2] 1039.9).[26] Ovid implies that large-breasted women who wear the strophium are more attractive (Ovid, *Rem. am.* 337–8, cf. *Ars am.* 3.622). In Roman wall paintings, most women in sexually explicit scenes wear the strophium, perhaps to heighten feeling or call attention to the breasts.[27] Another use of the strophium was to bind the orator's or actor's chest, perhaps to give him a stronger, more projecting voice.[28]

A severe form of body modification was sometimes practiced on children. By confining them in small cages or jars during infancy, children could be made permanently dwarfed (Ps.-Longinus, *Subl.* 44.5; Sen. *Controv.* 10.40).[29] The practice apparently continued into early modern Europe.[30] Dwarves were thought sexually humorous and appropriate for oral sex (Mart. 9.7.1–10, 11.61.1–14; Suet. *Tib.* 44). Indeed, a man could develop a fetish for dwarf women (Pliny, *NH* 8; Suet. *Galba* 3; Hesych. s.v. *nannaristēs*).

VIOLENCE AND PAIN

As it is today, so it was in antiquity: violence was often associated with sexual pleasure. Because men wielded great power over their inferiors, hurting them was thought to be natural, if opprobrious (Ovid, *Am.* 1.7). The common Greek verb for "to have intercourse" (*binein*), implies "violence" (*bia*), and the Latin *irrumatio* denotes a rape of the mouth. Aphrodite/Venus, the goddess of sex, is, after all, the lover of Ares/Mars, the god of war.

Rape was a common theme in both life and fiction. A Greek marriage (*gamos*; the word also means "intercourse") assumed the bride's acquiescence, not her assent. In Roman law, rape was only a crime against a freeborn citizen. In war, the victors conventionally raped and enslaved all female enemies—and killed their sons.

Rape is standard in myth; I give here only some notorious examples. Mars rapes the vestal virgin Rhea Silvia to produce Romulus and Remus. Jupiter gives Lara, her tongue ripped out, to Mercury to rape. Eros rapes Ganymede. Satyrs characteristically accost maenads[31]; centaurs rape women and youths. Boreas rapes the nymph Oreithyia; Hades rapes Persephone. Hephaestus unsuccessfully tries to rape Athena; so, too, the giant Tityos tries to rape Leto. Peleus rapes Thetis. Theseus assaults the nereid Amphitrite, and he and Pirithoüs rape the twelve-year-old Helen. Achilles rapes Troilus to death, and Ajax rapes Cassandra at the altar of Athena at Troy, personalizing the rape of the city.[32]

A few females also rape. Eos, goddess of dawn, abducts the Trojan prince Tithonus, and bears him Memnon. Tithonus begs Zeus for immortality so he can live with Eos, but he forgets to ask for eternal youth; so he shrivels up like a cicada and she locks him in a room and throws away the key. Eos then abducts Cephalus, the son of Hermes, and bears him Phaëthon, whom Aphrodite rapes. And Eos abducts Orion as he goes hunting—for his acquiescence, Artemis kills him.

Men interpreted women's fear of rape as attractive—a common trope in Ovid: "fear itself became" Leucothoë and "chaste tears became" Lucretia (Ovid, *Met.* 4.230; *Fasti* 2.757).[33]

Both men and women could inflict pain on their partner during sex by slapping them with sandals, but only men caned, whipped, and burnt women with oil lamps. Since men beat only prostitutes, such violence also expressed differences in class and status, as well as the differences that existed between citizen men and all women. Theoretically, at least, the difference in status that was eroticized was also made violent.[34]

Slapping with sandals is commonly depicted in Greek art and referred to in Greek literature (*Anth. Pal.* 5.202, 503).[35] In Roman depictions of sexual activity, removed sandals can be prominent.[36]

It is no surprise, then, that sandals became a sexual symbol, whether on or off the feet. Wearing them ensured that the feet stayed warm (male) and moist

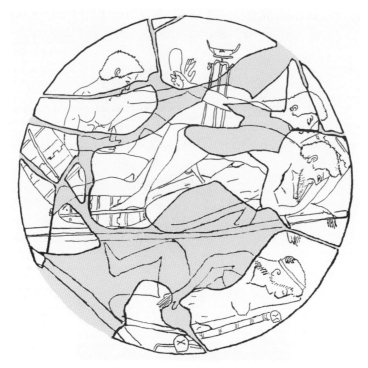

FIGURE 4.5: Tondo of an Athenian red-figure kylix depicting a woman slapping a man with a sandal, while a boy above and a woman below masturbate, by the Thalia Painter (ca. 500 B.C.); Berlin and Florence (reconstructed drawing, author).

(female), conducive to the proper expenditure of sexual fluids. The Greek verb *bainein* (to walk) implied sexual intercourse, particularly between men.[37] Similarly, taking sandals off signaled a desire and readiness for sex ([Arist.] *Probl.* 4.5). One of the more famous late Hellenistic statue groups from Delos shows a flaccid Pan accosting Aphrodite, who raises her sandal as if threatening him; Eros tugs at one of Pan's horns.[38]

A fetishistic desire for feet was also known in antiquity. Antiphanes finds pleasure in a woman rubbing his feet. Vitellius used to carry around one of Messalina's sandals (Suet. *Vit.* 2). The Severans Alciphron and Philostratus wrote letters that praise feet and footprints.[39]

It is possible that the juxtapositions "barefoot: impulsive" and "shod: sexual" had further implications (compare the story of Oedipus, who wears only one sandal when he meets his father and kills him). Dio Chrysostom attributes Socrates' condemnation to a connection between his bare feet and his corruption of minors (Dio Chrys. 66.25, 26), and several Greek vase paintings

FIGURE 4.6: Hellenistic statue group of
Aphrodite, Pan, and Eros, from Delos
(second c. B.C.); Athens National Museum
(photo, author).

show couples in erotic situations—the adult men shod, the prostitute women
or youths without shoes.[40]

Pain during sex could also involve caning or whipping. An Etruscan tomb
painting depicts a man caning a woman while he has *a tergo* (rear-entry)
intercourse with her and she fellates another man.[41] To the right of this scene,
a nude youth and a nude man both wield whips while a woman cowers. An
Athenian kylix (a cup used for drinking wine) by the Brygos Painter depicts
an orgy: a man canes a kneeling woman; another man carries a woman while
having frontal intercourse with her and while another man holds a burning
oil lamp to her buttocks; and a man spanks a kneeling woman with a sandal
(*ARV*[2] 372.31).[42]

Inflicting pain was also thought appropriate for instigating conception.
Unsuccessful Arcadian hunters flogged a statue of Pan to incite him to be more
fertile (Theoc. 7.106–8). And during the Lupercalia, young men ran around the
base of the Palatine, whipping women who wished to conceive. In one panel of

FIGURE 4.7: Etruscan tomb painting depicting a man having *a tergo* intercourse with a woman and caning her while she fellates another man; Tomba
delle Fustigazione, Tarquinia (photo, author).

the Great Fresco from the Villa of the Mysteries at Pompeii, a woman initiate
(possibly to marriage) sneaks a peek into a *fascinum* (a draped, erect, apotropaic phallus; Pliny, *NH* 28.39), and in a subsequent panel she is caned.[43]

HAVING SEX

When having penetrative sex, it was not common for partners (of either sex) to
look at each other—the missionary position was rare. Penetrative sex *in more
canum* (rear-entry, *a tergo*) was usual. It has been suggested that the inequality
of the sexes—including the skepticism about men being capable of loving
women—might have resulted in men not wanting to regard their partner while
penetrating them.[44] Such avoidance might also result from the common attitude that penetration is a violent act, one better perpetrated impersonally.

The other common sex position, "equestrian," had the penetrated partner
sitting on the man's lap (again, facing away being more common than facing
towards him).

FIGURE 4.8: Athenian black-figure kylix depicting men having *a tergo* sex with women; Rhodes Archaeological Museum (photo, author).

FIGURE 4.9: Roman wall painting depicting a man and woman having equestrian sex; in the Lupanar, Pompeii (computer-enhanced photo, author).

Both hetero- and homosexual encounters employed the *a tergo* and equestrian positions. Such positions for sex were featured in circulating sex manuals and in depictions in portable art, like Greek vase paintings and mould-made bowls, and Roman lamps, as well as in Roman wall paintings. Ovid briefly lists these sex positions, gives them names based on mythological figures, and attributes their preference, not to which gives more sexual pleasure, but to which part of the woman's body is thereby more pleasant to watch—her face is not mentioned (*Ars am.* 3.773–88).

Indoctrinating a youth into Greek male society could involve his introduction into the military by an adult male (see Daniel Ogden, Chapter 3). The custom of two men sharing a military cloak while on duty seems to have been common enough to inspire the sexual metaphor "to share the cloak," which we read in Plato and see on many Greek vases (Pl. *Symp.* 219b; Ath. 5.219b, 13.603e-4d). We also see between two and five women sharing a cloak on Greek vases, and some of these scenes have obvious sexual implications.[45]

Natural penetration was of a woman's vagina or a man's anus (or of a youth's thighs). Penetration of the woman's anus would occur primarily for birth control, but not at the beginning of a marriage—it was assumed that a young, married woman would quickly become pregnant. When Agariste II (mid-sixth century B.C.) complains to her mother that her new husband, Peisistratus, is practicing "unnatural intercourse," it is presumably because he wants to avoid fathering a child with the daughter of his political rival, Megacles (Hdt. 1.61, 6.131).

Masturbation was considered natural for boys ([Arist.] *Probl.* 30.1), men, and, apparently, women.[46] There are several Greek and Roman depictions of boys and men masturbating, and one Greek depiction of a woman (Figure 4.5; *Priap.* 63.17).[47] Masturbating in public was apparently not out of bounds for Diogenes the Cynic: caught doing so in the marketplace, he is said to have commented, "If only one could satisfy one's hunger by rubbing one's stomach" (Plut. *Mor.* 1044b). A graffito from Pompeii concurs: "When my worries oppress my body, with my left hand I release my pent up fluids" (*CIL* 4.2066).[48] Similarly, masturbation can express deep emotions: Petronius describes how the viewer of a beautiful painting by Apelles can only masturbate to express his admiration. There was also the conceit that statues of beautiful women, like the Aphrodite of Cnidus, could cause men to ejaculate on their thigh (Lucian, *Imag.* 4; *Am.* 15–16; Val. Max. 8.11.4; Pliny, *NH* 7.127, 36.20–1; Tzetzes, *Chil.* 8.375).

We hear just one mention of men—those who were born under the conjunction of Venus, Mercury, and Saturn—masturbating between a woman's breasts (Manetho 4.312). But surely more men were into this than the rare astral occurrence could explain: a terracotta of a woman's chest depicts a phallus between the breasts.[49]

Oral sex in antiquity included all kinds—fellatio, autofellatio, cunnilingus, and analingus, though the last was apparently not as common as it seems to be today. The associated Greek and Latin verbs meant "to lick" (*laikazein* in Greek, *lambere* in Latin; Mart. 11.58.12, 9.27.14). But there were common circumlocutions, such as *lesbiazein* (to do it Lesbos-style), and puns: since oral sex stops the performer from speaking, it could be said to shut a person up (*arrhētopoiein*)—that is, to be something unspeakable. Latin had several more circumlocutions: "to defile every orifice of the body" (Suet. *Nero* 29), to have an "impure mouth," to do something "shameless" (cf. Eur. *Ba.* 1062), "to offer the mouth" (*os praebere*), "to offer the head" (*caput praebere,* cf. *capiti non parcere,* Cic. *Har. resp.* 59), and "to devour a man's middle" (Cat. 80.6). Catullus also refers to autofellatio: "to eat himself with his head lowered" (Cat. 88.8).

Cunnilingus had a special circumlocution: "to deny nothing," conveying its extreme nature. For instance, "I deny nothing to you, Phyllis: deny nothing to me" (Mart. 11.50.12). A parallel remark is attributed to the wife of the tyrant Agathocles; as he was dying, she lamented, "What did I not do to you? What did you not do to me?" (Polyb. 12.15.104).

Just as today, fellatio was a common and quick sex act that could be performed anywhere. Thus, at Pompeii, both male and female prostitutes

FIGURE 4.10: Roman wall painting depicting a man having anal intercourse with a man being fellated by a woman, on whose vagina another woman performs cunnilingus (after Jacobelli 1995: pl. VIII); from the Suburban Baths, Pompeii (computer enhancement, author).

advertise fellatio cheaply—usually for two *asses*, occasionally for fewer (cf. Juv. 3.66, 6.365), but occasionally for more: Euplia offers fellatio for five *asses*. Cunnilingus is advertised by prostitutes at the same low price: Glyco (probably female) advertises cunnilingus for two *asses* (*cunnum lambet,* outside her cell; Pompeii III.1.27); Maritimus advertises it for four asses.

Latin had two words for fellatio: *fellatio* itself refers to the sucking action of the mouth, while *irrumatio* conveys the action of the penis—a rape of the mouth. To Martial, *irrumatio* is virile (compare the threat in Cat. 16), and a woman fellatrix has a "hot mouth" (Mart. 2.28.4, 2.82, 2.83, 4.17, 4.50, 7.55). In Pompeii, good fellators are congratulated: "Myrtis, you suck well"; "Secundus is an excellent fellator" (*CIL* 4.2273 + p. 216, 4.9027).[50]

As today, fellation could substitute for vaginal intercourse, preserving virginity and acting as a contraceptive (cf. Mart. 4.84.1–4) and also, as today, it might not be considered "sex" at all.[51] Martial plays on this conceit: "She's chaste a thousand times. She doesn't put out, but she doesn't deny men anything, either." Undoubtedly, the satirist would have appreciated the irony in Judge Webber Wright's 1998 definition of sex that allowed President Clinton to deny he had sex with Monica Lewinsky (since he did not touch her genitals). Because she did touch his, however, she, by definition, had sex with him. Similarly, abstinence from intercourse was practiced by ancient singers (Hor. *Ars P.* 414, cf. Suet. *Dom.* 10), but they could still perform fellatio and cunnilingus (Ar. *Eq.* 1278 ff., and scholiast; Juv. 6.73; Mart. 7.82, 11.75, 14.215).

Fellatio and cunnilingus were both considered appropriate activities for the elderly: "even an old wife, Simylus, sucks" (*Anth. Pal.* 5.38 [37], cf. Hor. *Epod.* 8; Mart. 4.50.2); "he cannot get an erection; so now he licks" (Mart. 6.26.1–3, cf. 3.81, 11.25, 11.47).

The few depictions of fellatio—all heterosexual—appear in terracottas, metal tokens, and wall paintings.[52] There were a couple of famous erotic paintings with this subject: Parrhasius's *Atalanta fellating Meleager,* which Tiberius owned (Suet. *Tib.* 44), and Chrysippus's *Hera fellating Zeus,* which was later sophistically interpreted as an act of creation: "Hera stands for matter that receives seminal *logoi* (principles) from the deity" (Origen, *Cels.* 4.48; Theophilus, *Ad Autolycum* 3.3 and 8).

Two partners practicing oral sex on each other simultaneously is common today (sixty-nine), but in antiquity this was only rarely depicted or referred to—and it always involved a man and woman (cf. Ovid, *Ars Am.* 2.703–32).[53]

Analingus may also have been rare. I know of only three graffiti from Pompeii that refer to it—and those references are merely insults: "Popilus canis

cunnum linget Reno" ("Popilus licks Renus's 'cunt' [i.e., anus] like a dog").
"Priscus Extalio cunnum" ("Priscus [licks] Extalius's 'cunt'"). "Fortunata,
linge culu<m>" ("Fortunata, lick ass") (*CIL* 4.4954, 8843, 8898).

Cunnilingus, however, was common. Since the associated words (*leichein*
in Greek, *lambere* in Latin) started with an *l*, they could easily be invoked with
just the letter (Auson. *Epigr.* 87.7; Varro, *Sat. Men.* 48 B, 70 Cèbe). Thus, the
lambda on Spartan shields was a joke.[54] To perform cunnilingus was to do it
"Phoenician-style" and to do it from the rear was to assume the "puppy" position (cf. Figure 4.10; Hesychius s.v. *skylax*).

Even though common, both fellatio and cunnilingus were considered vile,
with fellatio more so for men than for women (Mart. 2.50, 9.63). The mouth
was "defiled" (*os impure*), the lips white (Cat. 80), the breath so bad that smelly
food could not disguise it (Ar. *Ecc.* 647; Mart. 3.77.5–10, 10.22, 12.55). Cicero
charges Marc Antony with an *incesto ore* (unchaste mouth) and Quintus Apronius with bad breath (Cic. *Phil.* 11.5; *Verr.* 2.3.9, 23). Greeting a fellator with a
kiss was to be avoided (cf. Cat. 79.4; Mart. 6.55.5, 6.66.1–9, 12.85).

Because the vagina was thought to have a strong smell, like salted fish
(Auson. *Epigr.* 82.1–6),[55] cunnilictors were also accused of having bad breath.
So Martial accuses Athenagoras (Mart. 9.95+95a, cf. *Anth. Pal.* 12.187.1–6).
Performing cunnilingus on menstruating women was considered especially vile
(Galen 12.249 Kühn). Seneca characterizes a certain Natalis for having "a
wicked as well as a stinking tongue" and "a mouth in which women purged
themselves" (Sen. *Ep.* 87.16, cf. *Ben.* 4.31.2–5). Similarly, cunnilingus on
pregnant women was the subject of jokes. When Nanneius did it and heard
"the babies wailing within," "a shocking sickness paralyzed" his tongue
(Mart. 11.61.1–14). Ausonius (*Epigr.* 86.1–2) says of the schoolteacher Eunus,
"when licking the strong-smelling cunt of your pregnant wife, you're trying to
teach *glossae* [languages, tongues] to your not-yet-born children."

There are few depictions of heterosexual cunnilingus, and only one that
shows two women performing it on each other.[56]

VIEWING SEX

Most Greek plays had some sexual content, but Greek comedies and satyr
plays were awash with it. In Aristophanes' *Lysistrata*, for instance, women
refuse to have sex until the men stop fighting; consequently, both women
and men are randy, and the men all brandish erections. Satyr plays, originally one per tragic trilogy, featured sexually excited satyrs as the primary
actors and chorus. After satyr plays were produced by themselves (in the

mid-fourth century B.C.), they began to influence the development of other sexually comedic forms, especially in Italy.

Mime (short popular plays with dance and song) were put on by traveling troupes, both in public and in private residences.[57] In the third century B.C., Theocritus and Herondas wrote mimes with sexual content, and some of these might have included autofellatio (Ath. 14.622a-d, quoting Semus, floruit 200 B.C., concerning erotic *autokabdaloi*; *kubda* means "bent-over"). Pantomimes were introduced to Rome from the east; they starred a single actor who silently danced all roles in a silk gown and a mask with closed lips. The stories, such as the rape of Leda or Procne (Juv. 6.63, 7.92), all had strong sexual content—because of this, the actors were often thought effeminate (Pliny, *Pan.* 54.1)[58] and desirable (Pliny, *Ep.* 7.24)[59]; Maecenas, for example, was said to have been smitten with the mime Bathyllus (Tac. *Ann.* 1.54.3).

Magodiae included actors dressed like women and making indecent gestures while acting the parts of adulteresses and pimps (Ath. 14.621bd, cf. Herod. 36 and 40 Teubner). The southern Italian *phlyax* parodied myths, and featured men with long phalli either dangling or tied up in an exaggerated dog knot.[60] The Italian *fabulae* relied on sexual jokes and sex acts: the *palliata* reworked Greek plays into Latin with standard jokes; the *Atellana* was a short piece with stock characters that depicted town life. During the Floralia festival, the *fabulae Atellanae* featured nude women (Lactantius 1.20.1), and one play, by the Roman Afranius (mid-first century A.D.), included a scene where prostitutes masturbated men (Ausonius, *Epigr.* 79).

The Greeks and Romans conducted orgies in somewhat formalized environments. In the Greek symposium, men drank together, reclining on couches, while young males and females played music, danced, and performed sexually. In Plato's *Symposium* the men send away the "flute-girls" so they can concentrate on their conversation—which, nonetheless, is about the nature of Eros. These drinking parties, however, could devolve into orgies, as depicted on Athenian vase paintings (e.g., the Brygos Painter's kylix) and Etruscan wall paintings (e.g., Tarquinia Tomb 4260).[61] Another tomb at Tarquinia (Tomba delle Bighe)[62] shows two pairs of youths engaged in anal intercourse under bleachers full of proper Etruscan men and women watching a boxing match.

Roman parties were similar to the Greek ones, but added a new element: voyeurism.[63] In the sexually explicit paintings from Campania, a man and woman have sex almost always with someone present—usually, a room servant (*cubicularius*) stands nearby or in an open doorway.[64] (This custom was depicted in the television series *Rome.*) Voyeurism obviously added excitement: "Always with doors wide open and unguarded, Lesbia, you receive

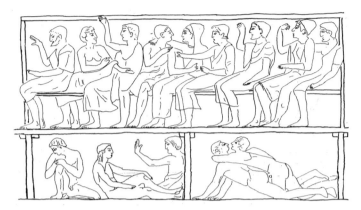

FIGURE 4.11: Etruscan tomb painting depicting two youths having anal intercourse beneath bleachers holding an audience watching a boxing match; Tomba delle Bighe, Tarquinia (drawing, author).

your lovers; you do not hide your vices. The beholder gives you more pleasure than the lover" (Mart. 1.34). Even watching oneself have sex was exciting: Horace decorated his bedroom with mirrors (Suet. *Poet.* 24.62–64), and Hostius Quadra was infamous for setting up a large mirror to watch himself be penetrated while performing cunnilingus (Sen. *Q nat.* 1.16).

Indeed, voyeurism seems an important part of Roman life in general. Many Campanian wall paintings of the Second to Fourth Styles include upper wall zones that depict small balconies containing anonymous small figures looking down and watching the real inhabitants of the room below.[65] While Greek houses concealed the interior from visitors, Roman houses often had the main entrance directly opposite the master's office (the *tablinum*), so passersby could see him at work in the distance, beyond the atrium. We—as well as the Greeks—might ask someone who stares at us, "What are you looking at?" A Roman would ask, "Do you like what you see?" Being viewed imparted importance.

We can call depictions of voyeurism in Roman sex "pornographic" in the modern sense (*pornographos* was first used to describe "the painters Aristeides, Pausias, and Nicophanes," who painted prostitutes, or *pornai*; Ath. 13.567b).[66] Modern definitions of pornography assume that its producers intend only to arouse an audience sexually. Can we know the intention of those who, in antiquity, produced sexually explicit scenes?[67]

We do know of the ancient sexual genres: sex manuals (such as those written by "Philainis")[68]; sexually explicit plays, verses, and entertainments performed by actors who emphasized the sexual content; literature that explored

FIGURE 4.12: Wall painting (from the painting,
Herrmann-Bruckmann 1904–1950: pl. 39);
House of the Vettii, triclinium *p*.

erotic feelings (such as Ovid's poetry, the Menippean satire *Satyrica*, by
Petronius, and episodes in Greek novels and in the Latin novel *Golden Ass*,
by Apuleius); and portable art such as *tabellae* (paintings on small wooden
diptychs),[69] erotic lamps, cameos, mirrors, and mold-made bowls.

Pornography depends on at least three premises: the sex act needs to be perceived, the audience needs to feel it is being performed for them, and orgasm
needs to be anticipated or perceived. For the first premise, many depictions strive
to make the sex act perceptible: a mirror cover from Corinth positions the couple
so we clearly see the man's penis entering the woman's vagina[70]; in Roman wall
paintings, the man tucks his near hand behind his back or places it on his hip, so
as not to interfere with our viewing the actual moment of penetration[71]—for the
same purpose, such hand placements are common in modern pornography.

For the second premise, modern pornography places the sex act in a con-
trived setting (platforms, obvious sets, convenient paraphernalia, costumes),
introduces a third party that stands for the audience (often not intimately par-
ticipating), and provides formulaic exclamations that are repeated theatrically

FIGURE 4.13: Roman wall painting from Campania depicting a
man having frontal intercourse with a woman, whose hand gesture may signal her orgasm (after Marcadé 1965: pl. on p. 59,
computer enhancement, author).

in order to focus the audience's attention on the activity. In Roman depictions of
sexual activity, a stage setting often appears: a curtain is drawn behind the participants, isolating them, along with the audience, from the rest of the world.[72]
Roman art also introduces the third party: the *cubicularius*. Repetitive exclamations are inscribed over the sex scene: on vases ("hold still," "let me!" and
"stop!"), in paintings ("push it in slowly"), and on several mold-made bowls.[73]

For the third premise, orgasm can be stated in literature, and it occasionally
is in Pompeian graffiti. In static art, orgasm is difficult to convey, so Roman
painting devised a convention: the man or woman stretches one hand out, as if
conveying tension and release.[74]

TRANSGRESSIONS

Transvestism seems to have been a socially sanctioned aspect of some rites
of passage:[75] male transition to adulthood most commonly employed it.

The Dorian *Ekdysia* (undressing, or stripping) was a Cretan festival in honor of Leto that involved youths who were becoming citizens changing clothes. (The verb *ekduō* was used for taking the oath of citizenship in several Cretan cities; compare the Roman custom of assuming the *toga virilis*). At Lyttos, the festival took place in September and October (compare Athens's *Oschophoria*) and had another name, the *Periblēmaia* (putting the woman's cloak on). In Sparta, another Dorian city, youths spent a period in isolation that ended in a race, a beating, and a procession in women's dress.

The Ekdysia has mythological transsexual explanations: Lamprus of Phaestus marries Galateia, and she becomes pregnant; he orders his wife to expose the child if it is a girl. During his absence, Galateia delivers a daughter but tells her husband it is a son, named Leucippus, and so keeps the child's true sex a secret. When the girl matures, Galateia prays to Leto to change her daughter into a son, and Leto does so. (On the eve of their wedding, grooms slept next to the statue of Leucippus; Antoninus Liberalis 17.) Another version concerns the girl Iphis, who is in the same predicament. At thirteen, "he" is betrothed to, and falls in love, with another girl, Ianthe, but as the wedding draws closer, Iphis begins to feel her love is unnatural (Ovid, *Met.* 9.666–797, incorporating a Lesbian version of the Leucippus story). She then calls out to the gods for help, and they transform her into a man so he can marry Ianthe.

In Athens, graduation from the ephebeia (the first stage of military service) at age twenty may also have involved a change of dress since, in Aristophanes' *Wasps*, Philocleon can see the ephebes' genitals. The autumn Athenian festival, the Oschophoria, remembers a mythological transvestism: two youths dress up as women to imitate the companions of Theseus, who dressed as women to kill the Minotaur.[76]

Other myths mask coming-of-age rites. Achilles dresses as a girl to avoid induction into Agamemnon's army, but Odysseus and Palamedes drop armor in front of him, which attracts his attention and reveals his true identity (Apollod. 3.13.8). Theseus enters Athens, wearing a chiton and long hair; this leads to his being mistaken for a maiden, which he corrects by throwing a bull into a sanctuary (Paus. 1.19.1).

Some marriage rites also called for transvestism. In Sparta and Cos, grooms don women's clothes on their wedding night (Plut. *Lyc.* 15; *Mor.* 304cd). In Argos, brides wear a false beard (Plut. *Mor.* 245ef)[77], and at another festival, the Hybristica, the Argives switch clothes to commemorate the female poet Telesilla, who led an army of women to defend Argos against Cleomenes of Sparta (ruled 520 to 489 B.C.; Plut. *Mor.* 245cf).

FIGURE 4.14: Statue from
Motya, Sicily (late 5th c.
B.C.), perhaps depicting
an actor (with *strophium*)
portraying Theseus (heroic
hairstyle); Mozzia Museum
(photo, author).

Men could be humiliated when wearing women's clothes. Surena, the victor
of Carrhae, mocked Crassus by dressing a man as a woman, labeled with the
latter's name, in his triumphal procession (Plut. *Crass.* 32.4–6). And there is
Heracles, dressed as a woman, doing women's work for Omphale as punishment (Ovid, *Her.* 9.53–118; *Fasti* 2.318–24; Plut. *Mor.* 304cd).

Transvestism could be dangerous. Twice at Thebes, beardless men dressed as
women—first to kill the Persian embassy (Hdt. 5.10), and later to kill the
Spartan garrison (Xen. *Hell.* 5.4.4). In myth, Dionysus dresses Pentheus as a
woman to infiltrate the Theban bacchants; his mother dismembers him. Both
Apollo and a certain Leucippus fall in love with Daphne, a companion of Artemis's, but she shuns men. Leucippus thereupon dresses as a maiden so he can
be in her party. Then one day, Daphne goes to bathe. Leucippus is reluctant to
strip and join in, however, so her girl-comrades undress him, see that he is a
man, and kill him (Paus. 8.20.2–4; Ovid, *Met.* 1.462–567).

Theater incorporates another aspect of socially accepted transvestism; until at least the late fourth century B.C., men played all roles—and several roles each within a play. Thus, Hippolytus could confront the sexuality of both father and stepmother if the same actor played Theseus and Phaedra in Euripides' *Hippolytus*.[78] Concert musicians also assumed long robes appropriate to women.[79] Compare Phaedrus's remark about Orpheus being effeminate, because he sang and played the kithara (Pl. *Symp.* 179d).

Transsexuality and hermaphroditism were, like transvestism, common topics in story—as well as an occasional reality. Lucius Mucianus claimed to have seen two transsexuals at Argos and Smyrna, Pliny reports four in 171 B.C., and he himself inspects one from Thysdrus (*NH* 7.23; Aulus Gellius, *NA* 9.4.12ff.). Phlegon of Tralles reports hermaphrodites in Greece (*Mirabilia 2*). In Rome, they were routinely killed from 207 to 92 B.C. (Livy 27.11.4, cf. Augustine, *Trinity* 6.8), but by Pliny's time, hermaphrodites were thought to have only a physical abnormality.[80]

In myth, Hermaphrodite was created when the water nymph Salmacis was united with Hermaphroditus, the son of Hermes and Aphrodite (Ovid, *Met.* 4.285–399). The conventional image of Hermaphrodite assumes a woman with female breasts and male genitals (contrast Priapus, who has a male body but often dresses like a woman). A famous Hellenistic statue plays with the viewer, who, based on their view from the rear, expects the likeness of a woman, but then discovers that, in front, "she" has male genitals.[81] Similarly, Roman paintings depict satyrs accosting Hermaphrodite and recoiling in surprise.[82]

A couple of well-known myths concern transsexuality. The Boeotian prophet Teiresias sees two copulating snakes and turns into a woman; when he sees them again, he turns back into a man (Hesiod fr. 275 M-W; Apollodorus 3.6.7).

FIGURE 4.15: Statue of a hermaphrodite, rear view; Athens National Museum (photo, author).

FIGURE 4.16: Statue of a hermaphrodite, front view; Louvre (photo, author).

Since he knows what it is like to be both sexes, he is asked who enjoys sex more. He answers, "Women, by a third." In another myth, Poseidon falls in love with the Lapith maiden Caenis and promises to grant her anything. She asks to be a man, Caeneus, to whom Poseidon gives immortality as well. At Pirithoüs and Hippodamia's wedding, the guests include centaurs and Caeneus (among other heroes); when the centaurs become drunk, they attack other guests, including Caeneus, but since he is immortal they resort to hammering him into the ground to kill him (Ovid, *Met.* 12.189–209; Apollonius 1.57 scholiast; Homer, *Iliad* 1.264 and 2.746 scholiast; Hyginus 14.4; Pindar fr. 150 Bowra).

Male gods change sex to seduce a mortal woman. Helius, the sun god, enters Leucothoë's bedroom disguised as her mother, Eurynome, and rapes her (Ovid, *Met.* 4.217–35). Phoebus Apollo and Hermes both want the girl Chione (Ovid, *Met.* 11.301–7); Hermes causes her to fall asleep, then rapes her. Later that night, Apollo, disguised as an old woman, also rapes her. Callisto is an Arcadian nymph dedicated to Artemis; when Zeus, disguised as Artemis, rapes her, she delivers the boy Arcas and is turned into a bear (or shot) by the goddess (Ovid, *Met.* 2.409–40, 4.217–33, 11.310, 14.654–771; *Fasti* 2.155–92; Apollod. 3.101; [Eratosthenes] *Catasterismi* 1.1.1–11).

There is little real evidence for ancient bestiality.[83] Non-mythological depictions are limited to a man having sex with a doe (*ABV* 469.71)[84] and to women copulating with horses, mules, or donkeys[85]—as Semiramis is said to have done (Pliny, *NH* 8.64)—and crocodiles mounting negro pygmies.[86] The last is, no doubt, meant to be a joke.

Instead, bestiality figures prominently in myth: Cronus, as a horse, rapes Phillyra, and she bears the centaur Chiron. As an eagle, Zeus has intercourse with Asterie and abducts Ganymede. As a swan, he rapes Leda, wife of Tyndareus, the king of Sparta; she produces Helen and Polydeuces (Pollux) from an egg, and, from an almost simultaneous union with Tyndareus, Castor and Clytemnestra. The egg was on view in Sparta (Paus. 3.16.1). Poseidon, as a horse, mates with Demeter in Arcadia, and she bears him the horse Arion or the local goddess Despoina of Lycosura (Paus. 8.25.4, 42.1).

In art, Pan attacks the shepherd Daphnis (*ARV*[2] 550.1),[87] and has frontal intercourse with a nanny goat.[88] Satyrs mostly rape maenads,[89] but occasionally also a male donkey.[90]

The two most famous myths with bestiality concern Europa (Ovid, *Met.* 2.844–75) and Pasiphaë. As a white bull, Zeus abducts Princess Europa of Tyre while she is playing on the shore. He takes her swimming across the sea

FIGURE 4.17: Roman discus lamp depicting a donkey having intercourse with a woman (first c. B.C.–first c. AD); Olympia Museum (photo, author).

to Crete, where she bears him two sons, Minos and Rhadymanthus, and, in later accounts, Sarpedon. Minos marries Pasiphaë, who conceives a passion for a bull sent to Minos by Poseidon. The court artisan, Daedalus, constructs a hollow bronze cow for her to fit into so she can have intercourse with the bull; she bears the Minotaur, a bull-headed man. A couple of Campanian wall paintings depict Daedalus bringing Pasiphaë the cow,[91] while Nero is said to have presented a live staging of Pasiphaë and the bull (Suet. *Nero* 12).

Copulating with a snake was said to produce great sons: Aristodama bore Aratus (Paus. 2.10.3), Olympias bore Alexander the Great, Avia bore Augustus. Scipio's mother, too, was said to have mated with a snake.

We have only two instances of ancient necrophilia, one possibly mythological and one presumably real. In epic poems that deal with events later than those in the *Iliad*, Achilles kills Penthesileia, the queen of the Amazons. As she dies, he falls in love with her.[92] The Byzantine scholar Eustathius of Thessalonica (*Il.* 1696.52) goes one step further and has Achilles consummate his love with Penthesilea's corpse.

Herodotus (5.92G1–4) records an odd story about Periander, tyrant of Corinth. When he consults the Oracle of the Dead on the river Acheron in Thesprotia, his dead wife, Melissa, appears and complains that she is cold because he has not burnt the clothing she wore when buried, and, she adds, because he had "put his loaves into a cold oven," referring to his intercourse with her dead body. Periander then orders all the Corinthian women to come to the temple of Hera, wearing their most beautiful garments; he orders them to strip, and, praying to Melissa, has the clothes burnt.

A final note to this summary of Greek and Roman sexual practices and attitudes: almost every real sexual activity we moderns do (phone sex being unreal) seems to have its ancient analogue—except one, fisting (inserting the hand through the vaginal or anal opening). This is probably the only new, post-antique sexual activity, an invention of the late twentieth century.[93]

CHAPTER FIVE

Sex, Religion, and the Law

ESTHER EIDINOW

INTRODUCTION: WRITTEN AND UNWRITTEN

While on a pilgrimage in Crete, an Athenian meets with two other travelers—a Spartan and a Cretan—and the three start to discuss the kinds of laws that would help establish the best possible state. This is the setting for *Nomoi* (*Laws*), probably Plato's final treatise. The three men are not aiming to create a utopia; this is a more pragmatic project. As they discuss regulating the sexuality of their imagined city's inhabitants, the Athenian observes how legislation alone cannot change people's behavior. Instead, drawing lessons from the way most people regard incest, he describes how the city authorities must ensure that state laws are supported by public opinion (*phēmē*). For this to work effectively, the city authorities must instill in the population a belief that, as with athletes, self-discipline will gain average citizens glory (by achieving "victory over pleasures"), reinforced by a fear of capitulating to behavior that is "never, in any way holy." Finally, he suggests that in case people still cannot control themselves, custom and "unwritten law" must be used to establish a second "law," or common standard: the conviction that any bad behavior must be conducted in private. In this way, the state can "hem in" those who have corrupt natures with godly fear, love of honor, and desire for virtue.[1]

The complexity of the processes the Athenian describes quashes ideas that legislation on its own regulates behavior, and that it simply asserts a consensual social order. First, his discussion prompts profound questions about the nature, role, and power of what we think of as laws. The Greek word for law (*nomos*) means not just legislation, but also particular customs or traditions, and can even indicate something akin to our word *taboo*: "a ritually sanctioned prohibition against contact with a thing, a person, or an activity."[2] The Athenian also mentions "unwritten law," or *agraphos nomos*—a phrase without a precise definition, usually used by the Greeks to indicate widely held moral and social rules.[3] Clearly, "laws" comprise a variety of mechanisms that regulate behavior. These are not only susceptible to variation over time and place between societies, but also—as the Athenian hints—to variations within societies, including gender and status. This leads, in turn, to questions about the personnel of regulation, and their relative powers: who gets to impose what kinds of regulation on whom—and why?[4] How, and why, might certain behaviors be deemed desirable, while others are not? How do different groups within society negotiate different forms of regulation?[5]

In this chapter, I attempt to answer some of the questions regarding the regulation of sex in the ancient world. I will discuss the evidence for explicit mechanisms of regulation, such as legislation, along with the evidence for more implicit mechanisms (by which I mean some of the core social attitudes and ethical concepts that shaped people's behavior), and I will examine the relationship between these two. It is impossible to be comprehensive, so I discuss the identification and treatment of two sexual crimes, adultery and rape—why these two crimes should be discussed side by side will become apparent—at particular times and places across Greek and Roman culture. In the interest of brevity, I will focus on the regulation of sexual crimes between men and women: sexual crimes between men, although obviously related, is a subject that merits discussion in its own right. The legal evidence discussed comprises a law-court speech from Athens, dating probably to the very end of the fifth century B.C.; civic law codes and sacred regulations from other Greek cities; and the *lex Julia de adulteriis coercendis* of Augustus (18 B.C.). Other material, used to place this evidence in context, is drawn from across Greek and Roman literature.

This paper does not attempt to chart comprehensively the development of social attitudes and legal instruments across antiquity: the difficulties posed by the evidence are well known. For Greek law, most of our evidence comes from Athens and cannot automatically be taken to represent the situation in other cities. Within democratic Athens, laws were decided by the Assembly and inscribed, but *nomoi* (permanent rules) were not distinguished from *psēphismata* (decrees) until 403 B.C., and only then was an archive (the *Mētrōon*), constructed to house them. There are no technical legal writings, and we are largely dependent on the partisan interpretations of particular laws given by forensic speeches. The mysterious seventh-century B.C. figure Draco, and the historical but over-venerated early-sixth-century B.C. Athenian states-man Solon are both credited with laws that were probably drafted far later. Turning to Roman law, we find that the Digests provide more specific legal information; but they were assembled in the sixth century A.D. and give no firm indication of how rules and attitudes changed over time. Any evidence for changing social attitudes is also limited insofar as it inevitably provides the experiences and opinions of only a small social group.

Nevertheless, there are patterns in the approach to regulation that recur across the evidence: for example, there are commonalities in the underlying attitudes toward women, and in the constructions of socially outrageous be-havior in Greek and Roman societies. But the evidence also brings to light sig-nificant changes over time in approaches to regulation: in particular, to draw on Foucault's descriptions of the development of regulation in much later his-torical periods, the ancient evidence implies a shift in the use of regulation of sexual behavior, from its employment as a method for imposing discipline on the individual body (in the form of punishment), towards its application as a political instrument to the population as a whole. The ancients' approach to the regulation of sexuality may be, historically, closer to ours than we think.

Recent scholarship on ancient sexual crimes tends to start with a discussion of the difference between modern Western approaches to sex crimes (which emphasize the consent of the victim) and ancient approaches (in which the consent of the female party was seldom the criterion for categorizing a sexual crime).[6] At first sight this is both clear-cut and correct, but it is far too simple. It risks not only introducing into the ancient world an idea of female autonomy that is largely irrelevant (which is not the same as saying that women were not autonomous in their daily lives), but also suggesting that our modern legal systems' treatments of sex crimes and the question of consent are straightfor-ward and objective.

In fact, in both theory and practice, this is seldom the case: modern legisla-tion may itself be discriminatory, defining rape from a male perspective, while the attitudes of those who apply it all too often depend on popular gender ste-reotypes and myths about sexual behavior.[7] Rape trials themselves frequently demonstrate the difficulties of identifying what is to be counted as consent and the "distance between most intimate violations of women and the legally perfect rape," while the way trials are conducted has led to the process being termed "secondary," or "judicial" rape.[8] We can trace links between ancient and modern values and attitudes, but my concern in raising this particular point is to draw attention to the *current* difficulties in describing and regulating the boundaries of sexual behavior—and to remind us of the close relationship of implicit social attitudes with legislation in this area across cultures, both ancient and modern.

THE ATHENIAN LAW COURT

Honor and Shame

In ancient Greek there is no single word that directly translates as "rape." A variety of terms appear across the literary genres: some simply use cognates of *bia* (force), but others provide more information about cultural perceptions of such an attack. For example, in New Comedy, the verb *phtheirō* and noun *phthora* are used, meaning "destruction," or "ruin," with the extended notion of "corruption," or "spoiling"—all of which describe not just the attack, but its implications for the victim.[9]

In most literary sources, the word *hybris* seems to come closest to indicating an act of rape.[10] Its victims are usually women and youths, attacked in contexts of physical violence—although it was also understood that fear alone could act as a coercive force.[11] However, *hybris* is far more than a simple descriptor of the physical act of rape. In modern use, we know it as a description of overweening arrogance; in ancient Greece, it was used to describe any action (not just sexual) that crossed the boundaries of acceptable behavior, and which, when directed against another, was intended to bring dishonor and shame upon them.[12] In Athens, to commit *hybris* (sexual or not) against a male citizen was a very serious matter indeed; it could be prosecuted by *ho boulomenos* (anyone who wished) by means of a public suit, the *graphē hybreōs*. Prosecutions could even be brought on behalf of slaves, demonstrating the extent to which the behavior and attitudes comprising *hybris* were considered intolerable. If we think of *hybris* in terms of what was suitable behavior for a citizen, we can understand how activities that involved consensual sexual relations could be described as *hybris*, and how one could even be described as committing *hybris* against oneself.[13]

The notion of *hybris* seems to have worked differently for women, free or not. Although it was certainly possible for women to be described rhetorically as committing *hybris* if they behaved in a way that transgressed social norms, we do not hear of any woman committing *hybris* against herself.[14] Legally, the status of women in Greek society meant that they could not perpetrate *hybris*;

they could only suffer it. Based on the literary use of the term, we might expect to find examples of this in the forensic texts, and it has been argued that it was possible to bring a *graphē hybreōs* against a rapist. (This may also have been one of the principal methods of regulating sexual activity that included children—although how exactly this would have worked in a culture of pederastic relationships is unclear—and perhaps slaves.) Nevertheless, the few cases of sexual violence for which we have evidence are committed against noncitizen women, and none results in a *graphē hybreōs*.

A speech by the orator Dinarchus does describe three cases that may involve *hybris* (although the term is only used explicitly of one of them). The first involves a miller killed for keeping a freed slave boy in a mill; the second centers around the execution of one Themistius of Aphidna because he committed *hybris* against a Rhodian lyre-player; and the last addresses the execution of Euthymachus for "putting the Olynthian girl in a brothel."[15] But we have no clear assurance that any of these cases involved rape. As another case, mentioned by Demosthenes, suggests, Themistius may also have assaulted a state official, which may have had a greater bearing on his punishment.[16] As well as the *graphē hybreōs*, a number of other legal procedures may have been used to prosecute rape, including the *dikē biaiōn* (private case against acts of violence), but, again, the evidence remains tentative.

Considering the absence of examples, it is perhaps surprising that the earliest legislation concerning rape is Draco's homicide law, dating as far back as the seventh century B.C., although it was apparently reinscribed in 409/8 B.C.[17] As reported, the law is not specifically concerned with sexual crimes, but describes situations in which a man who has killed someone cannot be condemned for homicide. These include warfare, sporting competitions, and, as described by Demosthenes, when a man catches another man with "his [the discoverer's] spouse or sister or daughter or a concubine whom he keeps for free children."[18]

As such, the law gives no weight to any factor other than the discovery by a male home-owner of another man in his house; it does not appear to distinguish between rape and adultery. A legal distinction may have developed later: other sources suggest Solon ruled that, while adulterers could be killed, rape and procurement could be punished privately with fines to be paid to the plaintiff (the victim's *kyrios,* her male guardian).[19] A technical term for adultery also develops in the classical period: *moicheia* is now generally accepted as having this meaning, although it may, as Draco's law, have had a wider application than simply illicit sexual behavior with another man's wife.[20] But the practical distinction behind the legislation may have been more difficult to prove: In

Euripides' *Trojan Women*, Hecuba argues that, because Helen didn't make a loud protest at the time of her abduction, she cannot claim to have been carried off by force (998–1001). Similar myths about how victims of rape typically respond are still prevalent, and may give us some idea of the complex social attitudes surrounding this crime in the ancient world.[21]

These, in turn, may help to provide an explanation of the paucity of examples of rape cases. It may be a matter of the survival of evidence, but the influence of social attitudes is also likely to play a part. A variety of ancient sources enable us to understand how sexual escapades—especially those of a woman—were perceived to undermine the honor of her male relatives, and how gossip about such matters would have spread through an ancient city.[22] Most of our examples are about adulterous women, but the same social constraints could haunt young men.[23] In Athens, at least, we can trace how this implicit form of regulation could become directly involved in litigation. For example, Apollodorus's case against Neaera ([Dem.] 59) rests on a compelling, often salaciously vivid narrative of her scandalous exploits; the same is true of Aeschines' prosecution of Timarchus for living in a way that disbarred him from public life.

It may be that Aeschines had discovered a new method or standard of proof; on the other hand, we know that similar prosecutions were threatened, presumably on a similar basis, some earlier than this case.[24] Surely such threats were powerful: even without much basis, a looming court case would be an effective way of starting rumors and attacking an enemy's reputation.[25] Even if it never came to court, the "case" would still be tried by citizens—just in the streets rather than the courts. Allowed to flourish, such accusations could have more dramatic consequences than mere fodder for gossip; no wonder ancient Athenians would often choose to attack their opponents on personal grounds.

Rules and Rhetoric

The preceding discussion of rape and the implications of social expectations provides some context for the discussion of a case of adultery presented in a law-court speech by Lysias. Euphiletus has killed a man he found in bed with his wife and is defending himself against a charge of murder. His defense turns on the argument that his action was not only perfectly justified, but was in fact demanded by the law precisely because this was a seduction (i.e., adultery), which all men judge to be the worst kind of *hybris*. He draws a comparison between the penalty for adultery, which he would have us believe is death, and that for rape, which, he announces, is limited to a fine. At first sight, the legislation seems as clear-cut as he presents it, but we must be on our guard: Euphiletus is facing a murder charge and is therefore pleading to save his own life. He sets the scene carefully: he records the evidence of others (the information provided by an old woman and his wife's maid); he mentions again the idea of *hybris* done to him by the adulterer's presence and activities in his house; he describes how the man is caught in bed with his wife, is seen naked by other witnesses, and admits his own guilt. Only after this does he introduce the three laws, which, he argues, justify his actions.

Unfortunately, none of the laws survives as quotations in the text, which means it is not clear what part, or how much, of the law is quoted. In the case of the first quotation, it is not even clear what law is being cited. After it has been read, Euphiletus reiterates Eratosthenes' confession, so it seems likely that this was critical to the legal procedure that followed. Some have argued that the law in question is the *kakourgōn apagōgē*—a procedure by which the Eleven (officials responsible for prisons and executions) oversaw summary executions of wrongdoers (possibly including adulterers) who were caught in the act.[26] This would explain why, despite Eratosthenes' confession, Euphiletus remains liable for a homicide charge, because he had carried out the sentence himself on the spot, rather than allowing for due legal process. Others argue that the law was the *nomos moicheias*, which specifically concerned adultery.[27] It may have included the possibility of summary execution following confession, but whether this could be carried out by an aggrieved husband rather than by city officials is unknown, and Euphiletus does not mention this aspect—rather suggesting it was the latter! The law almost certainly included alternatives to instant execution, including holding the perpetrator to ransom, or physically abusing him.[28] Again, Euphiletus makes no mention of these, either.

Euphiletus's following remarks give the impression that the law dictated that an adulterer who was caught in the act and confessed must be killed. He treats the second law quoted, the Draconian homicide law, in the same way, describing it as laying down the obligation for a man to kill an adulterer found with his wife, rather than providing a context for excusing such action. In keeping with this approach of painting adultery as the sexual crime that incurred the most severe penalty, Euphiletus then compares it with the treatment of rape in a *dikē biaiōn* (l.32), claiming that, whereas adultery was punishable by death, rape simply incurred a fine. In fact, as described above, just as there were other, more lenient penalties for *moicheia*, there were more severe penalties for rape: prosecuted under the *graphē hybreōs*, the latter could potentially incur the death penalty.

The creativity Euphiletus shows in his handling of the relevant laws demonstrates the fluidity of Athenian law.[29] But even if we cannot get a clear picture of the relevant legislation, Euphiletus's rhetoric illuminates popular attitudes: for example, his emphasis on the *hybris* he has suffered because of Eratosthenes' presence in his house, and the dangers that adultery poses to the city and its inhabitants. He argues that, while rape is only an attack on a woman's body, *moicheia* corrupts a woman's mind. Some have seen here a possible reference to a loss of affection between the partners,[30] but it is more likely that this is to do with the popular understanding of the nature of woman that we find expressed more explicitly elsewhere across Greek literature. For instance, a woman who has been adulterous is considered unable to remain faithful, endangering the purity of the family; a corrupting force, she must be kept away from other women.[31] By the fifth century B.C., this was expressed in law: adulterous women were not allowed to attend public sacrifices, risking a beating if found there, and they could not wear ornamentation in public. Their husbands had to divorce them or lose their civic rights.[32] Because women participated unlikeable in community life through familial and religious activities, these sanctions would certainly have made a woman's life unbearable.[33]

Nevertheless, Euphiletus's comparison of the social impacts of rape and adultery is likely to be specious: the evidence suggests that husbands may have felt the same way about a wife who had been raped as about one who had committed adultery. The Solonian law of uncertain date, quoted by Plutarch and already mentioned briefly above, mentions various penalties for the perpetrator of the crimes of rape, adultery, and procurement. It goes on to deny a father or brother the right to sell a sister or daughter into prostitution "unless he found her, an unmarried woman, having sex with a man." This may not be trustworthy evidence of historical legislation, but it is illustrative of social attitudes, and it makes no distinction between rape and adultery.[34]

Despite the plethora of possibilities for legal procedure, it remains unclear what kind of legal distinction existed between rape and adultery in ancient Athens, or how it would have been made. It surely did not turn on legal definitions, nor was it concerned with notions of female consent. Indeed, the evidence suggests that it was the wronged husband (or father, or brother) who decided the nature of the crime and selected the appropriate legal procedure.

However, there may be a clue to changing attitudes in what seems to be something of a clash of civic values in the background to this speech. When he appeals to his audience, Euphiletus emphasizes the importance of personally avenging *hybris,* safeguarding one's status, maintaining the integrity of one's household. However hard he tries to conceal it, his behavior conflicts with the demands of legal procedure.[35] Euphiletus emphasizes the ideal of self-help and the right of a citizen to defend his family, honor and status (enshrined in the Draconian justification of murder)—in contrast to the state's demand for oversight of the private realm, the regulation of violence, the protection of the legitimacy of offspring and the status of the family, through civic procedures rather than individual actions.[36] We can believe that some would have welcomed litigation as a far less risky course of action than self-help. Plato's reformulation of the penalties for rape in his *Laws* may show yet another view: he restricts self-help to those cases where force is used, while adultery is relegated to the realm of relatively minor offenses.

Silence and Signal

The voices of the victims of these crimes remain more or less silent. Scouring the evidence may reveal the odd signal, but even these tend to be heavily filtered. Examples include the character of Creusa, the Athenian princess raped and, as far as she knows, forsaken by Apollo, in Euripides' *Ion* (around 412 B.C.). Her account of the rape itself is brief, but includes some poignant details; in contrast Xuthus and Ion merely refer to it in passing. She gives an anguished description of how she gave birth and, with no mortal or divine support, was forced to abandon her child. It is plain that Creusa feels that the rape has destroyed her life, her agony compounded by the knowledge that she will die childless. Euripides' presentation of Creusa's own feelings was surely innovative, but the rest of her portrayal is far from straightforward. Throughout her laments, the audience knows that, in fact, her anger against Apollo is partially misplaced. While she and the chorus deny that women are a bad lot and are undeserving of male suspicion, and while they call for poets to tell the truth about men's sexual activities, the climax of the play is still her plot to poison Ion, and, in the course of events, we are constantly reminded of the uncontrolled and dangerous nature of women.[37]

Another example, dating a century or so later, is perhaps more surprising. In Menander's plays, rape is a frequent plot device, the "mistake" of a parade of wealthy young men who attack poor young women during nighttime festivals and then, finally, marry them, making everything right. These plays focus on the emotional journeys of their male leads, from rapist to respectable married man; the female characters in these plays are seldom, if ever, heard.[38] But there is an exception: in *Epitrepontes* (*Men in Arbitration*), the hero Charisius has, unknown to them both, raped his own wife, Pamphile, at a festival, before they were married. When he hears she has given birth, he assumes she is unfaithful and moves in with a *hetaira*, Habrotonon. Pamphile refuses to leave him, though urged to do so by her family. Meanwhile, Charisius is tricked by Habrotonon, who pretends to be the woman he raped. In response, as reported by his servant, Charisius seems to undergo a startling transformation: the discovery of his own transgression whips up the realization of his own double standards, as well as his guilt that his "adulterous" wife is still defending their marriage.[39] Does Charisius provide us with evidence of a changing sensibility in Greek society that perhaps reflects the changing role of women?[40] He still takes little responsibility for the rape, describing what happened to his wife as a "mischance"—that is, an involuntary action. However, he does abuse himself as uncivilized and immoral: a barbarian and a "sinner" (*alitērios*). Is this because of his act of rape or his abandonment of the marital home?[41] More intriguing still is the description of the aftereffects of the rape that Habrotonon provides, which, although brief, manages to evoke the violence of the act. In later conversation with Charisius—and still pretending she was the victim—Habrotonon mentions the violence of his actions with admiration. The audience knows this is a trick, that these are not her real feelings: is she subverting just *his* attitude, or attitudes to rape in general?[42]

LAWS BEYOND ATHENS

Civic Codes

From outside Athens, evidence for the regulation, implicit or explicit, of sexuality is limited. A brief passage in Xenophon's *Hiero*, set in Sicily, mentions the same concern as Euphiletus's about the corruption of a wife by seduction, using it to explain the fact that many Greek states sanction the killing of adulterers (and only adulterers) with impunity, on the grounds that being seduced must corrupt a wife's feelings for her husband.[43] Xenophon is certainly exaggerating: as we have seen, there were other crimes within Athens alone that incurred the death penalty, but other cities may well have sanctioned the killing of adulterers. Xenophon makes no explicit mention of what happens to the wives in such situations. However, we can elicit some idea from what he does go on to say. The passage switches subjects, going on to point out that if the wife's lapse is *kata symphoran* (the result of some accident), the husbands should continue to honor their wives as before. The implication is that in situations of seduction, the opposite occurs. Again, nothing is said about who judges the event to be an accident, or on what grounds.

From Crete comes the earliest evidence for legislation regarding rape and adultery: Gortyn's *The Great Code* (*IC* iv 72; c. 450 B.C.).[44] Column II 2–45 comprises material on rape, seduction, and adultery. It employs a variety of different terms for these offenses, but provides no explanations of what each term means, or how each differs from the others. The impression is of a series of regulations, assembled over time, identifying and tackling a variety of likely scenarios of illicit sexual behavior, rather than a single code drafted to provide comprehensive prescriptions.

In the code, both rape and adultery are dealt with as private matters rather than as public crimes; and the women involved are not only wives.[45] Both crimes incur the same level of fines, with the amount dependent on the status of victim and offender; in neither case is a penalty described for the victim. In the case of adultery, the affected family can hold the offender to ransom for five days, then do what they like with him once that time has passed. The fine is reduced by half if the offense took place somewhere other than in the house of the woman's father, brother, or husband (ll. 28–36). The code is organized according to the status of offender and victim, with slave offenders paying twice as much as freedmen. It does not provide penalties for all the different possible combinations of victim, agent, status, and offense it describes. However, the code does provide explicit legislation with regard to slaves, with a fine for adultery between slaves and between a slave and a freedwoman, for rape between serfs, and for rape of a household slave (depending on whether the slave had already been seduced by night or by day). By probably a century later, adultery became a publicly punishable offense: the offender came to court and was punished not only with a fine, but also with the loss of civil rights and public employment.[46]

Finally, the highly fragmentary remains of an inscription recording a treaty between the cities of Delphi and Pellana (third century B.C.) seem to include provisions for the regulation of sexual violence. If the reading is correct, the fine for rape is 1000 drachmas (50 if the victim is a slave). There may also be reference to a doubling of the penalty for theft when such violence is involved.[47]

These civic law codes share a marked absence of legal categories and definitions, and little, if any, information on legal procedure. It may be that we can draw a parallel with the fluidity of ancient Athenian law and presume that the lack of strict legal classifications across these codes indicates similar possibilities for the individual selection of legal procedure. However, their details regarding status (of victim and perpetrator), although not systematic, show a marked difference from the Athenian laws as they have survived, which are concerned primarily with the rights of citizens (although in Athens, too, slaves could be guilty of *hybris*).

Sacred Regulations

Did those committing sexual offenses risk *miasma* (pollution) and becoming ritually impure?[48] The most obvious candidate for incurring such pollution is incest, introduced by the Athenian in the passage from Plato's *Laws* discussed earlier, to indicate the kind of strong social feeling that is needed to support legislation on sexual behavior. This seems to be an example of an "unwritten law," since, though incest does not seem to have been illegal in Athens, there is plentiful evidence of strong social disapproval. (However, as modern commentators, we need to be aware that the definition of incest was not always the same as our own: across Greece, there existed varieties of what we think of as incestuous relationships.)

We might expect to find some guidance on incest—or, indeed, any sexual crime—among the laws classified as "sacred" by modern commentators, especially the ones describing the ideal state of purity for those entering sanctuaries.[49] These offer ample instruction regarding the treatment of impurity arising from sexual intercourse, most of it aimed at men. They are of a very general nature, usually stipulating some kind of delay and washing before entering a sanctuary in order to avoid "pollution."[50] Some regulations specify different rules for sleeping with someone other than your wife, but these differences are minimal and turn on the time that must pass before the man can enter the sanctuary.[51] No suggestions are made that there is anything wrong with sexual activity in itself. It is more as if these rules are intended to draw a boundary between two separate realms: the mundane and physical, and the sacred. The potential danger seems to lie in the idea of (bodily) matter being out of place.[52] Other activities meriting *katharsis* (purification) are menstruation, childbirth, abortion, contact with a corpse, and contact with certain foods. But as with the civic codes discussed previously, these sacred laws seem to build on customary practice, focusing on possible problems and their solutions, rather than defining the nature of transgressions. Unlike the codes, these regulations do not mention the civic body responsible for them, nor do they specify what kind of penalty there might be for transgressing these rules, who would enforce it, or how.[53]

The idea of matter being out of place may help to explain the use of "pollution" to describe an offender's disgraced social status, for example, those of convicted adulteresses and male prostitutes.[54] We might argue that these individuals were potentially offensive to the gods, which is why they were banned from public religious ceremonies, but there is no evidence that their offenses were regarded as "sins" in a religious sense. Rather, they were transgressions of social norms and boundaries, seen as threatening to the structure and institutions of the city and its inhabitants. Those who committed them had to be excluded from the citizen body, and this would necessarily have meant exclusion from participation in the sacred.

AUGUSTAN LEGISLATION

Tradition and Innovation

In Rome, after 18 B.C., under the *lex Julia de adulteriis coercendis,* the exclusion of adulterers, both men and women, took a more dramatic form.[55] The couple was deprived of property (the woman lost half her dowry and a third of her property; the man lost half his property), and they were sent to separate islands (*relegatio ad insulam*), although the period of banishment is unknown. In addition, the man was denied his civic privileges; the woman was forbidden to remarry and was required to wear the toga—the costume of the prostitute, when worn by a woman; and both genders lost the right to give evidence in court.[56] They would be lucky if they stayed alive to suffer these punishments.

   Pre-Augustan legislation against sexual crimes punished those who threatened or damaged their victim's *pudicitia,* a concept that is often translated as "chastity," or "modesty," but that also includes elements of both social and moral standing and integrity. Under the Lex Aquilia, an action for outrage (*iniuria*) could be taken against anyone who made sexual advances against a person, free or enslaved, male or female (but not a prostitute), which threatened their *pudicitia*, including by using flattery, removing an attendant, or following someone around in silence.[57] The charge could be brought by the victim (male or female) or by a husband or father, any of whom could prosecute, even if the victim had consented to the acts in question.[58] The term *stuprum* described illicit sexual relations, including both rape and seduction, although its early use seems to have applied to more general shame-inducing actions, like the Greek *hybris*. Under the Julian laws on violence, the rape (*per vim stuprum*, or "intercourse by force") of a freed boy, a young girl, or a single or married woman was a capital offense. The victim could bring a charge, as could a third party, if the father failed to prosecute.[59]

   The legislation of 18 B.C. had a different focus: Augustus's self-professed aim was the strengthening of Roman society, for the sake of Rome and her future, through a return to traditional values and customs; however; his motives may have been more nuanced than this suggests.[60] The law against adultery was passed soon after a law that prohibited marriage between members of certain social groups. The public demonstration of opposition by the *Equites* (the only act of opposition of its kind during Augustus's reign, which led to the *lex Papia Poppaea* in 9 A.D.) suggests his attempts were not widely appreciated.[61] He may have tried similar measures before (possibly around 28 B.C.), but there is no evidence for a law against adultery in the Republic, when, apart from a number of sensational trials, most cases seem to have been dealt with by the family.[62] One explanation for Augustus's change of approach may be gathered from the growing "narrative of decline" in Roman authors, from the second century B.C. onward, describing the disintegration of Roman moral integrity and demonstrating concern with the dangers of uncontrolled sexual activity (particularly that of women) and its damage to marriage and family.[63]

Our information about the Lex Julia is pieced together from literary sources and excerpts from five of the nine or more chapters it comprised. It is very difficult to separate the original provisions from later discussion and development, but, along with the penalties described earlier, the fundamental statutes seem to have carefully delineated the permitted and expected responses of a father or a husband to the discovery of his wife's or daughter's adultery. Perhaps unsurprisingly, the law dealt in detail with the right of a husband or father to kill, or spare, the woman and her lover.

If he found his wife and her lover together in his own house, a husband was allowed to kill a lover of low status (the legislation defined particular groups), but the pair must be caught in the act.[64] Other forms of degrading punishment may also have been permitted.[65] Otherwise, an aggrieved husband was allowed to hold the adulterer for twenty hours while he gathered evidence to take him to court, and he could recapture him if he escaped within this time.[66] The husband was not allowed to simply kill his wife (although there is evidence that if he did, he would be treated with relative leniency), but he was not permitted to forgive her, either. He was to divorce her, or risk prosecution for *lenocinium* (pimping).[67] No such limits were applied to the father of an adulterous woman. So long as he was the head of the household, he could kill both his daughter and her lover, whatever the latter's status. However, there were some circumstantial restrictions: the father had to find the lovers in the house in which he lived; they had to be caught in sexual congress; and, finally, the father had to kill the couple in one action.[68] Once a lover was convicted, a husband or father could bring an accusation against his wife or daughter within sixty days. Otherwise, any third party could bring a charge (including against the husband for complicity). All rights of accusation lapsed after five years.[69]

Thus, Augustus established crucial oversight of sexual activity, establishing a standing criminal court to deal with matters that, it seems, had previously rarely concerned the state.[70] The Lex Julia tackled not only *adulterium* (that is, illicit sexual relations with a married woman), but also *stuprum*, narrowing its definition to indicate sex with a boy or an unmarried woman or widow. Indeed, the emperor's own daughter, Julia, was convicted for this crime and exiled to the island of Pandateria.[71] In this way, *stuprum* was redefined as a consensual act, as incriminating for both partners as adultery—as a matter of fact, the jurists complain that the law did not distinguish between the two terms.[72] The constraints the law imposed from a male point of view were, in the end, not tremendous: there were four categories of women to which the law did not apply, and a fifth was added by the jurists.[73] A man could still have legal sexual relations with slaves and prostitutes of both genders. His wife could not accuse him of adultery.[74] Rather, it was the sexual activities of free, respectable women that were now highly constrained—on pain of severe penalties. By defining who could be prosecuted by whom, this legislation established a hierarchy of those whose sexual integrity was of concern to the state.

The jurists provide us with some idea of the nature of the oversight that followed, examining questions about the location and status of each party and their liability for prosecution; the timing of prosecutions; the collection of evidence; and the application of penalties. Such questions may illustrate the difficulties of implementation or describe test cases: either way, they reveal a new state focus on the details of private lives. One of the areas of discussion was the question of the liability of a woman compelled to have sex—a situation that, for a modern reader, would be a crime of rape. The law deemed culpable anyone who committed *stuprum* or adultery "knowingly," but how did this apply, for example, to women in time of war, or subjected to force by an enemy?[75] In fact, the concerns demonstrated by the law and the jurists are likely to have been part of a larger cultural disquiet about the dangers of female sexuality.

Stories and Rumors

Contemporary literature also reveals anxiety about female sexuality, adultery, and the question of consent. For example, the question of a woman's role in a situation of adultery is vividly examined in an *exemplum* Livy retells about the rape of Lucretia, set in 509 B.C. *Exempla* were stories that drew on key events in Roman history and were used in education and literature to encourage reflection on questions of morality and to communicate common values. The lessons of Livy's version of this story are intriguing.

Unlike his contemporaries, Livy emphasizes the role of Lucretia's consent to the rape, and its implications. Lucretia lays down her life in fear of damage to her reputation. She dies because she fears becoming an excuse for unchaste women, who will escape the penalty of *stuprum* on the grounds that they, too, were forced. With this version of Lucretia's story, Livy draws attention to the difficulties (and dangers) of distinguishing between those whose sexual integrity (*pudicitia*) deserves to be protected and avenged, and those who have forgone this protection because of their own appetites. In this story, *pudicitia* is a fragile quantity, difficult to protect and easily undone. Lucretia surrenders hers not because she is physically forced to do so, but in the face of what she perceives to be an even greater threat: damage to her reputation. Livy's telling of this story demonstrates how, without the moral strength of a Lucretia—and who possesses *that?*—the sexuality of women inevitably threatens the state.

Livy's description of Rome almost establishes rape as a state-building tool.[76] His account is dominated by stories of rape (of Rhea Silvia, the vestal virgin; of the Sabine maidens; of Lucretia; of Roman prostitutes by Sabine youths) and attempted rape (Verginia). In each case, the attack on an individual (and subsequent reactions) produces a crucial change for the city and society of Rome. Perhaps such a view is not so far-fetched in light of contemporary gossip gleaned from Suetonius: alongside the story of his legislation were stories of Augustus's own, very deliberate, adulteries, rumored to be perpetrated for state purposes: to discover his enemies' plots. It suggests a far more nuanced view of Augustus's character—and his view of the crime of adultery—than that suggested simply by his legislation.[77]

CONCLUSION: BODY AND POPULATION

Sexuality may be rooted in biological drives, but how and why are these mediated—constrained, accepted, feared, or welcomed? How does regulation become imposed, and by whom and through what mechanisms? What purposes can the regulation of sexual behavior serve?

In Plato's *Laws,* the Athenian reveals a sophisticated understanding of the ways in which the categorization (and regularization) of sexual behavior can be used as a method of controlling individuals and populations. We find it echoed in much later writers: Michel Foucault, although not the first, has been the most influential figure to examine the intersection of sexuality with modes of discipline. But, surprisingly, in Foucault's schema, the cultures of the Greeks and Romans were seen as free of such controls, allowing individuals (specifically, men) to fashion themselves in the absence of any kind of fixed moral code. Foucault argued that sexuality became the focus of state power later, in two key stages: first, through the discipline of the individual body, established during the seventeenth century and in the course of the eighteenth; then, during the second half of the eighteenth century, through more far-reaching regulation targeting the entire population, in which certain biological processes (birth, death, production, illness) were treated as a political matter. Foucault called this "biopolitics," and described it as a "new technology of power."[78]

Foucault's view of ancient sexuality has been challenged from many quarters from a variety of standpoints: critics have commented on his literal use of evidence, his curious omission of his own "archaeological method," his lack of reference to (or apparent interest in) the situations and viewpoints of women.[79] Even these brief case studies demonstrate how the sexual behavior of the ancient world was heavily regulated, both explicitly, through legislation, and implicitly, by powerful social dynamics and complex notions of moral and physical integrity (for example, *hybris*, *stuprum* and *pudicitia*). But although we may reject his conclusions about the ancient world, Foucault's descriptions of the development of regulation (or what he called "techniques of power") in later European cultures may be relevant and provocative for the purposes of this investigation.

Explicit and Implicit

The earliest evidence for the regulation of sexual behavior shows it targeting the individual. Outside Athens, sparse material limits our conclusions, but law codes seem to have developed as a result of rulings given to resolve private conflicts, which were then instantiated within communities. The state's discipline reinforces the status relations between individuals and (in rape and adultery cases) recognizes the need of the wronged citizen (husband, father or brother) to exact vengeance, providing a range of ways in which this might be obtained, even sanctioning violence in some cases. By exerting discipline over individuals (not just the discipline of punishment over the offender, but also the discipline of legal process over the offended), the state reasserted the implicit contract made between individuals in its social body.

A similar ethos seems to have prevailed, at least to begin with, in Athens, underlying Draco's homicide law, which oversees the relationship between individual and society, and shaping Euphiletus's appeals to his fellow citizens as he struggles to appeal to implicit social values, presumably in an attempt to overrule existing legislation. However, evidence suggests gradual changes in the nature of the regulation of sexual behavior, from a concern to discipline the behavior of individuals in order to maintain the social order, to a more politicized concern with the sexual processes of citizens, to the regulation of the population as a whole.

For example, although we don't have a date for these laws, the fact that sexual misdemeanors such as *moicheia* and *hybris* could be tried as *graphai* (public cases) and prosecuted by anyone who wanted to do so, not just the victim or their family, moves these crimes out of the private realm and into the glare of the public, and they become matters of state concern. Of course, the line between state and citizenry in ancient Athens cannot be drawn cleanly: thus, in the case against Timarchus, we find the state (embodied in a private citizen) using the city's law to attack a citizen in order, ostensibly, to protect the state (the citizens).

As for targeting the population, a first example is found in Solon's laws for punishing a woman (who was not a prostitute) involved in a sexual misdemeanor. Such a woman may be sold into prostitution by her male relatives: her behavior has barred her from state protection, presumably because she is no longer eligible to produce citizen children.[80] At first sight, this is simply the punishment of an individual. But the aim of the ruling is more far-reaching than just the discipline of any particular woman: its underlying aim is control of the (nature of the) population. Under Pericles, this aim is made more explicit in the citizenship law (451/0 B.C.), which was intended to secure the purity of the population by establishing the status of women who could have citizen children. This, again, was not about training the individual body; instead, it was a mechanism intended to regulate the effects of the sexual activities of the wider population.[81]

Of course, I am not arguing that the Greeks began gathering statistical data in order to monitor relevant phenomena, as Foucault describes happening in the eighteenth century. Nevertheless, these laws show a change of focus away from discipline of the individual body and toward a more far-reaching concern with safeguarding the population as a whole, through regulation of the effects of biological (specifically, sexual) processes. We can also make a further observation (one that Foucault was unlikely to have noted) about the gender roles that implicitly shape the structure and targets of this legislation: both Solon's and Pericles' laws cast women as merely the biological settings for male activity, giving them no politically or socially significant agency of their own.

The gradual changes we observe in Greek regulation of sexuality can also be seen, far more clearly, in the Augustan legislation. The *lex Julia de adulteriis coercendis* changed adultery from a personal matter that was resolved by the family to a public concern at a stroke.[82] Whereas Euphiletus appealed to his audience's sense of outrage that the adulterer was in his house, Augustus's legislation made it a matter of public, legal concern—even taking care to define, in the case of a father, which of his houses qualified as his home, and ruling on the appropriate level of violence in his response.

But this legislation targeted more than the individual: Augustus imposed his law on an unwilling population with the explicit intention of fundamentally restructuring social attitudes toward sexuality. It demanded that all citizens safeguard not their immediate family, but Roman society more generally, sometimes even sacrificing their immediate family for its sake. Moreover, this responsibility extended beyond the immediate family: anyone could bring a prosecution for adultery, and penalties were imposed even on those who were only indirectly involved in the crime (for example, someone who took a bribe to keep quiet). And, finally, Augustus's legislation, like that of the Greeks, gave the male agency, while the nature of his crime was defined in terms of the status of the woman, the biological facility with whom he transgressed. The law may have limited the types of women with whom a man could have sexual relations outside marriage, but it denied a woman any kind of sexual activity outside marriage. Whereas Pericles' citizenship law did not acknowledge an active role for women, Augustus's Lex Julia implicitly recognized and removed it.

In the case of this law, at least, later discussion and refinements among the jurists does suggest a growing acknowledgment, over time, of the idea of female agency. But reading the jurists' concerns about women is not the same as reading the expressions of women themselves. We know the law: a wife in Athens had no legal status, and so could not bring her husband to court; in Rome, wives were forbidden to prosecute their husbands. But their actual experiences, as with slaves', remain largely hidden. All is not completely lost: there are occasional clues scattered throughout ancient literature (albeit not in their own words) about wives' attitudes to their husbands' transgressions.[83] We can weigh these against a few more specific examples, such as the story of Vistilia, a member of a high-ranking family, who attempted in 19 A.D. to avoid impending prosecution for adultery by registering as a prostitute. (The Senate closed that loophole by passing a decree that no woman of the upper classes could prostitute herself.) Very rarely, we locate a female voice: the poetry of the first-century B.C. noblewoman Sulpicia gives us a vivid sense of a woman about whom we otherwise know very little. She not only tells off her lover Cerinthus for preferring a slave girl to her, but also states she would rather have a good lover than a good reputation.[84]

Implicit, explicit, unwritten, unspoken, unheard—the regulation of sexual behavior in any community across the ancient world comprised a multitude of regulatory mechanisms, from formal legislation to informal gossip, shaped, as these case studies have demonstrated, by complicated concepts of moral and physical integrity. We can describe the different aspects of this regulation, but attempts to understand how these mechanisms worked, together or in con-flict, must try to take into account how the experience, and negotiation, of these regulations, varied not just by time and place, but also according to age, gender, and social status. Any attempt at creating a single, simple narrative is likely to prove deceptive—although, all too often, we can only imagine what the other storylines might have added. Looking to our own time and beyond, we face similar challenges in our attempts to understand sexual behavior and its regulation, and we are left asking whose voices are not heard now.

CHAPTER SIX

Sex, Medicine, and Disease

HELEN KING

Ancient medicine, concerned with all aspects of the body and the environment, regarded sexuality as falling firmly within its purview: "what the medical texts provided were biological reasons for individuals to conform to their society's code of sexual behavior."[1] The texts discussed the causes and treatments of sexual disorders. The effects of sexual activity on the body could lead to disease or could restore health, depending on the state of the body itself and, as we shall see, on its gender. As well as describing the effects of sexual intercourse, the medical writers of antiquity put forward theories to explain the sex of the child that intercourse ideally produced, and some used this as an opportunity to explain that gender was more complicated than a simple male/female opposition. The passions were a concern of ancient medicine—with "evacuation" (the discharging of waste matter, especially from the bowels), they formed one of the six "non-naturals" of the humoral body. Medical writers were interested in the nature of desire, as well as in the nature of love, as the symptoms it caused in the body suggested it could be classified as a disease.

Medical involvement in sexual matters also raised questions about the extent of the doctor's role. The young doctor who makes his female patients feel a lot better—by having sex with them—is an established source of Roman humor; in one of Martial's epigrams, Leda claims to her elderly husband that she is *hysterica,* or affected by her womb, in order to ensure some young doctors are called in to "treat" her. Patricia Watson has argued that, although in general Martial reflects the sexual preferences as well as the views of the Roman elite male, he gives a rather unusual portrayal of the *matrona*. For example, Martial talks about how a wife should be Lucretia all day, but Lais all night.[2] The sexually demanding and sexually aware woman of the *Epigrams* would, however, for most ancient male writers, be seen as a joke, and a rather worrying one at that.

But sex as therapy was more than a joke, even though it was usually performed only within marriage. For example, a Hippocratic medical prescription is given for a woman suffering from an inability to maintain a pregnancy for more than a couple of months because her womb could not grow large enough to accommodate the fetus (*Steril.* 3.238, 8.452 L.). As the culmination of a complicated regimen of remedies—both applied directly to the womb and taken orally—the final instruction is, "Let her mix with her husband." The Hippocratic treatises, dating from the fifth century B.C. onward, may represent earlier oral traditions. Their aim is to achieve pregnancy, because, "if they become pregnant, they will be healthy" (*Virg.* 8.468 L.). The medical writers do not recommend sexual positions—other than advising that, depending on the desired sex of the child, the man should tie up either his right or his left testicle, and the woman should lie on her right or left side (e.g., Arist. *Gen. An.* 765a21–25). Nonmedical writers were less reserved, though they still followed the same mechanical principles. Lucretius noted that pregnancy was most easily achieved by having sex doggy-style, and that achieving it was less likely if the woman used sexy gyrations during intercourse, because these would stop the seed from entering the womb.[3]

The omission of detailed advice on sexual positions reflects the concerns raised by the medical treatment of women by men in the ancient world. These are exemplified by the late-third-century B.C. treatise *The Doctor* (Loeb VIII 302), which points out that the physician "meets women, maidens, and possessions very precious indeed." The Hippocratic *Oath* famously requires the doctor to make a solemn vow not to have intercourse with anyone he may meet as a result of entering the households of his patients. Such concerns explain why, when the ancient Greek doctor examined a female patient, he often did so through an intermediary, or asked the woman to examine herself and report back to him on whether, for example, the mouth of her womb was wet or dry, hard or soft.[4] In *Diseases of Women* (*Mul.* 1.68, 8.144 L.), the intermediary is a midwife (*iatreousa* in Greek); Nancy Demand has argued that some midwives would have improved their status by acting as assistants to Hippocratic doctors, and midwives are also associated with the "secret parts" in texts such as the *Dream Book* of Artemidorus.[5] Yet, there are some cases in which the doctor himself would perform an intimate examination, commenting, for example, on the "mouth of the womb," that, "if you touch, it seems to be like a stone ... and it does not admit the finger" (*Mul.* 2.156, 8.330 L.). Such cases are more common when the woman is regarded as being "experienced" as a result of having given birth, rather than with virgins vulnerable to assault.[6]

In such sensitive professional situations, how far could a doctor go in recommending sex as therapy? What about a woman who did not have a husband with whom to "mix"? Would it be acceptable to assist a woman whose recovery required orgasm by masturbating her? Before looking at these and related questions raised by medical interest in sexual matters, we need to consider the place of medical texts within knowledge about sex in the ancient world.

SEX AND THE BODY

Writing about medicine and the body was not restricted to what we would today classify as "medical texts": treatises written by people theorizing about, and practicing, medicine, and who claimed to be able to heal diseases. Those claiming the authority to treat the body were not necessarily very different from those they treated. Good examples are the Roman encyclopedists Celsus and Pliny the Elder—who had no medical training, but who included medical information in the manuals they produced as a summary of the knowledge expected of a male head of household in the Roman elite.[7]

In both the Greek and Roman worlds, the terminology used by doctors often overlapped with that used in ordinary language. Many of the words we now use as technical terms were originally coined by medical writers by analogy with everyday objects: for example, retina comes from the Latin *rete,* or "net."[8] Some of the terms used for the sexual organs appeared in both comedy and scientific writing, while others—including metaphorical terms for the vagina that associated it with both damp places and seed, comparing it to a garden, a plain, or a meadow—were only found outside the realm of technical treatises.[9] Medical writing on sexual matters placed itself in relation to other writing by a complicated pattern of overlap and distance that reflected the need to speak the common language, in order to connect with patients—while contributing something new—in order to make a case for the superiority of the medical view.

Sex was understood within the wider context of the fluids and temperatures of the body. The medical writers of the Hippocratic Corpus, while holding a range of views about the way in which the body works, commonly regarded disease as the result of an imbalance in these constituent fluids. Though we will focus here on Greek and Roman beliefs, there is evidence that other Mediterranean and Near Eastern cultures shared the conviction that the effects of sexual activity on the body were to be considered "medical" in the sense of altering the body's "heat." The medical role of the four qualities—hot, cold, wet, and dry—is most famous as part of the system of the four humors, cited in the Hippocratic treatise *On the Nature of Man* but extended and systematized by Galen over five hundred years later. Galen's extensive oeuvre mentioned women many times, but, in contrast to the Hippocratic Corpus, did not include any one text dedicated to the female body.

Thomas Laqueur argues that Galen's "one-sex model" of the body dominated Western medicine until the eighteenth century.[10] In this model, men and women were seen as two versions of a single sex, with the same organs. While men's greater heat meant that their organs were pushed to the outside, women—seen as the colder sex—retained theirs within their bodies. The penis becomes the analogue for the vagina. Laqueur's model, as we shall see, pays too much attention to homology and too little to fluids.

The model has been widely criticized over the past twenty years.[11] For one thing, it glosses over the various models of similarity and difference between the sexes found in the ancient world and, indeed, in later historical periods.[12] Laqueur made much of the passage in *On the Usefulness of Parts of the Body* (*UP* 14, 2.630 Kühn), in which Galen described the female genitalia as male genitalia, stating that heat, "Nature's primary instrument," causes men's organs to be pushed outside because men are hotter than women.[13] In seventeenth-century English medical writing, this belief was often repeated— for example, in Helkiah Crooke's *Microcosmographia* (1615) and in Jane Sharp's *The Midwives Book* (1671). Crooke observed that "it was the opinion of Galen ... that women had all those parts belonging to Generation which men have."[14] Sharp, using Crooke as one of her sources, noted, "Galen saith that women have all the parts of Generation that Men have, but Mens are outwardly, womens inwardly ... the parts are either thrust forth by heat, or kept in for want of heat."[15] But while such passages support Laqueur's argument that this inside/outside model of one sex was widespread before the eighteenth century, this was far from being the whole story. In the "controversies" with which he ended each section of his work, Crooke included information on "How the parts of generation in men and women do differ," concluding that, although stories of sex change from female to male had been used to support an inside/outside model (because the genitalia could move from inside to outside if the level of heat increased), the evidence from observation and reason suggested that there was much that challenged it. There are, he said, parts in men that simply do not exist in women, and others where the number of the parts differs between the sexes, while, "howsoever ... the neck of the womb [i.e., the vagina] shall be inverted, yet will it never make the virile member" because the latter is made of three hollow bodies, the former only of one. He added that those arguing for the clitoris as the female analogue for the penis were also mistaken, because the clitoris is small, not linked to the bladder, and has no passage from which it can emit seed.[16]

Katy Park has recently pointed out that this is the sole passage in Galen's enormous output arguing for an inside/outside relationship. Therefore, that model is hardly the Galenic view; furthermore, she stresses that it is essential to work out when this ancient text was, and was not, available as a resource for those constructing an image of sexual difference or homology. Park notes that *On the Usefulness of Parts of the Body* "had relatively little circulation in Latin Europe before the late fifteenth century and was not published until 1528. ... References to the homology between the male and female genitals were conspicuously absent from medieval anatomical texts and images before the thirteenth century."[17]

But heat and cold have far more significance to medicine and sexuality than Galen's comment on the location of the sexual organs. In ancient medicine, sexual activity in general "heats." For example, a Ugaritic myth describes how, "by kissing, there was pregnancy, by embracing, heating."[18] To say that a disease is "hot," and that "cooling" foods are needed to restore the body's balance is not necessarily to say something based on the actual physical characteristics of the food, but, rather, something that is far more complicated. Sexual activity not only affected the nonsexual parts of the body, but could also be used to counteract the effects of other externals—such as the seasons or the environment—on the body. Wet and dry were also as important as hot and cold. The Hippocratic writers advise men to have more intercourse in winter, because the wetness of the season means that more moisture needs to be removed from the body.[19]

SEED, GENERATION AND HEALTH

Central to medical theories about sex was the question of whether both men and women produced "seed." In humoral theory, as developed in its fullest form by Galen, the four fluids making up the body were blood, phlegm, yellow bile, and black bile. Both semen and menstrual blood were seen as products of blood, while breast milk was considered an intermediate stage between them. In generation, Aristotle argued, it was only the man's semen that could impose form on the shapeless mass of menstrual blood; only men were hot enough to cook, or "concoct," their blood into semen. This diverged from a traditional Greek idea that women were merely containers in which the male seed was placed; the woman was imagined as a field that was "ploughed" and "sown" by a man.[20] Galen suggested that both men and women produced forms of seed: that of the woman was more watery and weak. Lucretius, too, believed in female seed. This was perhaps because he associated pleasure with ejaculation—and, because women appeared to feel pleasure, he assumed they had seed[21]; Aristotle, however, explicitly denied that either a female's enjoyment of sex or her production of fluid meant that she could produce seed (*Gen. An.* 727b34–728a1).

Seed theory was important in understanding how the sex of the unborn child, and its gender identity, were formed. In the Hippocratic treatise *On Generation/Nature of the Child,* the process of sex determination in the womb was seen in terms of the polarities of strength and weakness, quantity and absence.[22] Here, perhaps six centuries before Galen, both sexes were thought to produce a seed, with the sex of the child decided according to the relative strength and quantity of the seminal material produced by the parents. For this Hippocratic writer, male and female were believed to exist on a continuum that included at its center the intermediate categories of the manly woman and the womanly man; instead of merely two genders, there were many variations. The seed was imagined to come from all over the bodies of the parents, with the physical characteristics of the child an outcome of the dominance, at the time of conception, of the seed from one parent's nose, ear, eye, and so on. This accounted for children of the same parents who looked very different from one another, and was also a model used outside medical writing, most notably by Lucretius. However, in the Hippocratic Corpus, seed theory was never used to suggest that women should be stimulated sexually; their pleasure, or its absence, made no difference in whether or not they conceived.[23] In a variation of the model of seeds mingling, put forward by Caelius Aurelianus, sexual preference as well as physical features could be explained by the mixing of the parental seeds; those who felt sexual desire for both men and women did so because, when their parents' seeds mingled, they had failed to fuse fully into one.[24]

Other parts of the Hippocratic Corpus played down female seed. The *Diseases of Women* treatises rarely mention seed: for them, the most important contribution of the mother to generation rested instead with the raw material provided by the blood. Here, women are seen not as a weaker version of men, but as a different sex entirely, their wet and spongy flesh absorbing more fluid from their diet, which would be transformed into a child. If no male seed had come into the womb, the blood was evacuated in a heavy menstrual loss.

Another treatise, *Places in Man*, concentrates on the generic male body—until its final section, where the female body is introduced with the statement that "the womb is the origin of all diseases in women" (*Loc.* 47).[25] In *Diseases of Women*, the difference between the genders lies in female flesh: for *Places in Man*, that difference is located in the womb. This method of treating men as normal, but adding a special section on women, is replicated in treatises such as *Aphorisms*, which group together medical conditions surrounding the womb and menstruation toward the end of the text (*Aph.* 5.29–62, 4.542–56 L.).

For those who believed in female seed, an important question was raised. If retention of seed was a medical condition, in that it affected the rest of the body, then was masturbation an acceptable therapy? For Galen, it was, due to his belief that, for women, it was more dangerous to retain seed than it was to hold menstrual blood. In a famous passage in his treatise *On the Usefulness of Parts of the Body*, where he argues that every part has its *telos* (purpose, or goal), Galen tells the story of a woman who suffered from the retention of her "female seed" after being a widow for a long time (*UP* 6.5, 8.421–4 Kühn). Her midwife told her that the symptoms she suffered were due to her womb's being "drawn up," and then applied "the customary remedies"—unspecified here—for the condition. When these substances were rubbed in, the woman felt the "pain and at the same time the pleasure" associated with sexual intercourse, and passed a large amount of thick "seed."

Taken with a passage in the Hippocratic *Diseases of Women*, this appears to be therapeutic masturbation. In a passage from the second book of *Diseases of Women* (*Mul.* 2.201, 8.384 L.), "very fragrant" substances are rubbed on the inner thighs of a woman suffering from "uterine suffocation" (*hysterikē pnix* in Greek). This was a condition in which the womb moved and caused symptoms throughout the body. The belief in womb movement was favored for a long time, despite anatomical discoveries that should have quashed it. Aristotle and the Hippocratics did not dissect humans, instead basing their beliefs about the interior of the body on what came out of it. But in third-century-B.C. Alexandria, Herophilus and Erasistratus opened the body and discovered, among other things, the uterine ligaments and the ovaries.[26] These organs were not fully understood, however, and the idea that the womb could move survived by attributing to the ligaments holding it in place a high degree of elasticity that allowed the womb to move up the body. This position was put forward by Aretaeus of Cappadocia in the first century A.D. (*CMG* 2.32–3).[27] The condition of "uterine suffocation" did not transform into "hysteria" until the nineteenth century. Before then, the origin of such "symptoms" was seen as entirely physical, coming from the womb (*hystera* in Greek), the precise symptoms varying according to the location to which the womb traveled.[28] Sexual intercourse was a cure because it drew the womb back to its proper place. In *Diseases of Women*, then, the intention of the therapy is to mimic sexual activity and thus restore a disordered womb to a better position in the body, from where it could more effectively lose blood and admit male seed.

In Galen's writings, it is a midwife who applies the substances: in the Hippocratic passage, the writer uses very neutral language, saying only that "it is necessary" (*dei* and *chrēn* in Greek) to rub the inner thighs in this way. In early modern medicine, there was surprise at Galen's apparent support for masturbation as well as considerable controversy regarding whether or not a doctor could carry out this therapy. Catholic physicians such as the Spanish Luis de Mercado (1525–1611), a convert from Judaism and the personal physician to Philip II and Philip III, condemned the practice.[29] Other early modern medical texts instead followed Galen in recommending dietary control—in particular, restricting the consumption of meat and other blood-producing foods—in order to prevent the buildup of semen and blood in the first place.

A medical condition affecting women, but which was believed by many ancient writers to result from a failure of male seed, was the uterine mole: a shapeless, failed pregnancy. It was sufficiently well-known outside medical writing that Plutarch could use it when drawing an analogy between the inability of women to make a child without male input and the "strange and evil schemes" hatched by women's minds if not properly controlled by their husbands (*Mor.* 145d).[30] The first description of the mole of pregnancy in medical writing, found in the Hippocratic *Diseases of Women* (*Mul.* 1.71, 8.148–50 L.), opens with the question of cause: "Concerning the *aition* of the mole of pregnancy". Its explanation concerns the polarity of abundance and lack, strength and weakness. The mole manifests when plentiful menses receive a scanty and sickly seed that is too weak to make an impression on the menstrual blood. In contrast, the other Hippocratic account, which concerns treatments for the condition, says of its cause only that a mole "develops on account of the thickness of the retained seed" (*Mul.* 2.178, 8.360–2 L.). No alternative manuscript reading "thinness" exists, so this passage may come from a different tradition, in which the male seed is not too thin, but too thick.

The inadequacies of the male seed can thus lead to a medical condition in women, which requires treatment if they are to recover. In *Diseases of Women*, fumigation of the womb is followed by washing to encourage blood to flow down. The writer argues that "it may be possible to set in motion the mass which appears to be an embryo" by warming up the woman via a drug.

However, this does not involve "motivating" the mole into any form of life, but simply moving it enough for it to leave the body.

The etymology of the word mole (*mylē* in Greek) links it to the word meaning "millstone." This is explicit in Soranus, writing in the second century A.D., who argues that this is because the millstone is heavy and immobile (*Gyn.* 3.36).[31] He followed the ancient Methodist medical sect, according to which all diseases in both sexes were caused by looseness or constriction—the womb being made of the same basic material as any other part of the body. His explanation for the mole is very different from that of the Hippocratics. Rather than being due to a failure in the process of conception, he removes it entirely from childbearing and suggests that, even though its symptoms mimic pregnancy, it is due to a prior inflammation of the womb or to an ulcer. His treatments involve warming, softening, raising the swollen belly, and removing blood in the acute stage. While in remission, the whole body should be strengthened, and heat and rubefacients should be applied. This suggests that Soranus saw the condition in terms of a hot/cold polarity—which is not prominent in the Hippocratic texts on moles, but instead is featured in Aristotle (*Gen. An.* 776a2–4).

SEXUAL DISORDERS

Hysterical suffocation and the uterine mole are only two of the conditions described in ancient medicine that have sexual connections, and those affecting men will be described later in this chapter. But what of the various vaginal discharges we could regard as evidence of sexually transmitted infections? Many such discharges of various colors and consistencies are discussed in detail in the *Diseases of Women* treatises, but, in the absence of any theory of infection, they are interpreted as inadequately formed menstrual blood. "The whites," in particular, are seen as very difficult to treat: *Diseases of Women* (*Mul.* 2.116–20, 8.250–62 L.) includes a section consisting of detailed descriptions of "the whites," which is seen as something different from the loss of "seed" discussed in an earlier chapter (*Mul.* 1.24, 8.64 L.). It is not possible to diagnose these discharges. Grmek has noted that "the diagnosis of gonorrhea is compatible with certain ancient descriptions," but he concludes that "for none of those descriptions is it the sole interpretation possible."[32] In any case, what ancient writers explicitly label as gonorrhea does not have to represent an infection; Soranus stated that gonorrhea, seen as an involuntary "flow of seed," could affect both men and women (*Gyn.* 3.14),[33] while Caelius Aurelianus defined gonorrhea as "a continual and involuntary escape of semen without any tension of the sexual organs" (*On Chronic Diseases* 3.18).[34]

On other occasions, Grmek is more optimistic about retrospective diagnosis: for example, he believes that genital herpes is the subject of passages in *Diseases of Women* (*Mul.* 1.90, 8.214–18 L.) and *Nature of Woman* (*Nat. Mul.* 108, 7.422 L.) because they describe ulcers on the labia.[35]

In the absence of any knowledge of the transmission of disease between individuals, Greek and Roman ideas of what counted as a "sexual disorder" were very different from our own. The texts of *Diseases of Women* focus on the failure to menstruate because it was from menstrual blood that the fetus was formed—a process discussed in the treatise *On Generation/Nature of the Child*. Indeed, it is not simply intercourse that the mobile womb desires, but conception: female sexuality is seen in terms of reproduction. To us, the absence of menstruation can be evidence of pregnancy, meaning that we interpret ancient remedies given to "draw out" the blood as abortions. To the ancient Greeks, such an absence was worrying for entirely the opposite reason. That is, because amenorrhea meant that conception could not take place, remedies were intended to flush out the blood from wherever in the body it was hiding.

Instead of being regarded as a possible source of disease, sex is presented as therapeutic for women, the remedy for many conditions being intercourse followed by pregnancy. As *On Generation* puts it, "Another point about women: if they have intercourse with men their health is better than if they do not" (*Genit.* 4, 7.476 L.).[36] While sex both keeps the womb open so it can menstruate and stimulates fluids in their movement around the body, the process of giving birth acts as a valuable purge. This contrasts with medical advice for men, who are more commonly advised to abstain from sex while recovering from a disease.

SEX AND DRUGS

Both magic and medicine offered users ways of attracting sexual partners, and of improving their sexual performance. Amulets that make the wearer seem more enticing are associated with Aphrodite, and Faraone has argued that the *kestos* worn by Aphrodite was similar to objects knotted and tied around a woman in the Near East around 1000 B.C.[37] Along with the charms and spells used to affect potency, a number of foodstuffs believed to enhance sexual desire were often prescribed. A Lydian gourmet sauce called *kandaulos* was described in a fragment of Menander as *hypobinētionta brōmata* ("food that makes one somewhat desirous of a screw.")[38] Certain foods, including bulbs and particular herbs, were believed to increase desire in a man; some were believed to affect women (e.g., Theophr. *HP* 9.18.9, cf. Pliny, *NH* 26.99).

Aphrodisiacs and antaphrodisiacs were very closely related, and could even be found in the same plant. For example, the *orchis* was thought to have two roots: one large and one small, one an aphrodisiac, the other able to undo such effects (Theophr. *HP* 9.18.3). Pliny includes over sixty aphrodisiac and antaphrodisiac preparations,[39] discussing drugs either to increase desire, or to stop the flow of seed and reduce it. For instance, statements that onions are aphrodisiacs are found in a wide range of literary genres.[40] Athenaeus, citing Heracleides of Tarentum, states that bulbs, snails, and eggs "produce semen, not because they are filling, but because their very nature in the first instance has powers related in kind to semen." This is presumably a reference to the sticky fluids they contain, or can produce. In Roman medicine, drugs were often accompanied by chants or other magical techniques. For example, Pliny places his advice on the application of a poultice to treat an unspecified abscess between a chapter on inguinal tumors and one on antaphrodisiacs, suggesting that the abscess is in the area of the genitalia.

> Those with experience (*experti*) have assured us that it makes all the difference if, while the patient is fasting, the poultice is laid upon him by a maiden (*virgo*), herself fasting and naked, who must touch him with the back of her hand and say, "Apollo tells us that a plague cannot grow more fiery in a patient if a naked maiden quench the fire," and with her hand so reversed she must repeat the formula three times and both must spit on the ground three times. (*NH* 26.93)

Bearing in mind the comments of ancient writers about the power of viewing a beautiful sexual object—whether male or female—in stimulating sexual desire,[41] it seems most unlikely that the practice Pliny outlines would "quench the fire."

The line between "food" and "drug" is not worth drawing in ancient texts: in some circumstances, one could argue that what separates them are the purposes behind their use. But in the case of sexual prescriptions, doctors simply relied on what was already believed about different foods—though they sometimes delivered a substance by means other than dietary.[42] As Christopher Faraone has shown, penis creams feature in Athenian comedy, scientific writing, and magical recipes.[43] Laurence Totelin has further explored the links between Hippocratic recipes and Attic comedy, demonstrating that a wide range of ingredients that do not seem to us obviously sexual would have carried a strong sexual charge in fifth-century B.C. Greece. For instance, *krithē* (barley) was a term invoked by comic writers to designate the penis—not only because of its bearded appearance, but also because of its associations with fertility (it was the main ingredient in the *kykeōn* that was drunk in the Eleusinian Mysteries).[44]

One theme that runs through medical discussions of drugs to stimulate sexual performance is their associated dangers. Faraone argues that love potions carried two different risks for men. The first was that the increase in desire could lessen a man's self-control; the second was that the plants that could arouse were also believed to cause permanent impotence if given at the wrong dosage.[45] More generally, doctors and laypeople alike were aware of the variable effects, depending on dosage, of the substances they applied to the body. For example, the Hippocratic writer of *Places in Man* was well aware that *mandragoras,* used in love potions, is antispasmodic in a small dose and cures insomnia in a moderate dose, but leads to delirium in a larger dose—and also that the line between small and large is not easy to recognize. Faraone cites the mistake made by the mistress of Philoneus in Antiphon 1.19, when she gives the object of her desire a love potion—but ups the amount of the drug a little, in hopes of making him love her all the more, and inadvertently kills him.[46]

According to Themison, eating too much of the aphrodisiac satyrion was a cause of the unpleasant medical condition called satyriasis (a permanent erection). He attributed many deaths in Crete to the use of satyrion: "and this is believed to have been due to ignorance about food, for in many cases people ate copiously of the plant satyrion." Pliny also mentions this plant as a sexual stimulant, including one type which, if held in the hand, arouses desire—but if drunk in dry wine, is even more arousing (*NH* 26.98). Caelius Aurelianus, who preserves fragments on satyrion from Themison in his work *On Acute Diseases,* states that the generic Greek words for drugs to arouse sexual desire were *satyrika* and *entatika* (*On Chronic Diseases* 3.18).[47] *Satyrika* included preparations "to engender boys/girls" or "to have a strong baby," as well as "to excite," suggesting that sexual pleasure was not necessarily divorced from fecundity (*Sor. Gyn.* 3.3).[48]

Caelius Aurelianus also states that those (of either sex) who eat the satyrion plant become aroused, attributing to Themison an account of female usage: "he also tells of seeing a young woman in Milan who died from eating satyrion. She had previously been quite modest and was married to a person of high status."[49] However, there are limits to human performance, even when it is enhanced with drugs. Pliny cites as "incredible" Theophrastus's comments on a certain plant that allows a man to perform seventy times in a row (*NH* 26.99; *HP* 9.18.9).

What about drugs to end an unwanted pregnancy? Some recent scholarship on ancient pharmacology has argued for a separate medical tradition associated with women: the handing down of knowledge, especially relating to abortives and contraceptives, from mother to daughter.[50] But it would be misleading to assume that all women had such information. For example, the Hippocratic *On Generation/Nature of the Child* includes the story of the slave entertainer who was encouraged to jump up and down to abort an unwanted child (*Nat. puer.* 13, 7.488–90 L.).[51] This girl is described as finding herself pregnant and telling her owner, a woman. Far from having access to "women's oral tradition," the owner, who does not know how to solve the problem herself, goes to her kinsman, the Hippocratic writer of the text. The remedies offered by all healers, whether female or male, relied on theories intended to account for women's symptoms—such as the theory that the womb was too dry and had risen up the body in search of moisture. If the patient did not believe in the theory, she would not be encouraged to follow the regimen offered as a cure. Rather than seeing theories of the nature of woman and remedies to treat their diseases as either women's or men's knowledge, a third option is probably nearer the truth: namely, that the image of women presented in these texts was one that both men and women would recognize and accept, while both sexes had knowledge of, and access to, the plant substances used to treat sexual diseases.

MEN'S DISEASES?

Men's sexual disorders—from swollen testicles to loss of desire—also came within the doctor's sphere of activity. In the third century A.D., Quintus Serenus included remedies for swollen testicles and impotence in his collection of popular remedies,[52] while Pliny (*NH* 26.89) gave remedies for swollen testicles using *hyoscyamus* (henbane) or the root of *acoron* (*calamus* in Latin).

As discussed already, there is no "one-sex" model in Greek or Roman medical writing—although, alongside claims that women are so different from men that they require a special branch of medicine (*Mul.* 1.62, 8.126 L.), we do find overlap between the diagnosis and treatment of the sexes. In the ancient medical texts on diseases of the genitals, some designations are applied to both male and female conditions in a way that suggests analogy. For instance, *phimōsis,* derived from the word for a bridle, could be a condition in which something blocked the penis, but it could also be applied to a narrowing of the mouth of the womb.[53]

Satyriasis is the most striking example of a sexual disorder primarily associated with men but linked as well to women by some writers. The origin of the disease label was thought to lie either in the ithyphallic satyr, or in the drug satyrion (however, the plant/drug may well have taken its name from the satyr). In the ancient debate about whether some medical conditions existed in only one of the sexes, writers who held to the Methodist position claimed that satyriasis is simply a disease of constriction that, as such, could also affect women.[54] In his *Gynaecology,* Soranus stated that the condition occurred more often in men—but, when it arose in women, it would cause itching, an irresistible urge for intercourse, and mental disturbance (*Gyn.* 3.3).[55]

Soranus's lost treatise on acute diseases was the source for Caelius Aurelianus, who stated that the two disorders were similar: satyriasis could affect both men and women, and, although the symptoms stopped when there was ejaculation of semen, they would come back again.[56] Women with satyriasis, he noted, "accost all who come to see them, and on their knees beg these visitors to relieve their lust."[57] Among the medical writers, Aretaeus was unique in denying that women could suffer from satyriasis. It was not possible, he said, because women are cold and lack "erectile parts."[58] For him, hysterical suffocation was the female equivalent of satyriasis. In ancient medicine—and, indeed, in pre-germ-theory medicine more widely—diseases could transform into other, more severe, conditions. Rufus of Ephesus claimed that satyriasis could become spermatorrhea (a condition of excessive, involuntary ejaculation), while lying on one's back irritated the genital organs and led to erotic dreams.[59] Nocturnal emissions were not seen as a disease, but could be an antecedent cause of gonorrhea: they were to be treated as a mild case of this condition, and so the patient, encouraged all the while to take his mind off sex so he would dream of something else, was made to lie on his side on a hard bed while cold juices were injected into his urethra. Falling asleep with a full bladder was recommended, as it made it less likely that the patient would fall into a deep sleep. An alternative was to tie up a big toe or thumb tightly—so the ensuing pain would have a similar effect.[60]

And what of priapism? Ancient medical writers disagreed about the difference between satyriasis and priapism: in particular, did only one of them involve desire? Aetius argued that priapism was when the penis became stiff in the absence of any sensation of desire.[61] Caelius Aurelianus (*On Chronic Diseases* 3.18)[62] repeats a story from Demetrius of Apamea.

In his book *On the Signs of Diseases,* Demetrius of Apamea mentions priapism. He says that he saw an old man who suffered from the disease and who sought, without any success, to obtain relief by masturbation. There was, he says, a powerful erection but with such little sensation that the organ might have been made of horn; and this condition remained unchanged for many months and did not yield to any medical remedy, but after a long period of time was fully relieved.

Medicine, then, was rendered impotent in the face of this erection. In contrast, doctors could offer hope to sufferers of satyriasis. Caelius Aurelianus recommends rest in a warm room, avoiding the stimulus of receiving visitors. (In keeping with ancient views about the stimulus of seeing a desirable object, young women and boys, in particular, were not to be admitted to the sickroom.) Once in remission, the patient could be given a regimen of bloodletting, leeches, cupping, poultices, heat applied with sponges, and warm olive-oil clysters (enemas)—these would release constriction. For female patients, an additional treatment was the insertion of a vaginal plug soaked in warm olive oil; Caelius Aurelianus added that this should be done by "a woman attendant."[63]

DESIRE AND PLEASURE

Male desire was aroused by the sight of beauty—or by an idea—but was this also true for women?[64] In the *Historia Augusta* version of the life of the emperor Marcus Aurelius, his wife, Faustina, is stricken with *amor* after seeing a gladiator walk by. After she confesses her condition to her husband, the Chaldeans advise that the gladiator be killed, and that Faustina wash in his blood before having intercourse with her husband (SHA, *Marcus Aurelius* 19).[65] As in the Hippocratic texts, sex is part of the cure. This story raises issues of desire and of love as a sickness.

The myth of the seer Tiresias, who experienced being both male and female, tells how he annoyed the goddess Hera by using his dual experience to reveal to her husband, Zeus, that women experience ten times the pleasure of men in sexual intercourse. However, the Hippocratic text *On Generation* argues that men feel more pleasure—though a woman's is of longer duration, peaking when the male seed reaches her womb (*Genit.* 4, 7.476 L.). Lesley Dean-Jones has shown that other Hippocratic gynecological treatises proposed that women generally do not feel desire. Instead, they are driven to sexual intercourse by their wombs, their desire only physiological in nature, and therefore not associated with any particular sexual object.[66] While men need to avoid having too much sex (the Hippocratic texts prescribed abstinence rather than sex for them), women are prescribed more sex, and pregnancy is their most healthy state: "let her lie with her husband," because, "if she becomes pregnant, she becomes healthy" (*Nat. mul.* 2, 7.314 L.). As Laurence Totelin has pointed out, the instruction to have sex at the end of a regimen of treatment is almost always in the imperative third person singular, "indicating that the woman should and must know when the appropriate time for the sexual encounter has come."[67] The only time when abstinence is advised is in order to prepare for sex. This recalls the mixed imagery of chastity and fertility in the Thesmophoria, the three-day Greek festival of Demeter when married women abstained from sex in order to become more fertile in the future.[68] Why is sex regarded as being so good in general for women? The Hippocratic texts show that it is because sex keeps the womb open and in the correct position, while agitating and moving the blood.

It is noteworthy that Galen's story of masturbation involves a widow. In the gynecological treatises, virgins and widows were seen as particularly susceptible to illness. There was a further debate in ancient medicine as to whether virgins suffered from desire.[69] The description of blood moving around the body of a young girl in *Diseases of Virgins* because the "orifice of exit" is not yet open suggests that, for the Hippocratic writers, "women have a physiological appetite for intercourse before they even know what it is."[70] The cure for the mental and physical disturbances suffered by these girls, who are "ripe for marriage" but not yet married, is to make the blood leave their bodies. The Hippocratic author suggests that the solution is "to lie with a man." Orgasm is not enough; masturbation or a dildo cannot provide the semen that the female body needs. Objects shaped like a penis, such as worms, cucumbers (of the squirting kind), and horns are commonly used in ancient treatments for women.[71] For example, in a treatment for a woman who has lost her ability to conceive, given in a section of *On Barren Women* (*Steril.* 222, 8.430–2 L.), the dry gourd used after a series of injections into the womb is explicitly "just a little smaller than the male organ" (*andros aidoion* in Greek), and the woman "sits herself on the glans [*balanos* in Greek, meaning "acorn"] of the gourd."[72] But, for the Hippocratic writers, such measures are often regarded as preparation, rather than a substitute, for sex.[73] In a remedy to enable a woman to conceive, the crushed testicle of a beaver is inserted into her vagina and left there overnight. In the morning, she is instructed to "go to her husband" (*Steril.* 221, 8.428 L.). Both deer horns and stag penises were used in powdered form to encourage fertility; the latter could also be used to encourage the quick delivery of a child.[74]

Recommending the health benefits of perpetual virginity for both women and men, Soranus[75] summarized the different views—but, in keeping with his

Methodist approach to medicine by which disorders were either *status laxus* (loose), *status strictus* (constricted), or *status mixtus* (features of both), held that sex relaxed the body too much to be good for it. As Pinault has noted, these chapters of Soranus did not find their way into the versions of his work later made by Theodorus Priscianus, Caelius Aurelianus, and Mustio.[76]

LOVESICKNESS

Desire was seen by Soranus, in his recommendations of perpetual virginity, as "creating suffering in the body." If there was no possibility of fulfillment, could desire be regarded as a disease? As Mary Wack has shown, the diagnosis of lovesickness became increasingly important during the medieval period, originating from Constantine the African's Latin adaptation of al-Jazzâr, in whose work "passionate love" was categorized as a disease.[77] In 1610, Jacques Ferrand composed a treatise on the condition, in which he traced it back to the classical world; this went into several editions.[78] Peter Toohey has, however, shown that there is very little written about lovesickness in ancient medicine or literature until the first century A.D.[79] After this date, philosophers began to see love as a "disease of the soul" that was more dangerous than any "disease of the body" and was best treated by philosophical arguments that could "cauterize" the soul.[80] While philosophers believed that love needed to be cured, the poets of Latin love elegy regarded it as something to be celebrated, despite the fact that it was an illness. Propertius, for instance, says that Gallus's love for Cynthia leads to him suffering "a truly debilitating emotional and physical condition."[81] For these artists, poetry, travel away from the beloved, the gods—and wine—can alleviate the symptoms.[82]

What of ancient medicine? Stories are told of both Hippocrates and Erasistratus in which their diagnostic skill enables them to recognize unrequited love as the cause of disease. The first story in which medicine takes control of love is that of Erasistratus, who diagnoses the love of the prince Antiochus for his stepmother, Stratonice. In the earliest version, that of Valerius Maximus (7.7.3 ext. 1), this love is described as a wound (*vulnus* in Latin) that causes the "utmost desire and the deepest shame."[83] Unable to act on his desire, Antiochus lies in bed as if he is dying. In the later version, by Plutarch (*Demetr.* 38), the verb *nosein* (to be ill) is used, and Antiochus stops eating in order to hasten his death. In most versions, his sickness is diagnosed by Erasistratus as a "condition of the mind" (Appian, *Roman History* 11.10). The physician arrives at this conclusion after checking Antiochus's reactions to the different people who enter his room: when his stepmother enters, Antiochus exhibits those "signs of which Sappho sings" (Plut. *Demetr.* 38). Sappho's fragmentary account of the physical reactions she experiences when seeing the object of her desire with another partner has traditionally been taken—even by ancient authors—as the first reference to the condition of lovesickness. However, though Sappho does describe how her body reacts, there is no sense in her writing that love is properly within the domain of medicine. Plutarch describes how, once King Seleucus was given Erasistratus's diagnosis, he took the responsibility for administering the treatment, saying that, "as father, husband and king, he was himself at the same time the best physician of his household." Seleucus then surrendered his wife to Antiochus. At some point before the second century A.D., the story was transferred to Hippocrates and King Perdiccas.[84] Galen adapted it "to enhance his own prestige as a master of diagnosis,"[85] telling how he diagnosed his patient's insomnia as being caused by a passion for the dancer Pylades by feeling her pulse.[86] In other stories of doctors confronted by lovesickness, some identify the condition from the pulse; others do so after feeling the movement of the heart by touching the patient's chest. In some accounts the whole point is that the doctor is unable to detect the true cause of the symptoms.[87]

At least in the realm of medical biography, even love can be regarded as a treatable ailment. While working for the satisfaction of the male patient's desire, preparing a woman for fruitful intercourse, or simulating the actions of sexual congress may not seem to us to be strictly "medical" remedies, within the context of Hippocratic medicine (in which "let her go to her husband" is a regular refrain), we can see that ancient practitioners regarded such actions very differently. As well as explaining the benefits of sex—and, in the case of women, of pregnancy—to their users, the writers of the medical texts brought into play the popular beliefs of their time, adding in an extra level of explanation and showing how the effects of sexual activity on the body varied according to age and gender. Just as the language in which they discussed sexual matters oscillated between that of their patients and a more selective sexual vocabulary appropriate to the medical profession, so their theories and therapies owed much to other branches of knowledge—while claiming a greater control of the field. They were well aware of the care they needed to take in intervening in this area of life that was at once very personal—and very important to the state.

CHAPTER SEVEN

Sex, Popular Beliefs, and Culture

HOLT PARKER

DEFINING THE POPULAR

In some ways this chapter ought to be blank. We scan the records of antiquity in vain for traces of a distinct, autonomous area of sexual beliefs, practices, or classifications we can label "popular." There are four reasons for this. First, it is difficult to define with any precision what might have constituted the "popular" in Greece or Rome.[1] Nearly all definitions of popular culture take as a given that it is a phenomenon dating from, or indeed caused by, the Industrial Revolution.[2] Greece and Rome have most often furnished the models of a unified, organic *Gemeinschaft* ever since Herder invented the terms "folksong" (*Volkslied*) and "popular culture" (*Kultur des Volkes*).[3]

Popular culture is like pornography: we may not be able to define it, but we know it when we see it.[4] None of the common definitions of popular culture can be applied with any ease to antiquity.[5] The ancient "popular" cannot be situated in opposition to an urban mass,[6] in part because it is precisely the urban mass we are interested in, and in part because we are so woefully uninformed about conditions outside the cities. Nor can ancient popular culture be contrasted with mass culture—a commercialized, commoditized "culture industry"[7]—since we are dealing with precapitalist formations.

Class is a tricky concept at the best of times and is especially difficult to demarcate in antiquity.[8] Plato maintained that the city was really two hostile cities, that of the rich and that of the poor (*Resp.* 4.422e). For classical Athens, Aristotle and others make binary oppositions between "the many," "the people," and similar terms, and "the notables," "the well-born," and "the few." But it is usually fruitless to attempt assigning individual Greeks (much less their cultural productions) to one side or the other.[9] Where to place, for example, Socrates, son of a herm-carver and a midwife, friend of the lower-lower Simon the shoemaker and the upper-upper Alcibiades the chariot-backer?

We seem to be on firmer ground in Rome. SPQR: there was the senate, and then there was the *populus*. A nice division, but can we really classify everyone outside those 600 or so families as "popular"?[10] Even if we toss in the knights (*equites*) we are still only talking about a minute fraction of the empire, which leaves 99.9 percent of everyone (by one rough estimate) as "the people."[11] The polarities of patricians versus plebeians, *optimates* versus *populares, honestiores* versus *humiliores* seem clearly marked—but here, too, we run into trouble. These dichotomies fail to line up cleanly and there is considerable overlap between categories.[12] Where to place fantastically wealthy and powerful imperial freedmen, whether real (Pallas) or fictional (Trimalchio)? Where to place actors, officially marked as social outcasts (*infames*), but at the heart of cultural production? Or Horace, for that matter?[13]

Second, it is difficult to associate any particular text or object with any broadly conceived class. Texts are especially problematic, since their very state of having been written is frequently interpreted as making them elite. The idea of popular culture is largely negative. Once you have eliminated elite texts and other sorts of evidence, there may not be much to go on. We have precious little of popular culture in the sense created by Herder—folksongs and the like.[14] Objects, too, present immense difficulties for interpretation. Movable goods (for instance, Attic pots) circulated around the world. It has been claimed that erotic content on Attic pots was intended to satisfy an Etruscan taste for porn.[15] Even the basic question of whether Attic painted pottery represents cheap mass-produced items or elite luxury goods is fiercely debated.[16] For immovable goods, how exactly are we to class Pompeian wall paintings? Where do the citizens of Pompeii fall in the *Roman* social order? Can we equate the elite of Rome with the elite of Pompeii? (No, says Cicero with a smirk: *Fam.* 7.1.3.) Does provincial, but wealthy, equal popular?

Third, we may be misled by false analogies to the modern period. Graffiti, for example, are sometimes taken uncritically as the production of the masses, and some may well be so.[17] But, even today, graffiti need not be the unmediated outpourings of the people—nor does every scrawl on a wall represent popular taste.[18] The magic spells have sometimes been taken as direct access to the lower-class mind. But magical practices, too, cut across class lines.[19]

Further, attempts to isolate a popular culture as "the culture which is left over after we have decided what is high culture"[20] may run aground on a mistaken idea of what constituted "high culture." Greek tragedy might appear to be a clear example of elite culture (*Oedipus Rex* is a talisman of the West), but tragedies were no less a part of the citywide festival of the Dionysia than were comedies.[21] Both were addressed to the widest possible citizen body—and beyond: to women, metics, and foreigners. The Romans carved the theatre and the circus into socially stratified seating, but everyone watched the same shows.[22]

Equally, isolating popular from elite culture may imply a distinction between the *Kultur des Volkes* and the *Kultur der Gelehrten* that is also anachronistic. A search for "popular" beliefs about the body implies the existence of a separate "professional," or even "scientific," discourse about sex and the body that simply is not applicable to the ancient world.[23]

Fourth, and most importantly, we are looking for something that may not have existed. There is nothing to show that the lower classes (whoever they may have been) held substantially different beliefs about how their bodies functioned or how they wanted their bodies to function from those of the elites (define them how you will). Sexuality, therefore, falls not under the heading of "popular" culture, but of "common" culture[24]—a set of knowledge and practices shared by nearly everyone, regardless of status.

REDEFINING THE POPULAR

We can, however, be cheerful in our search for the popular by approaching it in two ways. First, we may have more luck if we turn away from a Marxist model (with a focus on production) to a more Weberian model (with a focus on consumption), and turn from class to status.[25] We can cease to worry if we are truly isolating what "the people" produced—and turn our attention instead to what the people consumed. We may look at what was "popular" in the popular sense: what was directed at the vast majority of the population. It is here that we can get our best sense of what was widely believed and practiced—or believed to be practiced. Under this definition of the popular, we can turn back to the graffiti (and other genres) mentioned earlier—not as *produced* by just about anyone, but as *addressed* to just about anyone. Graffiti are on the same footing, then, as tombstones or public inscriptions, except that they are more likely to tell us about sex. Magic is back, not as the writings of the humble, but as a widely practiced belief system.

Under this definition, two genres in particular come to the fore: comedy and oratory. Comedy is privileged over other forms of popular entertainment because it can deal with sexual matters and has to appeal to the widest possible audience. Comedy is a dangerous source since it is based on exaggeration (Arist. *Poet.* 1448a16–18)—but, nonetheless, it is valuable because it reveals clearly the audience's shared fundamental assumptions.[26]

Greek private orations, though they may have been composed by a professional (*logographos*) such as Lysias or Demosthenes, were delivered by the defendant or plaintiff himself to a jury ranging from 201 to 2,501 of his fellow citizens, chosen by an elaborate system whose purpose was to make the jury represent the *dēmos* (the ordinary people of the city). An Athenian speech needed to convince the man in the street.[27] Similarly, at Rome: though the *patronus* may have delivered the speech for his *cliens*, the speech had to convince a Roman jury.[28]

Second, I would like to venture a new way of looking at popular culture, which may serve less as a functional definition than as a heuristic tool. Rather than looking at capital in the purely economic sense, we can turn to Bourdieu's idea of cultural capital.[29] It may be fruitful to define popular culture as the productions of those without cultural capital. Popular culture is "unauthorized utterance." That is, popular art consists of the paintings of those not recognized as artists by the art world,[30] the poems of those not recognized as poets by the cultural system responsible for recognizing poets, the medicine of those not recognized as physicians, the religion of those not recognized as priests. It is cultural capital and the institutions that control it that transform a painter into an artist and a writer into an author, in the full etymological sense, that confer authority, that make the scribbler authorized.[31] In this definition of "popular," Parrhasius and Apelles are out; Attic vases and the wall painters of Pompeii are in. Aristophanes and Horace are out; Attic folksongs and the wall poets of Pompeii are in.

We can thus distinguish three levels of discourse: (1) the unauthorized utterance, the voice of the subaltern, of those without access to cultural capital (graffiti, curses); (2) the authorized utterance seeking as large an audience as possible (Aristophanes, Plautus); and (3) the elite speaking to the elite (Theognis, Propertius). The examples that follow show that the public ideology of sex was remarkably similar across all three levels of discourse.

NEGATIVE FINDINGS

The lack of a distinct popular sphere is, in itself, quite important. For example, there is a persistent idea that "homosexuality" (by which is usually meant the custom of pederasty) was confined to the Athenian upper classes.[32] The reasons for this are varied. One, beginning with the Victorians, has been to protect the golden Greeks from charges of immorality.[33] Other reasons have more to do with our own ideologies, identity politics, anxieties, and a discourse of "decadence" than with the facts. However, one important reason is the nature of the data. We may be led by elite written sources into thinking that a desire to fuck boys was confined to the elite. This view is reinforced—via a form of circular argument—by the visual evidence: decorated pottery was sympotic; the symposium was elite; therefore, the pederastic scenes on the pottery were a custom confined to the elite. However, not all pottery was intended solely for use at the symposia, nor were all symposia elite—and, even if they were, the conclusion would not follow.[34]

The upper classes did, of course, desire to fuck pretty boys, but what the sources clearly show is that everyone assumed *any* normal healthy man would desire to fuck pretty boys (and women), provided he could get them.[35] The most obvious example is the newly rejuvenated Demos (whose name simply means "The People") in Aristophanes' *Knights*. He is offered various gifts by the Sausage-Seller (1384–6).

> So now in celebration, take this comfy chair,
> and this boy (who's still got his balls) to carry it for you
> and if you like, use him as a comfy chair. [36]

Demos is also offered two beautiful women, the embodiment of thirty-year-long peace treaties, and whom he also wants to "ratify."[37] The low-class Sausage-Seller could not be more explicit. He presents himself as a rival lover for Demos (casting "Mr. People" as a desirable youth), complaining (736–40):

> For you are like those beloved boys (*erōmenos*).
> You don't admit the noble and good
> but give yourself to lamp-sellers and shoe-repairmen,
> to shoemakers and tanners.[38]

Philocleon, tempting his father in *Wasps* (578), shows the same desires as those of Aristophanes and his friends (1025–8), as well as Heracles (*Ran.* 56–7). So, too, Euelpides in *Birds* (137–42), and Kinsman in *Thesmophoriazusae* (35, 59–62): all express a desire to fuck (or, at least, get to examine in detail) beautiful youths.

There will indeed be differences between rich and poor.[39] The rich will be able to afford the luxury of the best *hetairai* (the more sophisticated type of entertainers and sexual workers), while the poor will have recourse to whores (*pornai*) in democratic brothels traditionally founded by Solon, but both still liked women.[40] The poor may not have been able to bag the prettiest or most nobly born boys, but rich and poor both still liked boys.[41] So, too, for Rome: a verse graffito—found both in Nero's Domus Aurea and at Remagen on the German frontier—complains:

> Who loves boys and girls without end
> has no regard for his purse.[42]

Likewise, Athenian public speeches draw on the basic fact that every normal male in the citizen jury is attracted to beautiful (or, at least, available) boys and women.[43] It was an embarrassment to be seen spending too much time or money in the pursuit of love—and older men ought to be steadier about sex than the flighty young—but, as the defendant says in a case involving a violent fight over a pretty boy, appealing to the jury's sympathy: "For you know that desire is innate in all human beings, and he is the best and most self-controlled who can bear what befalls him in the most orderly way."[44] Far from casting pederasty as an elite pursuit, the orator Aeschines, who came from a nonelite background, makes a carefully controlled praise of carefully controlled pederasty central to his speech against Timarchus (1.132–57).[45] He claims that it is his opponents who despise the demos (1.141) and are attempting to cast him as someone who is trying "to bring the practice into disrepute and danger" (1.135). He too invokes Solon, making him not just the regulator but the encourager of pederasty. Solon forbade "slaves to love and follow a free boy," but, says Aeschines, "that same lawgiver ... did not forbid a *free* man to love and associate with and follow boys" (1.139). The pursuit of a boy is worthy of a free man. Aeschines holds up the Tyrannicides—the older Aristogeiton, "an adult male of the people, a middle citizen," and his beloved, the young aristocrat Harmodius[46]—"as the ideal examples of chaste and democratic eros."[47] Aeschines assumes that the ordinary citizens of the jury will agree with him: pederasty is democratic.

It is here that we can cite one of our few genuine folksongs from ancient Greece. The Tyrannicides, as Athenian culture heroes, were the subject not just of public sculpture,[48] but of a drinking song so well-known that Aristophanes lampooned it (*Vesp.* 1225–7). It is sung by the very nonelite chorus of old men in *Lysistrata* (632). This song exists in multiple versions.

In a myrtle branch I will carry my sword.
Like Harmodius and Aristogeiton
when they killed the tyrant
and made Athens a city of equal rights.[49]

As these examples show, we find the same sets of beliefs and practices reflected
with surprisingly little variation—not only from the top to the bottom of society, but also from Greece to Rome, and for a period of more than a thousand
years. The sex/gender systems of both Greece and Rome were remarkably
stable (one of the best examples of the *longue durée* I know of) with, for
instance, the same sort of epigrams being written on the proper age limits
for boys to be used for sex from Solon (archaic) to Eratosthenes Scholasticus
(Byzantine).[50]

Whatever the difficulties of the popular sources, the elite ones also point
to a societal uniformity of beliefs about sexuality. There is an interesting lack
of complaint from the upper classes about the sexual beliefs and practices of
the lower classes—something we find in other eras ("peasants copulate like
animals," and the like). Trimalchio perhaps comes closest: a creation of the
elite imagination who is unashamed by what he should be ashamed of.

Thus, we do not find much in the way of a Gramscian resistance to an imposed hegemony. In fact, the few voices we do hear raised in opposition are
those of the most elite of the elite: emperors and the like—those so powerful
they can declare themselves above the rules. Instead, unauthorized sources
show a remarkable conformity and uniformity. There are almost no examples of someone—even in the anonymity of graffiti—bucking the system and
proclaiming, "I'm a *cinaedus* and proud of it." Rather, we find second- and
third-person attacks: "You're a *cinaedus*. He's a *cinaedus*."

This could, of course, be the fault of the sources. To articulate opposition
to hegemony takes an articulate voice and the means to make it heard (that is,
access to cultural capital). Further, the media through which we might hear the
subaltern speak are not conducive to talk about sex. A tombstone is not the
place to list one's sexual preferences. However, the glimpses we are given into
common culture show continuity with elite sources. Indeed, this continuity is
deeply embedded in Greek culture and is the basis for Aristotle's method of
"saving the appearances."[51]

There is a shared view of the body and sexuality. For example, the author
of the Hippocratic *On Generation/Nature of the Child* examines the miscar-
riage of a slave girl. "This musician had heard the sorts of things that women
say to each other: that when a woman is going to conceive in her womb the

seed does not come out but stays inside."[52] Far from criticizing this piece of folk belief, the physician assumes it is true, as does the author of *On Generation*.[53] Similarly, everyone knows that a woman's womb can wander about in her body. It can go crashing into various organs, causing hysteria and other diseases—which can be cured by intercourse, pregnancy, and luring the womb back down to its proper place by either fumigating the vagina with sweet smells or driving it back down with unpleasant odors in the nose.[54] The only difference between the folk belief found in the magical spell "For the Ascent of the Uterus" and the one in Plato's *Timaeus* (90e-1d) or the Hippocratic Corpus is its philosophical deployment in the former and the search for a causal explanation in the latter.[55] Likewise, everyone knows that virgins are susceptible to a form of hysteria that drives them to hang themselves. One could blame the gods or a poisonous atmosphere, but doctors knew the cause was really a buildup of blood in the womb that could be cured with intercourse.[56] Hesiod (perhaps the only authentic voice of the small farmer) tells us that women are hornier in the summer and men in the winter. The aristocrat Alcaeus, the philosopher Aristotle, one of his followers, and the Roman knight Pliny the Elder all concur.[57] The difference is that the pseudo-Aristotle ventures some reasons why this might be so. Pliny also tells us that a menstruating woman turns a mirror dark just by looking at it—a clear folk belief—but, then, so does Aristotle.[58] The difference is that Aristotle mentions this well known fact in the course of proving a theory of vision. Indeed, the continuity of high and low is perhaps best seen in Pliny. This is not just because Pliny is indiscriminate and uncritical of his sources—though he is—but because he is reporting commonly held beliefs.[59]

At a less sophisticated level, popular sources confirm the standard image of women's bodies as wet, leaky, and dirty.[60] So says a verse graffito from Pompeii:

> Here just now I happened to fuck a pretty girl
> praised by many, but there was muck inside.[61]

This matches up with a poem:

> I'd need ten handfuls of aphrodisiac
> just to grind the ditch of your groin and bang
> the swarming worms of your cunt. (*Priap.* 46.8–10)

And three mixtures in a Greek magical manuscript ("To Stop Liquid in a Woman")[62] match up with similar recipes in the quasi-magical *Cyranides*

(1.18.12–24) that promise dryness and sexual pleasure, as well as with numerous prescriptions in the medical writings for the same thing.[63]

One place where a suppressed—or ignored—sexuality might speak are two magic spells where one woman binds another.[64]

I adjure you, Euangelos, by Anubis and Hermes and all the rest down below; attract and bind Sarapias whom Helen bore, to this Herais, whom Thermoutharin bore, now, now; quickly, quickly! By her soul and heart attract Sarapias herself, whom Helen bore from her own womb, etc.[65]

And a wonderful lead tablet, which reads, in part:

By means of this corpse-daemon inflame the heart, the liver, the spirit of Gorgonia, whom Nilogenia bore, with love and affection for Sophia, whom Isara bore. ... Burn, set on fire, inflame her soul, heart, liver, spirit with love for Sophia, whom Isara bore. Drive Gorgonia, whom Nilogenia bore, drive her, torment her body night and day, force her to rush forth from every place and every house, loving Sophia, whom Isara bore, she, surrendered like a slave, giving herself and all her possessions to her, because this is the will and command of the great god.[66]

The language of the woman forcing—indeed, torturing—another woman to love her is exactly the same as that of other binding spells used by men on women and by women on men.[67] A vivid example comes from a third-century A.D. lead tablet from Hadrumentum in Tunisia (in part).

Bring Urbanus, to whom Urbana gave birth, and unite him with Domitiana, to whom Candida gave birth, loving, frantic, tormented with passion (*erōs*) love (*philia*), and desire (*epithymia*) for Domitiana, whom Candida bore; unite them in marriage and as spouses in love (*erōs*) for all the time of their lives. Make him obey her like a slave, in love (*erōs*), so that he will desire no other woman or girl except Domitiana alone, to whom Candida gave birth, and will keep her as his life-partner for all the time of their lives. Now, now! Quickly, quickly![68]

Faraone perceptively remarks:

This startling flexibility in the victim's constructed gender seems to presuppose a belief that men and women are essentially of the same species and partake of the same nature (*physis*), a belief associated with Aristotle and with later medical writers such as Herophilus, Soranus, and Galen.[69]

Here, too, we see the continuity of high and low.

ORGANIZATION OF SEX

The scattered nature of the unauthorized utterances does not lend itself to a systematic treatment of how Greeks and Romans regarded sex.[70] Nonetheless, the popular sources do provide fitful illumination. For example, a binding spell sets out the image, found equally in elite texts, of the female body as a set of three holes: vagina, anus, and mouth.[71] The order, too, seems to reflect a "scale of humiliation," with oral sex the most defiling to the person who is used.[72]

> I bind you, Theodotis, daughter of Eus, unto the tail of the snake, unto the mouth of the crocodile, and by the horns of the ram, and by the poison of the cobra, and by the hairs of the cat, and by the forepart (penis) of the god so that you cannot ever have sex with (*symmignymi*) any other man, nor be fucked (*bineō*), nor be butt-fucked (*pygizō*), nor suck (*laikazō*), nor have pleasure with any other man except me alone, Ammonion the son of Emitaris.[73]

Unauthorized sources also give vivid witness to the classification of sex along the lines of active versus passive. We see the same valorization of the active penetrator and the same denigration of the passive penetrated that is described in literary texts.

Greece

As soon as the Greeks learned the alphabet, they began to write insults to each other. On the rocks above the gymnasium on Thera, we find a graffiti war dating probably around 700–650 B.C.[74] For example

> By Apollo Delphinius, here Crimon did the son of Bathycles, brother of …
> Crimon did Amotion.
> Pheidippidas did it.
> Timagoras and Entheres and I did it.
> Empedocles was banged here and made to dance, by Apollo.[75]

To use someone for your sexual pleasure was a reason for boasting; to be used by someone was a mark of shame. Boys and men who submitted could be called whores. In between the names Pheidippidas and Enpylus, someone has added "Whore" (*pornos*), a term applied in high literature as well to boys and men who submitted.[76] These simple assertions of phallic power are important—for implicit in the claim, "I fuck," is the claim "and am not fucked." The goal is to be the fucker and not the fucked: the doer and not the done.

At roughly the same time (around 650 B.C.), someone scratched on a drinking cup one of the earliest examples of writing in Athens:

Nicodemus, son of Philaeus, takes it up the ass (*katapygōn*).[77]

Katapygōn continues to be one of the most frequent insults in graffiti (and in high literary texts), well into the Roman Empire:[78]

Themistocles, son of Neocles, takes it up the ass.[79]

Titias, the Olympic victor, takes it up the ass.[80]

Sosias takes it up the ass. Euphronius, who wrote this, says so.[81]

Sydromachus, with his gaping asshole (*lakkoprōktos*), took it (*etlō*).[82]

Democritus has a wide asshole.[83]

Not to mention Sosias, Alcaeus, Eucles, and Aristomenes—who were all *katapygōn*, according to the graffiti.[84]

The threat—or boast—of anal rape (sometimes jocular, sometimes not) is frequent in elite literature, popular literature, and public sources.[85] A cup from Sicily says:

Porcus donates this cup to the in-laws' club. If he loved Phryne, no one else would take her. The writer will butt-fuck (*pygizō*) the reader.[86]

On a wall in Karnak (second century B.C.) is written:

They fucked him in the alley. Ptolemaeus, son of Abdaeus: They butt-fucked him in this very alley. The one who butt-fucked him ... [87]

On a first-century A.D. Roman-manufactured plate:

This belongs to Olympas. Whoever takes it will get butt-fucked.[88]

In the midst of all of this name-calling, we find two inscriptions that reflect idealized pederasty.

> Lysitheus says he loves (*phileō*) Micion above all others in the city, for he
>   is manly (*andreios*).[89]

> Here a man, having fallen in love with a boy, swore on oath
> To join in strife and tearful war.
> The soul of Gnathius perished in [battle]. I [the tombstone] am sacred
> To the hero … [90]

The language recalls closely Phaedrus's speech in the *Symposium* (178d-9b) that praises Love for inspiring lovers to deeds of bravery before their beloveds, and that wishes for an army of lovers and their boys.

Greece is also obsessed with the impure mouth. Women are routinely insulted as orally defiled:

> Arisemus is beautiful. Polytime is a cocksucker (*laikastria*).[91]

> Theodosia sucks cock well.[92]

> … and a cocksucker [feminine].[93]

On a long tablet that curses some hundred people, including leading citizens:

> Cleinis: cocksucker. Scylla: cocksucker. Sophronis: cocksucker. Archis:
>   cocksucker. Euphroniscus: cocksucker.[94]

Men, of course, are also accused of having impure mouths.[95] For example, Polybius, in the course of refuting the historian Timaeus, upbraids him for taking at face value an insult from the comic poet Archedicus. What is interesting is not just the charge, but the defense (12.13.1–2) and the mining of comedy for history:

> Timaeus says that Demochares [Athenian orator, around 360–275 B.C.] acted like a *hetaira*[96] with the upper parts of his body, was not worthy to blow on the holy fire, and that, in his practices, he had outdone the handbooks of Botrys, Philaenis, and the other obscene writers.[97] Not only would no cultured man ever make this kind of abuse or suggestion, but neither would anyone from a house of men who make their living from their bodies.

Polybius goes on to refute the charge (12.13.3–12.14.7): It cannot be true because Demochares was well-born, well brought-up, and had been appointed general. And even if it were true, it was rude of Timaeus to repeat it.

Cunnilingus was viewed as especially degrading and disgusting. This is a place where we can see the cultural continuity (high and low, Greek and Roman) especially clearly. Galen gives fascinating evidence (12.249 Kühn).

> Drinking sweat or urine or a woman's menstrual blood is an outrage and disgusting, and dung no less than these. Xenocrates describes what it can do when rubbed on the area around the mouth and throat and taken in a drink into the stomach. He also prescribes drinking earwax. Personally, I would never endure drinking it, not even if it meant that I would never become sick again. More disgusting than that is to eat dung. It is an even greater shame for a man in his right mind to be called a dung-eater than one who gives oral sex (*aischrourgos*) or anal sex (*kinaidos*).[98] And even among those who give oral sex, we consider those who give cunnilingus (*phoinikazō*) more disgusting than who give fellatio (*lesbiazō*). I think that someone who drinks menstrual blood subjects himself to something just like that.[99]

It is important to notice the context. Galen is not telling his readers about sexual practices, nor is he railing against perversion. He is arguing against Xenocrates and other doctors who make medical use of human waste products by appealing to common sense, to the things everyone knows: that eating shit is disgusting, that people who give oral sex are disgusting, and that cunnilingus is even more degrading than cocksucking. Galen naturally assumes the equation of the two forms of oral sex, one of which we would label heterosexual, and the other homosexual. Galen thinks that a man who could bring himself to do the one would do the other. Comedy and less elite sources agree completely. So Aristophanes launches an attack on Ariphrades as a cunt-licker and makes him "the object of three savage descriptions unmatched anywhere else in the remains of comedy for coarseness and scabrous detail."[100] So, in *Knights* (1282–9):

> He's not merely bad, or I wouldn't have noticed,
> nor completely bad, but he's actually discovered something beyond that:
> He defiles his tongue with shameful pleasures
> and in brothels he licks up the disgusting dew,
> staining his beard and stirring the hearth[101]

and doing the deeds of Polymnestus and joining with Oeonichus.[102]
Whoever does not utterly detest such a man,
never let him drink from the same cup as us![103]

In Hellenistic Egypt we find a graffito: "Sobibius, son of Cuntlicker," one time
with the joke name scratched out.[104]

Rome

For Rome and the empire, the record is even richer. A popular graffito from
Pompeii (in this case, on a tavern wall) pretty much sums up all possible roles
for a Roman male—both for reading and for sex.

> He who writes, loves (*amat*). He who reads is butt-fucked (*pedicatur*).
> He who hears, itches. He who passes by is a passive *(pathicus)*.
> Septumius, the butt-fucker (*pedicator*), writes this.[105]

To restate: "The writer fucks. If you read this, you're fucked up the ass. If
someone reads it to you, you want to be fucked up the ass. If you don't read
it, you take it in the ass or mouth." Notice here that loves (*amat*) is simply the
opposite, or active, of *pedicatur:* "The writer fucks. He isn't fucked."[106] The
same contrast is in another graffito:

> Servilius loves. May he not have a chance. Servilius, lick cunt![107]

The graffiti are a rich source of boasts of phallic power, of assertions that the
writer is active, not passive, and able to use other people's vaginas (*futuo*), anuses
(*pedico*), and mouths (*irrumo*) for his pleasure.[108] So, from Pompeii (*futuo*):

> When I got here, I fucked, then I went home.[109]

> I fucked many girls here.[110]

> Gaius Valerius Venustus, soldier, First Cohort, Rufus's century,
>   Praetorian Guard—best fucker.[111]

> Victor, be well, you who fuck well.[112]

> Nicopolis, I fucked you, so did Proculus and Fructus, slave of Holconius.[113]

> Horny boy, how many women have you fucked out (*defutuo*)?[114]

> It's better to fuck a hairy cunt than a smooth one. It holds in the steam
>   and brushes your cock.[115]

> Dionysius can fuck them open (*chalare*) anytime he wants.[116]

The walls of the Domus Augustiana in Rome bear the same sorts of boasts of being active—not passive—but in others' asses (*pedico*):

Perigenes the Greek: I butt-fuck.

Felix: I butt-fuck.

Bassus: I butt-fuck (*pygizō*).

Willingly butt-fucking.[117]

And from Pompeii:

Secundus butt-fucked pretty boys.[118]

I want to butt-fuck.[119]

The graffiti confirm the Roman prejudice that a boy's anus might give greater pleasure than a woman's vagina:

Cunt, you can cry or threaten the whole night long
but asshole has stolen what used to be your booty.[120]

Grieve, girls.
I want to butt-fuck. Proud cunt, farewell.[121]

However, *pedicare* is not confined to the use of boys. A graffito from Capua:

[Cly]mene, my dove. Shit so we can have a good sleep ... and to butt-fuck your white, dimpled ass cheeks. I'll rub your cunt. My fingers will help the itch.[122]

And from Pompeii:

Here, with my mistress, her butt opened, I did it
But it was naughty to write such verses.[123]

For oral sex, the active and passive roles are neatly summed up in a line of verse from the walls of Pompeii.

I'd rather have my friends suck me than my enemies fuck me in the mouth.[124]

There are the same simple active boasts:

[I am a] mouth-fucker.[125]

I fuck in the mouth.[126]

Above which someone has added:

Cocksucker.[127]

Cocksucking is, of course, desired by men:

Rufa, be well, since you suck cock well.[128]

But, more often, it is merely deployed as an insult against women and men:

Sabina, you suck cock. You're doing something that's not nice.[129]

Myrtis, the cocksucker.[130]

Myrtis, you suck cock well.[131]

Romula, with her man, sucks here and everywhere.[132]

Narcissus Cocksucker Maximus.[133]

The walls of Pompeii and Rome attest to the same kind of attacks on men for being passive that form a staple of Roman oratory and comedy.[134]

On 9 September, Quintus Postumius asked Aulus Attius if I could butt-fuck him.[135]

Surianus, who wrote this, butt-fucked Maevius.[136]

Ampliatus, Icarus butt-fucked you. Salvius wrote it.[137]

The citizens of Pompeii called each other *cinaedus* with mind-numbing frequency:

Cosmus, slave of Equitias, is a great *cinaedus* and cocksucker (*fellator*), with his legs spread.[138]

Vesbinus is a *cinaedus*. Vitalio has butt-fucked [him].[139]

Albanus is a *cinaedus*.[140]

As are Secundus, Antiochus, Lattario, Januarius, Restitutus, Natalis, Julius, Eros, Albanus, Publicus, Mus, Celer, Titinius, Amandio, Fuscus, and Phoebus—not to mention, apparently, all the male members of the leading families of the Cornelii and Caesii.[141]

Passive men are also attacked for submitting to oral abuse, whether from men (*fellator/irrumatus*) or women (as a *cunnilingus*).[142]

I fuck you in the mouth, Sextus.[143]

Under a painted election poster that reads MARTIALIS ASKS THAT YOU MAKE EPIDIUS SABINUS AEDILE, someone has scratched, "Martialis, you suck Proculus" (the latter is another candidate).[144] Also from Pompeii, a simple verse:

When a man farts out a prick, what do you think he's eaten?[145]

Pompeian graffiti routinely attack men as *cunnilingi*:[146]

Jucundus licks Rustica's cunt.[147]

Tiopilus, you dog, please don't lick girls' cunts up against a wall.[148]

Sollemnis, you lick cunt.[149]

Maritimus licks cunt for four *asses*. He admits virgins.[150]

Glyco supposedly undercuts him:

Glyco licks cunt for two *asses*.[151]

And we see the now familiar assumption that a man who would perform one act would perform the other:

Satyr, don't lick cunt outside of the opening, but inside the opening. Harpogras asks you to lick his cock. But, cocksucker, what … [152]

A mosaic in the passage between two rooms in a bath complex in Ostia reads STATIO CUNNULINGIORUM (Office for Cunt-lickers). Though treated as a serious possibility by some, it is a joke, similar to the wild sex scenes painted in the Suburban Baths of Pompeii, and probably serving the same function.[153]
Rome also attests threats of rape (anal and oral) as punishment.[154]

Batacarus, I'm going to butt-fuck you.[155]

L. Habonius wounds [and] fucks Caesius Felix in the mouth (*irrumare*).[156]

Some of the most vivid testimony comes in the strange form of lead sling bullets fired by the troops of Octavian (the future emperor Augustus) and of Lucius Antonius (Marc Antony's brother) at the siege of Perugia in 41–40 B.C. The bullets are rather phallic themselves, and their name, *glans* (acorn), was and is used to designate the head of the penis. Some are inscribed:

Hello, Octavian. You suck [cock].

I seek Octavian's asshole.

Loose Octavian, sit on it [with an image of a phallus].

And the bullets fired back:

I seek Fulvia's clit.

Bald Lucius Antonius and Fulvia, open your asshole.[157]

LOTS AND LOTS OF POTS

Classicists are obsessed with Greek pots: not because they necessarily have any intrinsic value, but because they survive and in prodigious numbers. Because John R. Clarke ably discusses the visual evidence in Chapter 9, I will confine myself to four observations on the Greek side.

First, Attic pots (our major source) were not exclusively sympotic, not exclusively erotic, not exclusively elite, and not exclusively intended for export.

Second, it is clear that we cannot simply accept the paintings on Attic vases as snapshots of real life.[158] Even snapshots are controlled, selected, intended to convey one picture of reality and not another—and it would take a very naive viewer indeed to accept our own pornography as a depiction of what people actually do, or even of our usual way of thinking about sex. The pots were not created to illustrate the texts and the world they do depict is different in many interesting respects.

For example, the literary sources have much praise for boys' thighs, but there is almost no direct mention or description of interfemoral intercourse.[159] Instead, it is illustrated on pottery, but less often than is supposed.[160]

On the other hand, when both literary and popular sources are explicit, they assume that the only form of intercourse between males is anal.[161] However, there are very few examples of males in the act on Attic pottery; instead, "there seems to have been a strong taboo against depiction in the visual arts of anal intercourse between males."[162]

"It was shocking if an *erastēs* was younger than his *erōmenos*."[163] From the world of pottery we have two examples—though they seem to present deliberate violations of the norms.[164]

The literary and popular written sources make numerous boasts, claims, and threats of men using other men's mouths, but there is not a single surviving depiction of men fellating other men.[165] Nor, despite the attacks on men as cunt-lickers, are there any images.[166] Who, then, is being more polite: the literary sources, by generally veiling actions in euphemisms, or the artistic sources, for generally avoiding "beastliness"?

Another area in which we have a conflict between the world as represented on the vases and the one found in literary sources is that of group sex. The vases depict various sexual acts as occurring in the same space, yet Theophrastus, in his *Character Sketches*, says of "The Obnoxious Man": "He goes shopping for himself and hires flute-girls and shows what he's bought to everyone and invites them to share." Of "The Tasteless Man," he writes, "Over the wine, he says, 'A delight has been prepared for the guests.'" If they ask for it, he says, "The slave will send for *her* from the pimp immediately, so that we may be played to by her and be pleasured."[167] It seems clear from these passages that asking the guests to share was considered tasteless. Plato concurs: "And when it comes to sex, we would all contend that it's the sweetest thing, but if you're going to do it, you have to do it so that no one sees, since it's the most shameful thing to be seen."[168] Apollodorus charges that the loathsome Phrynion "used her [the *hetaira* Neaera] shamelessly and outrageously, taking her with him to dinner whenever he drank, always partying with her, and openly having intercourse whenever and wherever he wished, making a display of his power over her to the onlookers."[169] Are we merely looking at pictorial convention, at what actually happened (despite the decorum of the texts), at fantasy, or at comic exaggeration?[170]

We can, however, make some interesting conclusions from largely negative findings. If the Greeks never once represent women having sex with each other, we may reasonably conclude that this is because Greek men simply didn't find "lesbians" sexually arousing.[171] No penis, no penetration, no danger of bastards: woman-woman sex was therefore neither threatening nor interesting.[172]

Third, are the sexual scenes meant to be normal or outrageous? Some images (however disturbing to us) might be ones of deliberate excess—intended to be amusing, satiric, cautionary, or apotropaic, as Clarke has suggested.[173] We might compare the numerous scenes of men vomiting (some of which swim up from the bottom of your drinking cup) or otherwise behaving badly, and the similarity of the group scenes to those featuring satyrs points in this direction.[174] We have certain images featuring violence, which have been compared to modern pornography.[175] Yet, these constitute only a tiny fraction of erotic images and seem confined to a handful of painters.[176] Nor is the violence itself straightforward: Spankings with slippers may have been intended to be titillating rather than to represent abuse. Furthermore, boys are threatened with slippers by men, and men by women.[177]

Fourth, and perhaps most troubling for a straightforward interpretation of Greek visual culture: no one has a good explanation for either the sudden beginning of erotic images in black-figure pottery (around 560 B.C.), or for their even more surprising cessation in red-figure pottery (around 460 B.C.).[178] We do not believe that the Athenians suddenly gave up sex (or, alternatively, that the Etruscans suddenly ceased to like porn). Are we dealing with a change in ethics and/or aesthetics—the rise of a new sensibility? The erotic scenes peter out at around the same time interior scenes of women start to proliferate.[179] There is a contemporaneous change in the shapes of pots: "away from the cups and large kraters [mixing-bowls]" and toward smaller shapes (lekythoi, et cetera).[180] Are certain shapes less suitable for erotic art? At roughly the same time, scenes of work, manufacture, and symposia also start to fade in number.[181] Have painters simply exhausted the artistic possibilities of a genre, finding that they have nothing further to say, even about sex?

CHAPTER EIGHT

Prostitution

ALLISON GLAZEBROOK

Prostitution in antiquity was pervasive. Freeborn, slave, ex-slave, male, female, citizen, foreigner—all openly practiced prostitution. According to the literary sources, prostitution occurred in private and in public, in secular and nonsecular contexts. Access to prostitutes was easy, even for slaves: the prices were cheap (an average of three obols in Athens and a common price of two *asses* in Pompeii),[1] and prostitutes were readily available in various and diverse venues. It is only recently, however, that a history of prostitution has gained the attention of serious scholarship. No longer "the literature of deviancy and crime,"[2] studies on prostitution reveal much about the gender hierarchies and attitudes of a culture and add to analyses of social and economic history. A history of ancient prostitutes, however, is difficult to write, since the voices of prostitutes themselves are lost. In their place exist the musings of elite male writers and legislation on ancient sexuality. In both cases, the prostitute is only of secondary concern: an image invented, constructed, and manipulated—frequently, for social and political ends. Greek writers especially, such as Anacreon, Athenaeus, and Lucian, whether from the Greek or Roman world, had a tradition of fetishizing the prostitute. Visual representations of prostitutes are frequently products of male fantasy, designed with male viewers in mind. The large numbers of brothel workers, streetwalkers, and other types of prostitutes should not lead us to believe that prostitution was an acceptable activity, or an acceptable profession for everyone. While the ancients did not have a moral aversion to prostitution and those who sought them out, prostitutes could be socially and/

or politically disadvantaged, and clients were criticized for having too much enthusiasm for their pursuit.

DEVELOPING AN APPROACH

For ancient Greece, much of the discussion of prostitution has centered on the *hetaira* (sexual companion; commonly translated as courtesan) and the sacred/ temple prostitute. Such foci have obstructed the study of prostitution in ancient Greece. For example, the impression of the *hetaira* as beautiful, educated, and witty is based on anecdotes (such as those from Pausanias and Athenaeus), written at least a few hundred years after any such woman likely lived—and that have little bearing on the reality of the *hetaira* in classical Greece. The contemporary context of these texts (in particular, those of Lucian, Machon, and Athenaeus) reveals that the *hetaira* represents the loss of a golden age and a unified Hellenic culture not recoverable for the Greeks living under the Romans. She represents the fragmentary nature of Greek culture and the focus on artifice in the literature of the Second Sophistic.[3] As such, she is a literary device that critiques the contemporary culture and thus has little to tell about prostitution or sexuality in her own period, let alone in classical or Hellenistic Greece.

While there are only two contemporary references to what might be interpreted as sacred prostitution at Corinth, the study of prostitution in this ancient city has remained focused on temple prostitution, neglecting the many references to prostitution at Corinth in general. But was there a class of prostitutes serving the goddess Aphrodite and working in her sanctuaries? Such a conclusion is highly problematic and controversial.[4] Ignoring the importance of context and prioritizing one type of evidence over another combined to create false dichotomies between *hetairai* and *pornai* (common prostitutes) and sacred and nonsacred prostitution. The result is the modern idealization of the *hetaira* and the sacred prostitute. In Roman studies, research has shown, in contrast, how prostitution is connected to larger social issues such as women's place in society, laws on marriage and sexuality more generally, ideas of social privilege, and hierarchies of gender. The study of prostitution as a sociocultural reality has advanced more rapidly for Rome than for ancient Greece because of the amount of available archaeological evidence from such sites as Pompeii. The willingness of Roman historians to apply comparative material to understand prostitution in Rome has also aided the scholarship.[5]

This chapter aims to refocus the discussion of prostitution for ancient Greece, as well as to compare and contrast the social, legal, and cultural practices of Greek and Roman prostitution. Both cultures covered a vast geographical and temporal area, but the focus will be on the places for which we have the most evidence: classical Athens, republican and imperial Rome and Pompeii. For the same reason, while we know that Greeks and Romans frequented male as well as female prostitutes, the emphasis is primarily on female prostitution. While a universal definition of prostitution is difficult and much debated, the basic definition of prostitution used here is any sexual activity in which payment, through hard currency, gifts, or other personal benefit, to a pimp, slave owner, or prostitute outweighs the concern for personal pleasure on the part of the individual prostitute. My examination of terminology, practice, law, and the impact of prostitution on women (and men more generally) reveals the varying sociocultural attitudes toward—and the significance of—prostitution in these parts of the ancient Mediterranean.

GREEK AND ROMAN TERMINOLOGY

The ancients had various terms for prostitutes.[6] Our own conceptions of prostitution—and the terminology we use to translate the ancient terms—often bias our scholarly interpretations and confuse the novice—so a discussion of terminology is necessary. In Greek, the lexicographers list the "ground-beater" (*chamaitypē*), "bridge-girl" (*gephyris*), and streetwalker (*spodēsilaura, peripolis, dromas*): all terms that suggest prostitutes could ply their trade throughout the city. Common terms from the classical period for a prostitute were *pornos/ pornē, paidiskē, hetaira*, and *pallakē. Pornē* likely comes from the verb *pernēmi* (to sell), and nicknames and slang terms such as *Obolē* (one obol), *Didrachmon* (twelve obols), and *chalkiditis* (penny whore) emphasize the material nature of the prostitute-client relationship, the low cost of such women, and their communal accessibility. While there is the possibility that independent, high-priced prostitutes (*megalomisthoi*) such as Phryne (Ath. 13.567e, 591d) and Rhodopis (Hdt. 2.135) did exist, these women were far fewer in number than we should imagine. *Mysachnē* (polluted one) and *pornoboskos* (pimp; from *boskō*—to feed or tend—commonly used in the case of cattle) imply the low regard some ancients had toward prostitutes.

Modern scholarship generally assumes that *pornai* worked for a fee in brothels and were of slave status, while *hetairai* were longer term companions who could be freed or freeborn, and who were often paid in kind rather than in cash.[7] The ancients, however, did not so clearly distinguish between the two. For example, the orator Apollodorus regularly refers to the prostitute Neaera as slave and freed, as receiving pay for her services and as available to anyone: though sometimes branded a *pornē*, she is nonetheless most commonly labeled a *hetaira* ([Dem.] 59). *Pornē* is clearly the more pejorative term, and was regularly used as a term of abuse, making it a mistake to associate terminology with a particular status or experience. Each prostitute's experience varied: overnight, she could go from being a regular partner of one man to working in a brothel. The sources speak of a *pallakē* of slave status whose lover plans to hand her off to a brothel (Antiph. 1.14–15). In a converse example, Alce begins her career as a *paidiskē*, a young slave prostitute in a brothel, but she is eventually freed and becomes the favorite of a wealthy Athenian (Isae. 6.19–20). Plutarch comments that *hetaira* was simply an Athenian euphemism for *pornē*—just as "contributions" was one for tribute, and "protectors" was one for garrisons posted in cities (*Sol.* 15.3). Cognates of *hetaira*, a term first appearing in the sixth century B.C., are related to *hetairos* (a man's war companion): they hint at the affection and regular association that could exist between a prostitute and her client. The term *hetaira* may have been an elite invention of archaic Greece, a time of much social and political tension. Participants in the aristocratic symposia (male drinking parties) assimilated prostitutes as fellow celebrants—but, at other times, put the *hetaira* in her place by differentiating the symposiasts from the prostitute via the use of *pornē*.[8] In each case, the motivation was political: we should not mistake the depiction for an accurate reflection of everyday life. While it is too simplistic to assume that there were no actual differences between prostitutes, it is our mistake to impose a strict taxonomy of prostitution that positions *pornē* at the bottom and *hetaira* at the top.

There is not as much confusion surrounding Latin words for prostitutes in republican and imperial Rome. The most popular terms were *meretrix* and *scortum*. *Scortum* was a common word for both male and female prostitutes from the second century B.C. onward;[9] it was more disparaging than *meretrix*. Neither term is obscene, neither refers to a particular class of prostitute—but *meretrix* would be preferred for a more sophisticated prostitute (Cic. *Verr.* 2.1.136–9), even though it is also used to identify the brothel prostitute (Cic. *Verr.* 2.1.101, 2.4.83, 2.5.38). The root of *meretrix*, *mereo* (to earn or to buy), like *pornē*, highlights the economic aspect of prostitution. But the term also indicates a prostitute with whom a client might have a regular association or deep affection. Another euphemistic term that also may indicate more of an affectionate bond between the prostitute and client is *amica*, "female friend" (Plaut. *Merc.* 923–5), but even this term is pejorative in certain contexts. Cicero refers to the matron Clodia as *amica omnium*, "a friend of everyone," to suggest her behavior is like a prostitute's (Cic. *Cael.* 32). A similar term is simply *puella*, which by the late Republic becomes common when referring to a woman of easy virtue—that is, a prostitute (Hor. *Sat.* 1.5.82; Mart. 6.66.1).

It also appears in erotic graffiti in Pompeii (*CIL* 4.1516, 2175, 10197). Less common terms for prostitutes refer to their method of solicitation by either sitting in front of a brothel or inn or walking the streets: *proseda* (Plaut. *Poen.* 268), *sellaria* (Schol. Juv. 3.136), *prostibulum* (Plaut. *Aul.* 285), *prostituta* (Sen. *Controv.* 1.2.2, 5, 6, 2.7.8; Pliny, *NH* 10.172, 30.15; Suet. *Cal.* 36.1, 40) and *circulatrix* (*Priap.* 19.1). *Togata*, which refers to the female's toga worn by prostitutes and women who commit adultery, indicates that Romans liked to know from appearances where an individual fit in their social hierarchy. *Publica* refers pejoratively to the indiscriminate access and easy virtue of prostitutes (Sen. *Ep.* 88.37), but the most derogatory way to refer to a prostitute is *lupa*, or "she-wolf" (Cic. *Mil.* 55; Mart. 1.34.8). The term hints at prostitutes' predatory nature, their wildness, and their lack of sexual virtue (Serv. on Virg. *Aen.* 2.647).

PROSTITUTES, CUSTOMERS AND PIMPS

The visual and literary evidence (e.g., [Dem.] 59 and Xen. *Mem.* 3.11) highlights the ambiguous attitude toward prostitutes in Greek society, both idealized as

FIGURE 8.1: Attic red-figure kylix (ca. 510 B.C.), Pedieus Painter; Louvre: Louvre G 13, Interior (photo credit, Erich Lessing/Art Resource).

FIGURE 8.2: Attic red-figure kylix (ca. 510 B.C.), Pedieus Painter; Louvre: Louvre G 13, Exterior (photo credit, Réunion des Musées Nationaux/Art Resource).

companions and despised as "other" as illustrated on the interior and exterior of an Attic red-figure kylix (figs. 8.1 and 8.2).

In practice, prostitutes could be slave, freed, or freeborn. In Athens, they appear to be popular with elite and nonelite alike. They walked the streets, worked in brothels, entertained at drinking parties and special festivals—traveling from city to city—or were the personal companions of one or two men. These different situations did not correspond to their actual status (as noted earlier), or with their working conditions: the experience of each of these women or men would have been very different. Those working in brothels, in particular, were likely of slave status—but brothels were not necessarily the slum holes of the poor and unfree, as some scholars have assumed them to be.[10] The only extant remains of a brothel dating to the classical period are in the Ceramicus of Athens.[11] The archaeological remains of Building Z, as it is called, suggest that the prostitutes were adorned with jewelry and that the space itself was "commodious,"[12] with a garden courtyard, mosaic floors, ample water facilities, and drinking ware. The prostitutes likely also worked at looms and as servers when not with clients.[13] On occasion, brothel workers could end up quite well-off. Alce seems to have become a favorite of the Athenian Euctemon: he freed her, put her in charge of another of his *synoikiai* (rooming houses), took most of his meals with her rather than with his wife and family, enrolled one of her children (who may or may not have been his) in his phratry (kinship group, or clan), and eventually lived with her full-time (Isae. 6.21).[14] Symposia were another important context for prostitution. The guests of such parties expected to be entertained, so hosts hired female dancers, harp-players, and flute-players (*aulētrides*) to such purpose.[15] These women, often of slave status, doubled as prostitutes. Some guests brought along personal companions—but even these could be of slave status (Antiph. 1.16–19; [Dem.] 59.24).

Though some freeborn or freed prostitutes and ex-prostitutes may appear to have worked independently, working for or with a manager was common. Managers of female prostitutes and brothels were frequently freedwomen, likely prostitutes once themselves, sometimes working for their former master ([Dem.] 59.18; Isae. 6.18–20). Despite their own past status as slave and/or prostitute, the *pornoboskousai* were not necessarily sympathetic to their workers and did not guarantee a less exploited existence for their prostitutes. The freedwoman Nicarete, for example, appears to have taken possession of any gift given to one of her girls by an admirer ([Dem.] 59.21). If not working for a pimp, prostitutes might seek out a lover who could offer protection. Neaera, a prostitute from Corinth, sought the protection of the Athenian Stephanus ([Dem.] 59.37–9).[16] Sometimes, two men would purchase a favorite brothel prostitute and share her between them. Once again, Neaera is our example. She began work as a *paidiskē* who was owned by the *pornoboskousa* Nicarete ([Dem.] 59.19).[17] Two of her lovers bought her for a large sum of money— and thus had exclusive use of her. These two lovers eventually allowed her to purchase her freedom ([Dem.] 59.29–32). When working for themselves, prostitutes entered into elaborate contracts with lovers, often long-term, that specified their cost, maintenance, and/or terms of use. Legally termed *autē hautēs kyria* (her own master), Neaera entered into a contract in Athens whereby she agreed to spend a certain amount of time with each lover each week, with each lover agreeing to cover her costs ([Dem.] 59.46). Such sharing sometimes ended in disputes requiring arbitration or formal legal action. The male prostitute Theodotus entered into a contract with two men, who ended up in court when the arrangement did not work out to the satisfaction of either of them (Lys. 3).[18]

While the majority of prostitutes at Athens were foreign and of slave or freed status, male and female citizens did practice prostitution.[19] Such individuals gave up certain civic rights: men could no longer speak in the assembly, be an ambassador, or hold office (Aeschin. 1.19–20); women were no longer eligible for marriage. None of these privileges was likely as much a concern for the poorer citizens, and thus their loss was not a deterrent. Athenians, however, conveniently ignored the fact that their own citizens might become prostitutes (not to mention the reasons for taking on such a profession), especially in the case of citizen females ([Dem.] 59.112–14).[20] At the same time, a man working as a prostitute was no different from one working as a fishmonger or a carpenter in some Athenian eyes (Pl. *Chrm.* 163b); elites looked down on all who had to work for a living, especially if they were working for another, whatever the reason. If a male citizen were to prostitute himself, however, he was not charged or singled out as a prostitute unless he attempted to exercise his right, as an Athenian, to speak publicly and hold office. However, male visits to prostitutes—and especially to brothels—regardless of the client's age or status, were socially sanctioned and encouraged as a safer alternative to illicit liaisons with wives, daughters, or sisters of male citizens (Ath. 13.569af). Penalties for the latter were steep and included fines, corporal punishment at the hands of the injured party, or even death (Lys. 1.32; [Dem.] 59.65–6; Plut. *Sol.* 23). But too much affection for prostitutes was discouraged, and lavishing gifts on them was seen as a threat to a citizen's patrimony (Isae. 3.17; Aeschin. 1.42). Denigrating an opponent for such attentions was an effective strategy among Athenian orators (e.g., [Dem.] 48.53).

The situation in Rome was somewhat different. Once again, prostitutes could be slave, freed, or freeborn. Prostitutes could work independently, but contracts—like those, mentioned in the Athenian texts, that outlined the conditions of a longtime association between a prostitute and customer—appear to have been uncommon in Rome.[21] More frequently, prostitutes worked under a manager, a male pimp called a *leno,* who was frequently also their master if they were of slave status. Although *lenae* (female pimps) likely existed (*Dig.* 23.2.43.7), they seem rarer and less important in Rome than in Greece.[22] Prostitutes could also freelance in brothels (Juv. 6.115–32). As in Greece, prostitutes were highly mobile, traveling from city to city. They walked the streets and worked in brothels, but were also common in inns, taverns, and baths. They were a well-known fixture at festivals and public places of entertainment, such as the circus, theater, and amphitheater. Physical remains of a purpose-built brothel, a structure solely intended for prostitution, have been found at Pompeii. The structure, commonly known as the Lupanar, was located on a backstreet near the forum.[23] It had five rooms on the ground floor, and another five above that. Each room on the lower level had a masonry bed and erotic decoration (Figures 8.3 and 8.4). A *titulus* (inscription) above or beside the door indicated the price of an encounter (Sen. *Controv.* 1.2.1, 5, 7; Mart. 11.45.1; Juv. 6.123). Brothels also existed in conjunction with *cauponae* and *popinae.*[24]

FIGURE 8.3: Masonry bed (ca. 79 A.D.); Lupanar, Pompeii (photo, Fotografica Foglia, House of the Lupanare/photo credit, Scala/ Art Resource).

Prostitutes in Pompeii and other Roman cities could also be found in cribs.[25] Such structures were single rooms operated by one prostitute at a time. These rooms may have been rented out on a pay-per-use basis, with the price included as an extra cost to the prostitute's fee. As with the brothels, they are easily identified by a masonry bed and/or erotic art—but any stand-alone room with direct access to the street might have been a crib (there are currently eleven known cribs in Pompeii). Occasionally, these cribs appear in the back room of a shop or tavern (Plaut. *Pseud.* 214, 229).[26] There is no specific Latin term for such rooms, known as *cellae meretriciae* among modern scholars. Freelance prostitutes could solicit customers on the street or in the baths and bring them to these cribs. The Roman sources suggest such spaces were unpleasant (Plaut. *Poen.* 268; Hor. *Sat.* 1.2.30; *Priap.* 14.9; Sen. *Controv.* 1.2; Juv. 6.131), and the archaeological evidence does not seem to contradict this.

Prostitutes were not regularly brought into one's home as they were in ancient Athens.[27] They were not a standard feature of the *cena* (main meal of the day—the equivalent of a dinner party) because Roman wives regularly

FIGURE 8.4: Erotic painting (ca. 79 A.D.); Lupanar, Pompeii (photo, Fotografica Foglia, House of the Lupanare/credit, Scala/Art Resource).

attended these with their husbands. The presence of prostitutes at such banquets is portrayed negatively in elite sources (Cic. *Sen.* 42, *Cat.* 2.10, *Fam.* 9.26.2; Plut. *Cato Maior* 17.3; Sen. *Controv.* 9.2.2.pr; Val. Max. 9.1.8), except in the case of youths (Plaut. *Most.* 326–7, 341–3). However, while visiting prostitutes and brothels was acceptable for young men of any status, as long as they kept their visits to a minimum (Hor. *Sat.* 1.2.31–4; pseudo-Acro 1.20), prostitutes were more commonly associated with the nonelite.[28] In fact, prostitutes in late republican and imperial Rome were, along with actors and gladiators, *infames* (individuals who lacked honor, and could bring dishonor to certain Romans if they entered into their presence).[29] Roman priestesses avoided them in the street (Sen. *Controv.* 1.2.8), and it was considered dishonorable for noble citizens over a certain age to visit prostitutes—especially in brothels, where the various classes easily intermingled. The Roman censors could declass citizens who became prostitutes or pimps from their tribe, and mark them with *notae*. Such individuals could no longer remain members of the senatorial or equestrian orders and thus (when male) were disqualified from the offices and distinctions of those orders. They were also barred from serving in the military. Roman emperors could decide such issues themselves and brought in legislation that excluded prostitutes from the top ranks. Even among the lower ranks, according to McGinn, prostitutes were excluded from honors and declassed to Caerites and/or aerarii, which meant they lost the civic right to hold office or even vote.[30] Ancient Rome had a more visible social hierarchy than did classical Athens, and, as a result, being a prostitute in Rome had more serious socio-political consequences.

Despite the infamy of pimping, members of the Roman elite, like wealthy Athenians, became involved with prostitution because of the potential for high profits (e.g., Sen. *Prov.* 5.2). In fact, they were likely the prime beneficiaries of prostitution.[31] Romans had to be careful to involve themselves indirectly so they would not be identified with a pimp and suffer the social stigma and other disadvantages associated with this status. Citizens among the elite invested in property used for prostitution. They also employed intermediaries to deal with the business associated with such property. More direct involvement included setting up a pimp with slave prostitutes and/or space, in the same manner as they might do for any other business. They could be the owner or patron of the pimp, who acted as a social and legal buffer, providing the owner a necessary distance from the business in addition to its management. Such elite involvement, however, did not improve attitudes toward prostitutes or their working conditions—nor did it motivate beneficial legislation.

PROSTITUTION AND THE LAW

Little evidence exists for the regulation of prostitution in ancient Greece. A recently discovered inscription from Thasos, the so-called stèle du port, suggests that city restricted solicitation by prostitutes and their pimps. Dating to the late archaic period, the stele prevents male and female prostitutes from showing themselves to customers by climbing on the roof or by hanging out the windows of the brothel.[32] Thasos also had a law restricting female dress (no. 155 Pouilloux), as did other Greek cities: only prostitutes (male or female) could wear particular jewelry and bright or elaborate garments.[33] These laws attempted to regulate the dress of regular citizens by equating the transgressors with prostitutes, thus enforcing distinctions between prostitutes and non-prostitutes rather than regulating prostitution.

On close examination, the various laws frequently reconstructed as relating to prostitution in Athens are not specific to prostitution at all. Graham has recently suggested, based on the stèle du port from Thasos, that Aristotle records a law against solicitation (*Ath. Pol.* 50.2).[34] But taken in context, the regulation simply concerns restrictions on windows and their shutters.[35] Based on the same passage of Aristotle, Herter and Davidson have further argued that the *astynomoi* were responsible for setting and enforcing the price of a night with a prostitute.[36] The passage has no specific mention of prostitutes—only of *aulētrides* and other musicians, who often doubled as prostitutes, but who most likely charged an additional fee for intercourse. Prices of prostitutes, instead, were variable, depending on "the attractiveness of the prostitute and the resources and urgency of the customer."[37] There are two interesting cases involving Athenians put to death for crimes possibly relating to prostitution: for committing *hybris* (outrage) against a Rhodian lyre-player and for placing a *paidiskē* (young girl) in a brothel (Din. 1.23). In both cases, it does not appear that a law particular to prostitution was used, suggesting that, despite their profession, prostitutes obtained protection from the laws in general. The references, however, lack the details necessary for firm conclusions.

Protecting the integrity of the citizen body, as defined by marriage, was the prime motivator in legislating sexuality in Athens. The Athenians had laws on procurement that restricted the selling of Athenian children for the purpose of prostitution. Solon restricted the right of a father to prostitute his daughter by allowing only daughters found unchaste to be sold for such purposes (Plut. *Sol.* 23).[38] Punishments for such crimes were severe. A father was charged a heavy fine in the case of prostituting a son, and a professional procurer could face capital punishment (Aeschin. 1.14, 184). The laws on adultery helped define and legitimize prostitution by claiming that no one who had relations with a woman openly bought and sold could be charged with a sexual crime ([Dem.] 59.67; Plut. *Sol.* 23). This distinction is important: for both men and women, adultery had severe consequences (Aeschin. 1.183; Lys. 1.30–3; [Dem.] 59.73–6). It was adultery, not prostitution, that the polis focused on preventing. In fact, adulterous women—banned from all festivals and from any sort of adornment—were more restricted than prostitutes (Aeschin. 1.183; [Dem.] 59.86). The concern of these laws, dating back as far as Solon, is legitimacy, based on marriage in a restricted citizenry,[39] and the concern seems to have increased over time, as Pericles' citizenship law (451/0 B.C.) makes clear.

Laws against procurement also protected the full citizen rights of future citizens and protected the citizen body from a prostitute's influence. A male citizen who had acted as a prostitute—whether out of youthful folly or compulsion—lost his right to hold office, speak in the assembly and law courts, or act as an ambassador (Aeschin. 1.19–20; Dem. 22.30; Andoc. 1.100). The act of prostitution itself was not a punishable crime,[40] but Athenians distrusted any male who allowed himself to be penetrated[41]—or, as Aeschines explains it, who used his own body in an absurd way—just as they lost confidence in anyone who abused his parents or appeared to be a coward. In the case of this particular trial, Aeschines accuses Timarchus of prostituting himself to pay for his expensive habits, having previously squandered his patrimony. If he sells himself, wastes his own wealth, and is addicted to pleasures, how can he possibly be trusted? Prostitution is only one in a list of behaviors that prevent Timarchus from speaking in public. To members of the nonelite—those not likely to be speaking in the assembly and law courts or acting as ambassadors anyway—such restrictions were not a deterrent. The law, therefore, protected the citizen body from the influence of prostitutes rather than punishing such characters for their behavior. There do not seem to be any laws suggesting a moral aversion to prostitution and visiting prostitutes—or suggesting a legal approach to prostitution more generally. It is noteworthy, in contrast, that adulterers were prosecuted and punished as criminals for their sexual crime alone.

In Rome's history, there was never any law specific to prostitutes and prostitution either, and evidence for any regulation of prostitution by the aediles in the late Republic or early imperial period is only slight.[42] There is a single reference to an elite woman, Vistilia, registering herself as a prostitute with the aediles (Tac. *Ann.* 2.85). Such registration, however, is likely to exempt prostitutes from the crime of adultery (it is for this reason that she registers), rather than to monitor or otherwise regulate their behavior. As in Athens, the prostitute and the *leno* do come up in laws on marriage and adultery. Romans of the senatorial order faced restrictions on whom they could marry, but all free Romans were forbidden to marry prostitutes, *lenones, lenae,* or anyone convicted of adultery (*lex Iulia de maritandis ordinibus* [18 B.C.] and *lex Papia Poppaea* [9 A.D.]). The law on adultery equated a convicted adulteress with a prostitute by forcing her to wear the prostitute's toga (*lex Julia de adulteriis coercendis,* 18 B.C.).[43] A husband who remained married to a female adulterer could be charged with pimping. Such laws construct the female prostitute and *leno* as the exact opposites of the *matrona* and *pater familias,* thereby defining the appropriate behavior and obligations of the latter two: she is expected to be virtuous, and he is expected to protect and ensure her sexual virtue.

Enacted as early as the first century A.D., the *Ne serva prostituatur,* an important law relating to prostitution, restricted the sale of slaves so they would not be used for prostitution. The penalty was stipulated at the time of sale: the seller typically specified a material fine, or the right to reclaim the slave, if the covenant was violated by the buyer. The imposition of a covenant usually meant that the buyer procured a slave for a slightly lower price; in cases where no penalty was agreed upon, the jurists calculated a fine based on the estimated financial loss to the original seller at the time of sale. With a ruling of Vespasian, any second buyer was bound by the covenant, even if the original buyer had not informed the subsequent purchaser of the restrictive clause (Modestinus, *Dig.* 37.14.7). In such a case, the slave was also granted her freedom and became a freedwoman of the original vendor. This law, however, only related to female slaves, and it did nothing to benefit the slave who was already a prostitute. In fact, the law suggests that once a female was prostituted, she became tainted for other professions and could thus expect to remain a prostitute. Still, the purpose of the law was not consideration for the slave herself, but, as McGinn suggests, protection of the original vendor, who, as a respectable Roman citizen, depended on the sexual virtue of all the female members of his household (past and present) to uphold his honor.[44] It also protected the vendor from a charge of pimping (*lenocinium*).[45] After Hadrian, the interest of the slave herself may have become a factor in lawmaking: now, even the original vendor violated the covenant if he regained a slave and used her for prostitution. In such cases, he lost his right as her patron (Marcellin.-Ulp., 5 *ad edictum, Dig.* 2.4.10.1; Paulus, 5 *quaest., Dig.* 18.7.9). But even this change does not reflect a desire to protect and improve the conditions of prostitutes, or to discourage prostitution as a state policy: after all, it was up to the individual vendor whether or not to utilize the *Ne serva prostituatur*. Instead, it represents a way to reward a loyal slave, or punish one who is less deserving.[46]

Roman law further reflects social disapproval of prostitution, although the censure is economic rather than moral. There were no laws in force against visiting prostitutes, but anyone who lent money to a young man for the purpose of purchasing or lending to a prostitute could not take legal action for any default of payment (Ulp. *Dig.* 17.1.12.11, cf. Julianus, *Dig.* 41.4.8). The concern of the law was most likely to prevent young men from wasting their patrimony on such pursuits, an accusation leveled against them on the comic stage (e.g., Plaut. *Merc.* 42–3).[47] On the other hand, the law protected profits from prostitution for posterity: an inheritance could include rent collected from a property containing a brothel. Specific laws avowing the rights of prostitutes did not exist. Prostitutes and pimps were instead denied basic rights common to other Romans. For example, a pimp was unable to claim theft, as a citizen would do for a regular slave, if his prostitute was abducted out of lust (Ulp. 41 *ad Sabinum, Dig.* 47.2.39; Paulus, *Sent.* 2.31.12)—nor could he charge anyone with corrupting his slave. A prostitute could not take legal action for theft against a customer who caused her to be robbed (Ulp., 41 *ad Sabinum, Dig.* 47.2.39). The law, however, did ensure the right of prostitutes to inherit (Maecianus, *Dig.* 36.1.5), to bequeath (Ulp. *Dig.*

38.17.2.4), and to receive payment for their services (Ulp. *Dig.* 12.5.4.3).
While, as in Athens, there was no moral aversion to prostitution, citizens of
Rome suffered greater disadvantages and loss of reputation upon becoming
a prostitute.

Athens, Rome, and other Roman cities, such as Pompeii, show little evidence of zoning prostitution. Locales for prostitution, including brothels, do
not appear to have been restricted to one particular area in the Athenian
polis. Xenophon indicates that the streets of Athens were full of prostitutes,
and that brothels were common (*Mem.* 2.2.4). Philemon refers to brothels
in "various quarters" (Ath. 13.569e).[48] Building Z is located within the city
walls, in the Ceramicus, the onetime potters' quarters containing a significant graveyard by the Sacred Gate. According to Hesychius, the district had
numerous prostitutes in residence. Brothels mentioned in the sources were
also located in the Peiraieus. The Athenian Euctemon had at least two *synoikiai*, one in each location, managed by freedwomen (*pornoboskousai*), that
housed prostitutes (Isae. 6.19, 20). There also appear to have been *porneia*
near the agora (Aeschin. 1.74). Brothels seem to have occupied space common to other businesses: the orator Aeschines comments that the same space
could house at different times a surgery, a laundry, a carpenter's workshop, or
a *porneion* (Aeschin. 1.124). Such sites of business were not segregated from
residential areas, as they are in North America today—so a citizen might
easily find his house next to a brothel. Renters may also have found themselves in the same situation. A *synoikia* in the Peiraieus functioned as a rooming house while also keeping working prostitutes (Isae. 6.19). Workshop
and home could coexist in the same space.[49] Brothels did collect in certain
high traffic areas—such as the Peiraieus and Ceramicus—that is, in harbors
and near city gates. The fact that there was little stigma attached to having
prostitutes in one's own home—at a symposium, or even for a short-term
stay ([Dem.] 59.22)—may explain why brothel spaces were not segregated
from other parts of the city.

Brothels in Pompeii were not located on main roads, but on narrow
backstreets and on the blocks behind public baths.[50] Brothels and other
businesses of prostitution, such as inns and taverns, did not commonly appear on streets where the houses of the elite were found—at least, not near
their main entrances. Some scholars therefore assume that, if the location of
places of prostitution were restricted, the motivation must have been moral
disapproval.[51] Laurence argues that keeping prostitutes and their clientele
away from *matronae* (and elite children, in particular) was the motivation
for such locations, but this also meant that a Roman would only encounter

prostitution if he sought it out.[52] That prostitutes and pimps were *infames*, that an encounter with a prostitute in the street could bring dishonor to a priestess, and that elite Romans avoided places of prostitution for the same reasons all suggest some logic for zoning. McGinn argues in contrast that such a thesis is too restrictive: prostitution was common in many venues. The uncertainty of the archaeological evidence makes it difficult to posit any kind of zoning.[53] Places of prostitution, like taverns and inns, mixed with lower-class housing, while possible brothels and *cellae meretriciae* were not far from elite housing. Elite houses in Rome, for example, could be found in the Subura (a notorious district), where brothels are thought to have been common. As with Athens, there is no evidence of zoning for businesses in general in Pompeii or other cities—and, in the end, the evidence supports the conclusion that brothels were scattered throughout these areas.[54] Certainly, as with Athens, specific areas such as harbors, town centers, city gates, and other high-traffic areas likely had more such businesses—but accessibility and economic factors, rather than moral censure, explain such placement.[55]

The governments of Athens and Rome, however, did have an economic interest in prostitution: both taxed prostitutes. Athens collected a *pornikon telon* (prostitution tax; Aeschin. 1.119). The *pornoboskoi* and *pornoboskousai* in charge of prostitutes must have paid this tax as well. Caligula introduced a prostitution tax in the early part of his reign (Suet. *Cal.* 40; Cass. Dio 59.28.8), and evidence suggests it was collected throughout the empire until 498 A.D.[56] Unlike the Athenian tax, the Roman version seems to have been restricted to female prostitutes and pimps. Prostitutes were charged a daily or monthly rate equal to the cost of one sexual encounter.[57] The rate, especially if daily, was high—and may have deterred part-time prostitutes. It is not clear what pimps paid. The existence of a tax indicates the economic importance of the profession and gives some legitimacy to it, suggesting that these ancient societies were not, in principle, opposed to prostitution.[58] It was only under the Christian emperors that discomfort with collecting such a tax arose.

PROSTITUTION AND GENDER

Women who became prostitutes were thought to be naturally predisposed to their profession. Neaera, one of the prostitutes of Nicarete, began practicing well before puberty—an age considered young, even for a Greek ([Dem.] 59.22). The speaker ignores the fact that she is working out of compulsion and identifies her licentiousness as the motivation instead. Augustus's daughter Julia and Claudius's wife Messalina are accused of prostituting themselves because of their lustful dispositions (Sen. *Ben.* 6.32.1; Juv. 6.115–32).[59] Firmicus Maternus (fourth century A.D.) comments that a *meretrix* is a woman who understands the economic potential of her internal desires. While verb forms referring to prostitution are most commonly used to indicate a male working as a prostitute, a female prostitute in ancient Athens is referred to by the nouns *hetaira* and *pornē,* suggesting that—while for men prostitution is simply an activity for making a living—for women, prostitution is an identity.[60] A Roman prostitute's dress distinguished her from *matronae,*[61] indicating that being a prostitute was as much a status as being a patrician or a plebeian was. The fact that adulterous women also had to wear the prostitute's toga suggests that Romans envisioned prostitutes as being licentious by nature.[62] The distinction in terminology for male and female prostitutes in Athens, as well as the restrictions on dress for female prostitutes at Rome, reinforces the attitude that women were prostitutes by nature, and that being a female prostitute was more than simply a way to make a living.[63]

Both cultures used images of the prostitute to enforce particular behavior in women—especially in elite women—by developing an opposition between the prostitute and the marriageable woman; in Rome, this was also accomplished by equating adulterous women with prostitutes.[64] Sexual virtue was the most important quality for female citizens in both cultures. The Greeks judged women by way of concepts such as *aidōs* (shame, humility, modesty) and *sōphrosynē* (self-control, moderation), the near-equivalents of the Latin *pudor* and *pudicitia* (chastity and modesty). Certain rules were to be followed when respectable women ventured into public. The more elite the woman, the more such rules were in force. In Greece, this meant averting one's eyes in the presence of men, avoiding non-kin males completely, and wearing a veil. Women in Rome had more freedom to circulate, but they avoided being seen alone with non-kin males, and were encouraged (at least under Augustus) to wear the *stola* in public[65] and to be accompanied through the streets by an appropriate number of slaves. The prostitute was seen as the polar opposite of such behavior. Although differences between wives, sisters, daughters, and prostitutes may not have been apparent in everyday life, especially in Athens, in certain contexts, such as the law courts, the differences were exploited. Apollodorus's famous statement, "we have *hetairai* for pleasure, and *pallakai* for the daily services of our bodies, but wives for the production of legitimate offspring and to have a reliable guardian of our household property,"[66] divides women into those available for sexual enjoyment and those available for the production of offspring. In the course of the rest of the speech, Apollodorus distinguishes between wives and daughters and the *sōphrōn* behavior required of these women (chastity, prudence, and moderation), and the behavior that marks a woman, such as Neaera, as a prostitute: sexually available to anyone for pay, extravagant in her tastes, excessive, and even arrogant.[67] Constructing the prostitute as the exact opposite of the wife, sister, and daughter is also a strategy in other speeches: for example, Isaeus discusses a situation where inheritance rights are at issue. The speaker claims that the mother of Phile was the deceased's *hetaira*—sexually available to everyone for a fee, attendant at symposia, and excessive in her behavior—while her brother claims she was his legitimate wife. While speakers sometimes use accusations of prostitution against men, the consistency with which they are lobbied against women reveals how the existence of prostitution and prostitutes could work as a form of social control on female sexual behavior more generally. A woman (or the man in charge of her) would pay close attention to her behavior so she might not be labeled a prostitute. Such an identity was not simply an insult: it brought her status as wife, as well as the legitimate status of her children, into question.

The same is true for late republican and imperial Rome. The most famous example is the portrayal of Clodia in Cicero's *Pro Caelio*.[68] Here, the family and the status of the woman are distinguished,[69] but Cicero uses wit, innuendo, direct accusation, and terms such as *meretrix* and *amica* to establish her identity as no better than a prostitute.[70] Cicero constructs a boundary between two types of women—the *matrona* and the *meretrix*—and places Clodia on the side of the whore. An identity associated with the prostitute as promiscuous and available to all is used to defame and abuse Clodia and remove the jurors' confidence in her as a witness. A similar strategy appears in Seneca's *Controversiae*, a collection of rhetorical exercises by famous declaimers modeled on legal disputes from the early imperial period. Although often fictional cases, these exercises reveal the claims a speaker makes when he wants his audience to find favor with a woman or, in contrast, to dislike or distrust her, since a declaimer presents arguments on both sides of an issue. They reveal how easily a female crosses the boundary between sexual propriety and sexual impropriety—and how speakers manipulate such behavior to suggest her identity as a prostitute or a wife, thereby winning disdain or sympathy for her. In 2.4, a father recognizes his dying son's child, born to him by a woman working as a prostitute. Declamations disputing the legitimacy of the grandson emphasize the notoriety and promiscuity of the woman by claiming that the father of her child is uncertain, while she is herself known only too well. Supporting arguments present the woman as a mourning wife tending to a dying husband, claiming she does not have the character, only the label, of a prostitute. In 2.7, a husband is suspicious of a bequest left to his wife by a young man and accuses her of adultery. The declaimer, using the persona of the husband, comments that her dress, walk, conversation, and appearance are not those of a faithful wife and associates her with *lenocinium,* a prostitute's allurement. He claims that she negotiated, like the most shameful women do (suggestive of prostitutes), for a higher price by at first rejecting the young man. Opposing arguments are less detailed and less interesting, merely claiming that the wife behaved appropriately, with *pudicitia,* and ignored the advances of the young man. These declaimers construct the prostitute and wife as opposites, using behavior associated with the prostitute to defame any woman and to act as a check on female behavior and sexuality in general.

Visual imagery reinforces such distinctions among types of female behavior. Female prostitutes frequently appear in Attic vase scenes depicting symposia, popular in the late sixth and early fifth centuries B.C.[71] Their gestures and behavior suggest interesting possibilities for the Athenian concept of the female prostitute and her opposition to the Athenian wife.[72] These women recline with symposiasts, participate in erotic games and intercourse, and are often either in transparent garments or nude, their limbs extended and torsos exposed, conveying their sexual availability and lack of modesty. Take, for example,

FIGURE 8.5: Attic red-figure kylix (ca. 470–460 B.C.), Tarquinia Painter; Side A; Antikenmuseum Basel und Sammlung Ludwig, Inv. Kä 415/photo credit, Andreas F. Voegelin. (Photo Courtesy of Antikenmuseum, Basel.)

FIGURE 8.6: Attic red-figure kylix (ca. 470–460 B.C.), Tarquinia Painter; Side B; Antikenmuseum Basel und Sammlung Ludwig, Inv. Kä 415/photo credit, Andreas F. Voegelin. (Photo Courtesy of Antikenmuseum, Basel.)

an early fifth-century (around 470–460 B.C.) kylix, a wine-drinking cup on which prostitutes recline with symposiasts (Figures 8.5 and 8.6).[73] The women, completely nude, extend their arms in ways that expose a full frontal view of their torsos. They look directly into the eyes of male participants and/or have physical contact with them. In general, aside from the youths, the gestures of the prostitutes are more exaggerated than those of the men, suggesting these women's lack of restraint. The scenes do not necessarily present an accurate picture of prostitutes at symposia, but they do make clear the Athenian attitude that prostitutes were sexually available and unrestrained.[74] This attitude is shared, almost a hundred years later, by Greek orators.

While such images oppose the *sōphrōn* behavior expected of the female members of an Athenian's family, they, like images of satyrs,[75] also remind the male participants to keep control of themselves at symposia. A red-figure psykter (a pot that holds and cools wine) decorated with prostitutes banqueting alone enforces these women's role as a reminder to behave (fig. 8.7).[76] It depicts four women in different sympotic activities: playing the flute, playing a drinking game, and drinking. One of the women holds a drinking cup in each hand, staring out at the viewer as she drinks from a skyphos and cradles a kylix (both types of cups for drinking wine) in her right hand. The frontal gaze

FIGURE 8.7: Attic red-figure psykter (505–500 B.C.), Euphronios; the State Hermitage Museum, Saint Petersburg, B.1650. (Courtesy of the State Hermitage Museum, Saint Petersburg.)

is rare in Attic vase painting and is reserved for altered or bestial states. It highlights her lack of control and deviant excess, traits associated with the feminine in Greek thought. The gaze also directly engages the viewer, causing him to reflect on and check his own behavior.[77] In a society such as that of ancient Athens, where *sōphrosynē* (moderation) and *enkrateia* (self-control) were important elements of masculinity, such reminders had social importance. Doing anything in excess was looked down upon and reflected badly on the perpetrator's masculinity. The *hetaira* (as both prostitute and female) came to symbolize such excess. We have already seen this association in Athenian oratory. Stories of the wealth and attention lavished on *hetairai* are also used in Attic oratory to critique male opponents ([Dem.] 48.53; Dem. 36.45). They also point out corrupt Macedonian and Hellenistic rulers and their feminization.[78] For example, Demetrius Poliorcetes, Harpalus, Ptolemy II Philadelphus, and Ptolemy IV Philopater are all described as being controlled by their *hetairai* (Plut. *Demetr.* 19.4; Ath. 13.594e, 595bc; Ath. 13.577a; Plut. *Mor.* 753f). Similarly, Cicero focuses on *meretrices* in his attack against Verres:[79] the *meretrix* Chelidon, rather than Verres himself, ran things while the latter was *praetor urbanus* of Rome. Cicero claims that she had a dominating influence over Verres, and that anyone wishing to see him went to see Chelidon first (*Verr.* 2.1.136–7). In this case, the *meretrix* is symbolic of Verres' feminization and also his excess. Because such stories point out corrupt and feminine rulers, they tell more about the masculinity of the male subject than about the *hetaira* herself.

Male citizens who became prostitutes were automatically untrustworthy, forfeiting some of their civic rights. In addition to a lack of self-control, prostitutes had penetrable bodies—whereas, in elite ideology, Athenian and Roman citizens did not. The fact that women and slaves were penetrated meant that an Athenian citizen who took on the role of a prostitute (that is, allowing himself to be penetrated) became similar to slaves and to females (Aeschin. 1.110–11). In other words, a prostitute surrendered his masculinity—or, as Halperin comments, he surrendered his phallus, "the marker of one's socio-sexual precedence."[80] Thus, a prostituted male was an emasculated male who, having taken on the negative traits normally associated with women, could no longer be trusted to have the self-control required for public life. Similarly, in both the late Roman Republic and the Roman imperial period, male citizens were distinguished from other societal members—particularly slaves and women—by the fact that their bodies were physically impenetrable. They further embodied masculinity via their status and their sexual integrity as the penetrant, not the penetrated.[81] Like in Athens, a penetrated man was emasculated and thought to have endured being a woman (Sall. *Cat.* 13.3; Tac. *Ann.* 11.36). Being penetrated was further equated with being a slave; therefore, any penetrated man was also slavelike. There were laws protecting Roman youths from such unmanly relations.[82] While the Roman citizen's bodily integrity extended to not being subjected to beatings, a freeborn prostitute—even if Roman—was no more protected from any such assault than was a slave (Aul. Gell. *NA* 9.12.7). The prostitute was the opposite of the Roman male and the Roman concept of citizen masculinity.[83] As in ancient Greece, male opponents could therefore be defamed through charges of prostitution (Cic. *Phil.* 2.44–5). In both cultures, the prostitute was the reverse of the manly citizen and the virtuous wife and was thus intimately connected to concepts of gender and appropriate sexuality for both male and female citizens.

CONCLUSION

Greeks and Romans had various terms for prostitutes, but they did not place them in recognizable classes, such as that of the courtesan. More often than not, the terms indicate a particular tone, whether neutral or pejorative, rather than a status such as slave, freed, or freeborn—and they should be read in context, since the tones can change. While the terminology is generally somewhat euphemistic, it often relates to the economic aspect, or the locale or solicitation practices of prostitution—even if not to the specific practices of the individual prostitute herself.[84] Expressions such as *lupa* and *mysachnē* reveal that the ancients might have despised those who practiced the profession. The attitude revealed by such words in classical Athens is more neutral than that in Rome, where the term *togata* (female wearer of the toga) reveals the prostitute as a status that could be physically marked. The Romans wanted to know who was and who was not a prostitute—just as they wanted to know a person's rank—while the Athenians only cared at certain times. This difference, like many others, is explained by the hierarchical nature of Roman society.

Laws on prostitution in modern Western enclaves such as Amsterdam and Nevada, where prostitution is openly practiced, typically include age restrictions, zoning, solicitation, and controls to stop the spread of disease. In other modern Western states, prostitution is criminalized—a policy motivated by a sense that it is universally wrong and/or exploitative. But concern for the practicing prostitute was alien to legislation in the ancient world. The ancients were against certain members of the community working as prostitutes—but they were not against the reality of working prostitutes, who were often slaves. In Athens, a citizen woman working as a prostitute gave up her right to bear legitimate children, and a male citizen gave up part of his civic rights. An individual was not guilty before the law for practicing prostitution, but was only accountable for being a prostitute if they claimed such rights. On the other hand, a procurer—whether a parent or a professional—could be punished for pimping in the case of free boys and free women, since these two groups lost important civic rights, whether or not they had been coerced. In Rome, concern regarding who was practicing prostitution was even greater. Disincentives to working as a prostitute included being declassed and having the status of *infames,* both of which brought many legal disabilities and prevented marriage. In general, though, legislation on prostitution is indirect, which suggests that both the Athenians and the Romans accepted prostitution in their midst, but saw no need to regulate the profession.

The prostitute, especially among Greek writers, was sometimes idealized, sometimes degraded. In both Athens and Rome, the habit of portraying prostitutes as excessive, untrustworthy, and licentious—as well as that of citing the behaviors associated with them to denigrate others—reveals a double standard. While prostitution was accepted, many practicing prostitution were devalued and denigrated.[85] Both women and men had to watch their behaviors so as not to be confused with whores. In Athens, it was easy to misrepresent the relationship between a male and a female, or a man and boy. Such a blurring of boundaries made for great political cannon fodder. In Rome, the division between prostitute and wife was not so readily confused, since Roman women had more public presence. But the behaviors of both men and women could be equated with prostitution, and their reputations subsequently sullied. Prostitution was not a controversial issue in either Athens or Rome, but being a prostitute was, in certain contexts, problematic.

CHAPTER NINE

Erotica: Visual Representation of Greek and Roman Sexual Culture

JOHN R. CLARKE

Three fundamental obstacles complicate the interpretation of ancient visual representations having to do with sex: anachronism, the reliance on texts to explain visual representation, and—paradoxically—use of the images themselves as evidence of sexual practices.

Until very recently, the assumption underlying large-format picture books and scholarly works alike was that the ancient Greeks and Romans were "just like us" with regard to what we call sexuality. This so-called essentialist approach assumes, for example, that if sex between adult men and pubescent boys is taboo in contemporary Euramerican culture, it was taboo in ancient Greece and Rome as well. Following this anachronistic line of reasoning, the essentialist would posit that, if there are self-identified gay men in our culture, then there were gay subcultures in antiquity.[1] Wholesale revision of this essentialist approach came with Michel Foucault, who argued that sexuality is a cultural construct, and that—like all practices of a culture—it is subject to the process of acculturation, or attitude-formation.[2] This process, so deeply ingrained as to be invisible to individuals within the culture, results in rules that govern sexual behavior, making it impossible to superimpose the sexual acculturation of our society upon those of the ancient Greeks and Romans.

A group of scholars who followed Foucault's lead established, through careful study of ancient texts, how attitudes toward sexual practices in the ancient world differed not only from contemporary Euramerican attitudes, but also from one ancient social group to another. They found that the very words we use to define sexual preference find little resonance in ancient Greece and Rome. Although there are many terms for sexual acts and the people who perform them, the word *sexuality,* in the sense of "my sexuality," does not exist before the twentieth century. The word *homosexual* is even more fraught, having been used scientifically only since the 1890s[3]; so, too, the words *heterosexual* and *bisexual.* It is unlikely that ancient Greeks or Romans could have identified their sexuality—let alone whether they were heterosexual, homosexual, or bisexual.[4] Even the word *pornography,* in the sense of sexually stimulating literature or visual art, is an invention of the 1850s.[5] Cultural-constructionist studies have been especially useful in determining what we might call the sexual rules of engagement; what is more, they are fundamental for interpreting visual representations in terms that fit with the attitudes ancient viewers had toward what we call sexuality.

We find the greatest evidence of the anachronistic approach in the literature associated with collections of objects that represent sexual activity or sexual organs. Beginning with the Renaissance, wealthy collectors assembled Greek and Roman sculpture, vase paintings, mosaics, ceramics, small bronzes, amulets, and gems with sexual representations, calling them "erotica." The excavations of Herculaneum (1738) and Pompeii (1748), carefully controlled by the Spanish Bourbon monarchy, saw an explosive proliferation of such objects—particularly frescoes showing frank sexual intercourse and bronze phalli with bells (*tintinnabula*). Soon, the Royal Museum at Portici became the largest repository of ancient sexual objects. Although they were integrated into the collection, they were subject to the same rules as nonsexual objects. Admission, closed to all but gentlemen of high social standing, depended on the whim of the king and his ministers—who also forbade reproduction by anyone other than the official artists who created the engravings in the monumental, rare, and expensive publication *Le antichità di Ercolano* (Accademia ercolanese di archeologia 1757–1792). Publication of erotic objects was piecemeal: engravings of a number of bronzes (mostly *tintinnabula* and images of Priapus) appeared in the second of two volumes of *Le antichità di Ercolano* that were dedicated to bronzes.[6]

Of course, curiosity about the sexual representations grew because of the royal monopoly on their publication. When a fine marble statue of Pan penetrating a she-goat emerged from the excavations of the Villa of the Papyri at

Herculaneum in 1752,[7] King Charles III consulted the sculptor Luigi Vanvitelli, who judged it "lascivious but beautiful." The king, on the advice of his confessor, judged it "worthy to be ground to a powder," closing it up in a special case within the royal collection at Portici and ordering that it not be shown to anyone who didn't have special permission.[8] Not even Johannes Winckelmann—one of the first archaeological theoreticians—was permitted to see the sculpture, even though he visited Naples four times between 1758 and 1767.

In England, the Society of Dilettanti applied its wealth and prestige to the collection and study of Greek and Roman antiquities throughout the Mediterranean world. Founding member Richard Payne Knight saw fit to study sexual representations: his privately published essay exemplifies the anachronistic approach in its attempts to explain phallic objects by comparison to contemporary phallic cults.[9]

In 1819, after the entire collection had been moved to the Royal Bourbon Museum in Naples (the current seat of the Naples Archaeological Museum), Francis I Bourbon, the future king of Naples, ordered Michele Arditi to sequester all objects that could be considered obscene by the standards of the time. Arditi himself studied the phallic objects, properly recognizing their apotropaic nature.[10] However, publication of the full range of sexual representations in the Cabinet of Obscene Objects had to await the eighth volume of *Herculanum et Pompéi*, the first affordable, illustrated publication of the objects in the Royal Museum.[11] Its author, Louis Barré, was a serious philologist; in volume eight, called *Le Musée secret*, he attempted to find texts to explain the sexual representations—sometimes with recourse to bizarre and random associations. Henri Roux, the principal engraver, copied freely from earlier publications to produce the illustrations, which included images of paintings still in place at Pompeii, as well as the erotic objects from the Farnese Collection in Rome and the Borgia Collection in Velletri. (Strangely, he omitted the terracotta lamps.) Some of the engravings reproduce paintings and sculptures with sexual subject matter that have either been destroyed or were invented wholesale by Roux or the artists whose work he copied.[12]

As public museums began to form throughout Europe during the nineteenth century, other "secret museums" joined the ranks of the collection in Naples. For example, Knight's collection—along with other "obscene" objects—made its way to the Museum Secretum of the British Museum.[13] With the unification of Italy, Giuseppe Fiorelli promised to make the Cabinet of Obscene Objects open to the public—a short-lived initiative.[14] The vicissitudes of these collections mirrored changing conceptions of what the museums' directors thought might corrupt public morality. It was not until 2000 that the Naples Cabinet, now called the Pornographic Collection, went on permanent public view.[15]

As is clear from our brief overview of essentialist scholarship on images of sexual activity, the separation of "obscene" objects from their archaeological contexts in secret museums, as well as the practices surrounding their publication, created the categories of "erotica" and "pornography." Essentialist accounts consider ancient sexual representations at face value, judging them by contemporary standards of morality. They also tend to lump together—under the rubric of the obscene or the pornographic—representations that ancient viewers did not necessarily consider sexually stimulating: phallic objects meant to ward away evil spirits (*apotropaia*); representations of the sexual exploits of half-animal deities (e.g., satyrs, Pan); and deities such as Priapus and Hermaphroditus, who had unusual sexual characteristics. Although the clearest evidence comes from images of human beings engaged in sexual intercourse, all of these visual representations bear on the question of ancient sexual acculturation. Sexual humor, a kind of visual representation that was developed by many artists—especially those from the Roman imperial period—is yet another aspect of ancient sexual acculturation that specialist studies have tended to overlook.

ARCHAIC AND CLASSICAL GREECE

Although black- and red-figure vase-painting is the major source for study of ancient Greek visual representations of sexuality, it is anything but a straightforward record of sexual practices.[16] First and foremost, sexual representations appear on a limited number of ceramic types meant for use at symposia. Images of heterosexual intercourse on these vessels tend to focus on the orgies with female sex-workers (*hetairai*) that constituted one of the entertainments of these all-male parties. Images of adult male-on-male sex emphasize the Athenian institution of boy-love, or pederasty.[17] These genres of visual representation must be understood in terms of both artist and audience. In the symposium images, repeated depictions of men debasing women (forced fellatio, spanking, simultaneous vaginal and oral penetration) suggest that the elite male consumer viewed such acts as transgressive and perhaps humorous—a kind of carnival that overturned the usual rules of sexual behavior encoded in Athenian law and literature.[18] Representations of women fondling dildos or being penetrated by macrophallic satyrs reflect the classical Greek notion (found in texts written by men) that women were sexually insatiable.

Scholars have also questioned the use of pederastic images as documents of sexual practices between the *erastēs* (adult-male lover) and the *erōmenos* (adolescent-male love object). Artists unfailingly represent man-boy couples facing each other and fondling each others' genitals. Intercourse, when represented, is intercrural (that is, interfemoral, or between the thighs), rarely anal.[19]

It seems likely that such representations reflect an artistic convention rather than the actual sexual practices of Athenian elite male society in the late sixth and fifth centuries B.C.

Sexualized demigods play an important role in visual representation in this period. In particular, the wild sexual exploits of satyrs—chasing maenads and having anal intercourse with each other—constitute a major theme in black- and red-figure vase-painting. Scholars have variously cast these representations of sexual abandon among the retinue of Dionysus as an enactment of repressed sexual desire or as an index of Greek male attitudes toward women.[20] The macrophallic, unrestrained satyr is, however, a monster in relation to Greek somatic and sexual ideals; clear evidence from both texts and visual representation reveals that the ideal penis was small, with a tight foreskin.[21] Not only is the satyr's huge penis laughable, but his improper animal sexuality is as well.

Centaurs (like the satyrs, hybrid animal-human creatures) become famously incontinent at the wedding of Pirithoüs and Hippodamia. Their attempted rape of the Lapith women is an important theme in Greek visual art (depicted, for instance, on the east pediment of the Temple of Zeus at Olympia), and the battle of the Centaurs and Lapiths becomes a potent metaphor for the triumph of Greek civilization (and restraint) over foreign barbarity (and excess).[22]

The visual art of this period sees the creation of a yet another sexualized body—that of the pygmy. As Véronique Dasen has shown, Greek representations of the pygmy have nothing to do with the ethnic pygmy.[23] Instead, artists created a body with the characteristics of dwarfism to take on the role of the "other," the opposite, like the satyr, of Greek somatic ideals: short, misshapen, and macrophallic. In a broad range of visual representations, pygmies enact comic roles, victims of the animals they attempt to hunt and of their own rampant sexual drives. This is the type of the pygmy that finds unusually full development in the art of Rome.

THE HELLENISTIC WORLD, 330–27 B.C.

Visual representations of sexual activity among humans change significantly in the early Hellenistic period (late fourth century B.C.), when they all but vanish from vase-painting, reappearing in mass-produced, mold-made ceramics and elegant mirrors. In these media—representing both ends of the economic spectrum—the image of the male-female couple, alone in a richly appointed bedchamber, replaces the orgy at the symposium. Artists take pains to make both the man and the woman beautiful—and equals in their pursuit of sexual pleasure. Some scholars interpret this shift to one-on-one sexual representations as a reflection of the emphasis on the individual—rather than on the collective—in Hellenistic society.[24] These romantic images may also reflect the growth of the romance novel in this period.

The inclusion of the god Eros in some representations, such as that on the exterior of a mirror case from Corinth (now in the Boston Museum of Fine Arts), testifies to the widely held belief during this period that sex with a beautiful partner was a gift of the gods.[25] Yet, the case's interior art is entirely secular, emphasizing the woman's sexual prowess: she assumes the "lioness" position, raising her buttocks high while bending her torso low.[26] Scholars have proposed that the owner of the case was either a famous courtesan or—equally plausibly—a married or unmarried Corinthian woman. If she were a married woman, her uninhibited sexual participation and prowess would reflect the Hellenistic notion that, in marriage, a woman should play an active role—and Eros would symbolize the rewards of the woman's efforts.[27]

There are also serial depictions of couples engaged in a variety of sexual positions on a single object (e.g., molded-glass and terracotta vessels) that illustrate the couples' ability to perform advanced sexual positions.[28] Second-century B.C. terracotta vessels from Delos and Pergamon[29]—as well as a recently discovered molded-glass vessel[30]—present such serial sexual imagery. Scholars have framed these representations in terms of the lost sex manuals to which ancient authors have alluded, attributing most of them to accomplished female prostitutes who supposedly lived during the Hellenistic period.[31]

Man-boy visual representations take a turn toward the romantic as well. Whereas the pederastic images of late archaic and classical Athens are often set in public places, such as the gymnasium, and have both parties standing, Hellenistic man-boy couples lie on a bed. What is more, artists represent the act of anal penetration frankly, even while emphasizing the tender exchange of gazes.[32] Although the venue has changed, the rules of engagement remain: the proper same-sex love object for an adult man is a boy, not another adult man.

For this reason, the representation on the Leiden cameo (first century B.C.) is atypical, for it shows two adult men copulating beneath a tender poem addressed to one of them.[33] The artist posed the couple so the viewer could see the erect penis of the man being penetrated anally, a unique portrayal in the visual record that suggests (as does the poem) that this was a private commission for an explicit and transgressive representation of man-on-man sex.[34]

It is important to note that, in the Hellenistic period, the development of such a wide variety of sexual representations occurs at both ends of the economic spectrum: from expensive cut gems and cameo glass to mold-made, mass-produced terracotta objects such as lamps and vessels. The plurality of styles and content in lovemaking scenes that developed in the period between

Alexander and Augustus provides rich sources for the artists of the early Roman imperial period.

HERMAPHRODITUS

Scholars characterize the image of Hermaphroditus in literature and visual representation as yet another expression of Hellenistic curiosity about the different sexual experiences of men and women.[35] The myth of Tiresias—much earlier than that of Hermaphroditus—emphasizes that women take more pleasure in sex than men, a likely expression of the Greek male construct of the female: she lives for sex, and finds it more pleasurable than a man does (Ovid, *Met.* 4.300–50).[36]

The myths of Hermaphroditus reveal another attitude toward the sexual differences between women and men. Hermaphroditus starts life as a male child of Aphrodite and Hermes. The boy rejects the advances of Salmacis, the nymph of a spring, but when he swims in the spring, Salmacis surrounds him and begs the gods that the two might never part. Granting her wish, the gods fuse the boy and girl together (Ovid, *Met.* 4.285–388). Hermaphroditus is biologically both sexes at once and forever, a sign of gender fusion—and confusion. Two constants appear in visual representations of the god: the humorous double take and sexual frustration.

The artistic elaboration of Hermaphroditus during the Hellenistic period responded to a demand on the part of consumers for novel visual representations. It is a period that sees the multiplication of nonideal types in the visual arts, with some calculated, like Hermaphroditus, to amuse—or even shock—the viewer.[37] A good example is the sculptural type of the sleeping Hermaphroditus that portrays the god with his belly pressed into a mattress and his head turned to the right side.[38] A viewer would have first taken pleasure in the beautiful "woman's" face, back, buttocks, and legs. Moving around to the other side of the statue would then reveal the creature's female breasts, penis, and testicles. Scholars attribute the original sculpture to the second century B.C., some citing Pliny the Elder's mention of a bronze *Hermaphroditus nobilis* by the Greek sculptor Polycles (Pliny, *NH* 34.80).[39] Another oft-repeated type that appears in sculpture, paintings, and mosaics has Hermaphroditus struggling with a satyr. Like the sleeping Hermaphroditus, it is the element of surprise at identifying Hermaphroditus's dual sexual nature that constitutes the central theme.[40] So, too, with the frescoes from houses at Pompeii that show Silenus or Pan coming upon Hermaphroditus from behind as he/she lifts a veil to reveal breasts and erect penis.[41]

All of these artistic representations of Hermaphroditus bring to the fore the ambiguities in sexual differences between women and men, as well as those inherent in all sexual acts. If the myth of Tiresias is about clarity and distinction between the sexual experiences of men and of women, Hermaphroditus gives an eternally ambiguous answer to a man's curiosity about a woman's sexual experience—and vice versa. The fact that Hellenistic—and, later, Roman—artists always treat Hermaphroditus in terms of the viewer's discovery of the god's actual sexual identity points to a construct of gender as a curiosity about genitals. A similar fascination seems to underlie the portrayal of beings such as satyrs or pygmies as having monstrous penises. Yet, representations of Hermaphroditus are more sophisticated than those of comic satyrs and pygmies in that they invade the boundaries between the sexes and gender roles so important to the Greek and Roman cultures.

DIONYSUS

If the many representations of Dionysus (with his mate, Ariadne) index the god's function as both savior and lover of mortal women, the unique painted frieze decorating a large reception space of the Villa of the Mysteries at Pompeii emphasizes his role in relation to women's sexuality. The room, part of a suite in one corner of the villa, belongs with the so-called megalographic paintings that appear during the mature Second Style (60–40 B.C.), at the very end of the Hellenistic period. Scholars, supposing the composition reflects known models from the Hellenistic world, have assembled comparanda for some of its aspects.[42] But, to date, the frieze remains unique in its depiction of life-size figures of women carrying out rituals that include the reading of sacred texts, the unveiling of the phallus, flagellation, and ecstatic dance.

Though one can count at least thirteen different interpretations, the fundamental account remains that of Margarete Bieber.[43] She proposed that the purpose of the frieze was to prepare young brides-to-be for marriage. There are several good reasons for accepting Bieber's argument. All the human actors in the frieze are women (except for a small boy in the scene of reading), and the two women who do not take part in the narrative are located in corners to the left and right of someone entering the room. One of these, to the left, must be the mistress of the house (*domina*). She is a married woman with a ring on her finger, and she gazes out at the proceedings on the other three walls.[44] In the right corner is a young woman who is dressing her hair and who is attended by two cupids: several scholars believe she is the bride to be.

In contrast to these static, onlooker figures are the women who enact a narrative that runs from left to right around the other walls of the room. The story starts with a woman, dressed in outdoor clothing, interrupting a naked boy who is reading from a scroll to an adult woman. Scenes of carrying offerings and ritual washing follow, broken by a vignette of a hairy Silenus singing while a male Pan observes a female Pan giving suck to a goat. The central image on the principal, or rear, wall is that of the drunken Dionysus reclining in Ariadne's lap; to their right a woman unveils (or veils) a huge phallus in a basket (the *liknon*), while a winged female demon flagellates a nude woman across the right corner. Behind her, a second nude woman—perhaps the flagellant at a later moment—dances ecstatically.

Many women in the Hellenistic and Roman periods belonged to the cult of Dionysus. Though the mysteries of initiation were never divulged, the Mysteries room furnishes the most tantalizing hints, with its range of emotions—from terror to ecstasy—and sequence of revelations we cannot fully understand. Alongside the religious dimension, there is a sexual one. Dionysus himself sets the theme of his love for a mortal woman, a love that promises salvation to all his female devotees. The wine that makes the god drunk (and that the Silenus and Pans drink) may also engorge the phallus and fuel both the sadomasochistic flagellation and the ecstatic dance that follows it. Yet, in the end, the viewer returns to three images of calm and stability: Dionysus and Ariadne, model lovers; the married woman who surveys it all; and the bride preparing for her first sexual experience. The Mysteries frieze offers a glimpse into female participation in a cult that mixed sex with religious rites.

THE AUGUSTAN AND EARLY
JULIO-CLAUDIAN PERIODS (27 B.C.–30 A.D.)

The quantity and variety of objects with sexual representations increase greatly in the age of Augustus—a profusion caused by the headlong growth of both Rome and the provincial capitals during the early empire. As in the Hellenistic period, we see a diffusion of sexual imagery throughout the classes. In the period between 30 B.C. and 30 A.D., terracotta workshops based in Arretium (modern Arezzo) produced vessels decorated with sexual imagery quite similar to that found on expensive silver and silver-gilt drinking ware meant for wealthy buyers. Elegant compositions feature handsome couples on beds in a variety of sexual positions. What is more, these decorations often alternate scenes of male-female intercourse with lovemaking between a man and a boy, suggesting that Roman viewers of the lower classes accepted the predominant Hellenistic Greek notion that equated these two kinds of love.[45]

These humble, mass-produced vessels reflect the bisexual decorations on luxury items, such as a recently discovered cut-cameo glass perfume bottle, the Ortiz flask.[46] On one side, a man kneels on a bed while grasping his female partner's waist in the preliminaries of intercourse—on the other side, perhaps the same man is about to penetrate a boy. The boy's unusual hairstyle, combed in bangs over the forehead but with a long lock at the nape of the neck, appears as well on side B of the Warren Cup, a silver vessel dating, like the perfume bottle, to the Augustan period. Both images are variations of a much-repeated composition of a man having anal intercourse with a young boy. But, unlike the bisexual imagery of the Ortiz flask, both sides of the Warren Cup present images of male-on-male lovemaking.[47] Scholars have proposed that the boys' hairstyle indicates their slave status, underscoring the rule that elite males could properly penetrate only persons of nonelite status.[48]

Even though its exclusively male-on-male lovemaking imagery sets it apart, the fact that the Warren Cup finds resonance with other works of Augustan and early Julio-Claudian silver in style and sexual subject matter reminds us that elite Romans—like the buyers of the mass-produced Arretine vessels—prized drinking cups with sex scenes on them. The scene on side A, like the image on the Leiden cameo, is unique: it shows a young man lowering his buttocks onto another man's penis, with the aid of a strap, while a young male voyeur looks on.[49] The artist has emphasized the beauty of the protagonists, including their Augustan hairstyles and Polyclitan bodies.

These neoclassical features, as well as the luxury of the setting—lavish bed linens, a lyre resting on a shelf, and an attendant-voyeur—fit well with contemporary images showing male-female lovemaking. The finest examples in silver come from the hoard found in the House of the Menander in Pompeii. On two of the cups, male-female couples make love in elaborate garden bowers.[50] Drinking vessels decorated with explicit scenes of lovemaking were part of the equipment of the drinking party, where men and women must have been expected to comment on the imagery. The fact that both male-female and male-male lovemaking appears on these cups suggests the expectation—corroborated by elite literature—that the Roman man regularly enjoyed penetrating both sexes.

The series of erotic pictures included in the painted decorative schemes of three rooms of the so-called Villa under the Farnesina, dated on the basis of style to around 20 B.C., casts further light on the place of sexual representations in elite Roman culture. In these rooms, conceived as picture galleries, representations in fresco of erotic pictures hold pride of place alongside reproductions of Greek masterpieces from the archaic and classical periods.[51] Like the scenes of male-male intercourse on the Warren Cup, the male-female couples in the Farnesina make love on luxurious beds in well-furnished chambers.

The paintings of lovemaking in the Farnesina villa, no less than those on the Warren Cup, were trophies of the owner's good taste and sophistication. Both the subjects and the profusion of such sexually explicit visual art contrast sharply with the sexual morality promulgated by Augustan textual propaganda.[52] There are hints in the literature that Augustus's program of moral reform was—at the worst—hypocritical (e.g., Ovid, *Tristia* 2.521–8). It should come as no surprise that Augustan and early Julio-Claudian representations, given their context within the sphere of private entertainment and collecting practices, seem to register positive social attitudes toward sex—with beautiful partners of both genders—for recreation rather than for procreation.

LATE JULIO-CLAUDIAN AND FLAVIAN PERIODS (30–96 A.D.)

The accidental preservation of Pompeii and Herculaneum by the eruption of Vesuvius in 79 A.D. left a remarkable body of evidence for the cultural construct of sexuality. The many explicit erotic paintings decorating the walls of the houses covered by Vesuvius document a mentality similar to that of the patron who commissioned the decorative ensembles of the Villa under the Farnesina in Rome. We can document the steady production of images of male-female intercourse, at varying levels of quality, from the period of the late Third Style (30–45 A.D.) through the final days of Pompeii, Stabiae, and Herculaneum (August 24, 79 A.D.). The finest of these, like the paintings from the House of the Beautiful Impluvium (30–45 A.D.),[53] the House of the Centenary, and the House of Caecilius Jucundus—all in Pompeii—present handsome couples in richly appointed bedrooms.

In the case of the House of Caecilius Jucundus, the erotic painting includes a bedchamber servant, and the artist accented fabrics with applied gold leaf (which was lost when the painting was cut from the wall in 1875 and transferred to the Pornographic Collection in Naples). The painting's original position, at the heart of the entertainment area of renovated garden, indicates the owner's wish to display it to all invited guests.[54] Its theme of human love originally related to paintings of pairs of divine lovers in adjacent entertainment spaces. Like the erotic paintings in the Villa under the Farnesina in Rome, most Pompeian representations of explicit lovemaking come from domestic contexts; they attest to the owners' refined tastes. Rather than being hidden from view, they form part of proper domestic decoration. The fact that such paintings decorate rooms meant for intimate entertaining, as well as the semi-public spaces of the house, suggests that they represented elite cultural values.

The three preserved paintings in room 43 of the House of the Centenary, one of the largest and most lavishly decorated homes in the city, provide a fuller interpretive context than do those of the House of Jucundus. Only two of them represent lovemaking; the principal painting, opposite the entrance, shows the hero Hercules fallen into an inebriated sleep while cupids play with his weapons. Although the paintings on the right and left walls show explicit sex between male-female couples, they do not signal the use of this room—as some scholars have asserted—for prostitution.[55] This room, with its elegant anteroom, is adjacent to an elaborately decorated dining room; the three rooms together form a suite for entertaining like those found in many wealthy houses and villas of the period. Ancient Romans would probably have called it a *cubiculum*.[56] Recent scholarship on texts has established that ancient Romans looked upon the *cubiculum* not as a bedroom in the modern sense of the word, but, rather, as a place for—among other things—meeting special guests, private conversation, sleeping, and sex.[57] The room's combination of an image of sleep (Hercules) and two portrayals of sexual intercourse corroborates the textual evidence.

If the relationship of erotic paintings to other rooms and paintings in a house can provide an interpretive context, so, too, can archaeological context and the known purpose of an object throw light on an owner's attitudes toward sex. The image of male-female intercourse on the exterior of a bronze mirror cover found in a burial context on the Esquiline Hill in Rome provides an excellent example of how the artist—and, presumably, the woman who owned the mirror—wished to frame sexual experience.[58] The image on the mirror, packed as it is with elaborate, intricately detailed furnishings (including a shuttered erotic picture and the woman's pet dog)—and showcasing the beauty and passion of both the man and the woman—prompts speculation about the original owner. If the dog is the woman's pet, perhaps she instructed the artist to immortalize him even while showing herself in a moment of supreme pleasure, decked out in her favorite lovemaking jewelry. The other side of the mirror, which consists of the reflecting disk in a filigree border decorated with the signs of the zodiac, invites speculation as well. Is it a reminder that time—like the beauty the mirror reflects—passes quickly? Excavators believe that the mirror was buried along with the owner's ashes, a fitting memorial to the woman's beauty and a thank offering for the sexual gifts Venus had bestowed on her.

Returning to Pompeii, we find another class of paintings belonging to the realm of entertainment: the low end of artistic production, such as the paintings decorating Pompeii's Lupanar, or brothel.[59] The discovery of the Lupanar in 1862 caused a sensation because everything about the building addresses the business of sex. It is a tiny, two-story structure occupying a triangular plot at the intersection of two narrow streets. The ground-floor interior consists of a broad corridor with five cubicles opening off of it—each with a raised masonry platform that served as a bed with a pillow, also in masonry. Above the doorways excavators found paintings of beautiful male-female couples having sex on lavishly outfitted wooden beds.

Rather than depicting a sexual act, one of the paintings shows a couple contemplating an erotic picture with shutters, as if for inspiration.[60] The woman, fully clothed in a long green dress, stands beside the bed, while the man, naked and resting against the headboard, gestures toward the picture. Rather than depicting the realities of the rough-and-ready sex that took place in the five shabby cubicles with their masonry couches, the paintings of the Lupanar must be seen as an attempt to pretty up the establishment with images of upper-class sex. Although the Lupanar presents clear evidence in its architecture, graffiti, and painted decoration of what a brothel for poor, lower-class clients was like, it would be a mistake to see the paintings (as many have) merely as illustrations of the services clients would receive. For one thing, the artist put his lovers on pretty beds, with covers, in rooms furnished with erotic pictures and lamp stands. For another, he created scenarios that emphasized the preliminaries to lovemaking and that explored the different emotional states of the man and the woman. These are artistic conventions that point to situations far removed from the realities of the Lupanar, where a turn with a prostitute cost the equivalent of a cup of common wine (two *asses*).

VISUAL HUMOR AS INDEX
OF SEXUAL ACCULTURATION

In contrast to these essentially positive, romantic sexual representations are images of humorous sexual acts. One common comic device was to represent taboo sex acts, as in the eight little paintings found in 1986 in the dressing room of the Suburban Baths of Pompeii (62–79 A.D.).[61] These small images, each positioned above a representation of a numbered box in perspective, were amusing labels associated with the real boxes beneath, where bathers placed their things.[62] Their humor—and their value to our understanding of Roman sexual acculturation—lies in their candid representation of sexual acts that most ancient viewers would have considered debased: fellatio, cunnilingus, woman-on-woman intercourse, sexual threesomes and foursomes. These are the very acts that both invective and legal literature frame in terms of obscenity and moral depravity.

Three representations play with the distinction between the pure and the impure mouth (the *os impurum*). Because the mouth was the organ of public speech, a person—and especially an elite male—reputed to have used their mouth for oral sex polluted the public trust.[63] In the Suburban Baths, a woman incurs the *os impurum* by fellating a man[64]; another woman does so by performing cunnilingus on another woman—a unique representation in Greek and Roman visual art.[65] And though there are some representations of a man performing cunnilingus on a woman in return for fellatio,[66] one of the vignettes in the Suburban Baths is unique because the man eagerly performs cunnilingus on a woman without receiving fellatio in return.[67]

The vignettes in the Suburban Baths include several unique representations of women—all with beautiful bodies and fashionable hairstyles (the piled-up curls of the Flavian period)—performing debased sexual acts. A damaged but still legible image that depicts a standing woman adopting a well-known heterosexual position to penetrate a woman lying on a bed indexes the construct of the lesbian penetrant that we find in misogynist invective (Juv. 6.306–13; Mart. 1.90, 7.67).[68] Roman men believed that, in woman-on-woman sex, one of the women had to "play the man" and penetrate the other with a strapped-on dildo (Sen. *Controv.* 1.2.23). This clearly parodic image, like that of a woman performing cunnilingus on another in the same series, contrasts sharply with highly positive images of women making love from the same period.

The humor of the Suburban Baths also targets men who misbehave. A Roman man who liked to be penetrated was branded with the status of infamy (*infamia*): in two paintings from the Suburban Baths, we see this sexual monster, usually called the *cinaedus*, being penetrated by a man.[69]

The notion that the man must be the penetrant, but never the penetrated, is perhaps the most deeply ingrained Roman sexual construct. The elite male, at least, could properly suffer no form of sexual penetration. He could penetrate with impunity the mouth, anus, or vagina of persons of inferior, noncitizen status—principally slaves and foreigners. Married women, virgins, and freeborn boys were off-limits (an early source is Plaut. *Curc.* 35–8). The social expectation was that all males were bisexual to some degree, and that they would engage in considerable sexual experimentation before (and sometimes after) marriage.[70] The sexual use of one's personal slaves and of prostitutes was expected and encouraged as a social safety valve.

In one vignette in the Suburban Baths, the *cinaedus* is the man in the middle of a sexual threesome: he penetrates a woman.[71] His debasement would be shocking and funny to a Roman viewer because, though he properly penetrates a woman, he is simultaneously being penetrated by a man. This vignette may also encode the cultural expectation that the *cinaedus* is attractive to women; texts often accuse him of adultery with another man's wife.[72] In a painting of a foursome (unfortunately, poorly preserved because of subsequent over-painting), the penetrated *cinaedus* is being fellated by a woman.[73] She, in turn, receives cunnilingus from another woman. In the Roman scale of sexual debasement, the worst kind of penetration is forced fellatio of a man by a man (indicated by the verb *irrumare*),[74] and the most unusual kind of penetration is cunnilingus—for the Romans believed that the woman receiving cunnilingus was penetrating the mouth of the person performing cunnilingus.[75] These complex codes make the sexual foursome from the Suburban Baths a veritable compendium of Roman sexual taboos—and, therefore, we presume, highly comical.

More obviously comical are representations of sexual acrobatics, yet several paintings representing improbable sexual couplings once decorated the walls of the Tavern on the Street of Mercury at Pompeii (VI 10, 1–19). Although they are now destroyed, contemporary engravings preserve their compositions—reflections, perhaps, of the popular nude mime (*nudatio mimarum*), a regular, highly licentious feature of theatrical productions (Val. Max. 2.10.8; Mart. 1.1). The most famous of these depicts a woman bending over to pour wine from a jug into a glass while being penetrated from behind.[76]

THE APOTROPAIC PHALLUS

There is ample evidence that the Romans believed the phallus—either alone or attached to a dwarf, hunchback, or pygmy—protected humans from the evil eye and demonic forces. There is already abundant testimony in archaic and classical Greek culture for the protective power of the phallus. On the island of Delos, a row of monumental stone phalli line a sacred street. The ubiquitous stelae of Hermes—vertical stone pillars topped with a head of the god and showing his erect phallus—date back to the archaic period.[77] The form continues to be elaborated upon throughout the Roman period, when artists substitute portraits of the *pater familias* for those of Hermes/Mercury. The herm is a redundant image: the vertical pillar itself could be seen as an erect phallus, yet the carved phallus is always present, sometimes in the form of a bronze attachment. As the guardian of crossroads, Hermes becomes the protector of travelers and, by extension, commerce. Many shops in Pompeii featured images of Mercury, some of them sporting huge phalli.[78]

The belief in the power of male fertility to avert evil goes far back in the ancient Mediterranean. Where contemporary European and American cultures associate any open display of male genitals with obscenity and pornography, ancient Romans felt it was their duty to put up phallic displays where danger lurked. They were unusually inventive in creating art that presented the male genitals as good-luck charms. These displays, strategically placed in streets, businesses, houses, baths, and tombs, articulate an aspect of sexuality that has been lost to contemporary Euramerican culture.

Ancient Romans believed that the male organ (called the *fascinum,* from the word *fas,* "favorable") was a talisman of fertility and prosperity that could also ward off evil spirits. Noise was a protective charm as well: babies and domestic animals often had bells strung around their necks. One of the earliest finds from Herculaneum (1740) was a particularly inventive hybrid phallus with the hind parts of a lion, wings, and four bronze bells.[79] It would have hung in the house—wherever the owner wanted special protection from malevolent forces. Romans also wore small amulets made of coral and amber: many represented phalli, but some represented the hand, thumb between index and middle finger, the image of a penis in a vagina.[80]

In the Roman city, images of the phallus appeared where the danger was. At crossroads (protected by herms in classical Athens), they placed altars to the appropriate guardians (the *lares compitales*). Another popular way of safeguarding a street was to place a phallus there. At Pompeii, excavators found many large stone phalli set into the walls of streets and alleyways. One of these, found in 1880, is carved from tufa and measures 25 1/2 inches; much of its red paint still adheres. Set into the wall beneath it was a carved marble plaque with the words *hanc ego cacavi,* or "I shat this one out," adding a bit of obscene humor to the *apotropaion.*[81]

A terracotta plaque showing an erect phallus, found above the oven in a Pompeii bakery, bears the legend HIC HABITAT FELICITAS—"Here dwells happiness."[82] The context makes it clear that the baker was not thinking of the happiness of mere sexual arousal, but, rather, of the good luck that phallic fertility and power brought. He placed the phallic plaque over his oven to make his bread rise and his business prosper.

THE EMBODIED PHALLUS: UNBECOMINGNESS AND SALUBRIOUS LAUGHTER

Several classes of sexualized beings develop in the Roman period, often with clear apotropaic functions. One of these, Priapus, is an agricultural deity of Near Eastern origins. In the Roman period, writers and visual artists make him the offspring of Aphrodite and Dionysus (Paus. 9.31.2). In art, Priapus has much in common with the stelae of Hermes—who seems to give the newer god Priapus some of his functions, making him protector of gardens, and, by extension, the doorway to the house.[83] Priapus also stands for abundance, usually bearing the fruits of the land in his mantle, which is lifted to reveal his enormous phallus.

For the Romans, as is evident from Priapic poetry, Priapus becomes a sort of talking phallus, embodying both male fantasies of the omnipotent phallus and men's fears of impotence.[84] He is a phallic scarecrow: a human frame designed to support a gigantic penis. And he acts like a scarecrow, since his original and ongoing job is to protect gardens from thieves. The god's threat to those who steal the fruits of the garden is forcible penetration of the vagina, anus, or mouth.[85] But when statues of Priapus appear in country shrines, devotees of both sexes come to pray to him for fertility. Worshippers of Priapus show up frequently in the sacral-idyllic landscapes, a genre that appears in the late first century B.C. and continues well into the third. Besides having these serious roles, Priapus is a god who provokes laughter.

Amy Richlin has pointed out that, since Priapus is a fertility god with obscene features, the humor surrounding him is properly obscene.[86] It is a kind of sacred obscenity. It is also clear that Romans connected Priapus's huge member with the phallic *fascinum*, meant to incite the laughter that would dispel demonic forces and the evil eye. Ancient Romans believed (as do many inhabitants of the Mediterranean today) that someone who envied an individual's physical beauty or material prosperity could fix the evil eye upon that person and cause it to emit particles that could harm or even kill them.[87] Laughter, however, dispels the evil eye. The most effective visual means for inciting laughter is to represent *atopia,* or "unbecomingness": huge phalli attached to individuals who look and act wrong.[88] It is not surprising, then, that in the Hellenistic and Roman periods, artists create a host of hyperphallic beings who have body types outside accepted norms and who often perform obscene acts—all of them meant to incite salubrious laughter.

Crucial to the humor of Priapus (and of hyperphallic representations in general) is the belief (mentioned earlier in relation to representations of satyrs) that large penises were both ugly and comical—a belief that stems from the classical Greek definition of the ideal male body type and its opposite. In *The Clouds,* Aristophanes has the character "Better Argument" trying to persuade young men to abandon the school run by the Sophist philosophers: "If you do these things I tell you, and bend your efforts to them, you will always have a shining breast, a bright skin, big shoulders, a minute tongue, a big rump and a small prick. But if you follow the practices of youth today, for a start you'll have a pale skin, small shoulders, a skinny chest, a big tongue, a small rump, a big dick and a long-winded decree" (Ar. *Nub.* 1009–19).[89]

Visual representation overwhelmingly supports Aristophanes' judgment: in Greek and Roman visual art, the right-sized penis is small. The Romans viewed the overlarge penis as an unattractive physical peculiarity—just as they did the red hair of the German or the deformities of the dwarf and hunchback. All these peculiarities were fair game for derision, and artists used all of them to create the laughter that warded off evil.

A famous mosaic showing the evil eye being attacked by an array of weapons, among them the phallus of a hunchback, makes explicit the apotropaic role of misshapen, hyperphallic beings. That the mosaic decorated the entry to a house—an important liminal space—reminds us that the owner wished to dispel the effects of envy as a person entered the house.[90]

Like the images of the hypersexual Priapus, the hunchback, and the bisexual Hermaphroditus, the sexually exuberant pygmy served as an *apotropaion*.[91] Beginning with the late first century B.C., we find a rapid development of the pygmy in Roman visual art. He is often accompanied by the Aethiops, a normally proportioned person whose skin is black. The males of both types sport enormous penises and perform outrageous sexual acts. Unlike sexual representations of beautiful human couples making love in beautifully appointed bedchambers, pygmies have sex out in the open: either in a picnic setting along the banks of the Nile,[92] or on boats (where we find both male-male and male-female sex).[93] Throughout the first century A.D. frescoes of pygmies alone come to predominate, especially in the garden settings of Pompeian homes.[94] Representations of the hypersexual pygmy-clown have a long life throughout the Roman world, often in contexts that demonstrate their apotropaic role.[95]

SEXUAL HUMOR IN THE RHÔNE
VALLEY CERAMICS, 70–250 A.D.

As the Italian ceramic production around Arezzo ceased in the thirties A.D., workshops sprang up near Roman army installations on the Rhône. By the seventies, their output—which included lamps, bowls, plates, and wine jugs—was exported throughout the empire. Despite their importance in documenting the wide distribution and development of sexual art after Pompeii (they continued to be produced through 250 A.D.), the Rhône ceramics have received little attention. On these lamps and pots we find many original sex scenes that go beyond what we know from Pompeii and Rome. The ceramic artists, even while replicating time-honored sexual compositions, invented new positions and new combinations of lovers. Most interesting of all, they created a series of sexual scenes with captions. Some of these captions comment on the scene;

others put words in the protagonists' mouths—often in the form of one-line sexual jokes.

Quantitative analysis suggests that ceramics with sexual subjects consti-tuted a large share of production and consumption. In a catalog of 1,121 Roman lamps, most made in France but found in Switzerland, 159 have erotic scenes. The only other categories with a higher number are representations of ani-mals (233) and gladiators and their weapons (198).[96] Another study, of Roman lamps in the British Museum, corroborates the great popularity of sex scenes; by one estimate, they constitute the largest coherent group among the many subjects represented in the museum's vast collection.[97]

The finest and most original sexual images appear in the so-called *médail-lons d'applique*: artists made the medallions in molds and attached them to bulbous, hand-thrown jugs. The medallions range in size from 2 to 7 inches in diameter. During the firing process, the medallions bonded with the clay of the pot they decorated. The most recent count catalogs 440 different compo-sitions among 700 medallions or fragments of medallions found. Categories include images of deities, emperors and empresses, gladiators, actors, chari-oteers, mythological episodes, and sex scenes.[98]

The "applied relief" medallions all seem to be humorous in their intent. One of the problems in studying sexual humor is the lack of evidence in post-Pompeian wall-painting. The miraculous preservation of so much material from the area covered by Vesuvius skews the statistics, making it seem that representing sexual humor—and perversity—was some sort of specialty in the Bay of Naples during the first century. These fancy pots—some decorated with as many as four differ-ent medallions—were popular gift items, given, for example, at the Saturnalia.

A medallion found at Lyons shows a man pleading his case to his partner, who turns her head away from him.[99] He kneels at the foot of the bed, his face in profile. The woman leans back and parts her legs dramatically, although she turns her head away from the man. The first part of the caption is clear enough: *bene futuo*, or "I fuck well." The second part, *volvi ma*, probably means "I'm laying down my life for you." The man is pleading his case, even while boasting of his sexual prowess.

"Giving it all up" for the woman is the subject of another sexual joke, where the artist suggests that the man is a victorious charioteer.[100] He holds the palm of victory in his left hand and is about to crown the woman with a laurel wreath. The artist has him saying, "*tu sola nica*," or "You're the only victor." In other words, the woman has conquered him in sex.

Things get dicier in a medallion found in 1951 near Arles (now lost), where the woman actually turns the tables, taking up a soldier's weapons.[101] Using the familiar comic trope of role reversal, the artist has the woman—rather than the man—taking up sword and shield. She straddles him, as if about to assume the "woman riding" position (*mulier equitans*), but she is actually leaning back to brandish her—really, his—weapons. The man registers his alarm by raising his right arm to shield his face with his hand. The words *orte scutus est* mean "Look out! That's a shield."[102] In a reversal of roles, the woman has become the aggressor—the "soldier" in the battle of love. Though he should be armed with a sword (his erection), the man is, in fact, flaccid. He is powerless to defend himself against the woman's real weapons. Given the fact that many such medallions served to decorate vessels found in tombs of the Roman military, the images take on a further level of irony. The soldier looks at the "defenseless" woman in a situation where she could easily defeat (castrate) him, using his own weapons.

Another applied medallion combines a purely visual pun with intimate sexual commentary. A couple makes love beneath a shuttered picture showing a four-horse chariot, an image that puns on the *mulier equitans* position.[103] Here, the implication is that she is not just riding but galloping. What is more, the artist has put words in the woman's mouth that comment shamelessly on her partner's sexual performance: "*va ... vides quam bene chalas.*" Aside from the missing first word, probably her partner's name, this clearly translates to "Va ... ! You see how well you open me up."

The artist is reinforcing the composition's visual message, with the woman blithely bouncing on the man's penis while he stretches out passively beneath her. It is, once again, the brazen, "liberated" woman dominating the man in sex. She is "on top" in every way—a role reversal intended to be humorous. The only other clear parallel for the artist putting words into the sexual protagonists' mouths is a painting removed from a room of the tavern near the forum in Pompeii (VII 9, 33). The excavator who found this picture concluded that the entire tavern was a whorehouse—though it now seems clear that, at most, this was a single room for a prostitute, a so-called *cella meretricia*. In this picture, the woman—who has assumed the position for rear-entry sex—turns to her partner, who kneels behind her, to say, "Thrust slowly" (*lente impelle*).[104]

Sometimes the captions, rather than putting words in the protagonists' mouths, make punning comments on the action. A large and unusually well-preserved applied medallion recently unearthed near Lyons is still attached to the large jug that it decorates.[105] A man steers a boat with the rudder handle in his right hand—even as he grasps the woman's left flank with the other arm and pushes his penis into her ample, extended buttocks. She turns to him to touch his bearded chin—an age-old gesture of affection in ancient art.[106]

To the left, we read the words *navigium veneris,* or "the navigation of Venus." Romans often used the name of the goddess Venus for the concept of sexual love, so an ancient viewer would understand the caption less literally as "sexual steersmanship," or even "on course for sex." In any reading, it is an unforgettable image of what we identify as multitasking. It is a pun that connects steering a boat with steering the penis.

The lamps from Arles demonstrate the creativity of local ceramicists—intent it seems, on inventing new sexual jokes. Although preserved only in a terribly worn replica, a lamp with a man, a woman, and a winged cupid on the bed makes a joke of extreme sexual acrobatics—and it is the woman who is the star performer.[107] She is quite a bit smaller than the man, and perhaps this is why she does a shoulder stand, holding her lower body in a nearly vertical position so the man, standing on the bed, can penetrate her. We see his right leg as he seems to stride into position—and though his head is worn away, he seems to be gazing down at the woman. The most remarkable feature about this composition is the figure of the cupid, who pushes the man's buttocks with both arms to increase his pleasure in penetrating the woman.

BALANCING ACTS: EVIDENCE
FOR SEX SHOWS?

A number of compositions that focus on a woman performing a balancing act while engaging in sexual intercourse appear in the applied medallions, suggesting that—like the painting from the tavern in Pompeii—their reference is the *nudatio mimarum* or similar comic sex shows.[108] A small medallion in the Archaeological Museum at Nîmes gets its visual interest—and humor—by depicting two men and a woman in a complex balancing act.[109] Although much worn, the composition is legible: the woman reclines on the back of a man on the right, who holds a large object with a handle in his right hand (perhaps a lantern or a pail); a second man, on the left, parts the woman's legs. The artist complicated these acrobatics by making the woman hold a lamp in her outstretched hand—a delicate situation, since any slight motion might spill the oil and the flame. If the group achieves their feat, they could easily compete with the couple from the Pompeii tavern, where it is wine, rather than oil, that the woman is trying not to spill.

A lamp from Arles shows a liberated woman combining her weight training with sexual pleasure, while the man is powerless to control her.[110] The woman's pose, half-crouching, half-standing, over the man's erect penis as she holds a weight in each hand, is dynamic and even a bit menacing. As with the *navigium veneris* image, part of the humor lies in the difficulty of having sex while performing a different, unrelated task. The viewer has to laugh while trying to imagine how the woman is able to maintain the alternating rhythm of swinging the weights to and fro while controlling the in-and-out of the man's penis.

A final type of sexual acrobatics that extends beyond the Rhône Valley ceramics features women copulating with stallions and mules—carefully choreographed acts with trained performers—of both human and beast varieties—played for laughs.[111] Textual sources—most notably, Apuleius's *The Golden Ass*—explore both the psychodynamics and the amusement of woman-quadruped copulation. Their humor lies in breaking the taboo against bestiality while alluding to Roman male beliefs about the insatiability of women.

THE THIRD CENTURY AND BEYOND

Evidence dwindles significantly in the third century, partly because of accidents of preservation. Nevertheless, the remains of a program of erotic paintings (mostly destroyed now) in a room of the Insula of the Painted Vaults in Ostia (around 250 A.D.) suggest that artists and patrons still valued such decorations.[112] Sexual scenes on lamps, both male-female and male-male, have an unusually long life; they continue to show up as late as the sixth century. Mostly found in tombs—and often in areas of the Roman world where burning olive oil was a luxury (Britannia, Germania, Upper Pannonia)—the lamps seem to have constituted a proud proclamation of Romanness for the individuals who placed them there. So too, it seems, does the sexual imagery itself: yet another reminder of the essentially positive values both Greeks and Romans attached to visual representations of lovemaking.

Whether their purpose was to portray the delights of sexual intimacy or absurdities of the battle between the sexes over sex, visual representations of sexual activity were everywhere, for all to see. It is this social embrace of sexual representation that separates our own attitudes—formed as they are around nineteenth-century ideas of obscenity, pornography, and individual sexual identity—from those of ancient Greece and Rome.

NOTES

Chapter 1

1. For the *kestos himas,* see C. A. Faraone, *Ancient Greek Love Magic* (Cambridge, MA: Harvard University Press, 1999), 97–110. It seems to be a legacy from Aphrodite's eastern origins, depicted on statuettes from Mesopotamia, Anatolia, and Cyprus; see the illustrations in D. H. Garrison, *Sexual Culture in Ancient Greece* (Norman: University of Oklahoma Press, 2000), 76–78, figures 3.3–3.5. Now, "in day-to-day life Venus the goddess wears tight sweaters and skirts, but, and this is the most important feature, you can recognize her because there's usually an invisible star in the middle of her forehead, a silver one, that she hypnotizes you with"; C. Baxter, *The Feast of Love* (New York: Pantheon, 2000), 298.
2. Many of the same elements are present in Ovid's version of the story of Arachne (Ovid, *Met.* 6.1–145): a list of the gods' lovers, human pain, humor.
3. W. Scheidel, "Measuring Sex, Age and Death in the Roman Empire: Explorations in Ancient Demography," *Journal of Roman Archaeology* Supplement 21 (1996): 9–51; but see now the skeptical discussion in S. R. Huebner, "'Brother-Sister' Marriage in Roman Egypt: A Curiosity of Mankind or a Widespread Family Strategy?," *Joural of Roman Studies* 97 (2007): 21–49 and the response by J. Rowlandson and R. Takahashi, "Brother-Sister Marriage and Inheritance Strategies in Greco-Roman Egypt," *Journal of Roman Studies* 99 (2009): 107–39.
4. S. L. Ager, "Familiarity Breeds: Incest and the Ptolemaic Dynasty," *Journal of Hellenic Studies* 125 (2005): 1–34.
5. L. Watson, "Catullus and the Poetics of Incest," *Antichthon* 40 (2006): 35–48.
6. T. F. Scanlon, "The Dispersion of Pederasty and the Athletic Revolution in Sixth-Century BC Greece," in *Same-Sex Desire and Love in Greco-Roman Antiquity and in the Classical Tradition of the West,* ed. B. C. Verstraete and V. Provencal (Binghamton: Haworth Press, 2005), 63–85.
7. H. van Wees, "The Seleucid Army," *Classical Review* 47 (1997): 357.

8. "The Biochemistry of Love," available at www.eclecticexpression.com/emotions brain.htm (retrieved 13 July 2010).

9. Sappho fr. 130 Campbell.

10. M. Nelson, "A Note on the Olisbos," *Glotta* 76 (2000): 75–82; H. N. Parker, "Sappho Schoolmistress," *Transactions of the American Philological Association* 123 (1993): 309–51.

11. Readers might never forgive me if I failed to mention a particularly odd kind of cultural continuity in this area: Draper Doyle Ryan, the young hero of Wayne Johnston's *The Divine Ryans*, believes his penis—which he dubs "Methuselah"—once belonged to the Roman poet Virgil, his dead father's favorite writer (W. Johnston, *The Divine Ryans* [Toronto: Vintage, 1990], 49).

12. L. E. Talalay, "A Feminist Boomerang: The Great Goddess of Greek Prehistory," *Gender and History* 6 (1994): 165–83; B. A. Olsen, "Women, Children and the Family in the Late Aegean Bronze Age: Differences in Minoan and Mycenaean Constructions of Gender," *World Archaeology* 2 (1998): 380–92; C. Morris, "From Ideologies of Motherhood to 'Collecting Mother Goddesses,'" in *Archaeology and European Modernity: Producing and Consuming the "Minoans" (Atti del convegno, Venezia, 25–27 novembre 2005),* ed. Y. Hamilakis and N. Momigliano (Padua: Bottega d'Erasmo, 2006), 69–78.

13. M. R. Lefkowitz, "Predatory Goddesses," *Hesperia* 71 (2002): 325–44.

14. M. Leigh, "Introduction" in *The Comedies of Terence,* trans. F. W. Clayton (Exeter: University of Exeter Press, 2006), xxv.

15. K. J. Dover, *Greek Homosexuality* (Cambridge, MA: Harvard University Press, 1989), 125–35.

16. P. A. Watson, "*Non tristis torus et tamen pudicus*: The Sexuality of the *matrona* in Martial," *Mnemosyne* 58 (2005): 62–87.

17. C. Laes, "Desperately Different? *Delicia* Children in the Roman Household," in *Early Christian Families in Context: An Interdisciplinary Dialogue,* ed. D. L. Balch and C. Osiek (Grand Rapids, MI: Eerdmans, 2003), 318.

18. A brief overview of the history of scholarship on sexuality and gender in Greece and Rome may be found in M. Golden and P. Toohey, eds., *Sex and Difference in Ancient Greece and Rome* (Edinburgh: Edinburgh University Press, 2003), 1–20. Among the many recent publications, M. Skinner, *Sexuality in Greek and Roman Culture* (Oxford: Blackwell, 2005) offers an excellent and accessible survey; M. Johnson and T. Ryan, eds., *Sexuality in Greek and Roman Society and Literature* (London: Routledge, 2005), a useful collection of ancient texts. W. A. Krenkel, *Naturalia non turpia: Sex and Gender in Ancient Greece and Rome; Schriften zur antiken Kultur- und Sexualwissenschaft,* ed. W. Bernard and C. Reitz (Hildesheim: Olms, 2006) collects contributions, some hard to find, by a courageous and capable investigator.

19. B. S. Thornton, *Eros: The Myth of Ancient Greek Sexuality* (Boulder, CO: Westview Press, 1997), 1–47.

20. E. Livrea, "La morte di Clitorio (SH 975)," *Zeitschrift für Papyrologie und Epigraphik* 68 (1987): 23–24.

21. R. R. Caston, "Love as Illness: Poets and Philosophers on Romantic Love," *Classical Journal* 101 (2006): 271–98.

22. B. Kingsolver, *The Poisonwood Bible* (New York: Harper, 1998), 277.

23. B. Maire, "L'imprégnation par le regard ou l'influence des 'simulacres' sur l'embryon," in *Conceptions et Mirabilia. Représentations de l'extraordinaire dans le monde antique. Actes du colloque international, Lausanne, 20–22 mars 2003*, ed. O. Bianchi and O. Thévenaz (Bern: Peter Lang, 2004), 279–94.

24. Intimations of more reciprocal relations have, however, been found in Sappho and the later Greek novel.

25. S. Boehringer, "'Ces monstres de femmes.' Topique des thaumata dans les discours sur l'homosexualité féminine aux premiers siècles de notre ère," in *Mirabilia. Conceptions et représentations de l'extraordinaire dans le monde antique. Actes du colloque internationale, Lausanne, 20–22 mars 2003*, ed. O. Bianchi and O. Thévenaz (Bern: Peter Lang, 2004), 75–98.

26. Agatharchides of Cnidus in S. M. Burstein, ed. and trans., *Agatharchides of Cnidus: On the Erythraean Sea* (London: Hakluyt Society, 1989), 108.

27. V. Wohl, *Love among the Ruins: The Erotics of Democracy in Classical Athens* (Princeton, NJ: Princeton University Press, 2002), 30–72; V. Yates, "*Anterastai*: Competition in *eros* and Politics in Classical Athens," *Arethusa* 38 (2005): 41–45; Y. Yatromanolakis, "Poleos erastes: The Greek City as the Beloved," in *Personification in the Greek World: From Antiquity to Byzantium*, ed. E. Stafford and J. Herrin (Aldershot: Ashgate, 2005), 267–83.

28. R. Langlands, *Sexual Morality in Ancient Rome* (Cambridge: Cambridge University Press, 2006), 138–91.

29. Wohl, *Love among the Ruins*, 3–10.

30. C. Dougherty, *The Poetics of Colonization: From City to Text in Archaic Greece* (New York: Oxford University Press, 1993), 61–80.

31. Langlands, *Sexual Morality in Ancient Rome*, 37–77.

32. See Skinner, *Sexuality*, 151–54 and Helen King's account in Chapter 6, this volume.

33. E. M. Harris, "Did Rape Exist in Classical Athens? Further Reflections on the Laws about Sexual Violence," *Dike* 7 (2004): 41–83.

34. So too boys, old men, and eunuchs were colder and wetter than mature males. Their sexuality did not merely mirror women's, however. Boys were less demanding; the Tarentine pentathlete Iccus abstained from sex during training, not taking a woman "or even a boy" (Pl. *Leg.* 8.839e-40a). For their part, eunuchs were in demand because their inability to ejaculate sperm made them both tireless and sterile; P. Cordier, "Tertium genus hominum. L'étrange sexualité des castrats dans l'Empire romain," in *Corps romains*, ed. P. Moreau (Grenoble: Jérome Millon, 2002), 61–75.

35. A. Rousselle, *Porneia: On Desire and the Body in Antiquity*, trans. F. Pheasant (Oxford: Blackwell, 1988), 27–30; but cf. L. Dean-Jones, "The Politics of Pleasure: Female Sexual Appetite in the Hippocratic Corpus," *Helios* 19 (1992): 82–83.

36. N. B. Kampen "What Could Hadrian Feel for Antinoos?," in *Geschlechterdefinitionen und Geschlechtergrenzen in der Antike*, ed. E. Hartmann, U. Hartmann, and K. Pietzner (Stuttgart: Franz Steiner, 2007), 199–207.

37. J. L. Butrica, "Some Myths and Anomalies in the Study of Roman Sexuality," in Verstraete and Provencal, *Same-Sex Desire and Love*, 223–31.

38. J. M. Barringer, *The Hunt in Ancient Greece* (Baltimore: Johns Hopkins University Press, 2001), 104–12.

39. A. Schnapp, "Eros the Hunter," in *A City of Images: Iconography and Society in Ancient Greece*, ed. C. Bérard et al., trans. D. Lyons (Princeton: Princeton University Press, 1989), 71–88.

40. F. Frontisi-Ducroux, "Eros, Desire and the Gaze," in *Sexuality in Ancient Art: Near East, Egypt, Greece, and Italy*, ed. N. B. Kampen (Cambridge: Cambridge University Press, 1996), 81–100.

41. See K. DeVries, "The 'Frigid Eromenoi' and Their Wooers Revisited: A Closer Look at Greek Homosexuality in Vase Painting," in *Queer Representations: Reading Lives, Reading Cultures*, ed. M. Duberman (New York: New York University Press, 1997), 14–24, with the objections of D. M. Halperin, "Questions of Evidence: Commentary on Koehl, DeVries, and Williams," in Duberman, *Queer Representations*, 52.

42. M. F. Kilmer, "Painters and Pederasts: Ancient Art, Sexuality, and Social History," in *Inventing Ancient Culture: Historicism, Periodization, and the Ancient World*, ed. M. Golden and P. Toohey (London: Routledge, 1997), 36–49.

43. M. Golden, "Slavery and Homosexuality at Athens," *Phoenix* 38 (1984): 308–24.

44. S. L. Budin, "Pallakai, Prostitutes and Prophetesses," *Classical Philology* 98 (2003): 148–59.

45. Butrica, "Some Myths and Anomalies," 210–21.

46. M. I. Finley, "Was Greek Civilization Based on Slave Labour?," *Historia* 8 (1959): 145–64; cf. M. I. Finley, *Ancient Slavery and Modern Ideology* (New York: Viking, 1980), 65.

47. A. Richlin, "Sexuality in the Roman Empire," in *A Companion to the Roman Empire*, ed. D. S. Potter (Malden, MA: Blackwell, 2006), 352; see p. 331 for her justification for using such sources as evidence for Roman sexuality.

48. A. Paradiso, "Schiavitù femminile e violenza carnale: stupro e coscienza dello stupro sulle schiave in Grecia," in *Femmes-Esclaves. Modèles d'interprétation anthropologique, économique, juridique. Atti del XXI colloquio internazionale GIREA (Lacco Ameno-Ischia, 27–29 ottobre 1994)*, ed. F. Reduzzi Merola and A. Storchi Marino (Naples: Jovene, 1999), 145–62; C. A. Williams, *Roman Homosexuality: Ideologies of Masculinity in Classical Antiquity* (Oxford: Oxford University Press, 1999), 30–38.

49. The strategy was not risk free. One of Lysias's clients, on trial for murdering his wife's lover, recalls some banter involving his advances to their slave girl (Lys. 1.12). The exchange is meant to display him as a man of the world, not the sort to kill someone unless that person deserved it. But perhaps it was these attitudes and actions that prompted his wife's adultery.

50. Solon supposedly took thought for women who were claimed as heiresses too, requiring their husbands to have sex with them at least three times a month as a mark of esteem and affection likely to make the marriage—whatever its original motives—a success; Plut. *Sol.* 20.3.

51. A. Paradiso, "Gli Iloti e l' 'oikos,'" in *Schiavi e dipendenti nell'ambito dell' "oikos" e della "familia,"* ed. M. Moggi and G. Cordiano (Pisa: Edizioni ETS, 1997), 73–90.

52. J. R. Clarke, *Looking at Lovemaking: Constructions of Sexuality in Roman Art 100 B.C.–A.D. 250* (Berkeley: University of California Press, 1998), 72–78.

53. W. Fitzgerald, *Slavery and the Roman Literary Imagination* (Cambridge: Cambridge University Press, 2000), 72–78.

54. P. Chantraine, *Dictionnaire étymologique de la langue grecque. Histoire des mots* (Paris: Klincksieck, 1984), 677.

55. Louvre G13, *ARV²* 86, 510–00 B.C., M. F. Kilmer, *Greek Erotica on Attic Red-Figure Vases* (London: Duckworth, 1993), 156–57, fig. R156B.

56. R. F. Sutton, "Pornography and Persuasion on Attic Pottery," in *Pornography and Representation in Greece and Rome*, ed. A. Richlin (New York: Oxford University Press, 1992), 11–12.

57. J. Uden, "Impersonating Priapus," *American Journal of Philology* 128 (2007): 1–26.

Chapter 2

1. For the history of heterosexuality as an identity category, see J. N. Katz, *The Invention of Heterosexuality* (Chicago: University of Chicago Press, 1995).

2. For Roman marriage, see S. Treggiari, *Roman Marriage: Iusti Coniuges from the Time of Cicero to the Time of Ulpian* (Oxford: Clarendon Press, 1991), 8. For Athenian marriage, see A.-M. Vérilhac and C. Vial, *Le mariage grec du viᵉ siècle av. J.-C. à l'époque d'Auguste* (Paris: Dépositaire, 1998), 232–47; P. duBois, *Sowing the Body: Psychoanalysis and Ancient Representations of Women* (Chicago: University of Chicago Press, 1988), 65–78; and C. Patterson, "Those Athenian Bastards," *Classical Antiquity* 9 (1990): 39–73.

3. Spartan practices offer an exception to this norm, see further S. B. Pomeroy, *Spartan Women* (Oxford: Oxford University Press, 2002).

4. The monogamy norm may have been relaxed once at Athens because of the shortage of citizen men; see further Diogenes Laertius 2.26.

5. Robert Wright observes that 980 of the 1,154 known human societies practice polygamy in some form (*The Moral Animal: Why We Are, the Way We Are: The New Science of Evolutionary Psychology* [New York: Pantheon, 1994], 90). These figures are based on information from G. Murdock's *Ethnographic Atlas* published in twenty-nine installments in *Ethnology* between 1962 and 1980.

6. For the distinction between polygamy and polygyny, see further M. Daly and M. Wilson, *Sex, Evolution, and Behavior* (Boston: Willard Grant, 1983); Wright, *The Moral Animal*, 40–44.

7. For the hostility of tragic wives to husbands who seek to introduce concubines into the conjugal home, see D. Ogden, "Women and Bastardy in Ancient Greece and the Hellenistic World," in *The Greek World*, ed. A. Powell (London: Routledge, 1995); H. P. Foley, *Female Acts in Greek Tragedy* (Princeton, NJ: Princeton University Press, 2001).

8. See Ath. 13.556be; E. Hall, *Inventing the Barbarian: Greek Self-definition through Tragedy* (Oxford: Oxford University Press, 1989), 142–43, 201–3; D. Ogden, *Polygamy, Prostitutes and Death* (London: Duckworth, 1997); L. McClure, *Courtesans at Table: Gender and Greek Literary Culture in Athenaeus* (New York: Routledge, 2003), 19–20.

9. See L. Betzig, *Despotism and Differential Reproduction: A Darwinian View of History* (New York: Aldine, 1986); R. Alexander, *The Biology of Moral Systems* (Hawthorne, NY: Aldine de Gruyter, 1987), 71–73, with additional references cited.

10. See L. Betzig, "Roman Polygyny," *Ethnology and Sociobiology* 13 (1992): 309–49.

11. See I. Morris, "The Strong Principle of Equality and the Archaic Origins of Greek Democracy," in *Dêmokratia: A Conversation on Democracies, Ancient and Modern,* ed. J. Ober and C. Hedrick (Princeton, NJ: Princeton University Press, 1996); I. Morris, *Archaeology as Cultural History: Words and Things in Iron Age Greece* (Malden, MA: Blackwell, 1999); E. W. Robinson, *The First Democracies: Early Popular Government Outside Athens* (Stuttgart: Franz Steiner Verlag, 1997).

12. On egalitarianism in the Greek world, see Morris, "The Strong Principle of Equality"; Morris, *Archaeology as Cultural History*; J. Ober, *The Athenian Revolution: Essays on Ancient Greek Democracy and Political Theory* (Princeton, NJ: Princeton University Press, 1996); see also R. Dahl, *Democracy and Its Critics* (New Haven, CT: Yale University Press, 1989) on the prerequisites of political egalitarianism.

13. C. Boehm, *Hierarchy in the Forest: The Evolution of Egalitarian Behavior* (Cambridge, MA: Harvard University Press, 1999), 10.

14. Relevant here is Ian Morris's argument that a strong principle of equality emerged in ancient Greece in the late sixth century. This is the notion that "none are so definitely better qualified than the others that they should be entrusted with making the collective and binding decisions" ("The Strong Principle of Equality," 20, quoting Dahl, *Democracy and Its Critics,* 30–31). Transferring this idea to the matrimonial domain, we can say that each man agreed to take one and only one wife in the belief that no man was so much better or more deserving than others so as to merit possessing multiple wives. In other words, he would resent a man who took or tried to take more than one wife.

15. For Athenian marriage practices as a source of egalitarian ideology, see C. Leduc, "Marriage in Ancient Greece," in *A History of Women in the West vol. 1: From Ancient Goddesses to Christian Saints,* ed. P. S. Pantel (Cambridge, MA: Belknap Press of Harvard University Press, 1992); S. Lape, "Democratic Ideology and the Poetics of Rape in Menander's Comedy," *Classical Antiquity* 20 (2001): 79–120; S. Lape, "Solon and the Institution of the Democratic Family Form," *Classical Journal* 98 (2002/2003): 117–39; S. Lape, *Reproducing Athens: Menander's Comedy, Democratic Culture and the Hellenistic City* (Princeton, NJ: Princeton University Press, 2004).

16. For the relationship between envy and equality in democratic Athens, see D. L. Cairns, "The Politics of Envy: Envy and Equality in Ancient Greece," in *Envy, Spite, and Jealousy: The Rivalrous Emotions in Ancient Greece,* ed. D. Konstan and K. Rutter (Edinburgh: Edinburgh University Press, 2003), 240; N.R.E. Fisher,

"Let Envy Be Absent: Envy, Liturgies, and Reciprocity in Athens," in Konstan and Rutter, *Envy, Spite, and Jealousy.*

17. We can infer this from the Draconian law on justifiable homicide, which allowed an Athenian man to kill any man he found with his wife, mother, sister, daughter, or "concubine (*pallakē*) kept for producing free children (*eleutherois paisin*)" (Dem. 23.53). This provision tells us that both a man's wife and his concubine could produce socially useful (i.e., free) offspring. For the attribution of this law to Draco, see E. Carawan, *The Rhetoric and Law of Draco* (Oxford: Oxford University Press, 1998), 78 n. 80; for its ideological significance, see Lape, "Solon and the Institution of the Democratic Family Form."

18. At most, the nonlegitimate son could receive a small portion, or *notheia,* consisting of either 1,000 (Harpocration, s.v. *notheia*) or 500 drachmas (Ar. *Av.* 1650–56).

19. For the correlation of legitimacy and citizenship in Solon's laws, see H. J. Wolff, "Marriage Law and Family Organization in Ancient Athens: A Study of the Interrelation of Public and Private Law in the Greek City," *Traditio* 2 (1944): 77–79; S. C. Humphreys, "The *nothoi* of Kynosarges," *Journal of Hellenic Studies* 94 (1974): 90; J. K. Davies, "Athenian Citizenship: The Descent Group and the Alternatives," *Classical Journal* 73 (1977/1978): 114–15; D. Ogden, *Greek Bastardy in the Classical and Hellenistic Periods* (Oxford: Oxford University Press, 1996), 43; Lape, "Solon and the Institution of the Democratic Family Form."

20. Concubinage is infrequently attested in the classical period, see O. Müller, "Untersuchungen zur Geschichte des attischen Bürger- und Eherechts," *Jahrbuch für Classischen Philologie* 25 (1899): 710–32; A. Maffi, "Matrimonio, concubinato e filiazione illegitima nell'Atene degli oratori," in *Symposion 1985: Vorträge zur griechischen und hellenistischen Rechtsgeschichte*, ed. G. Thür (Cologne: Böhlau, 1989); C. Mossé, "La place de la *pallaké* dans la famille athénienne," in *Symposion 1990: Vorträge zur griechischen und hellenistischen Rechtsgeschichte*, ed. M. Gagarin (Cologne: Böhlau, 1991); Ogden, *Greek Bastardy,* 158–63; K. Kapparis, *Apollodorus, "Against Neaira" [D. 59]* (Berlin: Walter de Gruyter, 1999), 9–13; Lape, "Solon and the Institution of the Democratic Family Form."

21. On the *hetaira* and female sex workers more generally, see further J. N. Davidson, *Courtesans and Fishcakes: The Consuming Passions of Classical Athens* (New York: Fontana, 1997); S. Goldhill, "The Seductions of the Gaze: Socrates and His Girlfriends," in *Komos: Essays in Order, Conflict and Community in Classical Athens,* ed. P. Cartledge, P. Millett, and S. von Reden (Cambridge: Cambridge University Press, 1998); Glazebrook, this volume, chapter 8. On the *hetaira* in Greek culture and literature, see the major studies by Reinsberg 1989; L. Kurke, *Coins, Bodies, Games, and Gold: The Politics of Meaning in Archaic Greece* (Princeton, NJ: Princeton University Press, 1999); McClure, *Courtesans at Table.*

22. Davidson, *Courtesans and Fishcakes;* Kurke, *Coins, Bodies, Games, and Gold,* 186; McClure, *Courtesans at Table,* 18.

23. Davidson, *Courtesans and Fishcakes,* 112; Goldhill, "The Seductions of the Gaze."

24. For violence against *hetairai* and *pornai* in vase painting, see E. C. Keuls, *The Reign of the Phallus: Sexual Politics in Ancient Athens* (New York: Harper & Row, 1985); R. F. Sutton, "Pornography and Persuasion on Attic Pottery," in

Pornography and Representation in Greece and Rome, ed. A. Richlin (New York: Oxford University Press, 1992).

25. [Dem.] 59.33.

26. For *moicheia* as applying to all Athenian women, irrespective of their marital status, see A.R.W. Harrison, *The Law of Athens* (Oxford: Clarendon Press, 1968–1971), 1.36; S. G. Cole, "Greek Sanctions against Sexual Assault," *Classical Philology* 79 (1984): 97–113; E. Cantarella, "Moicheia: Reconsidering a Problem," in *Symposion 1990: Vorträge zur griechischen und hellenistischen Rechtsgeschichte*, ed. M. Gagarin (Cologne: Böhlau, 1991), 292–95; L. Foxhall, "Response to Eva Cantarella," in Gagarin, *Symposion 1990*, 297–303; C. Carey, "Rape and Adultery in Athenian Law," *Classical Quarterly* 45 (1995): 407–17; R. Omitowoju, *Rape and the Politics of Consent in Classical Athens* (Cambridge: Cambridge University Press, 2002). For examples in Menandrian comedy, see Men. *Sic.* 209–10, *Peric.* 357, 370, 390, 986, *Sam.* 588–92.

27. See further A. Glazebrook, "Prostituting Female Kin (Plut. *Sol.* 23.1–2)," *Dike* 8 (2005): 46.

28. Cf. Plut. *Sol.* 23.1–2; see further Cole, "Greek Sanctions against Sexual Assault," 107–8; D. Cohen, *Law, Sexuality, and Society: The Enforcement of Morals in Classical Athens* (Cambridge: Cambridge University Press, 1991); W. Schmitz, "Der nomos moicheias—Das athenische Gesetz über den Ehebruch," *Zeitschrift der Savigny-Stiftung für Rechtsgeschichte. Romanistische Abteilung* 114 (1997): 45–140; Glazebrook, "Prostituting Female Kin," 33–52.

29. [Arist.] *Ath. Pol.* 26.3, Plut. *Per.* 37.2–4; M. Broadbent, *Studies in Greek Genealogy* (Leiden: E. J. Brill, 1968), 67–74; C. Patterson, *Pericles' Citizenship Law of 451–450 B.C.* (Salem, NH: Arno Press, 1981); C. Patterson, "Athenian Citizenship Law," in *The Cambridge Companion to Ancient Greek Law*, ed. M. Gagarin and D. Cohen (Cambridge: Cambridge University Press, 2005); P. J. Rhodes, *A Commentary on the Aristotelian* Athenaion Politeia (Oxford: Oxford University Press, 1981), 331–35; A. L. Boegehold, "Perikles' Citizenship Law of 451/0 B.C.," in *Athenian Identity and Civic Ideology*, ed. A. L. Boegehold and A. C. Scafuro (Baltimore: Johns Hopkins University Press, 1994); K. Stears, "Dead Women's Society: Constructing Female Gender in Classical Athenian Funerary Sculpture," in *Time, Tradition, and Society in Greek Archaeology: Bridging the "Great Divide,"* ed. N. Spencer (London: Routledge, 1995); Ogden, *Greek Bastardy*, 59–69; R. Osborne, "Law and the Representation of Women in Athens," *Past & Present* 155 (1997): 3–33; R. E. Leader, "In Death not Divided: Gender, Family, and State on Classical Athenian Grave Stelae," *American Journal of Archaeology* 101 (1997): 683–99; Vérilhac and Vial, *Le mariage grec*, 55–60.

30. For marriage and the law, see Humphreys, "The *nothoi* of Kynosarges," 88–95; Rhodes, *A Commentary on the Aristotelian* Athenaion Politeia, 331–33; C. Patterson, *The Family in Greek History* (Cambridge, MA: Harvard University Press, 1998), 110; Patterson, "Athenian Citizenship Law."

31. A. Diller, *Race Mixture Among the Greeks before Alexander* (Urbana: University of Illinois Press, 1937), 92; Humphreys, "The *nothoi* of Kynosarges," 94; L. Gernet, *The Anthropology of Ancient Greece*, trans. J. Hamilton and B. Nagy (Baltimore:

Johns Hopkins University Press, 1981); G. Herman, *Ritualized Friendship and the Greek City* (Cambridge: Cambridge University Press, 1987), 36; L. Kurke, *The Traffic in Praise: Pindar and the Poetics of Social Economy* (Ithaca, NY: Cornell University Press, 1991); Ogden, *Greek Bastardy*, 67.

32. See further Aeschin. 3.172–6; J. Ober, *Mass and Elite in Democratic Athens: Rhetoric, Ideology, and the Power of the People* (Princeton, NJ: Princeton University Press, 1989), 266; Lape, "Solon and the Institution of the Democratic Family Form"; R. Parker, *Polytheism and Society at Athens* (Oxford: Oxford University Press, 2005), 454. Blok argues (contra E. E. Cohen, *The Athenian Nation* [Princeton, NJ: Princeton University Press, 2000], 50–63) that the Periclean law redefined *astoi*, shifting the meaning from an idea of "belonging to us" to "belonging by descent" ("Becoming Citizens: Some Notes on the Semantics of 'Citizen' in Archaic Greece and Classical Athens," *Klio* 87 [2005]: 18, 20). For the role of women's bodies in securing the boundaries constitutive of the nation-state, see N. Yuval-Davis and F. Anthias, *Woman-Nation-State* (New York: St. Martin's Press, 1989).

33. For the Periclean law and the gender system, see Osborne, "Law and the Representation of Women in Athens"; Leader, "In Death not Divided"; and Lape, "Solon and the Institution of the Democratic Family Form." In the fourth century, the Athenians passed additional laws that underline the interconnections between marriage, female sexuality, and citizenship. See [Dem.] 59.16, 65 with Kapparis, *Apollodorus*.

34. Cohen, *Law, Sexuality, and Society*, 102 with n. 91.

35. For the self-help punishments that could be inflicted on *moichoi* caught in the act, see [Dem.] 59.66, Ar. *Nub.* 1083; C. Carey, "The Return of the Radish or Just When You Thought it Was Safe to Go Back into the Kitchen," *Liverpool Classical Monthly* 18 (1993): 53–55; K. Kapparis, "Humiliating the Adulterer: The Law and the Practice in Classical Athens," *Revue internationale des droits de l'antiquité* 43 (1996): 63–77.

36. M. Skinner, *Sexuality in Greek and Roman Culture* (Oxford: Blackwell, 2005), 197.

37. For female consent to sex in Athenian law, see Lape, "Democratic Ideology and the Poetics of Rape in Menander's Comedy"; Omitowoju, *Rape and the Politics of Consent*; R. Omitowoju, "Regulating Rape: Soap Operas and Self-Interest in the Athenian Courts," in *Rape in Antiquity: Sexual Violence in the Greek and Roman Worlds*, ed. S. Deacy and K. F. Pierce (London: Duckworth, 2002). Sommerstein underlines that it is not a woman's lack of consent to sex that qualifies an encounter as illicit but rather precisely the fact that a woman presumes to consent to nonmarital sexual relations ("Rape and Consent in Athenian Tragedy," in *Dionysalexandros: Essays on Aeschylus and His Fellow Tragedians in Honour of Alexander F. Garvie*, ed. D. L. Cairns and V. Liapis [Swansea: Classical Press of Wales, 2006]). See further Cole, "Greek Sanctions against Sexual Assault," and Glazebrook, "Prostituting Female Kin."

38. For *moicheia* and rape in Athenian law, see Cole, "Greek Sanctions against Sexual Assault"; Carey, "Rape and Adultery in Athenian Law"; Omitowoju, *Rape and the Politics of Consent*; Omitowoju, "Regulating Rape"; *contra* E. Harris," "Did the Athenians Regard Seduction as a Worse Crime Than Rape?," *Classical Quarterly* 40 (1990): 370–77.

39. See C. Vatin, *Recherches sur le mariage et la condition de la femme mariée à l'époque hellénistique* (Paris: E. de Boccard, 1970), 42–43; A. Carson, "Putting Her in Her Place: Woman, Dirt, and Desire," in *Before Sexuality: The Construction of Erotic Experience in the Ancient Greek World*, ed. D. M. Halperin, J. J. Winkler, and F. I. Zeitlin (Princeton, NJ: Princeton University Press, 1990).

40. Ar. *Thesm.* 339–45, Lys. 1, Xenarchus fragment 4 K-A; see further D. Cohen, "The Social Context of Adultery at Athens," in *Nomos: Essays in Athenian Law, Politics, and Society*, ed. P. Cartledge, P. Millett, and S. Todd (Cambridge: Cambridge University Press, 1990); J. Roy, "An Alternative Sexual Morality for Classical Athens," *Greece and Rome* 44 (1997): 11–22.

41. For the application of ethnic, polis, and political identities to women in the case of Athens, see N. Loraux, *The Children of Athena: Athenian Ideas about Citizenship and the Division between the Sexes* (Princeton, NJ: Princeton University Press, 1993) with the criticism and qualifications of Blok, "Becoming Citizens." For the construction of women as sexual beings in material culture, see A. F. Stewart, *Art, Desire, and the Body in Ancient Greece* (Cambridge: Cambridge University Press, 1997), 171–81; D. H. Garrison, *Sexual Culture in Ancient Greece* (Norman: University of Oklahoma Press, 2000). For gender and kinship accounting for more of a woman's identity than a man's, see J. F. Collier and S. J. Yanagisako, "Toward a Unified Analysis of Gender and Kinship," in *Gender and Kinship: Essays toward a Unified Analysis*, ed. J. F. Collier and S. J. Yanagisako (Stanford, CA: Stanford University Press, 1987).

42. M. Golden, *Children and Childhood in Classical Athens* (Baltimore: Johns Hopkins University Press, 1990), 122, 136; but see also W. Ingalls, "*Paida nean malista*: When Did Athenian Girls Really Marry?," *Mouseion* 1 (2001): 17–29.

43. For Hippocratic gynecology, see A. E. Hanson, "The Medical Writers' Woman," in Halperin, Winkler, and Zeitlin, *Before Sexuality*; A. E. Hanson, "Conception, Gestation, and the Origin of Female Nature in the Corpus Hippocraticum," *Helios* 19 (1992): 31–71; G. Sissa, "Maidenhood without Maidenhead: The Female Body in Ancient Greece," trans. R. Lamberton, in Halperin, Winkler, and Zeitlin, *Before Sexuality*; L. Dean-Jones, *Women's Bodies in Classical Greek Science* (Oxford: Oxford University Press, 1994); N. Demand, *Birth, Death, and Motherhood in Classical Greece* (Baltimore: Johns Hopkins University Press, 1994); H. King, *Hippocrates' Woman: Reading the Female Body in Ancient Greece* (London: Routledge, 1998); S. G. Cole, *Landscapes, Gender, and Ritual Space* (Berkeley: University of California Press, 2004). For the cultural construct of women as belonging to their own gender species, see Loraux, *The Children of Athena*; King, *Hippocrates' Woman*.

44. Although the Hippocratic doctors were itinerant, some did visit Athens. See N. Demand, "Women and Slaves as Hippocratic Patients," in *Women and Slaves in Greco-Roman Culture: Differential Equations*, ed. S. Joshel and S. Murnaghan (London: Routledge, 1998), 72.

45. Ogden, *Polygamy, Prostitutes and Death*.

46. J. R. Clarke, *Looking at Lovemaking: Constructions of Sexuality in Roman Art 100 B.C.–A.D. 250* (Berkeley: University of California Press, 1998), 22.

47. See, for example, B. S. Thornton, *Eros: The Myth of Ancient Greek Sexuality* (Boulder, CO: Westview Press, 1997), 174.

48. For Athenian autochthony, see N. Loraux, *The Invention of Athens: The Funeral Oration in the Classical City* (Cambridge, MA: Harvard University Press, 1986); Loraux, *The Children of Athena*; N. Loraux, *Born of the Earth: Myth and Politics in Athens* (Ithaca, NY: Cornell University Press, 2000); V. Rosivach, "Autochthony and the Athenians," *Classical Quarterly* 37 (1987): 294–306; Ogden, *Greek Bastardy*; C. Dougherty, "Democratic Contradictions and the Synoptic Illusions of Euripides' Ion," in *Dêmokratia: A Conversation on Democracies, Ancient and Modern*, ed. J. Ober and C. Hedrick (Princeton, NJ: Princeton University Press, 1996); J. M. Hall, *Ethnic Identity in Greek Antiquity* (Cambridge: Cambridge University Press, 1997); H. A. Shapiro, "Autochthony and the Visual Arts in Fifth-century Athens," in *Democracy, Empire, and the Arts in Fifth-century Athens*, ed. D. Boedeker and K. Raaflaub (Cambridge, MA: Harvard University Press, 1998); S. Gotteland, "L' origine des cités grecques dans les discours athéniens," in *Origines Gentium*, ed. V. Fromentin and S. Gotteland (Paris: Diffusion de Boccard, 2001); M. Detienne, *Être autochtone: du pur Athénien au Français raciné* (Paris: Seuil, 2003).

49. For Xuthus' foreign status, see 290, 590, 607, 813.

50. For this point, see Loraux, *The Children of Athena*. See also Dougherty, "Democratic Contradictions and the Synoptic Illusions of Euripides' Ion" and Hall, *Ethnic Identity in Greek Antiquity*, 56.

51. See F. I. Zeitlin, *Playing the Other: Gender and Society in Classical Greek Literature* (Chicago: University of Chicago Press, 1996), 293 with n. 20.

52. See *Ion* 670–2. See further G. B. Walsh, "The Rhetoric of Birthright and Race in Euripides' Ion," *Hermes* 106 (1978): 301–15; Loraux, *The Children of Athena*; Lape, "Solon and the Institution of the Democratic Family Form."

53. For the general theme of rape and Roman foundation myths, see J. Hemker, "Rape and the Founding of Rome," *Helios* 12 (1985): 41–47; S. Joshel, "The Body Female and the Body Politic: Livia's Lucretia and Verginia," in Richlin, *Pornography and Representation in Greece and Rome*.

54. For the rape of Lucretia, see S. N. Phillipides, "Narrative Strategies and Ideology in Livy's 'Rape of Lucretia,'" *Helios* 10 (1983): 113–19; D. Konstan, "Ideology and Narrative in Livy, Book 1," *Classical Antiquity* 5 (1986): 197–215; P. K. Joplin, "Ritual Work on Human Flesh: Livy's Lucretia and the Rape of the Body Politic," *Helios* 17 (1990): 51–70; Joshel, "The Body Female and the Body Politic"; R. A. Bauman, "The Rape of Lucretia," *Latomus* 52 (1993): 550–56; T. J. Moore, "Morality as History and Livy's Wronged Women," *Eranos* 91 (1993): 38–73; J. A. Arieti, "Rape and Livy's View of Roman History," in *Rape in Antiquity: Sexual Violence in the Greek and Roman Worlds*, edited by S. Deacy and K. F. Pierce (London: Duckworth, 1997); J. Claassen, "The Familiar Other: The Pivotal Role of Women in Livy's Narrative of Political Development in Early Rome," *Acta Classica* 16 (1998): 71–103.

55. For lust (*libido*) as one of the unjust ruler's defining characteristics in Roman political rhetoric and thought, see Cic. *Verr.* 1.14, 2.4.116, *Rep.* 2.45; R. Dunkle, "The

Greek Tyrant and Roman Political Invective of the Late Republic," *Transactions of the American Philological Association* 98 (1967): 151–71.

56. Boehm's concept of a reverse dominance hierarchy is discussed previously (Boehm, *Hierarchy in the Forest*).

57. For the rape of the Sabine women, see Livy 1. 9–13, Plut. *Rom.* 20, Dion. Hal. *Ant. Rom.* 2.30–47, Ovid, *Ars am.* 1.101–32, Cic. *Rep.* 2.12–14; Hemker, "Rape and the Founding of Rome"; G. B. Miles, "The First Roman Marriage and the Theft of the Sabine Women," in *Innovations of Antiquity*, ed. R. Hexter and D. Selden (New York: Routledge, 1992); R. Brown, "Livy's Sabine Women and the Ideal of Concordia," *Transactions of the American Philological Association* 125 (1995): 291–319; M. Beard, "The Erotics of Rape: Livy, Ovid and the Sabine Women," in *Female Networks and the Public Sphere in Roman Society*, ed. P. Setälä and L. Savunen (Rome: Institutum Romanum Finlandiae, 1999); R. Langlands, *Sexual Morality in Ancient Rome* (Cambridge: Cambridge University Press, 2006).

58. For the foundation of marriage in Athenian myth, see Schol. Ar. *Plut.* 773, Ath. 13.555d; S. Pembroke, "Women in Charge: The Function of Alternatives in Early Greek Tradition and the Ancient Idea of Matriarchy," *Journal of the Warburg and Courtauld Institutes* 30 (1967): 1–35; Zeitlin, *Playing the Other*, 115–16.

59. *Off.* 1.54.

60. For the definition of *conubium*, see Ulp. *Topics* 5.3.

61. See Ulp. *Topics* 5.8; D. Cherry, "The Minician Law: Marriage and the Roman Citizenship," *Phoenix* 44 (1990): 245. For the provisions of the Minician law specifying that children born from parents lacking *conubium* would take the status of the inferior parent, see Cherry, "The Minician Law," 250–51.

62. Slaves did, however, live in long-term relationships (when possible) and employed the language of marriage to describe these relationships; see B. Rawson, "Roman Concubinage and Other *de facto* Marriages," *Transactions of the American Philological Association* 104 (1974): 279–305; S. Treggiari, *"Concubinae,"* *Papers of the British School at Rome* 49 (1981): 59–81; P.R.C. Weaver, "The Status of Children in Mixed Marriages," in *The Family in Ancient Rome: New Perspectives*, ed. B. Rawson (Sydney: Croom Helm, 1986); K. Bradley, *Slaves and Masters in the Roman Empire: A Study in Social Control* (New York: Oxford University Press, 1987).

63. See further Treggiari, *Roman Marriage*, 229–61; S. Dixon, "The Sentimental Ideal of the Roman Family," in *Marriage, Divorce, and Children in Ancient Rome,* ed. B. Rawson (Oxford: Clarendon Press, 1991). For possible changes in the importance of conjugal life as a source of self-identity during the empire, see P. Veyne, "La famille et l'amour sous le haut-empire romain," *Annales (ESC)* 33 (1978): 35–63; M. Foucault, *The Care of the Self*, trans. R. Hurley (New York: Vintage Books, 1988); with the criticisms of D. Cohen and R. Saller, "Foucault on Sexuality in Greco-Roman Antiquity," in *Foucault and the Writing of History*, ed. J. Goldstein (Oxford: Blackwell, 1994).

64. Treggiari, *Roman Marriage*, 11–13, 83–124; M. Corbier, "Constructing Kinship in Rome: Marriage and Divorce, Filiation and Adoption," in *The Family in Italy*

from Antiquity to the Present, ed. D. L. Kertzer and R. P. Saller (New Haven, CT: Yale University Press, 1991), 127–30. Marriage choice was also constrained by provisions against incest (Roman practice is more restrictive in this regard than Athenian).

65. See M. Myerowitz, "The Domestication of Desire: Ovid's *Parva Tabella* and the Theater of Love," in *Pornography and Representation in Greece and Rome*, ed. A. Richlin (New York: Oxford University Press, 1992); Skinner, *Sexuality in Greek and Roman Culture*, 262–63; Clarke, *Looking at Lovemaking*; and Clarke, this volume, chapter 9.

66. For marriage in early Rome, see Treggiari, *Roman Marriage*, 16–34.

67. Treggiari, *Roman Marriage*, 54.

68. S. B. Pomeroy, *Goddesses, Whores, Wives, and Slaves: Women in Classical Antiquity* (New York: Schocken Books, 1975), 157. On the meaning of *pater familias*, see R. P. Saller, "*Pater Familias, Mater Familias* and the Gendered Semantics of the Roman Household," *Classical Philology* 94 (1999): 182–97.

69. See Gaius, *Institutes* 1.55.

70. For *patria potestas*, see J. Crook, "*Patria potestas*," *Classical Quarterly* 17 (1967): 113–22; R. P. Saller, "*Patria Potestas* and the Stereotype of the Roman Family," *Continuity and Change* 1 (1986): 7–22; R. P. Saller, "Corporal Punishment, Authority, and Obedience in the Roman Household," in *Marriage, Divorce, and Children in Ancient Rome*, ed. B. Rawson (Oxford: Oxford University Press, 1991); R. P. Saller, *Patriarchy, Property, and Death in the Roman Family* (Cambridge: Cambridge University Press, 1994), 114–30; Saller, "*Pater Familias, Mater Familias* and the Gendered Semantics of the Roman Household"; J. F. Gardner, *Being a Roman Citizen* (London: Routledge, 1993), 52–55, 68–69, 71–72. For the rights of the *pater familias* over his children's marriages, see Treggiari, *Roman Marriage*, 170–76, 459–61.

71. Saller, *Patriarchy, Property, and Death*, for example, deemphasizes the influence of *patria potestas* on the affective character of the Roman family. For a critique of this revisionist view, see E. Cantarella, "Marriage and Sexuality in Republican Rome: A Roman Conjugal Love Story," in *The Sleep of Reason: Erotic Experience and Sexual Ethics in Ancient Greece and Rome*, ed. M. C. Nussbaum and J. Sihvola (Chicago: University of Chicago Press, 2002), 272.

72. *Pudicitia* (chastity) was an appropriate virtue for virgins and married women, see Langlands, *Sexual Morality in Ancient Rome*.

73. B. Severy, *Augustus and the Family at the Birth of the Roman Empire* (New York: Routledge, 2003), 39. See also T. Cornell, "Some Observations on the *crimen incesti*," *Le délit religieux dans la cité antique*, Collection de l'École française de Rome 48 (1981): 27–31; C. Edwards, *The Politics of Immorality in Ancient Rome* (Cambridge: Cambridge University Press, 1993), 44.

74. E. Stehle, "Venus, Cybele, and the Sabine Women: The Roman Construction of Female Sexuality," *Helios* 16 (1989): 143–64; Edwards, *The Politics of Immorality*.

75. See Livy 1.58, 3.42–58, 10.31.9, with Konstan, "Ideology and Narrative in Livy, Book 1"; Joshel, "The Body Female and the Body Politic"; Moore, "Morality as

History and Livy's Wronged Women"; Arieti, "Rape and Livy's View of Roman History"; Langlands, *Sexual Morality in Ancient Rome*. For the importance of female chastity, see Cic. *Scaur.* fr. 8, *Prov. cons.* 6.

76. See S. Joshel, "Female Desire and the Discourse of Empire: Tacitus' Messalina," *Signs* 21 (1995): 70.

77. See A. Richlin, ed., *Pornography and Representation in Greece and Rome* (New York: Oxford University Press, 1992), 164–209.

78. See A. Richlin, "Approaches to the Sources on Adultery at Rome," *Women's Studies* 8 (1981): 225–50; S. Dixon, *Reading Roman Women: Sources, Genres, and Real Life* (London: Duckworth, 2001).

79. For debate about the age of women's marriage at Rome, see K. Hopkins, "Contraception in the Roman Empire," *Comparative Studies in Society and History* 8 (1965): 124–51; B. Shaw, "The Age of Roman Girls at Marriage: Some Reconsiderations," *Journal of Roman Studies* 77 (1987): 30–46; A. A. Lelis, W. A. Percy, and B. C. Verstraete, *The Age of Marriage in Ancient Rome* (Lewiston, NY: Edwin Mellen Press, 2003).

80. Treggiari, *Roman Marriage*, 105, 234. The importance of the bride's virginity is a running theme in the Elder Seneca's *Controversiae* (1.2.5, 1.2.8, 9.1.1). Characters in Roman New Comedy also emphasize the importance of a woman's *pudicitia* as a qualification for marriage; it is unclear, however, whether this entails physical virginity, see Plaut. *Amph.* 839, *Aul.* 239, Ter. *Ad.* 345–6. For virginity in the Greek novel, see S. Goldhill, *Foucault's Virginity: Ancient Erotic Fiction and the History of Sexuality (The Stanford Memorial Lectures)* (Cambridge: Cambridge University Press, 1995).

81. Sissa, "Maidenhood without Maidenhead," 358.

82. D. Konstan, "Premarital Sex, Illegitimacy, and Male Anxiety in Menander and Athens," in *Athenian Identity and Civic Ideology*, ed. A. Scafuro and A. Boegehold (Baltimore: Johns Hopkins University Press, 1994).

83. *Gyn.* 1.7.30–2; O. Temkin, *Soranus' Gynecology* (Baltimore: Johns Hopkins University Press, 1956). For gynecology and women's health in Rome, see A. Rousselle, *Porneia: On Desire and the Body in Antiquity*, trans. F. Pheasant (Oxford: Blackwell, 1988), 24–46; R. Flemming, *Medicine and the Making of Roman Women: Gender, Nature, and Authority from Celsus to Galen* (Oxford: Oxford University Press, 2000).

84. *Gyn.* 1.8, 33, 60.

85. For Soranus' gender ideology as deeply conservative, see Flemming, *Medicine and the Making of Roman Women*, 238.

86. There is a large literature on the marriage law (*lex Julia de maritandis ordinibus*) and the *lex Papia Poppaea* of 9 A.D. The following works offer useful introductions to the law and critical issues: P. Csillag, *The Augustan Laws on Family Relations* (Budapest: Akademiai Kiado, 1976); A. Wallace-Hadrill, "Family and Inheritance in the Augustan Marriage Laws," *Proceedings of the Cambridge Philological Society* 27 (1981): 58–80; Treggiari, *Roman Marriage*, 60–80; T.A.J. McGinn, *Prostitution, Sexuality, and the Law in Ancient Rome* (New York: Oxford University Press, 1998): 70–104.

87. For the Roman aristocracy's failure to reproduce itself, see K. Hopkins, *Death and Renewal* (Cambridge: Cambridge University Press, 1983).

88. See further Wallace-Hadrill, "Family and Inheritance in the Augustan Marriage Laws"; McGinn, *Prostitution, Sexuality, and the Law*, 72–74.

89. On the new status of the *mater familias* created and implied in Augustus's legislation, see McGinn, *Prostitution, Sexuality, and the Law*, 153–56. For this term, see Saller, "*Pater Familias, Mater Familias* and the Gendered Semantics of the Roman Household."

90. See Gaius, *Institutes* 1.144–5. On the *ius liberorum*, see further McGinn, *Prostitution, Sexuality, and the Law*, 75–78.

91. On the effects of Augustus's social legislation on the traditional gender ideology, see L. C. Ruggini, "Juridical Status and the Historical Role of Women in Roman Patriarchal Society," *Klio* 71 (1989): 604–19; T.A.J. McGinn, "The Augustan Marriage Legislation and Social Practice: Elite Endogamy versus Male 'Marrying Down,'" in *Speculum Iuris: Roman Law as a Reflection of Social and Economic Life in Antiquity*, ed. J. J. Aubert and B. Sirks (Ann Arbor: University of Michigan Press, 2002); Severy, *Augustus and the Family*, 52–56; K. Milner, *Gender, Domesticity and the Age of Augustus: Inventing Private Life* (Oxford: Oxford University Press, 2005), 151.

92. See T.A.J. McGinn, "Concubinage and the *Lex Iulia* on Adultery," *Transactions of the American Philological Association* 121 (1991): 335–75; Saller, "*Pater Familias, Mater Familias* and the Gendered Semantics of the Roman Household," 194.

93. E. Cantarella, *Bisexuality in the Ancient World* (New Haven, CT: Yale University Press, 1992), 220; C. A. Williams, *Roman Homosexuality: Ideologies of Masculinity in Classical Antiquity* (Oxford: Oxford University Press, 1999), 18. On Roman masculinity, see also Richlin, *Pornography and Representation*; J. N. Davidson, "Dover, Foucault and Greek Homosexuality: Penetration and the Truth of Sex," *Past and Present* 170 (2001): 28–29; F. Dupont and T. Eloi, *L'érotisme masculin dans la Rome antique* (Paris: Belin, 2001); Skinner, *Sexuality in Greek and Roman Culture*, 197.

94. For Augustus's blending of the political and paternal, see W. K. Lacey, "*Patria potestas*," in *The Family in Ancient Rome*, ed. B. Rawson (London: Croom Helm, 1986), 139; Severy, *Augustus and the Family*, 56.

95. On the role of marriage laws in stating and shaping national character, see N. Cott, "Giving Character to Our Whole Civil Polity: Marriage and the Public Order in the Late Nineteenth Century," in *U.S. History as Women's History*, ed. L. Kerber et al. (Chapel Hill: University of North Carolina Press, 1995); J. Stevens, *Reproducing the State* (Princeton, NJ: Princeton University Press, 1999).

96. On this restriction, see Treggiari, *Roman Marriage*, 63–64; McGinn, *Prostitution, Sexuality, and the Law*, 91–104.

97. On the restricted categories, see McGinn, *Prostitution, Sexuality, and the Law*, 72.

98. The law did not actually invalidate unions that contravened the new guidelines, see McGinn, *Prostitution, Sexuality, and the Law*, 83.

 99. For the adultery law (*lex Julia de adulteriis coercendis*), see Csillag, *The Augustan Laws*; D. Cohen, "Sexuality, Violence, and the Athenian Law of *hybris*," *Greece and Rome* 38 (1991): 171–88; E. Cantarella, "Homicides of Honor: The Development of Italian Adultery Law over Two Millennia," in *The Family in Italy from Antiquity to the Present*, ed. D. Kertzer and R. Saller (New Haven, CT: Yale University Press, 1991); Edwards, *The Politics of Immorality*; McGinn, *Prostitution, Sexuality, and the Law*; McGinn, "The Augustan Marriage Legislation."

100. For the offenses covered by the law, see Edwards, *The Politics of Immorality*, 37–42; McGinn, *Prostitution, Sexuality, and the Law*, 140–215. For *stuprum*, see E. Fantham, "*Stuprum*: Public Attitudes and Penalties for Sexual Offenses in Republican Rome," *Echos du monde classique/Classical Views* 10 (1991): 267–91.

101. See, for example, P. E. Corbett, *The Roman Law of Marriage* (Oxford: Oxford University Press, 1930), 139; Edwards, *The Politics of Immorality*; 38; McGinn, *Prostitution, Sexuality, and the Law*, 141.

102. See Treggiari, *Roman Marriage*, 275–77; McGinn, *Prostitution, Sexuality, and the Law*, 141–42; G. Puccini-Delbey, *La vie sexuelle à Rome* (Paris: Tallandier, 2007), 83–101.

103. See McGinn, *Prostitution, Sexuality, and the Law*, 203–5.

104. For this court and its history, see P. Garnsey, "Adultery Trials and the Survival of the *quaestiones* in the Severan Age," *Journal of Roman Studies* 57 (1967): 56–60; R. A. Bauman, "Some Remarks on the Structure and Survival of the *quaestio de adulteriis*," *Antichthon* 2 (1968): 68–93.

105. For the *leno-maritus*, see V. Tracy, "The *Leno-Maritus*," *Classical Journal* 72 (1976): 62–64.

106. On the toga of adulteresses, see Edwards, *The Politics of Immorality*, 40–41; McGinn, *Prostitution, Sexuality, and the Law*, 156–71; *contra* K. Olson, "*Matrona* and Whore: Clothing and Definition in Roman Antiquity," in *Prostitutes and Courtesans in the Ancient World*, ed. C. A. Faraone and L. K. McClure (Madison: University of Wisconsin Press, 2006). Respectable women convicted of premarital sexual behavior (*stuprum*) faced a much less severe monetary penalty; Rousselle, *Porneia*, 80.

107. See McGinn, "Concubinage and the *Lex Iulia* on Adultery"; McGinn, *Prostitution, Sexuality, and the Law*; R. Friedl, *Der Konkubinat im Kaiserzeitlichen Rom von Augustus bis Septimius* (Stuttgart: Franz Steiner, 1996).

108. For the motives behind concubinage, see Treggiari, "*Concubinae*"; R. P. Saller, "Slavery and the Roman Family," in *Classical Slavery*, ed. M. I. Finley (London: F. Cass, 1987), 74–76; McGinn, "Concubinage and the *Lex Iulia* on Adultery." Any children born of a concubine would be free but illegitimate and hence lacking rights of succession; on *liberi naturales*, see J. Plassard, *Le concubinat romain sous le haut empire* (Paris: Tenin, 1921), 92; Rawson, "Roman Concubinage"; Weaver, "The Status of Children in Mixed Marriages."

109. Papin. *Digest* 48.5.6.1.

110. Mart. 2.91, 8.31, 10.102, Juv. 6.76–81.

111. Edwards, *The Politics of Immorality*, 50 with note 55. As R. Syme puts it, "It is not easy to produce an authentic bastard anywhere" ("Bastards in the Roman

Aristocracy," *Proecedings of the American Philosophical Society* 104 [1960]: 324). See, however, Plut. *Cic.* 25, 26.6–7.

112. For this maxim of Roman law, see Corbier, "Constructing Kinship in Rome," 135.

113. See Severy, *Augustus and the Family*, 56.

114. See Sall. *Cat.* 25, Cic. *Cael.* 29, Tac. *Hist.* 1.2; Richlin, "Approaches to the Sources on Adultery at Rome"; Edwards, *The Politics of Immorality*, 34–47.

115. See further McGinn, "The Augustan Marriage Legislation."

116. See Cic. *Cael.* 31, 36, 38, 39, Pliny, *Ep.* 6.31.4–6, Juv. 6.76–81, 279, 331–2, Mart. 6.39, 8.31, Petr. *Sat.* 69.3, 75.11; Richlin, "Approaches to the Sources on Adultery at Rome"; Edwards, *The Politics of Immorality*, 43–44; J. Evans-Grubbs, "'Marriage More Shameful Than Adultery': Slave-Mistress Relationships, 'Mixed Marriages' and Late Roman Law," *Phoenix* 47 (1993): 125–26.

117. Pomeroy, *Goddesses, Whores, Wives, and Slaves*, 160.

118. Edwards, *The Politics of Immorality*, 53.

119. For adulterers as effeminate, see Edwards, *The Politics of Immorality*, 63–97; Dupont and Eloi, *L'érotisme masculin dans la Rome antique*.

120. See Tac. *Ann.* 4.3; Edwards, *The Politics of Immorality*, 47–48, 91.

121. See Richlin, *Pornography and Representation in Greece and Rome*, 81–104; Severy, *Augustus and the Family*.

122. For adultery as commonplace, see Sen. *Ben.* 3.16.3, Cic. *Cael.* 29.

123. See Edwards, *The Politics of Immorality*, 36.

124. T. Habinek, "The Invention of Sexuality in the World City of Rome," in *The Roman Cultural Revolution*, ed. T. Habinek and A. Schiesaro (Cambridge: Cambridge University Press, 1997), 29.

125. Tac. *Ann.* 2.84, Suet. *Tib.* 35; Richlin, "Approaches to the Sources on Adultery at Rome," 233; Habinek, "The Invention of Sexuality," 29.

126. Suetonius's reference to this incident (*Tib.* 35) indicates that many women were giving up the rank of *matrona* to work as prostitutes; see B. Rawson, "The Roman Family," in *The Family in Ancient Rome*, ed. B. Rawson (London: Croom Helm, 1986), 35.

127. For abortion as a consequence of adultery, see Sen. *Ben.* 3.16, Juv. 6.594–601; Edwards, *The Politics of Immorality*, 50.

128. See Hopkins, "Contraception in the Roman Empire"; J. Riddle, *Eve's Herbs: A History of Contraception and Abortion in the West* (Cambridge, MA: Harvard University Press, 1997), 45–46. Wealthy women may have also been able to buy safe sex in the form of eunuchs who were castrated after puberty, see Juv. 6.366–80, Mart. 6.67; A. B. Bosworth, "Vespasian and the Slave Trade," *Classical Quarterly* 52 (2002): 350–57.

129. K. L. Gaca argues that Musonius's thought derives from Pythagorean rather than Stoic philosophy (*The Making of Fornication: Eros, Ethics, and Political Reform in Greek Philosophy and Early Christianity* [Berkeley: University of California Press, 2003]).

130. Fragment 12, C. Lutz, "Musonius Rufus: The Roman Socrates," *Yale Classical Studies* 10 (1947): 84.

131. See Veyne, "La famille et l'amour sous le haut-empire romain"; Foucault, *The Care of the Self*, 112–32; P. Brown, *The Body and Society: Men, Women, and Sexual Renunciation in Early Christianity* (New York: Columbia University Press, 1988), 17–22.

132. Jer. *Ep.* 77.3, trans. E. Clark, "1990 Presidential Address: Sex, Shame, and Rhetoric: En-gendering Early Christian Ethics," *Journal of the American Academy of Religion* 59 (1991): 231.

133. J. Evans-Grubbs, *Law and the Family in Late Antiquity* (Oxford: Blackwell, 1995), 316. Brown attributes the double standard's continuity to the practice of slave-holding (*The Body and Society*, 22–23).

134. Brown, *The Body and Society*, 59–60, cf. E. Clark, "Antifamilial Tendencies in Ancient Christianity," *Journal of the History of Sexuality* 5 (1995): 356–80; E. Clark, *Reading Renunciation: Asceticism and Scripture in Early Christianity* (Princeton, NJ: Princeton University Press, 1999); Gaca, *The Making of Fornication*.

135. Brown, *The Body and Society*, 21–22; see also Clark, *Reading Renunciation*, 177–204 on strategies of defamiliarization in the synoptic gospels and early Christian writers.

136. See Stevens, *Reproducing the State*, 121–22.

137. Brown, *The Body and Society*, 98.

Chapter 3

Readers should note that this chapter was composed prior to the appearance of J. N. Davidson, *The Greeks and Greek Love* (London: Weidenfeld and Nicolson, 2007), and therefore does not engage the rich and expansive arguments presented in that work.

1. The most helpful modern works of scholarship on Greek male homosexuality are K. J. Dover, *Greek Homosexuality* (Cambridge, MA: Harvard University Press, 1978); F. Buffière, *Éros adolescent: la pédérastie dans la Grèce antique* (Paris: Belles Lettres, 1980), which has been underrated; B. Sergent, *Homosexuality in Greek Myth* (London: Athlone, 1987); D. M. Halperin, *One Hundred Years of Homosexuality and Other Essays on Greek Love* (New York: Routledge, 1990); J. N. Davidson, "Dover, Foucault and Greek Homosexuality: Penetration and the Truth of Sex," *Past and Present* 170 (2001): 3–51; J. N. Davidson, *The Greeks and Greek Love* (London: Weidenfeld and Nicolson, 2007); and T. K. Hubbard, ed., *Homosexuality in Greece and Rome: A Sourcebook of Basic Documents* (Berkeley: University of California Press, 2003), a substantial sourcebook by various hands.

2. M. H. Hansen and T. H. Nielsen, *An Inventory of Archaic and Classical Poleis* (Oxford: Oxford University Press, 2004).

3. Dover had done important work on Greek homosexuality as early as 1964, but, as Davidson ("Dover, Foucault and Greek Homosexuality," 7–20) notes, revised his ideas radically in the meantime under the influence of G. Devereux, "Greek 'Pseudo-homosexuality' and the Greek Miracle," *Symbolae Osloenses* 42 (1967): 69–92.

4. This summary follows closely that developed at D. Ogden, "Homosexuality and War-fare in Ancient Greece," in *Battle in Antiquity*, ed. A. B. Lloyd (London: Classical Press of Wales and Duckworth, 1996), 107–9. Readers are invited to compare these pages with B. A. Sparkes, "Sex in Classical Athens," in *Greek Civilisation: An Intro-duction*, ed. B. A. Sparkes (Oxford: Blackwell, 1998): 255–57.

5. Typical age-band for *erōmenoi*: Buffière, *Éros adolescent*, 566, 606, 609–11; and E. Cantarella, *Bisexuality in the Ancient World* (New Haven, CT: Yale University Press, 1992), 36–44. The key statement of the notion of a progression through sexual phases strongly tied to age is that of Devereux, Greek 'Pseudo-homosexuality.'" Hunting gifts: G. Koch-Harnack, *Knabenliebe und Tiergeschenke: ihre Bedeutung im päderastischen Erziehungssystem Athens* (Berlin: Gebr. Mann, 1983). The importance of gifts in return for favors: Buffière, *Éros adolescent*, 631–34. Zero-sum game: this way of understand-ing pederastic sexual relations is vigorously argued for by D. Cohen (*Law, Sexuality, and Society: The Enforcement of Morals in Classical Athens* [Cambridge: Cambridge University Press, 1991], 171–202). Help in becoming an adult member of the com-munity: this particular aspect of Greek pederasty encourages many to derive it from an "initiation rite"; see the debates in J. N. Bremmer, "An Enigmatic Indo-European Rite: Pederasty," *Arethusa* 13 (1980): 279–98; H. Patzer, *Die griechische Knabenliebe* (Wiesbaden: F. Steiner, 1982); Sergent, *Homosexuality in Greek Myth*; K. J. Dover, "Greek Homosexuality and Initiation," in *The Greeks and Their Legacy*, ed. K. J. Dover (Oxford: Oxford University Press, 1988); W. A. Percy III, *Pederasty and Peda-gogy in Archaic Greece* (Urbana: University of Illinois Press, 1996); T. K. Hubbard, ed., *Greek Love Reconsidered* (New York: W. Hamilton, 2000); T. F. Scanlon, "The Dispersion of Pederasty and the Athletic Revolution in Sixth-century BC Greece," in *Same-Sex Desire and Love in Greco-Roman Antiquity and in the Classical Tradition of the West*, ed. B. C. Verstraete and V. Provencal (Binghamton: Haworth Press, 2005). Timarchus: Aeschines 1.157 accuses him of having been a prostitute man and boy; cf. Dover, *Greek Homosexuality*, 29, 39; N.R.E. Fisher, *Aeschines Against Timarchos* (Oxford: Oxford University Press, 2001), *ad loc.* The Sausage-seller at Aristophanes' *Knights* 1242 is also said to have earned his money by being buggered as an adult.

6. H. Mommsen, *Der Affecter* (Mainz: P. von Zabern, 1975); C. A. Hupperts, "Greek Love: Homosexuality or Pederasty? Greek Love in Black-figure Vase Painting," in *Proceedings of the 3rd Symposium on Ancient Greek and Related Pottery*, ed. J. Chris-tiansen et al. (Copenhagen: Nationalmuseet, Ny Carlsberg Glyptotek, Thorvaldsens Museum, 1988); M. Golden, "Thirteen Years of Homosexuality (and Other Recent Work on Sex, Gender and the Body in Ancient Greece)," *Echos du monde classique/Classical Views* 10 (1991): 337; Hubbard, *Homosexuality in Greece and Rome*, 5–6.

7. Pl. *Prot.* 315e, *Symp.* passim, Plut. *Mor.* 770c; cf. also Ael. *VH* 13.5. See Buffière, *Éros adolescent*, 613; Golden, "Thirteen Years of Homosexuality," 337.

8. Davidson, "Dover, Foucault and Greek Homosexuality." This article returns in part to ideas initially developed but then largely rejected by Dover in 1964, but more importantly builds on the wider understanding of classical Athenian atti-tudes to the desires and to consumption developed in J. N. Davidson, *Courtesans and Fishcakes: The Consuming Passions of Classical Athens* (New York: Fontana, 1997). See also Hubbard, *Homosexuality in Greece and Rome*, 10–14.

9. Dover, *Greek Homosexuality,* 98–100, with qualification at G. Vlastos, "Socratic Irony," *Classical Quarterly* 37 (1987): 96. See also Buffière, *Éros adolescent,* 123–48; Golden, "Thirteen Years of Homosexuality," 332; R. F. Sutton, "Pornography and Persuasion on Attic Pottery," in *Pornography and Representation in Greece and Rome,* ed. A. Richlin (New York: Oxford University Press, 1992), 13; H. A. Shapiro, "Eros in Love: Pederasty and Pornography in Greece," in Richlin, *Pornography and Representation,* 57.

10. Notably Davidson, *Courtesans and Fishcakes.* For *akrasia* see primarily Arist. *NE* 1145a-1152a, with J. J. Walsh, *Aristotle's Concept of Moral Weakness* (New York: Columbia University Press, 1964); M. Foucault, *The History of Sexuality: vol. 2, The Use of Pleasure,* trans. Robert Hurley (Harmondsworth: Viking, 1985), part 1 chapter 3; and G. S. Shrimpton, *Theopompus the Historian* (Montreal: McGill-Queen's University Press, 1991), 136–56.

11. On this passage compare, for example, Dover, *Greek Homosexuality,* 135; Buffière, *Éros adolescent,* 17; G. F. Pinney, "For the Heroes Are at Hand," *Journal of Hellenic Studies* 104 (1984): 181–83; Ogden, "Homosexuality and Warfare," 111, 133; Davidson, "Dover, Foucault and Greek Homosexuality," 25, 48.

12. [Arist.] *Phgn.* 808a7–11 and 809b8. For older views on the *kinaidos* see Dover, *Greek Homosexuality,* 75; Buffière, *Éros adolescent,* 435–49, 602, 617; J. J. Winkler, *The Constraints of Desire* (London: Routledge, 1990), 45–47, 50–54, 67, and index s.v; Halperin, *One Hundred Years of Homosexuality,* 33; M. W. Gleason, "The Semiotics of Gender: Physiognomy and Self-fashioning in the Second Century C.E.," in *Before Sexuality,* ed. D. M. Halperin et al. (Princeton, NJ: Princeton University Press, 1990), 396–99.

13. Davidson, "Dover, Foucault and Greek Homosexuality," 20–28.

14. Dover, *Greek Homosexuality,* 105–6; Ogden, "Homosexuality and Warfare," 163.

15. The primary contention of Ogden, "Homosexuality and Warfare."

16. Plut. *Pel.* 18–19. For the excavation of the tumulus of the Sacred Band at Chaeronea, see W. K. Pritchett, "Observations on Chaeronea," *American Journal of Archaeology* 62 (1958): 307–11. For a recent discussion, D. Leitao, "The Legend of the Sacred Band," in *The Sleep of Reason: Erotic Experience and Sexual Ethics in Ancient Greece and Rome,* ed. M. Nussbaum and J. Sihvola (Chicago: University of Chicago Press, 2002).

17. Phaedimus, *Anth. Pal.* 13.22; cf. Buffière, *Éros adolescent,* 99–100.

18. Diod. Sic. 12.70.1. See the discussion at Ogden, "Homosexuality and Warfare," 114–15. K. J. Dover ("The Date of Plato's *Symposium,*" *Phronesis* 10 [1965]: 13) perhaps therefore makes an unwarranted claim in his attempts to date the *Symposium* in asserting, "until 378 nothing had been done to justify dissemination of a belief that any Theban or Boeotian force was deliberately organised on an erotic principle." It may be relevant that [Dem.] 61 praises a desired boy for his success in an obscure sport in which one leaped from a chariot, a sport Harpocration (s.v. *apobatēs*) associates with Boeotia and Attica. I thank the editors for this reference.

19. Xen. *Symp* 8.34 (*erastai* and *erōmenoi*), *Hell.* 7.4.13, 16, 31 (elite force), *Lac.* 2.12 (Boeotian comparison), Pl. *Symp.* 182b. cf. Buffière, *Éros adolescent,* 89–91.

20. Ath. 13.565e, 609e (incorporating Theophr. F111 Wimmer). cf. Buffière, *Éros adolescent*, 90–91; Ogden, "Homosexuality and Warfare," 115.

21. Strabo 10.4.21, incorporating Ephorus *FGH* 70 F149. For these Cretan customs as "initiatory" see Bremmer, "An Enigmatic Indo-European Rite"; Sergent, *Homosexuality in Greek Myth, passim* esp. 7–39; Dover, "Greek Homosexuality and Initiation," 115–34; Cantarella, *Bisexuality in the Ancient World*, 3–8.

22. Xen. *Symp.* 8.35 (the principle; the text is misinterpreted by P. Cartledge, "The Politics of Spartan Pederasty," *Proceedings of the Cambridge Philological Society* 27 [1981]: 22), *Hell.* 4.8.39 (Anaxibius), Ath. 13.561ef.

23. Plut. *Lyc.* 17–18.

24. E. Bethe, "Die dorische Knabenliebe," *Rheinisches Museum* 62 (1907): 438–75. Cf. K. J. Dover, "Eros and nomos," *Bulletin of the Institute of Classical Studies* 11 (1964): 42 n. 35; Dover, *Greek Homosexuality*, 189 n. 12, 193, 202; Buffière, *Éros adolescent*, 56–57, 70, with n. 20; Bremmer, "An Enigmatic Indo-European Rite," 280–83, 293; Cartledge, "The Politics of Spartan Pederasty," 23–25, 31 n. 18.

25. Pl. *Leg.* 636b, 836ac. *Kysolakōn*: Hesychius s.v. An excess of idealism leads Xen. *Lac.* 2.13, and, in his wake, the Ps.-Plutarchan text at *Moralia* 237bc, to affirm the chastity of homosexual relationships at Sparta. See Dover, *Greek Homosexuality*, 187–89, 194; Buffière, *Éros adolescent*, 69–73; Bremmer, "An Enigmatic Indo-European Rite," 283; Cartledge, "The Politics of Spartan Pederasty," 19–20.

26. See Ogden, "Homosexuality and Warfare," 118–19, 139–47. For the Sambia more generally, G. H. Herdt, *Guardians of the Flutes: Images of Masculinity*, 2nd ed. (New York: McGraw-Hill, 1987).

27. For female homosexuality in the Greek world, see B. J. Brooten, *Love between Women: Early Christian Responses to Female Homoeroticism* (Chicago: University of Chicago Press, 1996), 29–186, and the essays collected in N. S. Rabinowitz and L. Auanger, eds., *Among Women: From the Homosocial to the Homoerotic in the Ancient World* (Austin: University of Texas Press, 2002). Brave but, alas, doomed attempts to find sex acts between women in the iconography are mounted by M. F. Kilmer, *Greek Erotica on Attic Red-Figure Vases* (London: Duckworth, 1993), 26–30, and N. S. Rabinowitz, "Excavating Women's Homoeroticism in Ancient Greece," in Rabinowitz and Auanger, *Among Women*. The closest we come is a red-figure vase from Tarquinia (Kilmer's R207), on which one *hetaira* perfumes the pubis of another.

28. Plut. *Lyc.* 18; cf. S. B. Pomeroy, *Spartan Women* (Oxford: Oxford University Press, 2002), 29. The Spartans were prepared to share sexual partners even, surprisingly, in the context of childmaking: see the evidence collected at D. Ogden, *Greek Bastardy in the Classical and Hellenistic Periods* (Oxford: Oxford University Press, 1996), 238–45.

29. Scholiast Theocritus 12, argument, incorporating Alcman F34 Page/Campbell.

30. *Suda* s.v. *Alkman*.

31. Alcman F1 lines 73–7 Page/Campbell. English readers may most conveniently access the fragments of Alcman through D. A. Campbell, *Greek Lyric*, vol. 2 (Cambridge, MA: Harvard University Press, Loeb Classical Library, 1988). See, in

general, C. Calame, *Choruses of Young Women in Ancient Greece* (Lanham, MD: Rowman and Littlefield, 1997).

32. Alcman F3 lines 61–85.
33. The best general introduction to Sappho's work and world remains A. P. Burnett, *Three Archaic Poets: Archilochus, Alcaeus, Sappho* (London: Duckworth, 1983). Much of the more recent writing on Sappho is unimpressive. See, however, Brooten, *Love between Women*, 29–41; J. M. Snyder, *Lesbian Desire in the Lyrics of Sappho* (New York: Columbia University Press, 1997).
34. For fragments that seem to refer to Sappho's school and those of her rivals, see Sappho F57 (the mistress of a rival school?), F150 LP/Campbell (where it is referred to as a "house of the Muses"), F261 lines 7–11 *SLG* = 214B Campbell (Sappho teaches the noblest girls of Ionia). See A. L. Klinck, "'Sleeping in the Bosom of a Tender Companion': Homoerotic Attachments in Sappho," in Verstraete and Provencal, *Same-Sex Desire and Love*, superseding H. N. Parker, "Sappho Schoolmistress," *Transactions of the American Philological Association* 123 (1993): 309–51.
35. Philostr. *Imag.* 2.1, incorporating F185 LP/Campbell. cf. Demetr. *Eloc.* 132, who indicates that Sappho's poetry typically consisted of gardens of nymphs, wedding songs, and love affairs.
36. Sappho F1 LP/Campbell; cf. F2 for another Hymn to Aphrodite, in a typically Sapphic meadow context.
37. Sappho F94 LP/Campbell.
38. Sappho F23 LP/Campbell.
39. Sappho F126 LP/Campbell.
40. Sappho F213 LP/Campbell.
41. Sappho F44 (the wedding of Hector and Andromache), 104 (the wedding night separates the bride from her mother), 111 LP/Campbell (carpenters are bidden raise the roof of the wedding chamber high, no doubt, at one level, so that the bridegroom, encumbered with suitably huge erection, may enter).
42. Thus Sappho F44a (the story of Artemis' determination to remain a virgin), 105a (a virgin ripening like a sweet apple, not forgotten by the apple-pickers, but high on the tree beyond their reach), 107 (a girl laments that she must lose her virginity so soon), 114 LP/Campbell (a girl laments in responsion with the personified virginity that must leave her).
43. Sappho F31LP/Campbell; for the physical effects of love or desire, cf. FF 47, 131.
44. Sappho F16 LP/Campbell.
45. Sappho F99 LP/Campbell = Alcaeus F303a V.
46. Alcaeus F130 LP/Campbell.
47. Ath. 13.610a, incorporating Theoph. F112 Wimmer.
48. Anacreon F358 Page/Campbell.
49. Pl. *Symp.* 191e. For the meaning of *laikastria*, see D. Bain, "Six Greek Verbs of Sexual Congress (*binō, kinō, pugizō, lēkō, oiphō, laikazō*)," *Classical Quarterly* 41 (1991): 74–77.
50. Asclepiades, *Anth. Pal.* 5.207.
51. For Roman male homosexuality see above all S. Lilja, *Homosexuality in Republican and Augustan Rome* (Helsinki: Societas Scientiarum Fennica, 1983); Cantarella,

Bisexuality in the Ancient World; A. Richlin, ed., *Pornography and Representation in Greece and Rome* (New York: Oxford University Press, 1992); C. A. Williams, *Roman Homosexuality: Ideologies of Masculinity in Classical Antiquity* (Oxford: Oxford University Press, 1999); Hubbard, *Homosexuality in Greece and Rome*, 308–532; J. L. Butrica, "Some Myths and Anomalies in the Study of Roman Sexuality," in Verstraete and Provencal, *Same-Sex Desire and Love*.

52. For example, Polyb. 31.25.2–5, Ovid, *Met.* 10.78–219 (Orpheus's invention of pederasty). Compare R. MacMullen, "Roman Attitudes to Greek Love," *Historia* 31 (1982): 484–502 (with care); Williams, *Roman Homosexuality*, 64–72; Hubbard, *Homosexuality in Greece and Rome*, 16, 311–12.

53. Thus Lutatius Catulus F1 *FLP*, (paying tribute to Callimachus, *Anth. Pal.* 12.73), Cat. 24 (a harsher Roman take on Theognis's poems to Cyrnus), Virg. *Ecl.* 2 (a Theocritean pastoral), *Aen.* 5.293–344, 9.176–449 (the tale of Nisus and Euryalus, reminiscent of many Greek tales of loving couples in war).

54. Compare Davidson, "Dover, Foucault and Greek Homosexuality," 28; Hubbard, *Homosexuality in Greece and Rome*, 6–14.

55. Plaut. *Rud.* 1073–5, *Persa* 284–6, *Pseud.* 1177–82, *Cas.* 449–66, Polyb. 31.25.2–5, Sen. *Controv.* 4 preface 10, Musonius Rufus 12, Mart. 12.96, Stat. *Silv.* 2.6, Aul. Gell. *NA* 15.12.2; cf. also Cat. 56. Butrica ("Some Myths and Anomalies," 210–21) contends that freedmen, by contrast, were not obliged to offer sexual services to their former masters. Hubbard's attempt (*Homosexuality in Greece and Rome*, 13–14) to absolve Roman homosexuality in general of the charge of exploitation will convince few. If the concept of exploitation is to be held relevant to the ancient material, and is to be applied to it, then we cannot deny that slaves were indeed sexually exploited. That a slave might use sexual submission to achieve eventual freedom does not alter this.

56. *Discourses* 2.10.14–20.

57. Cass. Dio 62.6.4.

58. Livy 8.28. A similar story featuring Plotius and Veturius is sited in the years after 321 B.C. by Val. Max. 6.1.9. See Butrica, "Some Myths and Anomalies," 214–15.

59. Val. Max. 6.1.7; Cantarella, *Bisexuality in the Ancient World*, 111–14; Williams, *Roman Homosexuality*, 119–24; Butrica, "Some Myths and Anomalies," 213–14.

60. Plut. *Mor.* 288a.

61. Val. Max. 9.1.7–8.

62. Plaut. *Curc.* 482–4. cf. also, perhaps, Pomponius Bononiensis, *Prostitute* F1R.

63. Cf. Butrica, "Some Myths and Anomalies," 221.

64. For example, above all, Cat. 16; so too Cat. 15, 21.

65. *CIL* 11.6721.

66. Suet. *Iul.* 2, 49 (cf. 52), Cass. Dio 43.20.4; cf. Cat. 29, 57.

67. Cic. *Red. Sen.* 11, *Har. Resp.* 42, 59.

68. Cic. *Cat.* 2.8.

69. Suet. *Aug.* 68.

70. Suet. *Nero* 28–9.

71. Cass. Dio 80.13–14, SHA, *Elagabalus* 10.

72. For Priapus and Priapea see H. Herter, *De Priapo* (Giessen: A. Töpelmann, 1932) (an extensive reproduction of the testimonia for the god, with commentaries, and a catalogue of the statuary then known); V. Buchheit, *Studien zum Corpus Priapeorum* (Zetemata 28: Munich, 1962); B. Kytzler, *Carmina Priapea: Gedichte an den Gartengott* (Zürich: Artemis, 1978); W. H. Parker, *Priapea: Poems for a Phallic God* (London: Croom Helm, 1988); E. M. O'Connor, *Symbolum Salacitatis: A Study of the God Priapus as a Literary Character*, Studien zur klassischen Philologie, Band 40 (Frankfurt am Main: Lang, 1989); C. Goldberg, *Carmina Priapea: Einleitung, Übersetzung, Interpretation und Kommentar* (Heidelberg: Winter, 1992); Richlin, *Pornography and Representation*, 116–27; and Williams, *Roman Homosexuality*, 18, 21–22, 86–95. Parker, *Priapea*, 3 and 9–11, lists 37 from the *Greek Anthology*, 80 from the Latin *Corpus Priapeorum*, a further 23 in Latin and one in both Latin and Greek.

73. *Priap.* 13, 28, 35.

74. For Roman female homosexuality see in general Brooten, *Love between Women* (critiqued at D. M. Halperin, *How to Do the History of Homosexuality* [Chicago: University of Chicago Press, 2002], 48–80); J. P. Hallett, "Female Homoeroticism and the Denial of Roman Reality in Latin Literature," in *Roman Sexualities*, ed. J. P. Hallett and M. B. Skinner (Princeton, NJ: Princeton University Press, 1997); F. Mencacci, "Päderastie und lesbische Liebe: die Ursprünge zweier sexueller Verhaltensweisen und der Unterschied der Geschlechter in Rom," in *Rezeption und Identität: die kulturelle Auseinandersetzung Roms mit Griechenland als europäisches Paradigm*, ed. G. Vogt-Spira and B. Rommel (Stuttgart: F. Steiner, 1999); Butrica, "Some Myths and Anomalies," 238–62.

75. Hor. *Ep.* 1.19.28 = Sappho T3 Campbell.

76. Phaedrus 4.16 = no. 515b Perry.

77. Lucian, *Dial. Meret.* 5, with discussion at S. P. Haley, "Lucian's 'Leaena and Clonarium': Voyeurism or a Challenge to Assumptions," in Rabinowitz and Auanger, *Among Women*; and K. Gilhuly, "The Phallic Lesbian: Philosophy, Comedy, and Social Inversion in Lucian's *Dialogues of the Courtesans*," in *Prostitutes and Courtesans in the Ancient World*, ed. C. A. Faraone and L. K. McClure (Madison: University of Wisconsin Press, 2006); cf. also Sen. *Ep.* 95.21.

78. Ovid, *Met.* 9.669–797; cf. D. T. Pintabone, "Ovid's Iphis and Ianthe: When Girls Won't Be Girls," in Rabinowitz and Auanger, *Among Women*.

79. Mart. 7.67 and 70. The name Philaenis is also used as iconic for female homosexual desire at [Lucian] *Am.* 28. The editors put it to me that in making Philaenis a wrestler poem 67 may jokingly assimilate two kinds of "rubbing": sexual and athletic. Athletes rubbed themselves with oil; the Greek term *aleiptēs* (which does not appear in this text), "gymnastic trainer," literally means "rubber" or (better) "anointer."

80. Mart. 1.90. For homosexuality in Martial see H. P. Obermayer, *Martial und der Diskurs über männliche Homosexualität in der Literatur der frühen Kaiserzeit* (Tübingen: G. Narr Verlag, 1998).

81. Hybreas at Sen. *Controv.* 1.2.23.

82. Soranus at Caelius Aurelianus, *On Chronic Diseases* 4.9.

83. [Lucian] *Am.* 28.

84. Compare Brooten, *Love between Women,* 73–113.

85. In R. W. Daniel and F. Maltomini, *Supplementum Magicum,* 2 vols., Papyrologica Coloniensia vols. 16.1 and 16.2 (Cologne: Westdeutscher Verlag, 1990–1992).

86. Winkler, *The Constraints of Desire,* 90 and 229 n. 32. The general implications of Winkler's review stand, although he did make some precarious guesses about the genders of some authors, accidentally double-counted one text, and missed others of relevance (and, of course, others again have come to light since he wrote).

87. See D. Ogden, "Binding Spells: Curse Tablets and Voodoo Dolls in the Greek and Roman Worlds," in V. Flint, R. Gordon, G. Luck, and D. Ogden, *The Athlone History of Witchcraft and Magic in Europe: Vol. 2. Ancient Greece and Rome,* (London: Athlone, 1999), 63–64.

Chapter 4

1. J. L. Butrica, "Some Myths and Anomalies in the Study of Roman Sexuality," in *Same-Sex Desire and Love in Greco-Roman Antiquity and in the Classical Tradition of the West,* ed. B. C. Verstraete and V. Provencal (Binghamton: Haworth Press, 2005), 210–21.

2. J. N. Davidson, *Courtesans and Fishcakes: The Consuming Passions of Classical Athens* (New York: Fontana, 1997), 65.

3. C. Johns, *Sex or Symbol: Erotic Images of Greece and Rome* (Austin: University of Texas Press, 1982), b/w fig. 104; O. J. Brendel, "The Scope and Temperament of Erotic Art in the Greco-Roman World," in *Studies in Erotic Art*, ed. T. Bowie and C. V. Christenson (New York: Basic Books, 1970), 3–107, figs. 34–36.

4. I. Bragantini and M. de Vos, *Le decorazioni della villa romana della Farnesina* (Rome: De Luca, 1982); J. R. Clarke, *Looking at Lovemaking: Constructions of Sexuality in Roman Art 100 B.C.-A.D. 250* (Berkeley: University of California Press, 1998), 120–29.

5. P. Schaff, "The Twelve Patriarchs, Excerpts and Epistles, The Clementina, Apocrypha, Decretals, Memoirs of Edessa and Syriac Documents, Remains of the First Ages," vol. 8 of *The Ante-Nicene Fathers: Translations of the Writings of the Fathers down to A.D. 325* (New York: Charles Scribner's Sons, 1899), 846–51, especially 850.

6. For example, B. MacLachlan, "Sacred Prostitution and Aphrodite," *Studies in Religion* 21 (1992): 145–62; R. A. Strong, "The Most Shameful Practice: Temple Prostitution in the Ancient Greek World," unpublished PhD dissertation, University of California at Los Angeles, 1997.

7. M. M. Henry, "The Edible Woman: Athenaeus's Concept of the Pornographic," in *Pornography and Representation in Greece and Rome,* ed. A. Richlin (New York: Oxford University Press, 1992), 262, using Ath. 13.559ab.

8. T.A.J. McGinn, "Pompeian Brothels and Social History," in T.A.J. McGinn et al., *Pompeian Brothels, Pompeii's Ancient History, Mirrors and Mysteries, Art and Nature at Oplontis, and the Herculaneum "Basilica." Journal of Roman Archaeology* Supplement 47 (2002): 62–85.

9. S. Riccobono et al., *Fontes juris romani antejustiniani* (Florence: G. Barbera, 1940–1943), 556–57; see also *Theodosian Code* 9.7.6.

10. K. J. Dover, *Greek Homosexuality* (Cambridge, MA: Harvard University Press, 1978), 124–35.

11. K. DeVries, "The 'Frigid Eromenoi' and Their Wooers Revisited: A Closer Look at Greek Homosexuality in Vase Painting," in *Queer Representations: Reading Lives, Reading Cultures,* ed. M. Duberman (New York: New York University Press, 1997), 14–24; D. M. Halperin, "Questions of Evidence: Commentary on Koehl, DeVries, and Williams," in *Queer Representations,* ed. M. Duberman (New York: New York University Press, 1997), 45–53.

12. S. Flory, "Dressed to Kill: The Aesthetics of Archaic and Classical Greek Hoplite Warfare," *American Journal of Archaeology* 98 (1994): 333.

13. N. B. Crowther, "Weightlifting in Antiquity: Achievement and Training," *Greece and Rome* 24 (1977): 111–20.

14. A. d'Ambrosio, ed., *Women and Beauty in Pompeii,* trans. Graham Sells (Los Angeles: 'L'Erma' di Bretschneider and J. Paul Getty Museum, 2001); H.-G. Mirabeau, *Errotika biblion* (Rome: De l'Imprimerie du Vatican, 1783), 183.

15. D. Sansone, *Greek Athletics and the Genesis of Sport* (Berkeley: University of California Press, 1988), 122–28.

16. D.E.E. Kleiner, *Roman Sculpture* (New Haven, CT: Yale University Press, 1992), figs. 48, 50, 106; E. D'Ambra, "The Calculus of Venus: Nude Portraits of Roman Matrons," in *Sexuality in Ancient Art,* ed. N. B. Kampen (Cambridge: Cambridge University Press, 1996), 219–32; K.D.S. Lapatin, "Review of *Polykleitos, the Doryphoros, and Tradition,* edited by W. G. Moon, *Sculptors and Physicians in Fifth-century Greece: A Preliminary Study,* by G.P.R. Métraux, and *The Aphrodite of Knidos and Her Successors: A Historical Review of the Female Nude in Greek Art,* by C. M. Havelock," *Art Bulletin* 79 (1997): 156.

17. D. Montserrat, *Sex and Society in Graeco-Roman Egypt* (London: Kegan Paul International, 1996), 61–79.

18. O. Meinardus, "Mythological, Historical, and Sociological Aspects of the Practice of Female Circumcision among the Egyptians," *Acta Ethnographica Academiae Scientiarum Hungaricae* ser. 9, 16 (1967): 389–90; A. S. Hunt and C. C. Edgar, *Select Papyri,* 4 vols. (Cambridge, MA: Harvard University Press, 1970), 1.31–33; U. Wilcken, *Urkunden der Ptolemäerzeit* (Berlin: Walter de Gruyter, 1978), text 2, 1.16; D. J. Thompson, *Memphis under the Ptolemies* (Princeton, NJ: Princeton University Press, 1988), 232–33; H. Brunner, "Review of R. and J. Janssen, *Growing Up in Ancient Egypt,*" in *Discussions in Egyptology* 21 (1991): 77–78.

19. W. Sweet, "Protection of the Genitals in Greek Athletics," *Ancient World* 11 (1985): 43–52; C. de Wit, "La circoncision chez les anciens Egyptiens," *Zeitschrift für Ägyptische Sprache und Altertumskunde* 99 (1972): 41–48.

20. E. M. Smallwood, "The Legislation of Hadrian and Antoninus Pius against Circumcision," *Latomus* 18 (1959): 334–47.

21. R. G. Hall, "Epispasm: Circumcision in Reverse," *Bible Review* 8, no. 4 (1992): 52–57.

22. R. S. Bianchi, "Tattoo in Ancient Egypt," in *Marks of Civilization,* ed. A. Rubin (Los Angeles: University of California, Los Angeles, Museum of Cultural History, 1988), 21–28; P. G. Preziosi and S. S. Weinberg, "Evidence for Painted Details in Early Cycladic Sculpture," *Antike Kunst* 13 (1970): 4–12; L. E. Talalay, "Body Imagery of the Ancient Aegean," *Archaeology* 44 (1991): 46–49; L. E. Talalay, *Deities, Dolls, and Devices: Neolithic Figurines from Franchthi Cave, Greece* (Bloomington: Indiana University Press, 1993), 161–68; E. Hendrix, "Some Methods for Revealing Paint on Early Cycladic Figures," in *Metron* (*Aegaeum* 24), ed. K. Foster and R. Laffineur (Liège: Université de Liège, 2003), 139–45; E. A. Hendrix, "Painted Early Cycladic Figures: An Exploration of Context and Meaning," *Hesperia* 72 (2003): 405–46.

23. B. Fowler, *Iceman: Uncovering the Life and Times of a Prehistoric Man Found in an Alpine Glacier* (New York: Random House, 2000).

24. B. Fellmann, "Zur Deutung frühgriechischer Körperornamente," *Jahrbuch des deutschen archäologischen Instituts* 93 (1978): 1–29; K. Zimmermann, "Tätowierte Thrakerinnen auf griechischen Vasenbildern," *Jahrbuch des deutschen archäologischen Instituts* 95 (1980): 163–96; M. Robertson, *Art of Vase Painting in Classical Athens* (Cambridge: Cambridge University Press, 1992), 157.

25. J. G. Younger, "Bronze Age Representations of Aegean Bull-games, III," in *Politeia* (*Aegaeum* 12), ed. R. Laffineur and P. B. Betancourt (Liège: Université de Liège, 1995), 507–45; J. G. Younger, "Waist Compression in the Aegean Late Bronze Age," *Archaeological News* 23 (1998–2000): 1–9.

26. T. F. Scanlon, *Eros and Greek Athletics* (Oxford: Oxford University Press, 2002), 190, fig. 7–7.

27. For example, J. Marcadé, *Roma Amor: Essay on Erotic Elements in Etruscan and Roman Art* (Geneva: Nagel, 1965), pl. on p. 107; P. G. Guzzo and V. S. Ussani, *Veneris figurae: Immagine di prostituzione e sfruttamento a Pompei* (Naples: Ministero per i Beni e le Attività Culturali, Soprintendenza Archeologica di Napoli e Caserta, 2000), fig. on p. 14; J. R. Clarke, *Roman Sex: 100 B.C. to A.D. 250, with New Photography by Michael Larvey* (New York: Harry N. Abrams, 2003), figs. 33, 38, 40.

28. Compare fig. 4. 14; for example, J. Guillaud and M. Guillaud, *Frescoes in the Time of Pompeii* (Paris: Guillaud Editions, 1990), fig. 242.

29. W. A. Krenkel, "Tonguing," *Wissenschaftliche Zeitschrift der Wilhelm-Pieck-Universität Rostock* 30 (1981): 37–54.

30. V. Hugo, *L'homme qui rit* [*By Order of the King*] (New York: The Co-operative Publication Society, 1869 [1920]); "Another Preliminary Chapter—The Comprachicos," 26–39.

31. R. Osborne, "Desiring Women on Athenian Pottery," in Kampen, *Sexuality in Ancient Art,* 78–80.

32. H. A. Shapiro, "Eros in Love: Pederasty and Pornography in Greece," in Richlin, *Pornography and Representation,* 65.

33. P. Gordon, "The Lover's Voice in *Heroides* 15: or, Why Is Sappho a Man?" in *Roman Sexualities,* ed. J. P. Hallett and M. B. Skinner (Princeton, NJ: Princeton University Press, 1997), 282; "Rape is a compliment paid to an attractive woman."

Also, A. Richlin, "Reading Ovid's Rapes," in Richlin, *Pornography and Representation*, 169; R. F. Sutton, "Pornography and Persuasion on Attic Pottery," in Richlin, *Pornography and Representation*, 30–31.

34. Sutton, "Pornography and Persuasion," 32.

35. M. F. Kilmer, *Greek Erotica on Attic Red-Figure Vases* (London: Duckworth, 1993), 108–10, 121–24; D. Levine, "*Eraton bama* ('Her lovely footstep'): The Erotics of Feet in Ancient Greece," in *Body Language in the Greek and Roman Worlds*, ed. D. L. Cairns (Swansea: Classical Press of Wales, 2005).

36. Marcadé, *Roma Amor*, pls. on p. 76; A. Varone, *Eroticism in Pompeii*, trans. Maureen Fant (Los Angeles: 'L'Erma' di Bretschneider and J. Paul Getty Museum, 2001), pl. 65.

37. J. Henderson, *The Maculate Muse: Obscene Language in Attic Comedy*, 2nd ed. (New York: Oxford University Press, 1991), 19 n. 70.

38. B. S. Ridgway, *Hellenistic Sculpture 2: The Styles of ca. 200–100 B.C.* (Madison: University of Wisconsin Press, 2000), 147–49.

39. A. R. Benner and F. H. Fobes, *Alciphron, Aelian, Philostratus: The Letters* (Cambridge, MA: Harvard University Press, 1949), nos. 18, 36, 37, and 31, respectively.

40. C. Reinsberg, *Ehe, Hetärentum und Knabenliebe im antiken Griechenland* (Munich: C. H. Beck, 1989), figs. 64, 89, 117; C. Johns, *Sex or Symbol: Erotic Images of Greece and Rome* (Austin: University of Texas Press, 1982), b/w figs. 81, 82, 109; E. C. Keuls, *The Reign of the Phallus: Sexual Politics in Ancient Athens* (New York: Harper and Row, 1985), figs. 37, 158, 196, 197, 254.

41. S. Steingräber, *Etruscan Painting: Catalogue Raisonné of Etruscan Wall Paintings* (New York: Harcourt Brace Jovanovich, 1985), cat. 67.

42. Reinsberg, *Ehe, Hetärentum und Knabenliebe*, figs. 51; Johns, *Sex or Symbol*, b/w figs. 93, 108; Keuls, *The Reign of the Phallus*, figs. 167–70.

43. Johns, *Sex or Symbol*, 114.

44. M. Marks, "Heterosexual Coital Position as a Reflection of Ancient and Modern Cultural Attitudes," unpublished PhD dissertation, SUNY-Buffalo, 1978.

45. H. A. Shapiro, "Courtship Scenes in Attic Vase-painting," *American Journal of Archaeology* 85 (1981): 133–43, no. 62; Reinsberg, *Ehe, Hetärentum und Knabenliebe*, fig. 96a-c.

46. W. A. Krenkel, "Masturbation in der Antike," *Wissenschaftliche Zeitschrift der Wilhelm-Pieck-Universität Rostock* 28 (1979): 159–78.

47. Reinsberg, *Ehe, Hetärentum und Knabenliebe*, fig. 52; Johns, *Sex or Symbol*, b/w fig. 117.

48. A. Varone, *Erotica Pompeiana. Love Inscriptions on the Walls of Pompeii*, trans. R. P. Berg (Rome: 'L'Erma' di Bretschneider, 2001), 94.

49. G. Vorberg, *Glossarium eroticum* (Hanau am Main: Müller & Kiepenheuer, 1965), 485.

50. Varone, *Erotica Pompeiana*, 77, 140.

51. S. A. Sanders and J. M. Reinisch, "Would You Say You 'Had Sex' If … ?" *Journal of the American Medical Association* 281 (1999): 275–77.

52. Reinsberg, *Ehe, Hetärentum und Knabenliebe*, fig. 83; Johns, *Sex or Symbol*, b/w figs. 115, 122; L. Jacobelli, *Le pitture erotiche delle Terme Suburbane di Pompei* (Rome: 'L'Erma' di Bretschneider, 1995), figs. 33, 34, 55, pl. IV.

53. Vorberg, *Glossarium eroticum*, 185, 582–85; Johns, *Sex or Symbol,* b/w fig. 116.

54. Eupolis 1, J. M. Edmonds, *The Fragments of Attic Comedy after Meineke, Bergk and Kock* (Leiden: Brill, 1957–1961); cf. Photius s.v. *lambda*.

55. Compare Davidson, *Courtesans and Fishcakes,* 10–11.

56. W. A. Krenkel, "Tonguing," 37–54, pls. 1, 2; Brendel, "The Scope and Temperament of Erotic Art in the Greco-Roman World," fig. 13; Vorberg, *Glossarium eroticum,* 129, 185; Johns, *Sex or Symbol,* b/w fig. 116; Jacobelli, *Le pitture erotiche delle Terme Suburbane di Pompe,* figs. 35, 46, pls. V, VIII.

57. Richlin, "Reading Ovid's Rapes," 158–79; cf. Xenophon's *Symposium*.

58. A. Richlin, *The Garden of Priapus: Sexuality and Aggression in Roman Humor* (New Haven, CT: Yale University Press, 1983), 92–93, 98.

59. S. Brown, "Death as Decoration: Scenes from the Arena on Roman Domestic Mosaics," in Richlin, *Pornography and Representation,* 180–83, 186–87; C. Edwards, "Unspeakable Professions: Public Performance and Prostitution in Ancient Rome," in Hallett and Skinner, *Roman Sexualities,* 67–68.

60. O. Taplin, "Phallology, *phylakes*, Iconography and Aristophanes," *Proceedings of the Cambridge Philological Society* 33 (1987): 92–104; A. Pontrandolfo, "Dionisio e personaggi fliaciei nelle immagine pertane," *Ostraca* 9 (2000): 117–34.

61. Steingräber, *Etruscan Painting,* cat. 156.

62. Steingräber, *Etruscan Painting,* cat. 47.

63. Varone, *Eroticism in Pompeii,* 74–80.

64. Compare wall paintings from the Farnesina Villa: Clarke, *Roman Sex,* figs. 9, 11; and from the house of Caecilius Jucundus: Marcadé, *Roma Amor,* pl. on p. 15; Clarke, *Roman Sex,* figs. 12–14; and the silver Warren Cup: D. Williams, *The Warren Cup* (London: The British Museum Press, 2006).

65. Compare J. Elsner, *Art and the Roman Viewer: The Transformation of Art from the Pagan World to Christianity* (Cambridge: Cambridge University Press, 1997); J. Elsner, *Roman Eyes: Visuality and Subjectivity in Art and Text* (Princeton, NJ: Princeton University Press, 2007).

66. W. A. Krenkel, "Zur Prosopographie der antike Pornographie," *Wissenschaftliche Zeitschrift der Wilhelm-Pieck-Universität Rostock* 19 (1970): 615–19.

67. Johns, *Sex or Symbol,* 96; H. N. Parker, "Love's Body Anatomized: The Ancient Erotic Handbooks and the Rhetoric of Sexuality," in Richlin, *Pornography and Representation,* 90–91.

68. Parker, "Love's Body Anatomized," 94.

69. J. G. Younger, *Sex in the Ancient World From A to Z* (New York: Routledge, 2005), s.v.

70. Johns, *Sex or Symbol,* figs. 95, 112; Clarke, *Roman Sex,* figs. 16, 17.

71. Marcadé, *Roma Amor,* pl. on p. 50; Clarke, *Roman Sex,* fig. 49.

72. For example, Johns, *Sex or Symbol,* b/w figs. 31, 65, color pls. 23, 37; Marcadé, *Roma Amor,* pls. on pp. 36, 59, 90, 107, 120, 123; Clarke, *Roman Sex,* figs. 33, 36, 37, 38, 40.

73. For example, Athenian kylikes, *ARV*[2] 444.241; Johns, *Sex or Symbol,* b/w fig. 111; Kilmer, *Greek Erotica,* R463; in a Pompeii wall painting, Clarke, *Roman Sex,*

fig. 107; and, for the bowls, G. Siebert, "Un bol à reliefs inscrit à représentations érotiques," *Antike Kunst* 27 (1984): 14–20; and I. M. Akamates, *Pulíes mêtres aggeíon apò tên Pélla. Sumbolê stê melétê tês ellênistikés keramikês* (Athens: Greek Ministry of Culture, 1993), nos. 322, 323.

74. For example, Vorberg, *Glossarium eroticum,* 230, 462–63; J. Marcadé, *Eros Kalos: Essay on Erotic Elements in Greek Art* (Geneva: Nagel, 1962), pls. on pp. 39C, 59, 119; Johns, *Sex or Symbol,* b/w figs. 95, 112, 117, and color pl. 37.

75. D. Leitao, "The Perils of Leukippos: Initiatory Transvestism and Male Gender Ideology in the Ekdusia at Phaistos," *Classical Antiquity* 14 (1995): 130–63.

76. E. Simon, *Festivals of Attica: an Archaeological Commentary* (Madison: University of Wisconsin Press, 1983), 89–92.

77. Compare Leitao, "The Perils of Leukippos," 163.

78. N. S. Rabinowitz, "The Erotics of Greek Drama: The Contribution of the Cross-dressed Actor," *Abstracts of One Hundred Twenty-Seventh Meeting, American Philological Association,* 132 (Worcester: American Philological Association, 1995); cf. Plautus, *Casina.*

79. M. Maas and J. Snyder, *Stringed Instruments in Ancient Greece* (New Haven, CT: Yale University Press, 1989), 118–19.

80. *NH* 11.262; cf. A. Ajootian, "The Only Happy Couple: Hermaphrodites and Gender," in *Naked Truths: Women, Sexuality, and Gender in Classical Art and Archaeology,* ed. C. Lyons and A. Koloski-Ostrow (London: Routledge, 1997), 220–42; L. Brisson, *Sexual Ambivalence: Androgyny and Hermaphroditism in Graeco-Roman Antiquity,* trans. J. Lloyd (Berkeley: University of California Press, 2002).

81. Johns, *Sex or Symbol,* b/w fig. 85; see John Clarke, this volume, Chapter 9.

82. Johns, *Sex or Symbol,* color pl. 29.

83. Johns, *Sex or Symbol,* 110–11.

84. Keuls, *The Reign of the Phallus,* fig. 161.

85. D. M. Bailey, *A Catalogue of the Lamps in the British Museum,* 3: *Roman Provincial Lamps* (London: British Museum, 1988), nos. Q2578, Q3271; cf. Priap. 53; Juv. 6.333 ff.; Apuleius 10.22.

86. Johns, *Sex or Symbol,* b/w fig. 91; Vorberg, *Glossarium eroticum,* 95 lower left, 601.

87. Keuls, *The Reign of the Phallus,* fig. 331.

88. Johns, *Sex or Symbol,* color pl. 1.

89. A. Henrichs, "Greek Maenadism from Olympias to Messalina," *Harvard Studies in Classical Philology* 82 (1978): 121–60.

90. Johns, *Sex or Symbol,* color pl. 26.

91. Varone, *Eroticism in Pompeii,* pl. 1.

92. Apollod. *Epitome* 5.1; cf. the early fifth century kylix by the Penthesilea Painter, *ARV²* 879.1; and the slightly later scene painted on the barriers to the throne of Olympian Zeus, Paus. 5.11.6.

93. E. Gregersen, *Sexual Practices: The Story of Human Sexuality* (New York: Franklin Watts, 1983), 56–57; cf. D. M. Halperin, *Saint Foucault: Towards a Gay Hagiography* (Oxford: Oxford University Press, 1996), 92.

Chapter 5

1. Pl. *Laws* 838a-41c; L. Strauss, *The Argument and the Action of Plato's Laws* (Chicago: University of Chicago Press, 1975).

2. T. Barfield, *The Dictionary of Anthropology* (Oxford: Blackwell, 2001).

3. Arist. *Rhet.* 1373b3–74a22; see M. Griffith, *Sophocles: Antigone* (Cambridge: Cambridge University Press, 1999), 201; M. Ostwald, "Was There a Concept *agraphos nomos* in Classical Greece?," in *Exegesis and Argument: Studies in Greek Philosophy Presented to G. Vlastos, Phronesis* suppl.1, ed. E. N. Lee, A.P.D. Mourelatos and R. M. Rorty (Assen: Van Gorcum, 1973).

4. L. Foxhall and A.D.E. Lewis, "Introduction," in *Greek Law in its Political Setting*, ed. L. Foxhall and A.D.E. Lewis (Oxford: Clarendon Press, 1996); M. Gagarin, *Early Greek Law* (Berkeley: University of California Press, 1986); V. Hunter, *Policing Athens: Social Control in the Attic Lawsuits* (Princeton, NJ: Princeton University Press, 1994).

5. B. Z. Tamanaha, *Realistic Socio-Legal Theory: Pragmatism and a Social Theory of Law* (Oxford: Clarendon Press, 1997).

6. For example, D. Cohen, "Consent and Sexual Relations in Classical Athens," in *Consent and Coercion to Sex and Marriage in Ancient and Medieval Societies*, ed. A. E. Laiou (Washington, DC: Dumbarton Oaks, 1993).

7. R. A. Miller, *The Limits of Bodily Integrity: Abortion, Adultery and Rape Legislation in Comparative Perspective* (Aldershot: Ashgate, 2007); D. Nicolson and L. Bibbings, *Feminist Perspectives on Criminal Law* (London: Cavendish, 2000); J. Temkin, "Rape and Criminal Justice at the Millennium," in *Feminist Perspectives on Criminal Law*, ed. D. Nicholson and L. Biddings (London: Cavendish, 2000); A. Wertheimer, *Consent to Sexual Relations* (Cambridge: Cambridge University Press, 2003).

8. C. A. MacKinnon, *Toward a Feminist Theory of the State* (Cambridge, MA: Harvard University Press, 1989), 179.

9. *Phtheirō*: V. Rosivach, *When a Young Man Falls in Love: The Sexual Exploitation of Women in New Comedy* (London: Routledge, 1998); *Bia*: Lys. 1.32, Plut. *Sol.* 23; for terms for rape see E. M. Harris, "Did Rape Exist in Classical Athens? Further Reflections on the Laws about Sexual Violence," *Dike* 7 (2004): 41–83.

10. Further discussion of *hybris*: D. Cohen, "Sexuality, Violence, and the Athenian Law of *hybris*," *Greece and Rome* 38 (1991): 171–88; Cohen, "Consent and Sexual Relations"; N.R.E. Fisher, *Hybris* (Warminster: Aris & Phillips, 1992); N.R.E. Fisher, "Violence, Masculinity and the Law in Classical Athens," in *When Men Were Men: Masculinity, Power, and Identity in Classical Antiquity*, ed. L. Foxhall and J. Salmon (London: Routledge, 1998); E. Harris, "Did the Athenians Regard Seduction as a Worse Crime Than Rape?," *Classical Quarterly* 40 (1990): 370–77; R. Omitowoju, "Regulating Rape: Soap Operas and Self-interest in the Athenian Courts," in *Rape in Antiquity: Sexual Violence in the Greek and Roman Worlds*, ed. S. Deacy and K. F. Pierce (London: Duckworth, 2002).

11. On fear: Xen. *Hiero* 1.27–38.

12. Fisher, "Violence, Masculinity and the Law"; Arist. *Rhet.* 1378b20, 1374a13.

13. Consensual: Dem. 22.58; Aeschin. 1.28–32, with 1.51–7, 185–6; Xen. *Mem.* 2.1.30. Against oneself: Aeschin. 1.29, 108, 186.

14. Further discussion of *hybris* and women: R. Omitowoju, *Rape and the Politics of Consent in Classical Athens* (Cambridge: Cambridge University Press, 2002).

15. Din. *Dem.* 23.7.

16. Dem. 21.36.

17. E. Cantarella, "Gender, Sexuality and Law," in *The Cambridge Companion to Ancient Greek Law,* ed. M. Gagarin and D. Cohen (Cambridge: Cambridge University Press, 2005); M. Gagarin, *Drakon and Early Athenian Homicide Law* (New Haven, CT: Yale University Press, 1981); R. S. Stroud, *Drakon's Law on Homicide* (Berkeley: University of California Press, 1968).

18. Dem. 23.53 with [Arist.] *Ath. Pol.* 57.3, Lys. 1.30–4.

19. Lys. 1.32 and Plut. *Sol.* 23.1–2; see discussion in A. Glazebrook, "The Bad Girls of Athens: The Image and Function of Hetairai in Judicial Oratory," in *Prostitutes and Courtesans in the Ancient World,* ed. C. A. Faraone and L. K. McClure (Madison: University of Wisconsin Press, 2006).

20. C. Carey, "Rape and Adultery in Athenian Law," *Classical Quarterly* 45 (1995): 407–17 (see also D. Cohen, *Law, Sexuality, and Society: The Enforcement of Morals in Classical Athens* [Cambridge: Cambridge University Press, 1991]; S. Todd, *The Shape of Athenian Law* [Oxford: Oxford University Press, 1993]); Omitowoju, "Regulating Rape."

21. C. Dyer, "Reforms Aim to Dispel Rape Myths and Increase Convictions," *Guardian Unlimited,* November 29, 2007, http://www.guardian.co.uk/crime/article/0,,2218536,00.html (accessed December 5, 2007).

22. See D. Cohen, *Law, Sexuality, and Society: The Enforcement of Morals in Classical Athens* (Cambridge: Cambridge University Press, 1991); Cohen, "Sexuality, Violence"; Hunter, *Policing Athens.*

23. Pl. *Phdr.* 231e–232b; Ar. *Wasps* 1023–8; [Dem.] 61.17; N.R.E. Fisher, *Aeschines Against Timarchos* (Oxford: Oxford University Press, 2001).

24. S. Todd, "Some Notes on the Regulation of Sexuality in Athenian Law," in *Symposion 2003: Vorträge zur griechischen und hellenistischen Rechtsgeschichte,* ed. H. A. Rupprecht (Vienna: Verlag der Österreichischen Akademie der Wissenschaften, 2006); but see Fisher, *Aeschines Against Timarchos.*

25. Aeschin. 1.71–3, 107; Arist. *Rhet.* 1373a30 and 35.

26. For example, D. Ogden, "Rape, Adultery and Protection of Bloodlines in Classical Athens," in *Rape in Antiquity: Sexual Violence in the Greek and Roman Worlds,* ed. S. Deacy and K. F. Pierce (London: Duckworth, 2002); Omitowoju, *Rape and the Politics of Consent*; see Aeschin. 1.91.

27. Carey, "Rape and Adultery"; the law is perhaps referred to by [Dem.] 59.87, also [Arist.] *Ath. Pol.* 59.3.

28. [Dem.] 59.66; Lys. 1.48–9; Ar. *Clouds* 1083–4 with scholiast.

29. R. Osborne, "Law in Action in Classical Athens," *Journal of Hellenic Studies* 105 (1985): 40–58.

30. See for discussion Carey, "Rape and Adultery."

31. Eur. *El.* 921–4; Aeschin. 1.182–3.

32. [Dem.] 59.87; Aeschin. 1.183.

33. Aeschin. 1.183.

34. Plut. *Sol.* 23; Lys. 10.15–19; cf. [Dem.] 59.67.

35. But see G. Herman, "How Violent was Athenian Society," in *Ritual, Finance Politics: Athenian Democratic Accounts Presented to David Lewis,* ed. R.Osborne and S. Hornblower (Oxford: Oxford University Press, 1994).

36. *Ath.Pol.* 26.3, 42.1–2; Plut. *Per.* 37.3; Dem. 57; Craterus, *FGH* 342 F4 ; see for discussion L. Foxhall, "Response to Eva Cantarella," in *Symposion 1990: Vorträge zur griechischen und hellenistischen Rechtsgeschichte,* ed. M. Gagarin (Cologne: Böhlau, 1991); D. M. Halperin, *One Hundred Years of Homosexuality and Other Essays on Greek Love* (New York: Routledge, 1990); K. Kapparis, "When Were the Athenian Adultery Laws Introduced?," *Revue international des droits de l'antiquité* 42 (1995): 97–122. Outside Athens: I. Arnaoutoglou, *Ancient Greek Laws: A Sourcebook* (London: Routledge, 1998), 18, no. 14.

37. K. Zacharia, *Converging Truths: Euripides' Ion and the Athenian Quest for Self-Definition* (Leiden: Brill, 2003).

38. E. Fantham, "Sex, Status and Survival in Hellenistic Athens, a Study of Women in New Comedy," *Phoenix* 29 (1975): 44–74.

39. Men. *Epit.* 878–907.

40. R. van Bremen, "Women and Wealth," in *Images of Women in Antiquity,* ed. A. Kuhrt and A. Cameron (London: Croom Helm, 1983).

41. Men. *Epit.* 894; S. Lape, *Reproducing Athens: Menander's Comedy, Democratic Culture and the Hellenistic City* (Princeton, NJ: Princeton University Press, 2004).

42. Rosivach, *When a Young Man Falls in Love,* 30.

43. Xen. *Hiero* 3.3–6.

44. J. K. Davies, "Deconstructing Gortyn: When Is a Code a Code?," in *Greek Law in its Political Setting: Justifications not Justice,* ed. L. Foxhall and A.D.E. Lewis (Oxford: Oxford University Press, 1996); J. K. Davies, "The Gortyn Laws," in *The Cambridge Companion to Ancient Greek Law,* ed. M. Gagarin and D. Cohen (Cambridge: Cambridge University Press, 2005); M. Gagarin, "The Organisation of the Gortyn Law Code," *Greek, Roman, and Byzantine Studies* 23 (1982): 129–46.

45. E. Cantarella, "Moicheia: Reconsidering a Problem," in *Symposion 1990: Vorträge zur griechischen und hellenistischen Rechtsgeschichte,* ed. M. Gagarin (Cologne: Böhlau, 1991).

46. Ael. *VH* 12.12.

47. F. Salviat and C. Vatin, "La répression des violences sexuelles dans la convention entre Delphes et Pellana, le droit d'Athènes et les lois de Platon," in *Inscriptions de Grèce Centrale* (Paris: Editions de Boccard, 1971).

48. R. Parker, *Miasma: Pollution and Purification in Early Greek Religion* (Oxford: Clarendon Press, 1983).

49. R. Parker, "What Are Sacred Laws?," in *The Law and the Courts in Ancient Greece,* ed. E. Harris and L. Rubinstein (London: Duckworth, 2004); E. Lupu, *Greek Sacred Law: A Collection of New Documents* (NGSL) (Leiden: Brill, 2005).

50. For example: *IG* 2^2 1565.23–5; *LSCG* 95.5; 124.9; 171.7.

51. *LSAM* 12.4–6 and 29.5–7. Greater detail could be taken to indicate a different sensibility to the body and/or social/gender dynamics, cf. L. Dean-Jones, *Women's Bodies in Classical Greek Science* (Oxford: Oxford University Press, 1994), 248.

52. M. Douglas, *Purity and Danger: An Analysis of Concepts of Pollution and Taboo* (London: Routledge and K. Paul, 1966).

53. Parker, "What Are Sacred Laws?"; R. Parker, "Law and Religion," in *The Cambridge Companion to Ancient Greek Law,* ed. M. Gagarin and D. Cohen (Cambridge: Cambridge University Press, 2005).

54. [Dem.] 59.86–7; Aeschin. 1.19.

55. For detailed discussion of the aspects of this legislation, see: C. Edwards, *The Politics of Immorality in Ancient Rome* (Cambridge: Cambridge University Press, 1993); J. F. Gardner, *Women in Roman Law and Society* (London: Croom Helm, 1986); R. Langlands, *Sexual Morality in Ancient Rome* (Cambridge: Cambridge University Press, 2006); T.A.J. McGinn, *Prostitution, Sexuality, and the Law in Ancient Rome* (New York: Oxford University Press, 1998); D. C. Moses, "Livy's Lucretia and the Validity of Coerced Consent in Roman Law," in *Consent and Coercion to Sex and Marriage in Ancient and Medieval Societies,* ed. A. E. Laiou (Washington, DC: Dumbarton Oaks, 1993); O. F. Robinson, *The Criminal Law of Ancient Rome* (London: Duckworth, 1995); R. Saller, "The Social Dynamics of Consent to Marriage and Sexual Relations: The Evidence of Roman Comedy," in Laiou, *Consent and Coercion;* M. Skinner, *Sexuality in Greek and Roman Culture* (Oxford: Blackwell, 2005); S. Treggiari, *Roman Marriage:* Iusti Coniuges *from the Time of Cicero to the Time of Ulpian* (Oxford: Clarendon Press, 1991); C. Vout, *Power and Eroticism in Imperial Rome* (Cambridge: Cambridge University Press, 2007).

56. *Dig.* 22.5.18 Paul.; *Dig.* 22.5.14 Pap.; *Dig.* 28.1.20.6 Ulp.

57. *Dig.* 47.10.1.2, 47.10.9.4, 47.10.15.15–26 Ulp.

58. *Dig.* 47.10.1.3 Ulp.

59. *Dig.* 48.6.5.2 Marc.

60. Suet. *Aug.* 34; *Res Gestae Divi Augusti* 8, but see Cass. Dio 54.16.3.

61. Suet. *Aug.* 34.

62. Possible allusions in Prop. 2.7 and Livy *praef.* 9, 12; R. Syme, "Livy and Augustus," *Harvard Studies in Classical Philology* 64 (1959): 27–87 (opposing, E. Badian, "A Phantom Marriage Law," *Philologus* 129 [1985]: 82–98).

63. E. Fantham, "*Stuprum*: Public Attitudes and Penalties for Sexual Offenses in Republican Rome," *Echos du monde classique/Classical Views* 10 (1991): 267–91.

64. *Dig.* 48.5.25(24) Macer.

65. Alluded to in Hor. *Sat.*1.2.37–46.

66. *Dig.* 48.5.23(22).4 Pap.; *Dig.* 48.5.26(25) Ulp.

67. Leniency: *Dig.* 48.5.38.8 Pap.; see also *Dig.* 48.5.2.2, 48.5.2.6 Ulp.

68. *Dig.* 48.5.21(20) and 23(22) Pap.; *Dig.* 48.5.24(23) Ulp.

69. *Dig.* 48.5.30(29).5 Ulp., *Dig.* 48.5.32(31) Paul.

70. Fantham, "*Stuprum.*"

71. Suet. *Aug.* 65; Tac. *Ann.* 1.53.

72. *Dig.* 48.5.6.1 Pap.

73. Treggiari, *Roman Marriage,* 278.

74. *CJ* 9.9.1; his behavior might still come under scrutiny: *Dig.* 48.5.14(13).5 Ulp.

75. *Dig.* 48.5.14(13).7 Ulp.; *Dig.* 48.5. 40(39) Pap.; Moses, "Livy's Lucretia," 58.

76. J. A. Arieti, "Rape and Livy's View of Roman History," in *Rape in Antiquity: Sexual Violence in the Greek and Roman Worlds,* ed. S. Deacy and K. F. Pierce (London: Duckworth, 2002).

77. Suet. *Aug.* 69.1.

78. M. Foucault, *The History of Sexuality: vol. 1, An Introduction,* trans. R. Hurley (London: Allen Lane, 1979); M. Foucault, *The History of Sexuality: vol. 2, The Use of Pleasure,* trans. R. Hurley (Harmondsworth: Viking, 1986); M. Foucault, *The Care of the Self,* trans. R. Hurley (New York: Vintage Books, 1988); M. Foucault, *Society Must be Defended: Lectures at the Collège de France 1975–6,* ed., M. Bertani and A. Fontana (London: Allen Lane, 2003); J. N. katz, *The Invention of Heterosexuality* (Chicago: University of Chicago Press, 1995).

79. D. Cohen and R. Saller, "Foucault on Sexuality in Greco-Roman Antiquity," in *Foucault and the Writing of History,* ed. J. Goldstein (Oxford: Blackwell, 1994).

80. See note 34.

81. Plut. *Per.* 37 and [Arist.] *Ath. Pol.* 26.3.

82. Treggiari, *Roman Marriage,* 267–68.

83. Lys. 1.12; Xen. *Symp.* 4.8.

84. Vistilia: Tac. *Ann.* 2.85; Sulpicia: Tib. 3.13–18 = Sulpicia 4.7–12.

Chapter 6

1. L. Dean-Jones, "The Politics of Pleasure: Female Sexual Appetite in the Hippocratic Corpus," *Helios* 19 (1992): 73.

2. P. A. Watson, "*Non tristis torus et tamen pudicus:* The Sexuality of the *matrona* in Martial," *Mnemosyne* 58 (2005): 62–87.

3. Ibid., 67.

4. D. Gourevitch, *Le mal d'être femme. La femme et la médecine dans la Rome antique* (Paris: Les Belles Lettres, 1984), 219.

5. N. Demand, *Birth, Death, and Motherhood in Classical Greece* (Baltimore: Johns Hopkins University Press, 1994); R. J. White, translator and commentary, *The Interpretation of Dreams: Oneirocritica by Artemidorus* (Park Ridge, NJ: Noyes Classical Studies, 1975), 166.

6. G.E.R. Lloyd, *Science, Folklore, and Ideology: Studies in the Life Sciences in Ancient Greece* (Cambridge: Cambridge University Press, 1983), 72–73; H. King, *Hippocrates' Woman: Reading the Female Body in Ancient Greece* (London: Routledge, 1998), 48–49.

7. A. Richlin, "Pliny's Brassiere," in *Roman Sexualities,* ed. J. P. Hallett and M. B. Skinner (Princeton, NJ: Princeton University Press, 1997), 198.

8. On the development of anatomical terminology, see Lloyd, *Science, Folklore, and Ideology*, 149–67.

9. F. Skoda, *Médecine ancienne et métaphore: Le vocabulaire de l'anatomie et de la pathologie en grec ancien* (Paris: Peeters/Selaf, 1988), 177.

10. T. Laqueur, *Making Sex: Body and Gender from the Greeks to Freud* (Cambridge, MA: Harvard University Press, 1990).

11. For example, K. Park and R. A. Nye, "Destiny Is Anatomy," *New Republic* 18 (1991): 53–57.

12. H. King, "The Mathematics of Sex: One to Two, or Two to One?," *Studies in Medieval and Renaissance History: Sexuality and Culture in Medieval and Renaissance Europe* 2 (2005): 47–58.

13. Laqueur, *Making Sex*, 28.

14. H. Crooke, *Microcosmographia: A Description of the Body of Man* (London, 1615), 216.

15. J. Sharp, *The Midwives Book*, ed. E. Hobby, *The Midwives Book, Or, the Whole Art of Midwifry Discovered* (1671; New York: Oxford University Press, 1999), 37.

16. Crooke, *Microcosmographia*, 249–50; K. Crawford, *European Sexualities, 1400–1800* (New York: Cambridge University Press, 2007), 109.

17. K. Park, *Secrets of Women: Gender, Generation and the Origins of Human Dissection* (New York: Zone Books, 2006), 186–87.

18. M. Stol, *Birth in Babylonia and the Bible: Its Mediterranean Setting* (Groningen: Styx/Brill, 2000), 6.

19. Dean-Jones, "The Politics of Pleasure," 77.

20. P. duBois, *Sowing the Body: Psychoanalysis and Ancient Representations of Women* (Chicago: University of Chicago Press, 1988).

21. R. D. Brown, *Lucretius on Love and Sex: A Commentary on* De rerum natura *IV, 1030–1287 with Prolegomena, Text, and Translation* (Leiden: Brill, 1987), on 4.1209 ff.

22. I. M. Lonie, *The Hippocratic Treatises "On Generation," "On the Nature of the Child," "Diseases IV"* (Berlin: de Gruyter, 1981).

23. Dean-Jones, "The Politics of Pleasure," 83.

24. *On Chronic Diseases* 4.9, in I. E. Drabkin, ed. and tr., *Caelius Aurelianus On Acute Diseases and Chronic Diseases* (Chicago: University of Chicago Press, 1950), 902–5.

25. E. M. Craik, ed., tr., and comm., *Hippocrates, Places in Man* (Oxford: Clarendon Press, 1998), 86.

26. H. von Staden, ed., tr., and comm., *Herophilus: The Art of Medicine in Alexandria* (Cambridge: Cambridge University Press, 1989).

27. King, *Hippocrates' Woman*, 230.

28. H. King, "Once upon a Text: The Hippocratic Origins of Hysteria," in *Hysteria Beyond Freud*, ed. S. Gilman, H. King, R. Porter, G. S. Rousseau, and E. Showalter (Berkeley: University of California Press, 1993).

29. W. Schleiner, *Medical Ethics in the Renaissance* (Washington, DC: Georgetown University Press, 1995).

30. S. B. Pomeroy, *Plutarch's* Advice to the Bride and Groom, *and* A Consolation to His Wife: *English Translations, Commentary, Interpretive Essays, and Bibliography* (New York: Oxford University Press, 1999), 13.

31. P. Burguière, D. Gourevitch, and Y. Malinas, ed., tr., and comm., *Soranos d'Éphèse, Maladies des Femmes,* 4 vols. (Paris: Les Belles Lettres, 1988–2000), 3.39–42.

32. M. Grmek, *Diseases in the Ancient World,* trans. M. Muellner and L. Muellner (Baltimore: Johns Hopkins University Press, 1989), 144.

33. Burguière, Gourevitch, and Malinas, *Soranos d'Éphèse,* 3.50–51.

34. Drabkin, *Caelius Aurelianus,* 412.

35. Grmek, *Diseases in the Ancient World,* 149.

36. On definitions of female health in the Hippocratic Corpus, see H. King, "Women's Health in the Hippocratic Corpus," in *Health in Antiquity,* ed. H. King (London: Routledge, 2005).

37. C. Faraone, "Sex and Power: Male-targeting Aphrodisiacs in the Greek Magical Tradition," *Helios* 19 (1992): 92–93.

38. D. Harvey, "Lydian Specialities, Croesus' Golden Baking-woman, and Dogs' Dinners," in *Food in Antiquity,* ed. J. Wilkins, D. Harvey, and M. Dobson (Exeter: Exeter University Press, 1995), 277.

39. Richlin, "Pliny's Brassiere," 207.

40. Aphrodisiac: for example, Mart. 13.34. Not conducive to kisses, for example, Ar. *Lys.* 798; see D. Gilula, "Comic Food and Food for Comedy," in Wilkins, Harvey, and Dobson, *Food in Antiquity,* 394.

41. Dean-Jones, "The Politics of Pleasure," 76–77.

42. H. King, "Food and Blood in Hippokratic Gynaecology," in Wilkins, Harvey, and Dobson, *Food in Antiquity,* 355–56.

43. C. Faraone, *Ancient Greek Love Magic* (Cambridge, MA: Harvard University Press, 1999), 18–21.

44. L. Totelin, "Sex and Vegetables in the Hippocratic Gynaecological Treatises," *Studies in History and Philosophy of Biological and Medical Sciences* 38 (2007): 535–36.

45. Faraone, "Sex and Power," 100–101.

46. Faraone, *Ancient Greek Love Magic,* 114–15. See also [Arist.] *MM* 1188b30–8.

47. Drabkin, *Caelius Aurelianus,* 410.

48. Burguière, Gourevitch, and Malinas, *Soranos d'Éphèse,* 3.76, n. 121.

49. 3.18; Drabkin, *Caelius Aurelianus,* 416; D. Gourevitch, "Women Who Suffer from a Man's Disease: The Example of Satyriasis and the Debate on Affections Specific to the Sexes," in *Women in Antiquity: New Assessments,* ed. R. Hawley and B. Levick (London: Routledge, 1995), 153.

50. J. Riddle, *Contraception and Abortion from the Ancient World to the Renaissance* (Cambridge, MA: Harvard University Press, 1992); *contra* King, *Hippocrates' Woman,* 132–56.

51. Lonie, *The Hippocratic Treatises,* 160–62.

52. R. Pépin, ed. and trans., *Quintus Serenus (Serenus Sammonicus) Liber Medicinalis* (Paris: Presses Universitaires de France, 1950), 35.

53. Skoda, *Médecine ancienne et métaphore,* 295–97.

54. Gourevitch, "Women Who Suffer."

55. Burguière, Gourevitch, and Malinas, *Soranos d'Éphèse,* 3.16–17.

56. Drabkin, *Caelius Aurelianus,* 410.

57. Drabkin, *Caelius Aurelianus,* 410; Gourevitch, "Women Who Suffer," 157.

58. Gourevitch, "Women Who Suffer," 158.

59. C. Daremberg and C. E. Ruelle, *Oeuvres de Rufus d'Ephèse* (Paris: Baillière, 1879), 66 ff., cited in Gourevitch, "Women Who Suffer," 159.

60. Caelius Aurelianus, *On Chronic Diseases* 4.9; Drabkin, *Caelius Aurelianus,* 958–62.

61. Gourevitch, "Women Who Suffer," 155.

62. Drabkin, *Caelius Aurelianus,* 412.

63. Ibid., 414.

64. Dean-Jones, "The Politics of Pleasure," 76–77.

65. P. Toohey, *Melancholy, Love and Time: Boundaries of the Self in Ancient Literature* (Ann Arbor: University of Michigan Press, 2004), 83–84.

66. Dean-Jones, "The Politics of Pleasure," 76; Gourevitch, "Women Who Suffer," 162.

67. Totelin, "Sex and Vegetables," 532.

68. M. Detienne, *The Gardens of Adonis: Spices in Greek Mythology,* trans. J. E. Lloyd (Hassocks: Harvester Press, 1977; first published as *Les Jardins d'Adonis* [Paris: Gallimard, 1972]), 78–82; M. Detienne, "The Violence of Well-born Ladies: Women in the Thesmophoria," in *The Cuisine of Sacrifice Among the Greeks,* ed. M. Detienne and J.-P. Vernant (Chicago: University of Chicago Press, 1989; first published as *La Cuisine du sacrifice en pays grec* [Paris: Gallimard, 1979]), 147).

69. For example, Soranus, *Gyn.* 1.9; Burguière, Gourevitch, and Malinas, *Soranos d'Éphèse,* 3.25–28; J. R. Pinault, "The Medical Case for Virginity," *Helios* 19 (1992): 126.

70. Dean-Jones, "The Politics of Pleasure," 78.

71. Totelin, "Sex and Vegetables," 532.

72. As Skoda, *Médecine ancienne et métaphore,* 161–63, and Totelin, "Sex and Vegetables," 535, show, *balanos* was used for the glans of the penis both by the writers of comedy, and by Aristotle, for example, *HA* 1.13.

73. Abstinence as preliminary to sex: *Mul.* 1.12 (8.48 L.); 2.143 (8.316 L.), 144 (8.316 L.) and 149 (8.326 L.); *Steril.* 230 (8.444 L.).

74. Totelin, "Sex and Vegetables," 534.

75. Burguière, Gourevitch, and Malinas, *Soranos d'Éphèse,* 3.25–28.

76. Pinault, "The Medical Case for Virginity," 124.

77. M. F. Wack, *Lovesickness in the Middle Ages: The Viaticum and its Commentaries* (Philadelphia: University of Pennsylvania Press, 1990).

78. For example, Jacques Ferrand, *De la maladie d'amour, ou maladie érotique. Discours curieux qui enseigne à cognoistre l'essence, les causes, les signes, et les remèdes de ce mal fantastique* (Paris, 1623; translated as *Treatise on Lovesickness,* tr. and ed. D. A Beecher and M. Ciavollella [Syracuse, NY: Syracuse University Press, 1990]).

79. Toohey, *Melancholy, Love and Time,* 59 ff.
80. R. R. Caston, "Love as Illness: Poets and Philosophers on Romantic Love," *Classical Journal* 101 (2006): 280–81.
81. Cited in Caston, "Love as Illness," 283.
82. Ibid., 284–85.
83. Lucretius 4.1030–1287 also uses medical terminology for the "wounds" of love; see Caston, "Love as Illness," 281.
84. J. R. Pinault, *Hippocratic Lives and Legends,* Studies in Ancient Medicine 4 (Leiden: Brill, 1992), 61.
85. Ibid., 69.
86. *Prog.,* V. Nutton, ed., tr., and comm., *Galen, On Prognosis* (CMG V. 8, 1) (Berlin: Akademie-Verlag, 1979), 101–4.
87. Pinault, *Hippocratic Lives and Legends,* 67–68. Toohey, *Melancholy, Love and Time,* 270–71, mentions a Vandal version of the story of Perdiccas, which ends with the patient hanging himself after Hippocrates has given up on the case. In Galen's version of the lovesickness of Antiochus, it is his father's concubine, rather than his step-mother, who is the object of his desire (Nutton, *Galen, On Prognosis,* 100; Pinault, *Hippocratic Lives and Legends,* 105–6).

Chapter 7

Abbreviations: *CIL* = *Corpus Inscriptionum Latinarum; IG* = *Inscriptiones Graecae* (*IG* 1³ is the third edition of the volume devoted to Attica); *PGM* = *Papyri Graecae Magicae,* K. Preisendanz, *Papyri graecae magicae; die griechischen Zauberpapyri,* 2 vols. (Leipzig: Teubner, 1928–1931), English translations in H. D. Betz, *The Greek Magical Papyri in Translation, Including the Demotic Spells,* 2nd ed. (Chicago: University of Chicago Press, 1992); *SEG* = *Supplementum Epigraphicum Graecum; SM* = *Supplementum Magicum,* R. W. Daniel and F. Maltomini, *Supplementum Magicum,* 2 vols. Papyrologica Coloniensia vols. 16.1 and 16.2 (Cologne: Westdeutscher Verlag, 1990–1992). Vases are listed by the system used in K. J. Dover, *Greek Homosexuality* (Cambridge, MA: Harvard University Press, 1978) and M. F. Kilmer, *Greek Erotica on Attic Red-Figure Vases* (London: Duckworth, 1993) (B = black-figure, R = red-figure). Others by their Beazley numbers: *ABV* = J. D. Beazley, *Attic Black-Figure Vase-Painters* (Oxford: Clarendon Press, 1956); *ARV*² = J. D. Beazley, *Attic Red-Figure Vase-Painters,* 2nd ed. (Oxford: Clarendon Press, 1963); *Para.* = J. D. Beazley, *Paralipomena: Additions to Attic Black-Figure Vase-Painters and to Attic Red-Figure Vase-Painters (Second Edition)* (Oxford: Clarendon Press, 1971); *Add.* = T. H. Carpenter, *Beazley Addenda: Additional References to ABV, ARV*² *& Paralipomena,* 2nd ed. (Oxford: Published for the British Academy by Oxford University Press, 1989).

A note on language: In translating, I use English's rather impoverished vocabulary of primary obscenities not for their shock value but to reflect as accurately as possible the meanings of primary obscenities in Greek and Latin. Thus, for example, *irrumo* does not mean "to have oral sex with" or the like. It is a (very) transitive verb and it takes a (very) direct object.

1. Tony Bennett, "Popular Culture: A Teaching Object," *Screen Education* 34 (1980): 18: "The concept of popular culture is virtually useless, a melting pot of confused and contradictory meanings capable of misdirecting inquiry up any number of theoretical blind alleys."

2. For example, R. Williams, *Culture and Society 1780–1950*, 2nd ed. (Harmondsworth: Penguin, 1971), 11; J. Storey, *Cultural Theory and Popular Culture: An Introduction*, 4th ed. (Athens: University of Georgia Press, 2006), 10.

3. For Greece, see, for example, Johann Gottfried Herder, "Über die Wirkung der Dichtkunst auf die Sitten der Völker in alten und neuen Zeiten," in *Herder. Werke, in fünf Bänden* 3, ed. W. Dobbek (Berlin: Aufbau-Verlag, 1964), 212–20; for "Zivilisation eines Volks" and "Kultur des Volkes" versus "Kultur der Gelehrten," see Johann Gottfried Herder, *Outlines of a Philosophy of the History of Man*, trans. T. Churchill (London: Printed for J. Johnson, by Luke Hansard, 1800; reprinted New York: Bergman Publishers), 311–12; Johann Gottfried Herder, *On World History: An Anthology*, ed. H. Adler and E. A. Menze, trans. E. A. Menze with M. Palma (Armonk, NY: M. E. Sharpe, 1997), 246. Herder translated the English "popular song" as *Volkslied* (1773), which was then back-translated as "folk song."

4. Potter Stewart, Concurring Opinion, Jacobellis v. Ohio, 378 U.S. 184 (1964).

5. For a survey, see Storey, *Cultural Theory and Popular Culture*, 1–12.

6. J. Storey, "The Popular," in *New Keywords: A Revised Vocabulary of Culture and Society,* ed. T. Bennett, L. Grossberg, and M. Morris (Malden, MA: Blackwell, 2005), 263.

7. M. Horkheimer and T. W. Adorno, "The Culture Industry: Enlightenment as Mass Deception," in *Dialectic of Enlightenment,* trans. J. Cumming (New York: Herder and Herder, 1972; German original 1944); M. Shiach, *Discourse on Popular Culture* (Cambridge: Polity Press, 1989), 22; J. Fiske, *Understanding Popular Culture* (Boston: Unwin Hyman, 1989), 24.

8. M. I. Finley, *The Ancient Economy*, 2nd ed. (Berkeley: University of California Press, 1985), 33–61, esp. 44–53; P. Cartledge, "Class Struggle," in *The Oxford Classical Dictionary*, 3d ed., ed. S. Hornblower and A. Spawforth (Oxford: Oxford University Press, 1996). Marx notoriously failed to provide a definition (see his sketchy remarks at *Capital* vol. 3, ch. 52) and explicitly ruled out applying "capitalism" to the slave-based economy of antiquity in *Pre-Capitalist Economic Formations*. See G.E.M. de Ste. Croix, *The Class Struggle in the Ancient Greek World from the Archaic Age to the Arab Conquests* (London: Duckworth, 1981), 45, 81–98, on "exploitation," and the criticisms of J. Vogt, *Ancient Slavery and the Ideal of Man*, trans. T. Wiedemann (Cambridge, MA: Harvard University Press, 1975), 89; Finley, *The Ancient Economy*, 35–61, esp. 49; P. Vidal-Naquet, *The Black Hunter: Forms of Thought and Forms of Society in the Greek World*, trans. A. Szegedy-Maszak (Baltimore: Johns Hopkins University Press, 1986), 159–67; J. Ober, *Mass and Elite in Democratic Athens: Rhetoric, Ideology, and the Power of the People* (Princeton, NJ: Princeton University Press, 1989), 25.

9. On the problems of defining the elite at Athens, see Ober, *Mass and Elite*, esp. 11–17, 192–205, 248–59.

10. The number decreed by Augustus and more or less maintained for several centuries; Cass. Dio 54.14, 53.17. On the difficulties of locating the Roman lower class, see N. Horsfall, *The Culture of the Roman Plebs* (London: Duckworth, 2003), 20–30; J. Toner, *Popular Culture in Ancient Rome* (Cambridge: Polity, 2009), 1–2.

11. R. MacMullen, *Roman Social Relations, 50 B.C. to A.D. 284* (New Haven, CT: Yale University Press, 1974), 88–89.

12. C. Nicolet, *The World of the Citizen in Republican Rome,* trans. P. S. Falla (Berkeley: University of California Press, 1980), 344: "Society was honeycombed with divisions and contrasts sometimes overlapping and sometimes not: between the poor, the less poor and the rich; between members of the higher and privileged orders—senators, knights and officials—and the rest; between city-dwellers and country-dwellers, 'new' and 'old' citizens, former slaves and the free-born." See esp. 49–88 on the all-important institution of the census, 343–81 on "Popularitas." A. Giardina, ed., *The Romans,* trans. L. G. Cochrane (Chicago: University of Chicago Press, 1993) provides a good overview of different Roman social types. For how this played out in Roman art history, see J. R. Clarke, *Art in the Lives of Ordinary Romans: Visual Representation and Non-elite Viewers in Italy, 100 B.C.-A.D. 315* (Berkeley: University of California Press, 2003), 2–9.

13. G. Williams, "*Libertino patre natus*: True or False?," in *Homage to Horace: A Bimillenary Celebration,* ed. S. J. Harrison (Oxford: Clarendon Press, 1995); R.O.A.M. Lyne, *Horace: Behind the Public Poetry* (New Haven, CT: Yale University Press, 1995), 1–11.

14. See the following for some examples. For an exhilarating survey of the "discovery of the people," see P. Burke, *Popular Culture in Early Modern Europe* (New York: Harper & Row, 1978).

15. F. Brommer, "Themenwahl aus örtlichen Gründen," in *Ancient Greek and Related Pottery: Proceedings of the International Symposion in Amsterdam 12–15 April 1984,* ed. H.A.G. Brijder (Amsterdam: Allard Pierson Museum, 1984), 181 (on the basis of four examples); R. F. Sutton, "Pornography and Persuasion on Attic Pottery," in *Pornography and Representation in Greece and Rome,* ed. A. Richlin (New York: Oxford University Press, 1992), 8; S. Lewis, "Shifting Images: Athenian Women in Etruria," in *Gender and Ethnicity in Ancient Italy,* ed. T. Cornell and K. Lomas (London: Accordia Research Institute, University of London, 1997); S. Lewis, *The Athenian Woman: An Iconographic Handbook* (London: Routledge, 2002), 116–29; S. Lewis, "Representation and Reception: Athenian Pottery in its Italian Context," in *Inhabiting Symbols: Symbol and Image in the Ancient Mediterranean,* ed. J. Wilkins and E. Herring (London: Accordia Research Institute, University of London, 2003); J. de La Genière, "Clients, potiers et peintres," in *Les clients de la céramique grecque,* ed. J. de La Genière (Paris: Académie des inscriptions et belles-lettres, 2006). Lewis now claims that nearly all Attic pottery was in fact made for the Etruscans, and specifically that the sexual scenes represent Etruscan orgies and not Athenian symposia ("Representation and Reception," 189–90). For detailed criticisms, see F. Lissarrague, "Voyages d'images: iconographie et aires culturelles," *Revue des études anciennes* 89 (1987): 268; N. Spivey, "Greek Vases in Etruria," in *Looking at Greek Vases,* ed. T. Rasmussen and N. Spivey (Cambridge: Cambridge

University Press, 1991); V. Stissi, "Production, Circulation, and Consumption of Archaic Greek Pottery (Sixth and Early Fifth Centuries B.C.)," in *The Complex Past of Pottery: Production, Circulation and Consumption of Mycenaean and Greek Pottery (16th to Early 5th Centuries B.C.)*, ed. J. P. Crielaard, V. Stissi, and G. J. van Wijngaarden (Amsterdam: J.C. Gieben, 1999); H. B. Hastrup, "La clientèle étrusque de vases attiques a-t-elle acheté des vases ou des images?," in *Céramique et peinture grecques: Modes d'emploi*, ed. M.-C. Villanueva-Puig, F. Lissarrague, P. Rouillard, and A. Rouveret (Paris: Documentation française, 1999); R. Osborne, "Why Did Athenian Pots Appeal to the Etruscans?," *World Archaeology* 33 (2001): 277–95; J. Boardman, *The History of Greek Vases: Potters, Painters, and Pictures* (New York: Thames & Hudson, 2001), 55, 226, 236–39; C. Reusser, *Vasen für Etrurien: Verbreitung und Funktionen attischer Keramik im Etrurien des 6. und 5. Jahrhunderts vor Christus* (Zürich: Akanthus, 2002), 149–50; M. Lee, "Review of Sian Lewis, *The Athenian Woman: An Iconographic Handbook*," *Bryn Mawr Classical Review* (September 28, 2003), http://ccat.sas.upenn.edu/bmcr/2003/2003-09-28.html; M. Stansbury-O'Donnell, *Vase Painting, Gender, and Social Identity in Archaic Athens* (New York: Cambridge University Press, 2006), 37–39; A. Steiner, *Reading Greek Vases* (Cambridge: Cambridge University Press, 2007), 234–36.

16. As nonluxury: M. J. Vickers, "Artful Crafts: The Influence of Metal Work on Athenian Painted Pottery," *Journal of Hellenic Studies* 105 (1985): 128; M. J. Vickers and D. Gill, *Artful Crafts: Ancient Greek Silverware and Pottery* (Oxford: Clarendon Press, 1994), 92. As luxury: A. M. Snodgrass, *Archaic Greece: The Age of Experiment* (Berkeley: University of California Press, 1980), 127; P. Cartledge, "'Trade and Politics' Revisited: Archaic Greece," in *Trade in the Ancient Economy*, ed. P. Garnsey, K. Hopkins, and C. R. Whittaker (Berkeley: University of California Press, 1983), 14; B. A. Sparkes, *The Red and the Black: Studies in Greek Pottery* (London: Routledge, 1996), 143; R. T. Neer, *Style and Politics in Athenian Vase-Painting: The Craft of Democracy, ca. 530–460 B.C.E.* (Cambridge: Cambridge University Press, 2002), 213; Reusser, *Vasen für Etrurien*, 119; J. H. Oakley, "Review of Richard T. Neer, *Style and Politics in Athenian Vase-Painting: The Craft of Democracy, ca. 530–460 B.C.E.*," *American Journal of Archaeology* 107 (2003): 510. "Among the cheapest decorated objects of the day," J. Boardman, "Sixth-century Potters and Painters," in *Looking at Greek Vases*, ed. Tom Rasmussen and Nigel Spivey (Cambridge: Cambridge University Press, 1991), 79; "Decorated vases were cheap on the home market, but not *that* cheap," J. Boardman, "Review of Michael J. Vickers, and David Gill, *Artful Crafts: Ancient Greek Silverware and Pottery*," *Classical Review* 46 (1996): 126; "a semiluxury," J. Boardman, "Review of Richard T. Neer, *Style and Politics in Athenian Vase-Painting: The Craft of Democracy, circa 530–470 B.C.E*," *Common Knowledge* 10 (2004): 353.

17. Dialectal and nonstandard elements in both Greek and Latin graffiti point in that direction. For Latin, see V. Väänänen, *Le latin vulgaire des inscriptions pompéiennes,* 3rd ed. (Berlin: Akademie Verlag, 1966).

18. For an overview, see M. Langner, *Antike Graffitizeichnungen: Motive, Gestaltung und Bedeutung* (Wiesbaden: Ludwig Reichert, 2001). For varying opinions about

Pompeii, see A. Mau, *Pompeii, Its Life and Art,* trans. F. W. Kelsey (New York: Macmillan, 1902), 491; H. H. Tanzer, *The Common People of Pompeii: A Study of the Graffiti* (Baltimore: Johns Hopkins University Press, 1939), 83; J. Lindsay, *The Writing on the Wall: An Account of Pompeii in Its Last Days* (London: Frederick Muller, 1960), 115; W. Harris, *Ancient Literacy* (Cambridge, MA: Harvard University Press, 1989), 261; J. L. Franklin Jr., "Literacy and the Parietal Inscriptions of Pompeii," in *Literacy in the Roman World,* ed. J. H. Humphrey (Ann Arbor: University of Michigan Press, 1991); Jozsef Herman, *Vulgar Latin,* trans. R. Wright (University Park: Pennsylvania State University Press, 2000), 18–20.

19. See the comments of C. Faraone, *Ancient Greek Love Magic* (Cambridge, MA: Harvard University Press, 1999), 3–10; D. Ogden, "Binding Spells: Curse Tablets and Voodoo Dolls in the Greek and Roman Worlds," in V. Flint, R. Gordon, G. Luck, and D. Ogden, *The Athlone History of Witchcraft and Magic in Europe: Vol. 2. Ancient Greece and Rome* (London; Athlone, 1999), 67–71.

20. Storey, *Cultural Theory and Popular Culture,* 5.

21. For the sources, see A. W. Pickard-Cambridge, *The Dramatic Festivals of Athens* 2nd ed. J. Gould and D. M. Lewis (Oxford: Oxford University Press, 1988), 263–78; A. J. Podlecki, "Could Women Attend the Theater in Ancient Athens? A Collection of Testimonia," *Ancient World* 21 (1990): 27–43; E. G. Csapo and W. J. Slater, *The Context of Ancient Drama* (Ann Arbor: University of Michigan Press, 1995), 286–305. On women in the audience: J. Henderson, "Women and the Athenian Dramatic Festivals," *Transactions of the American Philological Association* 121 (1991): 133–47; S. Goldhill, "Representing Democracy: Women at the Great Dionysia," in *Ritual, Finance, Politics: Athenian Democratic Accounts Presented to David Lewis,* ed. R. Osborne and S. Hornblower (Oxford: Clarendon Press, 1994); S. Goldhill, "The Audience of Athenian Tragedy," in *The Cambridge Companion to Greek Tragedy,* ed. P. E. Easterling (Cambridge: Cambridge University Press, 1997), 61–66, for a skeptical reading. On civic ideology, see J. J. Winkler and F. I. Zeitlin, eds., *Nothing to Do With Dionysos? Athenian Drama in its Social Context* (Princeton, NJ: Princeton University Press, 1989); W. R. Connor, "City Dionysia and Athenian Democracy," *Classica & Mediaevalia* 40 (1989): 7–32; C. Sourvinou-Inwood, "Something to Do with Athens: Tragedy and Ritual," in *Ritual, Finance, Politics: Athenian Democratic Accounts Presented to David Lewis,* ed. R. Osborne and S. Hornblower (Oxford: Oxford University Press, 1994).

22. H. N. Parker, "The Observed of All Observers: Spectacle, Applause, and Cultural Poetics in the Roman Audience," in *The Art of Ancient Spectacle,* edited by B. Bergmann and C. Kondoleon (Washington, DC: National Gallery of Art, 1999); R. C. Beacham, *Spectacle Entertainments of Early Imperial Rome* (New Haven, CT: Yale University Press, 1999).

23. G.E.R. Lloyd, *Science, Folklore, and Ideology: Studies in the Life Sciences in Ancient Greece* (Cambridge: Cambridge University Press, 1983).

24. Burke, *Popular Culture;* J. Storey, *Inventing Popular Culture: From Folklore to Globalization* (Malden, MA: Blackwell, 2003), 14, 17.

25. So Weber's notion of status shown by "style of life" (*Lebensstil*) and stylized consumption; most succinctly at Max Weber, *Economy and Society: An Outline*

of Interpretive Sociology, 2 vols. (Berkeley: University of California Press, 1978), 305–6 (also 932–33, 935–38): "With some over-simplification, one might thus say that 'classes' are stratified according to their relations to the production and acquisition of goods; whereas 'status groups' are stratified according to the principles of their consumption of goods as represented by special 'styles of life.'" See A. Giddens, *The Class Structure of the Advanced Societies* (New York: Harper & Row, 1973), 43–44. For Weber on the ancient world, see *Economy and Society*, 1340–72.

26. D. Konstan, *Greek Comedy and Ideology* (New York: Oxford University Press, 1995), 6; M. Heath, *Political Comedy in Aristophanes* (Göttingen: Vandenhoeck & Ruprecht, 1987), 40–41.

27. Rightly F. R. Earp, *The Way of the Greeks* (London: Oxford University Press, 1929), 11; K. J. Dover, *Greek Popular Morality in the Time of Plato and Aristotle* (Oxford: Blackwell, 1974), 5–8. See Ober, *Mass and Elite*, 141–44 for the composition of the juries.

28. Because the literary materials are more easily accessible and have considerable secondary studies, I will devote most space to graffiti and such.

29. For "symbolic" or "cultural capital" see P. Bourdieu, "Cultural Reproduction and Social Reproduction," in *Knowledge, Education and Cultural Change*, ed. R. Brown (London: Tavistock, 1973) (a definition on p. 73: "instruments for the appropriation of symbolic wealth socially designated as worthy of being sought and possessed"); also P. Bourdieu, *Outline of a Theory of Practice* (Cambridge: Cambridge University Press, 1977), esp. 177–97; and P. Bourdieu, "The Forms of Capital," in *Handbook of Theory and Research for the Sociology of Education*, ed. J. Richardson (New York: Greenwood Press, 1986). See also J. Guillroy, *Cultural Capital: The Problem of Literary Canon Formation* (Chicago: University of Chicago Press, 1993).

30. I draw on Dickie's "Institutional Theory of Art": "A work of art in the classificatory sense is (1) an artifact, (2) a set of the aspects of which has had conferred upon it the status of candidate for appreciation by some person or persons acting on behalf of a certain social institution (the artworld)" (G. Dickie, *Art and the Aesthetic: An Institutional Analysis* [Ithaca, NY: Cornell University Press, 1974], 464; G. Dickie, "What Is Art: An Institutional Analysis," in *Art and Philosophy: Readings in Aesthetics*, ed. W. E. Kennick [New York: St. Martin's Press, 1979], 89). For his later refinements on this idea see G. Dickie, *The Art Circle: A Theory of Art* (New York: Haven, 1984); G. Dickie, *Art and Value* (Malden, MA: Blackwell, 2001), 52–73. Dickie in turn draws on A. C. Danto, "The Artworld," *Journal of Philosophy* 61 (1964): 571–84, for the idea of "the artworld"; see also A. C. Danto, *The Transfiguration of the Commonplace* (Cambridge, MA: Harvard University Press, 1981), 45, 135. This is Bourdieu's institutionalized state of cultural capital ("The Forms of Capital," 47). Convenient overviews in D. Graves, "The Institutional Theory of Art: A Survey," *Philosophia* 25 (1997): 51–67; R. J. Yanal, "The Institutional Theory of Art," in *The Encyclopedia of Aesthetics*, ed. M. Kelly (Oxford: Oxford University Press, 1998).

31. The interesting problem then—but one beyond the scope of this chapter—is to identify the sources of cultural "anointing" in the ancient world. What/who made a poet a poet? What/who authorized an artist?

32. V. Ehrenberg, *The People of Aristophanes: A Sociology of Old Attic Comedy*, 3rd rev. ed. (New York: Schocken Books, 1962), 180; H. A. Shapiro, "Courtship Scenes in Attic Vase-Painting," *American Journal of Archaeology* 85 (1981): 133–43; H. A. Shapiro, "Eros in Love: Pederasty and Pornography in Greece," in *Pornography and Representation in Greece and Rome,* ed. A. Richlin (New York: Oxford University Press, 1992); M. Golden, "Slavery and Homosexuality at Athens," *Phoenix* 38 (1984): 320; Ober, *Mass and Elite,* 250, 253, 257–58, 263; J. N. Bremmer, "Adolescents, *symposion,* and Pederasty," in *Sympotica: A Symposium on the Symposion,* ed. O. Murray (Oxford: Oxford University Press, 1990); S. Todd, "Lady Chatterley's Lover and the Attic Orators: The Social Composition of the Athenian Jury," *Journal of Hellenic Studies* 110 (1990): 166; B. S. Thornton, *Eros: The Myth of Ancient Greek Sexuality* (Boulder, CO: Westview Press, 1997), 195–96; T. K. Hubbard, "Popular Perceptions of Elite Homosexuality in Classical Athens," *Arion* 6 (1998): 48–78; V. Yates, "*Anterastai*: Competition in *eros* and Politics in Classical Athens," *Arethusa* 38 (2005): 33–47; even Dover ("Eros and nomos," *Bulletin of the Institute of Classical Studies* 11 [1964]: 36–39; *Greek Homosexuality* [Cambridge, MA: Harvard University Press, 1978], 149–52) tends to view pederasty as the prerogative of the rich. See the criticisms of D. M. Halperin, *One Hundred Years of Homosexuality and Other Essays on Greek Love* (New York: Routledge, 1990), 91 (but cf. D. M. Halperin, "Plato and Erotic Reciprocity," *Classical Antiquity* 5 [1986]: 60–80; Halperin, *One Hundred Years of Homosexuality,* 4); V. Wohl, *Love among the Ruins: The Erotics of Democracy in Classical Athens* (Princeton, NJ: Princeton University Press, 2002), 6–7.

33. R. Jenkyns, *The Victorians and Ancient Greece* (Cambridge, MA: Harvard University Press, 1980).

34. N.R.E. Fisher, "Symposiasts, Fish-eaters and Flatterers: Social Mobility and Moral Concerns," in *The Rivals of Aristophanes: Studies in Athenian Old Comedy,* ed. D. Harvey and J. Wilkins (London: Duckworth and the Classical Press of Wales, 2000); J. Wilkins, *The Boastful Chef: The Discourse of Food in Ancient Greek Comedy* (Oxford: Oxford University Press, 2000), 202–13; B. Pütz, *The Symposium and Komos in Aristophanes* (Stuttgart: M&P Verlag für Wissenschaft und Forschung, 2003), 155.

35. N. Dunbar, *Aristophanes: Birds* (Oxford: Clarendon Press, 1995), 178 on Old Comedy.

36. The "comfy chair" was a piece of luxury furniture (Ath. 12.515c). The boy can be bent over, too. The point about him still having his balls is that he is not some foreign eunuch.

37. Henderson's clever rendering (*Aristophanes: Acharnians. Knights* [Cambridge, MA: Harvard University Press, 1998], 403).

38. A slap at Cleon (and other politicians, according to the scholiasts) for being in low professions to be sure; the point is that the low professions are assumed to share the tastes of everyone else.

39. One place where we might find an important difference is the seclusion of women. This belongs more properly to gender rather than sex as such, but public work could lead to accusations of being a public woman. See R. Just, *Women in Athenian Law and Life* (London: Routledge, 1989), 106–7, 113; D. Cohen, *Law, Sexuality, and Society: The Enforcement of Morals in Classical Athens* (Cambridge: Cambridge University Press, 1991), 146–54; see Arist. *Pol.* 1300a4–9, Dem. 57.30–1 (female workers in the agora open to insults).

40. Solon's move is called "democratic" (*dēmotikon*) by a character in Philemon's *Brothers* (Philemon 3 K-A = Ath. 13.569df). Halperin comments: "The assumption underlying this 'Solonian' reform would seem to have been that a society is not democratic so long as sexual pleasure remains the exclusive perquisite of the well-to-do" (*One Hundred Years of Homosexuality*, 100). Athenaeus also claims the authority of Nicander of Colophon (who may be drawing on Philemon or the same legend) and contrasts the "hetaerae with their huge prices."

41. On love as a rich man's pastime, see Semon. 7.57–70, Men. *Dys.* 341–4; cf. the tragedian Achaeus (*TGF* 6). For a survey of Greek prices, see H. Herter, "The Sociology of Prostitution in Antiquity in the Context of Pagan and Christian Writing," trans. L. DeLong, in *Sex and Difference in Ancient Greece and Rome*, ed. M. Golden and P. Toohey (Edinburgh: Edinburgh University Press, 2003), 71–78; Halperin, *One Hundred Years*, 107–12; for economics at Athens, E. E. Cohen, "Free and Unfree Sexual Work: An Economic Analysis of Athenian Prostitution," in *Prostitutes and Courtesans in the Ancient World*, ed. C. A. Faraone and L. K. McClure (Madison: University of Wisconsin Press, 2006). For Rome, T.A.J. McGinn, *The Economy of Prostitution in the Roman World: A Study of Social History and the Brothel* (Ann Arbor: University of Michigan Press, 2004). Poverty is the standard complaint of all the Roman elegiac lovers.

42. H. Solin, "Un epigramma della Domus Aurea," *Rivista di filologia e di istruzione classica* 109 (1981): 268–71; E. Courtney, *Musa Lapidaria: A Selection of Latin Verse Inscriptions* (Atlanta, GA: Scholars Press, 1995), 103 (no. 102), 313. Even this scrap of verse finds an elite echo in Nemesianus' *Eclogue* 4 (c. A.D. 280), where the two shepherds lament *parilisque furor de dispare sexu*, "the same madness for different sexes" (4.5). 4.56 has the same opening: *quisquis amat pueros, ferro praecordia duret* "Whoever loves boys, let him harden his heart with steel."

43. N.R.E. Fisher, *Aeschines Against Timarchos* (Oxford: Oxford University Press, 2001), 26–27, 58–62, 274–88.

44. Lys. 3.4. As in Aeschines' *Against Timarchus*, the basis of this case is that there is a right way and a wrong way to pursue those you are sexually interested in and a right way of settling disputes over pretty boys that doesn't involve public unrest. The sex of the sex object is not at issue. A similar case involves a fight over a courtesan: [Dem.] 59, and see Ath. 13.555a. See J. J. Winkler, *The Constraints of Desire* (London: Routledge, 1990), 49; D. Cohen, *Law, Violence, and Community in Classical Athens* (Cambridge: Cambridge University Press, 1995), 127–28; N.R.E. Fisher, "Violence, Masculinity and the Law in Classical Athens," in *When Men Were Men: Masculinity, Power, and Identity in Classical Antiquity*, ed. L.

Foxhall and J. Salmon (London: Routledge, 1998), 73–78. The author of the *Dissoi logoi* 4.2–5 takes it as axiomatic that, "For a boy in the flower of his youth to grant his favors to a good lover is good but shameful to a lover who is not good," a piece of commonsense as basic as the fact that adultery or men wearing makeup is bad.

45. Detailed analysis at Fisher, *Aeschines Against Timarchos,* 274–88.

46. See Thuc. 6.54–9. Aristogeiton killed the tyrant's son Hippias in part because he made an attempt to seduce (or abduct) Harmodius. The love between an elite and an ordinary citizen was taken as a founding model for the ideal of a legitimate democracy; see A. F. Stewart, *Art, Desire, and the Body in Ancient Greece* (Cambridge: Cambridge University Press, 1997), 73; Fisher, *Aeschines Against Timarchos,* 277; Wohl, *Love among the Ruins,* 4, 8.

47. Fisher, *Aeschines Against Timarchos,* 285. Hyperides 6.39 also places the love affair at the center of the story of democracy. So too Pl. *Symp.* 182c4–7, an elite text. [Arist.] *Ath. Pol.* 18 and Arist. *Rhet.* 1401b6–8 show just how much a given was the tie between the erotic and the democratic.

48. See Stewart, *Art, Desire, and the Body,* 70–75 for a reading of the erotics of the statues of the Tyrannicides.

49. *PMG* 893–6. Specifically said to have been sung not just at symposia but in the Prytaneum in which nearly all Athens' citizens would have at one time served (Schol. Pl. *Grg.* 451e2 = p. 462 Greene).

50. Solon 25 W., *Anth. Pal.* 5.277.

51. M. C. Nussbaum, *The Fragility of Goodness: Luck and Ethics in Greek Tragedy and Philosophy* (Cambridge: Cambridge University Press, 1986), 240–63; Arist. *Eth. Nic.* 1145b2–7.

52. Hippoc. *De natura pueri* 13.6 (7.490.6–8 L.).

53. *De Genitura* 5 (7.476.17–20 L.). See L. Dean-Jones, *Women's Bodies in Classical Greek Science* (Oxford: Oxford University Press, 1994), 28, for this example.

54. For surveys, see I. Veith, *Hysteria: The History of a Disease* (Chicago: University of Chicago Press, 1965); B. Simon, *Mind and Madness in Ancient Greece: The Classical Roots of Modern Psychiatry* (Ithaca, NY: Cornell University Press, 1978); M. R. Lefkowitz, *Heroines and Hysterics* (New York: St. Martin's Press, 1981); P. Manuli, "Donne mascoline, femmine sterili, vergini perpetue: la ginecologia greca tra Ippocrate e Sorano," in *Madre materia: sociologia e biologia della donna greca*, ed. S. Campese (Turin: Boringhieri, 1983); B. K. Gold, "Dionysus, Greek Festivals and the Treatment of Hysteria," *Laetaberis* 6 (1988): 16–28; A. E. Hanson, "The Medical Writers' Woman," in *Before Sexuality: The Construction of Erotic Experience in the Ancient Greek World*, ed. D. M. Halperin, J. J. Winkler, and F. I. Zeitlin (Princeton, NJ: Princeton University Press, 1990), esp. 319–21; S. Gilman et al., *Hysteria beyond Freud* (Berkeley: University of California Press, 1993); Dean-Jones, *Women's Bodies,* 69–77; M. S. Micale, *Approaching Hysteria: Disease and Its Interpretations* (Princeton, NJ: Princeton University Press, 1995); S. Föllinger, "*Skhetlia drôsi.* 'Hysterie' in den hippokratischen Schriften," in *Hippokratische Medizin und antike Philosophie,* edited by R. Wittern and P. Pellegrin (Zürich: Olms Weidmann, 1996).

55. *PGM* VII.260–71 (Betz, *The Greek Magical Papyri*, 123–24) for hysteria; *PGM* XXXVI.283–94 (Betz, *The Greek Magical Papyri*, 276) for opening and locking the womb.

56. Plut. *Mor.* 249bd, Hippoc. *Virg*, (8.466–70 L.). For translations, see M. R. Lefkowitz and M. B. Fant, *Women's Life in Greece and Rome: A Source Book in Translation*, 3rd ed. (Baltimore: Johns Hopkins University Press, 2005), 242–43, 259. See H. King, "Bound to Bleed: Artemis and Greek Women," in *Images of Women in Antiquity*, ed. A. Cameron and A. Kuhrt (Detroit: Wayne State University Press, 1983); Dean-Jones, *Women's Bodies*, 28.

57. Hes. *Op.* 586, Alcaeus 347a (*LP*), Arist. *HA* 9(7).542a32, [Arist.] *Prob.* 4.25 (879a27–36), 4.28 (880a12–22); Pliny, *NH* 10.172.

58. Pliny, *NH* 38.82; Arist. *Insomn.* 459b-60a.

59. For an example where Pliny disagrees, *NH* 24.18: juniper juice smeared on the penis is not in fact a good contraceptive. For the accommodation of folk beliefs into medical and philosophical systems, see Lloyd, *Science, Folklore, and Ideology*, 82–86, 168–82.

60. See A. Carson, "Putting Her in Her Place: Woman, Dirt, and Desire," in *Before Sexuality: The Construction of Erotic Experience in the Ancient Greek World*, ed. D. M. Halperin, J. J. Winkler, and F. I. Zeitlin (Princeton, NJ: Princeton University Press, 1990) for a brilliant reading of the Greek sources; J. Henderson, *The Maculate Muse: Obscene Language in Attic Comedy*, 2nd ed. (New York: Oxford University Press, 1991), 145–46. See, for example, Hipponax 57 (M. L. West, *Studies in Greek Elegy and Iambus* [Berlin: de Gruyter, 1974], 142). For Roman sources, see A. Richlin, ed., *Pornography and Representation in Greece and Rome* (New York: Oxford University Press, 1992), 26, 82.

61. *CIL* 4.1516; cf. *CIL* 4.1517. See Courtney, *Musa Lapidaria*, 308.

62. *PGM* XIV.970–84 ("A prescription to stop liquid in a woman"), Betz, *The Greek Magical Papyri*, 243.

63. For excessive moisture in the womb/vagina: Hippoc. *Mul.* 10 (8.42.2 L.), 17 (8.56.5–15), 18 (8.58.3); Arist. *HA* 582b26; [Arist.] *HA* 10.635b29–31; Aëtius 16.29, 16.31, 16.34, 16.104; Paulus of Aegina 3.74.5–7 (1.292.19–293.10 H.); Oribasius, *Synopsis* 9.43.27–31 (5.304.7–18 R.), Metrodora 21–2. For restoration of virginity: Galen 14.478, 485–6 Kühn; Aspasia in Aëtius 16.66; Metrodora 25.

64. B. J. Brooten, *Love between Women: Early Christian Responses to Female Homoeroticism* (Chicago: University of Chicago Press, 1996), 90–96, argues that *SM* 37, which twice uses the feminine pronoun, should be included, but the name of the intended victim, Pantous/Paitous, is masculine (rightly Faraone, *Ancient Greek Love Magic*, 148 n. 63; see G. Heuser, *Die Personennamen der Kopten* [Leipzig: Dieterich, 1929], 47; A. Gardiner, *Egyptian Grammar; Being an Introduction to the Study of Hieroglyphs*, 2nd ed. [London: Oxford University Press for the Griffith Institute, Ashmolean Museum, Oxford, 1950], 86 §111; A. Loprieno, *Ancient Egyptian: A Linguistic Introduction* [Cambridge: Cambridge University Press, 1995], 69; B. Layton, *A Coptic Grammar: With Chrestomathy and Glossary: Sahidic Dialect* [Wiesbaden: Harrassowitz, 2000], 97 §126 for details).

65. *PGM* XXXII, Egypt, Hawara, second century A.D. (Betz, *The Greek Magical Papyri,* 266). Euangelos is the dead man whose spirit is being used.

66. *SM* 42 = Daniel and Maltomini, *Supplementum Magicum* 1, 132–53; Egypt, Hermoupolis, third-fourth century A.D. See also Brooten, *Love between Women,* 73–113; Faraone, *Ancient Greek Love Magic,* 148–49.

67. Brooten, *Love between Women,* 103–5, I believe, soft-pedals this. I also differ somewhat in my reading from Faraone (e.g., *Ancient Greek Love Magic,* 146, 165) who sees a more marked difference in spells to produce affection (*philia*), which he finds to be used more by women on men, and those to induce passion (*erōs*), used more by men on women. However, as the previous example shows, the two are often combined, men frequently request *philia* or the even more domestic *storgē* and *agapē* from women (e.g., *PGM* 7.389, 10.7; *SM* 45, 47, 49), women request *erōs* from men, and a rigid distinction is hard to maintain (cf. Faraone's warning in *Ancient Greek Love Magic,* 165).

68. A.M.H. Audollent, *Defixionum tabellae quotquot innotuerunt, tam in Graecis Orientis quam in totius Occidentis partibus praeter Atticas in corpore inscriptionum Atticarum editas* (Paris: A. Fontemoing, 1904), 373–77, no. 271.39–47; J. G. Gager, *Curse Tablets and Binding Spells from the Ancient World* (New York: Oxford University Press, 1992), 112–15, no. 36 (his translation adapted).

69. Faraone, *Ancient Greek Love Magic,* 165; C. A. Faraone, "Agents and Victims: Constructions of Gender and Desire in Ancient Greek Love Magic," in *The Sleep of Reason: Erotic Experience and Sexual Ethics in Ancient Greece and Rome,* ed. M. C. Nussbaum and J. Sihvola (Chicago: University of Chicago Press, 2002), 415. See T. Laqueur, *Making Sex: Body and Gender from the Greeks to Freud* (Cambridge, MA: Harvard University Press, 1990).

70. Concise statements in D. M. Halperin, "Homosexuality," in *The Oxford Classical Dictionary,* 3rd ed., ed. S. Hornblower and A. Spawforth (Oxford: Oxford University Press, 1996); H. N. Parker, "Heterosexuality," in *The Oxford Classical Dictionary,* 3rd ed., ed. S. Hornblower and A. Spawforth (Oxford: Oxford University Press, 1996).

71. For example, a passage cut from the surviving text of [Dem.] 59, apparently as too racy, but preserved in Hermogenes, *On Style* 2.3 (p. 325.18–21 Rabe); Auson. *Epigr.* 75 (79), cf. Mart. 2.28, 2.47, 3.73, 3.83, 9.67; H. N. Parker, "The Teratogenic Grid," in *Roman Sexualities,* ed. J. P. Hallett and M. B. Skinner (Princeton, NJ: Princeton University Press, 1997), for further analysis.

72. Parker, "The Teratogenic Grid," 53.

73. *SM* 38. Same language and order at *SM* 46.9, 49.20–22; cf. *PGM* 4.351, *SM* 47.8–9, 48.8. Compare the epigrams in *Anth. Pal.* 5.49 (Gallus) and 11.328 (Nicarchus). For *laikazō,* see H. D. Jocelyn, "A Greek Indecency and its Students: *laikazein,*" *Proceedings of the Cambridge Philological Society* 26 (1980): 12–66; Henderson, *The Maculate Muse,* 249.

74. On the date, see L. H. Jeffery, *The Local Scripts of Archaic Greece,* rev. ed. with a supplement by A. W. Johnston (Oxford: Clarendon Press, 1990), 318–19 (as old as the Hymettus inscription), 323 (end of eighth century onward), 413 (Thera 1b).

75. *IG* 12.3.53, The verb "did" is the Doric *oipheō;* for emotive range see Dover, *Greek Homosexuality,* 123; Henderson, *The Maculate Muse,* 157; D. Bain, "Six Greek Verbs of Sexual Congress (*binō, kinō, pugizō, lēkō, oiphō, laikazō*)," *Classical Quarterly* 41 (1991): 72–74; and the gloss at Aristophanes of Byzantium 15 (Kock = Eust. *Od.* p. 1597.28). The verb for dance, *orkheō,* also contains a pun on testicle; one might translate with the English "ball." The other references to so-and-so being a good "dancer" need to be interpreted in this light.

76. Ar. *Plut.* 155; Xen. *Mem.* 1.6.13; Dem. 22.73, 24.181; Aeschin. 1.70, 123, 130, 157; Eupolis 92 K-A; Lucian, *Ind.* 25.

77. C. W. Blegen, "Inscriptions on Geometric Pottery from Hymettos," *American Journal of Archaeology* 38 (1934): 10–11; R. S. Young, "Graves from the Phaleron Cemetery," *American Journal of Archaeology* 46 (1942): 47 n. 14; M. K. Langdon, *A Sanctuary of Zeus on Mount Hymettos: Hesperia* Supplement 16 (Princeton, NJ: American School of Classical Studies at Athens, 1976), 22 (no. 36), 45–47; Jeffery, *The Local Scripts,* 69 (item 3b), 401.

78. Ar. *Vesp.* 84, 687, *Nub.* 529, 909, *Thesm.* 200. See H. N. Parker, "The Myth of the Heterosexual or the Anthropology of Sexuality for Classicists," *Arethusa* 34 (2001): 315 n. 7. For later examples, see Lucian, *Tim.* 22.4 and *Ind.* 23. For the graffiti, see M. J. Milne and D. von Bothmer, "Katapugôn, katapugaina," *Hesperia* 22 (1953): 215–24.

79. Athens, c. 575 B.C.: *SEG* 46:80. This is the great Athenian general, whose name is also found on many ostraca.

80. Athens, c. 525–500 B.C.: *SEG* 16:38; M. Lang, *Graffiti and Dipinti:* The Athenian Agora 21 (Princeton: American School of Classical Studies at Athens, 1976), 12 (C 5).

81. Athens, c. 485 B.C.: *SEG* 21:215.

82. Athens, c. 475–50 B.C.: Lang, *Graffiti and Dipinti,* 14 (C 23). For this term of abuse, see Ar. *Nub.* 1330, Eupolis 385.4 K-A, Cephisiodorus 3.4 K-A.

83. Egypt, Abydos, c. 475: *SEG* 26:1708.

84. Respectively, Lang, *Graffiti and Dipinti,* 13–14 (C18), (C 22), (C 24), all Athens c. 475–50 B.C.; (C26), Athens, c. 450–25.

85. A sampling of literary sources: Ar. *Nub.* 1083–1104, *Thesm.* 59–62, 157–8; Theoc. 5.41–3, 116–19 (*pygizō*), Lucian, *Peregr.* 5. Xen. *Mem.* 2.1.5 refers to nameless shameful evils.

86. Sicily, Montagna di Marzo, c. 500–475 B.C. (*SEG* 31:824).

87. Karnak, Wall of the Court of Bubastides. F. Preisigke et al., eds., *Sammelbuch griechischer Urkunden aus Ägypten* (Strassburg: K. J. Trübner, 1915–1993), 3.157–8 (no. 6840 A1); A. Bernand, *Le Delta égyptien d'après les textes grecques, I: Les Confins libyques,* 3 vols., Mémoires 91 (Cairo: Institut français d'Archéologie orientale du Caire, 1970), 918–19.

88. *SEG* 27:240, from Nikopolis.

89. *IG* 1³ 1401 (*IG* 1² 924), 475–50 B.C. See Dover, *Greek Homosexuality,* 123–24. Of course, we have no guarantee that Lysitheus put this up.

90. Elegiac couplet. Inscribed tombstone, Attica, Prospalta (Kalybia Kouvara), c. 525–500 B.C.?, *IG* 1³ 1399 (*IG* 1² 920). P. Friedländer, *Epigrammata: Greek In-*

scriptions in Verse from the Beginnings to the Persian Wars (Berkeley: University of California Press, 1948), 63–64 (no. 59) suggests that the unnamed boy may have put up this inscription. See Dover, *Greek Homosexuality*, 124.

91. *IG* 1³ 1402. Graffito, Greece, Piraeus, c. 450 B.C.?

92. Lang, *Graffiti and Dipinti*, 15, Agora C 33 on a skyphos, c. 350 B.C. Theodosia has been scratched out.

93. Lang, *Graffiti and Dipinti*, 15, Agora C34, on a spindle whorl, typically a woman's object, fourth century B.C.

94. Attica, c. 323 B.C. E. Ziebarth, "Neue Verfluchungstafeln aus Attika, Boiotien und Euboia," Preussische [Deutsche] Akademie der Wissenschaften, *Sitzungsberichte* (1934): 1024 (no. 1.B.16–20). Gager, *Curse Tablets*, 145–47 (no. 56) with improved readings by David Jordan. The last name is masculine.

95. Aristyllus (Ar. *Eq.* 647–48; his anus gapes: *Plut.* 314) and Cleisthenes (*Ran.* 423), a frequent butt; Agathon (*Thesm.* 49), The Sausage-Seller (*Eq.* 167), and all the leaders of Athens (*Ach.* 79). For other examples in comedy, cf. Alexis 244 K-A, Strattis 41 K-A.

96. See Dover, *Greek Homosexuality*, 21.

97. On these writers, see H. N. Parker, "Love's Body Anatomized: The Ancient Erotic Handbooks and the Rhetoric of Sexuality," in *Pornography and Representation in Greece and Rome*, ed. A. Richlin (New York: Oxford University Press, 1992).

98. *Aischrourgos < aischro-ergos*, literally "one who does what is shameful." This passage makes clear the technical meaning. *Kinaidos* is a general word for the sexually passive male, but in contrast with other terms refers to undergoing anal sex specifically. Compare Aeschin. 2.99 (similarly linking the two terms).

99. For *lesbiazō* see Dover, *Greek Homosexuality*, 182; Henderson, *The Maculate Muse*, 183–84; For *phoinikazō*, "do like the Phoenicians do," see Lucian, *Pseudol.* 28, where the two verbs are similarly linked. The meanings of the two verbs are clearly set out by W. Kroll, "Lesbische Liebe," *Real-Encyclopädie der klassischen Altertumswissenschaft* 12.2 (1925): 2100–2102. Compare *Anth. Pal.* 11.329.

100. Henderson, *The Maculate Muse*, 185.

101. The scholiast explains: "the lips of the female genitals," also Eust. *Od.* 1523.28, 1539.33.

102. The ancient commentators have only guesses as to what these two men got up to.

103. The man who doesn't hate Ariphrades shares his tastes and his mouth, too, would pollute a shared cup. Aristophanes shares vocabulary with Galen and others: *bdelyttai* "detest," *aischrais* "shameful."

104. Preisigke et al., *Sammelbuch griechischer Urkunden aus Ägypten*, 1, 288 (no. 4130); A. Bernand, *De Koptos à Kosseir* (Leiden: Brill, 1972), 52–53 (no. 23).

105. *CIL* 4.4008, that is, the writer is the only man. Courtney, *Musa Lapidaria*, 92–93, 301. Compare the same type of joke at *CIL* 4.1837, 8230, 8617, and—"Same back at you"—1623: *et qui scripsit fellat*, "Yeah, well the writer sucks, too!"

106. For *amare* in the bare meaning "fuck," see the substitution of *scortare* "go whoring" for *amare* in Ter. *Ad.* 32 and 102; cf. Plaut. *Mostell.* 22–3, 27; *Poen.* 661 (cf. 602); *Pseud.* 1271–2; *Stich.* 446–8.

107. *CIL* 4.4304, in the Gladiators' school (Pompeii V.5.3).

108. See Parker, "The Teratogenic Grid," for the triple vocabulary.

109. *CIL* 4.2246 (add. p. 465). On the walls of a brothel (Pompeii VII.12.18).

110. *CIL* 4.2175; same location.

111. *CIL* 4.2145.

112. *CIL* 4.2274.

113. *CIL* 4.8171.

114. *CIL* 4.5213.

115. *CIL* 4.1830 (add. pp. 212, 464). Verse (septenarii). D. R. Shackleton Bailey, "Notes on Minor Latin Poetry," *Phoenix* 32 (1978): 322.

116. *CIL* 4.8897. On *chalare*, see J. N. Adams, *The Latin Sexual Vocabulary* (Baltimore: Johns Hopkins University Press, 1990), 173.

117. Severan age. V. Väänänen, *Graffiti del Palatino*, 2 vols. (Helsinki: Institutum Romanum Finlandiae, *Acta*, vol. 3, 4, 1966), 1, 145 (no. 121), 200–201 (no. 230, 232), 247 (no. 364). Comparison makes it clear that *pedico* is the verb, not the noun.

118. *CIL* 4.2048 (add. 215). E. Diehl, *Pompeianische Wandinschriften und Verwandtes*, 2nd ed. (Berlin: de Gruyter, 1930), no. 622. See A. Varone, *Erotica pompeiana: Love Inscriptions on the Walls of Pompeii*, trans. R. P. Berg, with revisions by D. Harwood and R. Ling (Rome: 'L'Erma' di Bretschneider, 2002), 132–33; P. Moreau, "Review of Antonio Varone, *Erotica pompeiana*," *Antiquité classique* 64 (1995): 434 has the correct reading.

119. *CIL* 4.2210, Diehl, *Pompeianische Wandinschriften und Verwandtes*, no. 810: *pedicare volo*.

120. A. Vassileiou, "Un graffito métrique érotique de Villards d'Héria," in *Mélanges É. Bernand*, ed. N. Fick and J-C. Carrière (Paris: Les Belles Lettres, 1991), 369, from the baths at Villards d'Héria (France). Courtney, *Musa Lapidaria*, 102–3 (no. 100a), 311–12. cf. Strato, *Anth. Pal.* 12.7, Mart. 11.43, 12.96; Richlin, *Pornography and Representation*, 38, 41–42, 50, 54.

121. *CIL* 4.3932, Courtney, *Musa Lapidaria*, 311–12. The last part of a hexameter and the pentameter; written in charcoal and now vanished. Much of the rest of the transcription cannot be read (contra Varone, *Erotica pompeiana*, 134–35).

122. First century A.D.(?). *CIL* 10.4483, Diehl, *Pompeianische Wandinschriften und Verwandtes*, 31 (no. 508). For elite texts with *pedicare* used of women as objects, Mart. 11.104.17, cf. 11.99.2; Parker, "The Teratogenic Grid."

123. *CIL* 4.9246b. H. Armini, "Ad carminum epigraphicorum tertium uolumen adnotatiunculae," *Eranos* 34 (1936): 126 (cf. Juv. 11.182); Varone, *Erotica pompeiana*, 74–75. Not with Courtney, *Musa Lapidaria*, 101 (no. 97), 310, "my haunches heaving."

124. CIL 4.10030: *malim me amici fellent quam inimici irrument*.

125. *CIL* 4.1931: *ir irumator* (with a false start).

126. *CIL* 4. 4547: *ir<r>umo*; cf. *CIL* 4.2277, 1473.

127. CIL 4.4848: *fel<l>ator*.

128. *CIL* 4.2421.

129. Not with Varone, *Erotica pompeiana,* 77, "but you're not doing it right": *non belle facere* implies moral disapproval not technical incompetence; cf. Cic. *Att.* 5.17.6; Cat. 12.2; *Oxford Latin Dictionary,* s.v. 1b, citing this inscription.

130. *CIL* 4.2292.

131. *CIL* 4.2273 (add. p. 216).

132. H. Solin, "Die Wandinschriften im sog. Haus des M. Fabius Rufus," in *Neue Forschungen in Pompeji und den anderen vom Vesuvausbruch 79 nach Christi verschütteten Städten* (Recklinghausen: Bongers, 1975), 249 (no. 38).

133. *CIL* 4.1825a, as if a parody of a proper Roman name, but cf. *CIL* 4.9027: *Secundus fel(l)ator rarus.*

134. Oratory, for example, Cic. *Dom.* 25–6, 47, 83 (on Clodius); *Phil.* 2.44–7. For surveys, see Richlin, *Pornography and Representation,* esp. 87–104; C. Edwards, *The Politics of Immorality in Ancient Rome* (Cambridge: Cambridge University Press, 1993), 63–97; A. Corbeill, *Controlling Laughter: Political Humor in the Late Roman Republic* (Princeton, NJ: Princeton University Press, 1996), 99–127 (on impure mouths), 128–73 (effeminacy). In comedy, slaves especially taunt each other with having been used by their masters. So Plaut. *Cas.* 362, 455–65, *Epid.* 66, *Mostell.* 890, 894–5, *Persa* 284–6 (with a character named Paegnium "Boy-toy"), *Rud.* 1073–5. See C. A. Williams, *Roman Homosexuality: Ideologies of Masculinity in Classical Antiquity* (Oxford: Oxford University Press, 1999), 35–37, 78–81.

135. *CIL* 4.8805. The author changes from the third person to the first person.

136. Diehl, *Pompeianische Wandinschriften,* no. 1091. Third century A.D. Spain, Mérida. Verse (trochaic septenarius).

137. *CIL* 4.2375.

138. *CIL* 4.1825 (add. pp. 212, 464).

139. *CIL* 4.2319b (add. p. 216).

140. *CIL* 4.4917.

141. *CIL* 4. 1172, 1802, 2332, 2334, 2338, 3114, 4082, 4201, 4602, 4917, 5001, 5064, 5156, 8531, 10043, 10086b, 10143; 2312.

142. In classical Latin, *cunnilingus* is the actor not the act.

143. Arrentine ware plate. First century A.D. H. Comfort, "An Insulting Latin Graffito," *American Journal of Archaeology* 52 (1948): 321–22.

144. *CIL* 4.8841 under 4.7666.

145. *CIL* 4.1884; Courtney, *Musa Lapidaria,* 93 (no. 80), 301.

146. *CIL* 4.763, 1255, 1331, 1383, 1425, 1578, 2081, 2257, 3925, 3999, 4264, 4304, 4699, 4995, 5178, 5193, 5267, 8380, 8419, 8698, 8843, 8877a-b, 8898, 8939, 8940; *CIL* 10.5263, 8069.4.

147. *CIL* 4.4264.

148. *CIL* 4.8898: *Tiopilus, canis, cunnum lingere noli puellis in muro.* See H. Solin, "Pompeiana," *Epigraphica* 30 (1968): 115–18.

149. *CIL* 4.4995.

150. *CIL* 4.8939–40: *Maritimus cunnu[m] linget a. IIII, virgines ammitit.* M. Johnson and T. Ryan, eds., *Sexuality in Greek and Roman Society and Literature* (London: Routledge, 2005), 109, suggest "admit (free)."

151. *CIL* 4.3999. One must not be too quick to read these as offers rather than insults; rightly M. Panciera, "Alicaria in Plautus, Festus and Pompeii," *Classical Quarterly* 57 (2007): 303–6. See R. B. Ward, "Women in Roman Baths," *Harvard Theological Review* 85 (1992): 137 n. 48; McGinn, *The Economy of Prostitution*, 43 n. 213, 299.

152. *CIL* 4.2400 with add. pp. 221, 272 (no. 465); Solin, "Pompeiana," 117; Varone, *Erotica pompeiana*, 82. *Porta*: "gate" (of a city, etc.) but also of bodily openings: Cat. 15.18, *Priap.* 52.5 (anus; not in Adams, *The Latin Sexual Vocabulary*).

153. Terme della Trinacria. *Statio* is a business office; incommoding the passers-by is the least of the troubles with this idea. The paintings in the Suburban Baths served the simple (and funny) purpose of reminding the bathers in which niche they had left their clothes. See L. Jacobelli, *Le pitture erotiche delle Terme Suburbane di Pompe* (Rome: 'L'Erma' di Bretschneider, 1995), esp. 65–8, 99; J. R. Clarke, "Look Who's Laughing at Sex: Men and Women Viewers in the Apodyterium of the Suburban Baths at Pompeii," in *The Roman Gaze: Vision, Power, and the Body*, ed. D. Fredrick (Baltimore: Johns Hopkins University Press, 2002); Clarke, *Art in the Lives of Ordinary Romans*, 195; J. R. Clarke, *Roman Sex: 100 B.C. to A.D. 250, with New Photography by Michael Larvey* (New York: Harry N. Abrams, 2003), 115–33 (and also Clarke's early analysis: *Looking at Lovemaking: Constructions of Sexuality in Roman Art 100 B.C.-A.D. 250* [Berkeley: University of California Press, 1998], 212–40).

154. Cat. 15.18–19, 16; Juv. 10.314–17. Unspecified sexual abuse at Val. Max. 6.1.13.

155. *CIL* 4.2254 (add. p. 216).

156. CIL 4.10232a: *L. Habonius sauciat irrumat Caesum Felic[e]m*. For *sauciat*, see Adams, *The Latin Sexual Vocabulary*, 127, 152.

157. *CIL* 11.6721.7, 9, 11; 5, 14. See J. P. Hallett, "*Perusinae glandes* and the Changing Image of Augustus," *American Journal of Ancient History* 2 (1977): 151–71.

158. See for example, the criticisms of G. Ferrari, *Figures of Speech: Men and Maidens in Ancient Greece* (Chicago: University of Chicago Press, 2002), 1–7; G. Ferrari, "Myth and Genre on Athenian Vases," *Classical Antiquity* 22 (2003): 37–54. On the other hand, M. F. Kilmer, "Painters and Pederasts: Ancient Art, Sexuality, and Social History," in *Inventing Ancient Culture: Historicism, Periodization, and the Ancient World*, ed. M. Golden and P. Toohey (London: Routledge, 1997), 36–37.

159. For example, Solon 25 W., Soph. fr. 345 Radt, Aesch. fr. 135, 136 Radt, Anacreon 407, *Anacreonta* 17.32, [Lucian], *Am.* 53; *diamērizō* "part the thighs" does not refer to interfemoral sex per se and is used of both male and female objects: for example, Ar. *Av.* 669, 706; see Dover, *Greek Homosexuality*, 98. Women's thighs are praised as well, but we never read about or see depicted interfemoral sex with women.

160. Kilmer, *Greek Erotica*, 15: "Clear instances of male homosexual copulation are rare, as are scenes of imminent homosexual copulation." There are four good examples in black-figure: B114, B250, B486, B634 (B130, B458, B482 are likely

but damaged). A change in practice seems less likely than a change in genre scenes.

161. Dover, *Greek Homosexuality*, 88, 145.

162. Dover, *Greek Homosexuality*, 99; Kilmer, *Greek Erotica*, 23. The only examples known to me are black-figure, which generally speaking tends to be wilder and woollier than red-figure: (1) R. F. Sutton, "The Good, the Base and the Ugly: The Drunken Orgy in Attic Vase Painting and the Athenian Self," in *Not the Classical Ideal: Athens and the Construction of the Other in Greek Art*, ed. B. Cohen (Leiden: Brill, 2000), 187–89, fig. 7.2; T. K. Hubbard, ed., *Homosexuality in Greece and Rome: A Sourcebook of Basic Documents* (Berkeley: University of California Press, 2003), fig. 8. (2) Beazley *Para.* 68, 87; *Add.* 47; Sutton, "The Good, the Base and the Ugly," 188–9. The Affecter Painter does not show anal intercourse (H. Mommsen, *Der Affecter* [Mainz: P. von Zabern, 1975], 56–60; C. A. Hupperts, "Greek Love: Homosexuality or Pederasty? Greek Love in Black-figure Vase Painting," in *Proceedings of the 3rd Symposium on Ancient Greek and Related Pottery*, ed. J. Christiansen et al. [Copenhagen: Nationalmuseet, Ny Carlsberg Glyptotek, Thorvaldsens Museum, 1988], 260–62; M. Golden, "Thirteen Years of Homosexuality [and Other Recent Work on Sex, Gender and the Body in Ancient Greece]," *Echos du monde classique/Classical Views* 10 [1991]: 333). See note 164 for the other two examples.

163. Dover, *Greek Homosexuality*, 87, citing Xen. *An.* 2.6.28.

164. (1) *ABV* 102.100, *Para.* 38, *Add.* 27; G. Vorberg, *Glossarium eroticum* (Hanau am Main: Müller & Kiepenheuer, 1965), 466; Kilmer, "Painters and Pederasts," 44, plate 7; Sutton, "The Good, the Base and the Ugly," 185–86, fig. 7.1. (2) H. A. Shapiro, "Leagros and Euphronios: Painting Pederasty in Athens," in *Greek Love Reconsidered*, ed. T. K. Hubbard (New York: W. Hamilton Press, 2000), 16–18, fig. 5–6: "It is simply a riotous drunken revel, or kōmos (note the large bowl for wine) at which all inhibitions have broken down"; Hubbard, *Homosexuality in Greece and Rome*, fig. 5a.

165. Dover, *Greek Homosexuality*, 99; Kilmer, *Greek Erotica*, 70. All this could be changed, however, by a single new find. See Kilmer, *Greek Erotica*, 213–14 on the absence of certain types of images.

166. It would be quite easy to show cunnilingus unambiguously, but the painters choose not to. Florence V 34, R192, and R361, sometimes claimed, are not candidates: Dover, *Greek Homosexuality*, 101–2; Kilmer, *Greek Erotica*, 71; L. Kurke, "Inventing the Hetaira: Sex, Politics, and Discursive Conflict in Archaic Greece," *Classical Antiquity* 16 (1997): 133 = L. Kurke, *Coins, Bodies, Games, and Gold: The Politics of Meaning in Archaic Greece* (Princeton, NJ: Princeton University Press, 1999), 203–4.

167. J. Diggle, *Theophrastus: Characters* (Cambridge: Cambridge University Press, 2004), 318, 403–4; he is probably right not to see an obscene sense in "pipe" (the same passive is at 19.9 with no dirty overtones).

168. *Hipp. Maj.* 299a (which I will take as genuine). Again, the point is that Plato is not arguing about proper sexual activity; he is appealing to what everyone knows in order to prove the point that circumstances alter cases.

169. [Dem.] 59.33. Two epigrams refer to three men sharing one woman: *Anth. Pal.* 5.49 (Gallus) and 11.328 (Nicarchus) but such a scene may be more a poet's conceit than a good indication of practice.

170. Dover, *Greek Popular Morality,* 206; Sutton, "The Good, the Base and the Ugly," 183–84. Other examples are more about sex in the open (generally among barbarians) and the proper behavior of wives specifically: *Dissoi logoi* 2.4, Xen. *An.* 5.4.34. But for a slave looking on, see Ar. *Ran.* 542–8. Literary descriptions of symposia are very decorous.

171. Attempts to turn three pieces of ceramic into evidence of lesbian sex tend to resort to special pleading and occasional disingenuousness. See Kilmer, *Greek Erotica,* 28–30; Brooten, *Love between Women,* 57–60; N. S. Rabinowitz, "Excavating Women's Homoeroticism in Ancient Greece," in *Among Women: From the Homosocial to the Homoerotic in the Ancient World,* ed. N. S. Rabinowitz and L. Auanger (Austin: University of Texas Press, 2002) for surveys. See Lewis, *The Athenian Woman,* 38.

172. Rome seems to find the masculine woman more disturbing. See J. P. Hallett, "Female Homoeroticism and the Denial of Roman Reality in Latin Literature," in *Roman Sexualities,* ed. J. P. Hallett and M. B. Skinner (Princeton, NJ: Princeton University Press, 1997).

173. Compare Mary Beard on "Undermining the stereotype," "Adopting an Approach II," in *Looking at Greek Vases,* ed. T. Rasmussen and N. Spivey (Cambridge: Cambridge University Press, 1991), 26–30.

174. Sutton, "The Good, the Base and the Ugly," 193–94. In general we can get a good idea of what is not seemly for humans by looking at what satyrs get up to. See F. Lissarrague, "The Sexual Life of Satyrs," in *Before Sexuality: The Construction of Erotic Experience in the Ancient Greek World,* ed. D. M. Halperin, J. J. Winkler, and F. I. Zeitlin (Princeton, NJ: Princeton University Press, 1990).

175. E. C. Keuls (*The Reign of the Phallus: Sexual Politics in Ancient Athens* [New York: Harper & Row, 1985], 174–86) reads these scenes as abuse directed specifically at older, fatter prostitutes; so too Sutton, "The Good, the Base and the Ugly," 194–99; Ferrari, *Figures of Speech,* 163, 178; see, however, the critique by Lewis, *The Athenian Woman,* 124–25. See also Kurke, *Coins, Bodies, Games, and Gold,* 208–12.

176. M. F. Kilmer, "Sexual Violence: Archaic Athens and the Recent Past," in *Owls to Athens: Essays on Classical Subjects Presented to Sir Kenneth Dover,* ed. E. M. Craik (Oxford: Clarendon Press, 1990); Kilmer, *Greek Erotica,* 104, also 214–15; Lewis, *The Athenian Woman,* 124–25. R156: Pedieus Painter, R223: Nikosthenes; R513, 518: Brygos; R530: Foundry Painter. To these, we should add the unique scene of satyrs torturing a woman (African? A lamia?) by the Beldam Painter (*Para.* 292). In R518, a man is threatening the conjoined genitals of a man and woman with a lamp. Does this point in the direction of outrageous behavior or specifically male-on-female violence? F. Frontisi-Ducroux, "Eros, Desire and the Gaze," in *Sexuality in Ancient Art: Near East, Egypt, Greece, and Italy,* ed. N. B. Kampen (Cambridge: Cambridge University Press, 1996), 90, identifies him as a voyeur whose lamp is not threatening.

177. Kilmer, *Greek Erotica*, 104–24, 214–15. Boy about to be spanked: R18 (R596 shows satyrs and sexual content is dubious); woman spanking man: R192 (Thalia Painter, which also features the only certain scene with a woman masturbating by hand). In Hellenistic art, Aphrodite Slipper-Slapper (often threatening her son Eros) is a common theme.

178. Dover, *Greek Homosexuality*, 152–53; Kilmer, *Greek Erotica*, 2. The visual evidence dribbles away even as the literary evidence comes in floods.

179. L. Burn, *The Meidias Painter* (Oxford: Clarendon Press, 1987), 84–85; J. Boardman, *Athenian Red Figure Vases: The Classical Period: A Handbook* (London: Thames and Hudson, 1989), 219; Sutton, "Pornography and Persuasion," 33, speculate on changes in the status of or attitude to women. Jan Bažant, "Les vases athéniens et les réformes démocratiques," in *Images et société en Grèce ancienne. L'iconographie comme méthode d'analyse* (*Actes du Colloque international, Lausanne 8–11 février 1984*), ed. C. Bérard, C. Bron, and A. Pomari (Lausanne: Institut d'archéologie et d'histoire ancienne, Université de Lausanne, 1987) looked to democratic reform promoting interiority. Any such causal connection has its difficulties; see Lewis, *The Athenian Woman*, 131–32.

180. Lewis, *The Athenian Woman*, 132.

181. Similar appearances and disappearances of topics are common in vase painting: Fountain House scenes, for example, flourish only between 520 and 480. See Ferrari, *Figures of Speech*, 1–7; Ferrari, "Myth and Genre on Athenian Vases," 44–50; Lewis, *The Athenian Woman*, 1–4.

Chapter 8

I would like to acknowledge and thank the Social Sciences and Humanities Research Council of Canada and the Humanities Research Institute at Brock University for their generous support of my research.

1. W. T. Loomis, *Wages, Welfare Costs, and Inflation in Classical Athens* (Ann Arbor: University of Michigan Press, 1998), 185. See also 166–85 and D. M. Halperin, *One Hundred Years of Homosexuality and Other Essays on Greek Love* (New York: Routledge, 1990), 107–12 on prices in general. A laborer working on the Athenian acropolis in 408–7 B.C. earned one drachma per day, that is, six obols (*IG* I³ 374.404–17). For Rome see R. Flemming, "*Quae corpore quaestum fecit*: The Sexual Economy of Female Prostitution in the Roman Empire," *Journal of Roman Studies* 89 (1999): 48; and T.A.J. McGinn, *The Economy of Prostitution in the Roman World: A Study of Social History and the Brothel* (Ann Arbor: University of Michigan Press, 2004), 40–47, 55. Two *asses* equals the price of a loaf of bread. Prices of prostitutes were likely always negotiable and depended on the extent of the service.

2. T. J. Gilfoyle, "Prostitutes in History: From Parables of Pornography to Metaphors of Modernity," *American Historical Review* 104 (1999): 120.

3. L. McClure, *Courtesans at Table: Gender and Greek Literary Culture in Athenaeus* (New York: Routledge, 2003), 167–69. Also see K. Gilhuly on Lucian ("The Phallic Lesbian: Philosophy, Comedy, and Social Inversion in Lucian's

Dialogues of the Courtesans," in *Prostitutes and Courtesans in the Ancient World,* ed. C. A. Faraone and L. K. McClure [Madison: University of Wisconsin Press, 2006]) and L. Kurke on Machon ("Gender, Politics, and Subversion in the *Chreiai* of Machon," *Proceedings of the Cambridge Philological Society* 48 [2002]: 20–65).

4. In support see R. A. Strong, "The Most Shameful Practice: Temple Prostitution in the Ancient Greek World," unpublished PhD dissertation, University of California, Los Angeles, 1997. Contra: M. Beard and J. Henderson, "With This Body I Thee Worship: Sacred Prostitution in Antiquity," in *Gender and the Body in the Ancient Mediterranean,* ed. M. Wyke (Oxford: Blackwell Publishers, 1998) and S. L. Budin, "Sacred Prostitution in the First Person," in *Prostitutes and Courtesans in the Ancient World,* ed. C. A. Faraone and L. K. McClure (Madison: University of Wisconsin Press, 2006) and S. L. Budin, *The Myth of Sacred Prostitution in Antiquity* (Cambridge: Cambridge University Press, 2008).

5. McGinn has used such a framework in his important studies of Roman prostitution and the brothel (*Prostitution, Sexuality, and the Law in Ancient Rome* [New York: Oxford University Press, 1998] and *The Economy of Prostitution*). I rely on McGinn extensively in my discussion of Roman prostitution.

6. The best discussion of terminology for Greece is: McClure, *Courtesans at Table,* 11–18, and for Rome: Flemming, "*Quae corpore quaestum fecit,"* 47–48, and J. N. Adams, "Words for 'Prostitute' in Latin," *Rheinisches Museum für Philologie* 126 (1983): 321–58.

7. For an interesting recent rethinking of the *hetaira* see J. N. Davidson, *Courtesans and Fishcakes: The Consuming Passions of Classical Athens* (New York: Fontana, 1997), 120–26. For critiques of the idealized modern view of the *hetaira* see E. C. Keuls, *The Reign of the Phallus: Sexual Politics in Ancient Athens* (New York: Harper & Row, 1985), 188–200, and C. Reinsberg, *Ehe, Hetärentum und Knabenliebe im antiken Griechenland* (Munich: C.H. Beck, 1989), 80–86, 88–89.

8. L. Kurke, *Coins, Bodies, Games, and Gold: The Politics of Meaning in Archaic Greece* (Princeton, NJ: Princeton University Press, 1999), 175–219.

9. Plaut. *Curc.* 473; *Poen.* 17; Cic. *Dom.* 49; *Cat.* 2.10, 2.24; Petr. 9.6, 119.

10. See Davidson, *Courtesans and Fishcakes,* 83–85, on brothels as slum holes; contra A. Glazebrook, "*Porneion*: Prostitution in Athenian Civic Space," in *Greek Prostitutes in the Ancient Mediterranean, 800 B.C.E. to 200 C.E.,* ed. A. Glazebrook and M. M. Henry (Madison: University of Wisconsin Press, 2011).

11. The majority of scholars accept this identification. See B. A. Ault, "Housing the Poor and Homeless in Ancient Greece," in *Ancient Greek Houses and Households: Chronological, Regional and Social Diversity,* ed. B. A. Ault and L. C. Nevett (Philadelphia: University of Pennsylvania Press, 2005), 149–50; J. G. Younger, *Sex in the Ancient World From A to Z* (New York: Routledge, 2005), 27; N.R.E. Fisher, *Aeschines Against Timarchos* (Oxford: Oxford University Press, 2001), 261; Davidson, *Courtesans and Fishcakes,* 85; and H. Lind, "Ein Hetärenhaus am Heiligen Tor? Der Athener Bau Z und die bei Isaios (6, 20f.) erwähnte Synoikia Euktemons," *Museum Helveticum* 45 (1988): 158–69. But Knigge, the excavator, remains cautious, stating instead only that it kept prostitutes (*The Athenian Kerameikos,* trans. J. Binder, The German Archaeological Institute in Athens [Athens: Krene Editions, 1991] and *Kerameikos Bd.17: Bau Z* [Munich: Hirmer Verlag, 2005]).

12. B. A. Ault, "Housing the Poor and Homeless in Ancient Greece," 149.

13. On the spinning *hetaira* see Davidson, *Courtesans and Fishcakes*, 86–90, and Knigge, *Kerameikos Bd.17*, 49, 78.

14. Davidson suggests that this relationship with Euctemon proves Alce was never a *pornē* in a *porneion* (*Courtesans and Fishcakes*, 332 n. 55), but the mistake is our assumption that brothels were unsanitary and for customers of low status. Also note the example of Neaera, [Dem.] 59.29–30.

15. On flute girls see C. Starr, "An Evening with the Flute-girls," *La Parola del Passato* 33 (1978): 401–10; and Davidson, *Courtesans and Fishcakes*, 80–82.

16. We can use this and other speeches to talk about the sociocultural history of prostitution, but need to be cautious in what we accept as historically accurate for these women themselves. See A. Glazebrook, "The Making of a Prostitute: Apollodoros's Portrait of Neaira," *Arethusa* 38 (2005): 161–88 and A. Glazebrook, "The Bad Girls of Athens: The Image and Function of Hetairai in Judicial Oratory," in *Prostitutes and Courtesans in the Ancient World*, ed. C. A. Faraone and L. K. McClure (Madison: University of Wisconsin Press, 2006).

17. Nikarete is never described as *pornoboskousa* directly, but she manages a group of girls of slave status.

18. See also Lys. 4 for another dispute over a prostitute.

19. E. E. Cohen, *The Athenian Nation* (Princeton, NJ: Princeton University Press, 2000), 114–15, 136; E. E. Cohen, " 'Whoring under Contract': The Legal Context of Prostitution in Fourth-century Athens," in *Law and Social Status in Classical Athens*, ed. V. Hunter and J. Edmondson (Oxford: Oxford University Press, 2000), 157–58, 167 n. 66. Cohen lists Isae. 3, Dem. 22.61 and Lys. fr. 82 as support.

20. "Citizen female" refers to the partial citizenship of women that made them eligible for marriage, to bear sons that could become full citizens and to participate in certain cults such as the Thesmophoria.

21. McGinn, *The Economy of Prostitution*, 46, n. 229. Herter assumes the practice is the same for Greeks and Romans; H. Herter, "The Sociology of Prostitution in Antiquity in the Context of Pagan and Christian writing," trans. L. DeLong, in *Sex and Difference in Ancient Greece and Rome*. ed. M. Golden and P. Toohey (Edinburgh: Edinburgh University Press, 2003). A possible example is Mart. 9.32.3–6. An example from Roman comedy is Plaut. *Asin.* 746–809. But does it reflect Greek practices or Roman? The text uses a term based on Greek, *syngraphum* (236, 746, 802). See S. James, "A Courtesan's Choreography: Female Liberty and Male Anxiety at the Roman Dinner Party," in *Prostitutes and Courtesans in the Ancient World*, ed. C. A. Faraone and L. K. McClure (Madison: University of Wisconsin Press, 2006), 227, for the view that the contract does reflect Roman practice. James presents the contract as negotiated between the prostitute and her client, but it is actually between the client, the prostitute and her *lena* (746–47) and it is the *lena* who receives the payment (753–56).

22. See Flemming, "*Quae corpore quaestum fecit*," 43. Sources for the *lena* are mainly comedy and elegy (Plaut. *Mostell.* 157–279, *Asin.* 174–5; Tib. 1.5; Prop. 4.5; Ovid, *Am.* 1.8). Both are problematic. Her inclusion is influenced by her representation in Menander's plays. In elegy it is also programmatic rather than a reflection of everyday life; K. S. Myers, "The Poet and the Procuress: The *lena* in Latin Love

Elegy," *Journal of Roman Studies* 86 (1996): 3–4. Griffin suspects they are uncommon, simply a poetic creation (*Latin Poets and Roman Life* [Chapel Hill: University of North Carolina Press, 1986], 114).

23. *Lupanar* is common in "Pompeianist slang," but McGinn refers to it as the "Purpose-Built Brothel," claiming it is unique (*The Economy of Prostitution*, 232). Cf. A. Wallace-Hadrill, "Public Honour and Private Shame: The Urban Texture of Pompeii," in *Urban Society in Roman Italy*, ed. T. Cornell and K. Lomas (New York: St. Martin's Press, 1995), 51–52; and J. DeFelice, *Roman Hospitality: The Professional Women of Pompeii* (Warren Center, PA: Shangri-La Publications, 2001), 13. For details see McGinn, *The Economy of Prostitution*, 220–39, and J. R. Clarke, *Looking at Lovemaking: Constructions of Sexuality in Roman Art 100 B.C.–A.D. 250* (Berkeley: University of California Press, 1998), 196–206.

24. McGinn argues that the *caupona* brothel was the most popular form of brothel at Pompeii ("Pompeian Brothels and Social History," 37).

25. Some scholars argue for such structures in ancient Athens (Davidson, *Courtesans and Fishcakes*, 90–91), but there is no archaeological evidence for cribs like at Pompeii. See further Glazebrook, "*Porneion*," and see McGinn, *The Economy of Prostitution*, 291–94, for a list of possible cribs at Pompeii.

26. Pompeii VII.6.14–15.

27. On prostitutes at the *cena* see M. Roller, "Horizontal Women: Posture and Sex in the Roman Convivium," *American Journal of Philology* 124 (2003): 393–404, and McGinn, *The Economy of Prostitution*, 27.

28. Flemming, "*Quae corpore quaestum fecit*," 45, 56, 60; and Clarke, *Looking at Lovemaking*, 196–206. See Horace, *Sat.* 1.2.30 on slaves as customers. On brothels as disreputable places for the elite see McGinn, *The Economy of Prostitution*, 19, 25, 71–72, 84–86, 163; and McGinn, *Prostitution, Sexuality, and the Law*, 329–30.

29. See C. Edwards, "Unspeakable Professions: Public Performance and Prostitution in Ancient Rome," in *Roman Sexualities*, ed. J. P. Hallett and M. B. Skinner (Princeton, NJ: Princeton University Press, 1997), esp. 66–67; McGinn, *Prostitution, Sexuality, and the Law*, 19, 44–69.

30. McGinn, *Prostitution, Sexuality, and the Law*, 32–44. Contra E. Pólay, "Das *Regimen Morum* des Zensors und die sogenannte Hausgerichtsbarkeit," in *Studi in onore di Edoardo Volterra*, Vol. 3 (Milan: A. Giuffrè, 1971), 296; A. E. Astin, "Regimen morum," *Journal of Roman Studies* 78 (1988): 17–19, 23; and E. Baltrusch, *Regimen Morum: Die Reglementierung des Privatlebens der Senatoren und Ritter in der römischen Republik und frühen Kaiserzeit* (Munich: C. H. Beck, 1989), 24–25, 28, 47–48.

31. McGinn, *The Economy of Prostitution*, 30–36, 263. Contra Clarke, *Looking at Lovemaking*, 174. McGinn, *The Economy of Prostitution*, 49, 54, 71–72, notes it was not profitable for the poor or for prostitutes themselves.

32. A. J. Graham, "The Woman at the Window: Observations on the 'Stele from the Harbour' of Thasos," *Journal of Hellenic Studies* 118 (1998): 22–40; A. Henry, "Hookers and Lookers: Prostitution and Soliciting in Late Archaic Thasos," *Annual of the British School at Athens* 97 (2002): 217–21. Contra: H. Duchêne, *La*

stèle du port. Fouilles du port 1. Recherches sur une nouvelle inscription thasienne, Etudes Thasiennes 14 (Paris: de Boccard, 1992); and D. M. Lewis, "Keeping Roads Clean in Thasos," *Classical Review* 43 (1993): 402–3.

33. Locri Epizephyrii (Diod. Sic. 12.21), Syracuse (Ath. 12.521b) and Sparta (Clem. Al. *Protr.* 2.10 bis. 105). See A. Dalby, "Levels of Concealment: The Dress of Hetairai and Pornai in Greek Texts," in *Women's Dress in the Ancient Greek World*, ed. L. Llewellyn-Jones (London: Duckworth, 2002), 113–14; H. Mills, "Greek Clothing Regulations: Sacred and Profane?," *Zeitschrift für Papyrologie und Epigraphik* 55 (1984): 264–65; D. Ogden, "Controlling Women's Dress: Gynaikonomoi," in *Women's Dress in the Ancient Greek World,* ed. L. Llewellyn-Jones (London: Duckworth, 2002), 208–10.

34. Graham, "The Woman at the Window," 40.

35. P. J. Rhodes, *A Commentary on the Aristotelian* Athenaion Politeia (Oxford: Oxford University Press, 1981), 575.

36. H. Herter, "The Sociology of Prostitution in Antiquity," 72 and 107; Davidson, *Courtesans and Fishcakes,* 82. Also see Halperin, *One Hundred Years of Homosexuality,* 110.

37. Loomis, *Wages, Welfare Costs, and Inflation,* 184.

38. Glazebrook, "Prostituting Female Kin"; Herter, "The Sociology of Prostitution," 109–10.

39. S. Lape, "Solon and the Institution of the Democratic Family Form," *Classical Journal* 98 (2002/2003): 120–22.

40. But see Lape's recent interpretation of Aeschines 1 ("The Psychology of Prostitution in Aeschines' Speech against Timarchus," in *Prostitutes and Courtesans in the Ancient World,* ed. C. A. Faraone and L. K. McClure [Madison: University of Wisconsin Press, 2006], 139–60). She argues that Aeschines attempts to make morality the issue and make prostitution wrong for all citizens.

41. On penetration see Halperin, *One Hundred Years of Homosexuality,* 95–97; K. J. Dover, *Greek Homosexuality* (Cambridge, MA: Harvard University Press, 1978), 103–4.

42. Flemming, "*Quae corpore quaestum fecit,*" 54. In support see Edwards, "Unspeakable Professions," 81; cf. McGinn, *The Economy of Prostitution,* 149–54.

43. McGinn, *Prostitution, Sexuality, and the Law,* 156, 166, 168. Also K. Olson, "*Matrona* and Whore: Clothing and Definition in Roman Antiquity," in *Prostitutes and Courtesans in the Ancient World,* ed. C. A. Faraone and L. K. McClure (Madison: University of Wisconsin Press, 2006), 194–96.

44. McGinn, *Prostitution, Sexuality, and the Law,* 289, 300, 311–16. Compare Flemming, "*Quae corpore quaestum fecit,*" 53. Contra: K. Bradley, "Prostitution, the Law of Rome, and Social Policy," *Journal of Roman Archaeology* 13 (2000): 471.

45. B. Shaw, "Review of Thomas A. J. McGinn, *Prostitution, Sexuality and the Law in Ancient Rome,*" *Bryn Mawr Classical Review.* http://ccat.sas.upenn.edu/bmcr/1999/1999-09-22.html.

46. See McGinn, *Prostitution, Sexuality and the Law,* 321.

47. See McGinn, *Prostitution, Sexuality, and the Law,* 329 for other examples.

48. "Various quarters" is C. B. Gulick's translation of *kata topous* (Athenaeus, *The Deipnosophists,* vol. 6 [Cambridge, MA: Harvard University Press, 1937]).

49. B. Tsakirgis, "Living and Working around the Athenian Agora: A Preliminary Case Study of Three Houses," in *Ancient Greek Houses and Households: Chronological, Regional, and Social Diversity,* ed. B. A. Ault and L. C. Nevett (Philadelphia: University of Pennsylvania Press, 2005), 67, 69, 79.

50. R. Laurence, *Roman Pompeii: Space and Society* (New York: Routledge, 1994), 73; and Wallace-Hadrill, "Public Honour and Private Shame," 51, 55–57, believe there was some form of moral zoning. The latter sees an official zoning of the city, while the former only an informal arrangement for the benefit of individual members of the elite.

51. Laurence, *Roman Pompeii,* 73 and 75; Wallace-Hadrill, "Public Honour and Private Shame," 56–57.

52. Laurence, *Roman Pompeii,* 73 and 77.

53. T.A.J. McGinn, "Zoning Shame in the Roman City," in *Prostitutes and Courtesans in the Ancient World,* ed. C. A. Faraone and L. K. McClure (Madison: University of Wisconsin Press, 2006), 162–65.

54. Mart. 7.61 suggests restrictions on businesses, but not zoning.

55. See McGinn, *The Economy of Prostitution,* 181, 270.

56. On collection see McGinn, *Prostitution, Sexuality, and the Law,* 256–58, 282. Bradley suggests more diversity in the collection of the tax ("Prostitution," 470).

57. McGinn, *Prostitution, Sexuality, and the Law,* 264, argues for the daily rate. In support of the monthly rate see Herter, "The Sociology of Prostitution," 107, and J. F. Gardner, *Women in Roman Law and Society* (London: Croom Helm, 1986), 253.

58. McGinn, *Prostitution, Sexuality, and the Law,* 255 and n. 54. Contra Flemming, who argues it "exploits the situation in which prostitution is entirely licit, but its personnel are legally and socially compromised; not disallowed but disadvantaged" ("*Quae corpore quaestum fecit,*" 54).

59. See McGinn on the invective aspect of these passages (*Prostitution, Sexuality, and the Law,* 168–70).

60. McClure, *Courtesans at Table,* 15. But note the use of *pornos* at Ar. *Plut.* 153–9, Xen. *Mem.* 1.6.13, Aeschin. 1.130. In each case, the term is the highest insult.

61. See note 43. Olson comments that while the toga may not have been required of the prostitute, whores and *matronae* were likely still distinguishable by dress, adornment and comportment ("*Matrona* and Whore," 199–201).

62. Note Olson on the use of *togata* as "metonomy for the sexually licentious woman" ("*Matrona* and Whore," 196).

63. S. Lewis, *The Athenian Woman: An Iconographic Handbook* (London: Routledge, 2002), 99, points out the recently acknowledged distinction that "prostitution is a trade, not an identity."

64. Contra Flemming, "*Quae corpore quaestum fecit,*" 57–59. In support see Edwards, "Unspeakable Professions," 81; McGinn, *Prostitution, Sexuality, and the Law,* 140–215; and McGinn, *The Economy of Prostitution,* 4.

65. But note Olson, "*Matrona* and Whore."

66. [Dem.] 59.122, trans. C. Carey, *Apollodoros Against Neaira. [Demosthenes] 59* (Warminster: Aris & Phillips, 1992), 81.

67. Glazebrook, "The Bad Girls of Athens," and Glazebrook, "The Making of a Prostitute." On the excess of prostitutes see Herter, "The Sociology of Prostitution," 99.

68. See McGinn, *The Economy of Prostitution,* 161, and McGinn, *Prostitution, Sexuality, and the Law,* 168–70. Contra Flemming, "*Quae corpore quaestum fecit*," 57.

69. See M. Skinner, "Clodia Metelli," *Transactions of the American Philological Association* 113 (1983): 273–87, on Clodia and the representations of her in Latin literature in general.

70. Cicero openly calls Clodia a *meretrix* at 38. He indirectly alludes to her as one at 1, 37, 49 and associates her with the life and habits of a *meretrix* at 49, 50, 57. On Cicero's attack against Clodia and her portrait as a prostitute see T. Hillard, "On the Stage, behind the Curtain: Images of Politically Active Women in the Late Roman Republic," in *Stereotypes of Women in Power: Historical Perspectives and Revisionist Views,* ed. B. Garlick, S. Dixon, and P. Allen (London: Greenwood Press, 1992), and K. A. Geffcken, *Comedy in the Pro Caelio* (Leiden: Brill, 1973), 31–34, 37.

71. See Lewis, *The Athenian Woman,* 98–129, for a recent discussion of such scenes and 98–112 in particular on identifying prostitutes on Attic pottery. Although I do not agree with all her conclusions, especially her reluctance to view the scenes as depicting Athenian "mentality" (118–20) and her desire to argue away the significance of the abuse scenes (125), the discussion is thorough. See also J. Neils, "Others within the Other: An Intimate Look at Hetairai and Maenads," in *Not the Classical Ideal: Athens and the Construction of the Other in Greek Art,* ed. B. Cohen (Leiden: Brill, 2000), 208.

72. See E. D. Reeder, "Representing Women," in *Pandora: Women in Classical Greece,* ed. E. D. Reeder (Princeton, NJ: Princeton University Press, 1995), 123–26, esp. 124, 183–92. Also E. Keuls, "The Hetaera and the Housewife: The Splitting of the Female Psyche in Greek Art," *Mededelingen van het Nederlands Instituut te Rome* 44/45 (1983): esp. 30–38. Neils presents the *hetaira* (and maenad) as the "other" to the Athenian wife ("Others within the Other," 225–26).

73. Also note other kylikes with symposium scenes (Yale University Art Gallery, 1913.163, c. 510–500 B.C.; J. P. Getty Museum 86.AE.285, 490 B.C.), a *stamnos* with *symposium* scene (Brussels, Musées Royaux A717, 510 B.C.) and a fifth kylix showing a solicitation scene (Toledo Museum of Art, 1972.55 [490–80 B.C.]).

74. Contra: Lewis, *The Athenian Woman,* 115, who puts the emphasis on the status of the prostitutes as equal to the symposiasts rather than as objectified and sexually available, since such women are represented as just as active as the male participants.

75. F. Lissarrague, *The Aesthetics of the Greek Banquet: Images of Wine and Ritual* (Princeton, NJ: Princeton University Press, 1990), 91–92; and F. Lissarrague, "The Sexual Life of Satyrs," in *Before Sexuality: The Construction of Erotic Experience in the Ancient Greek World,* ed. D. M. Halperin, J. J. Winkler, and F. I. Zeitlin (Princeton, NJ: Princeton University Press, 1990).

76. Compare an Attic red-figure donkey-head rhyton, attributed to the Brygos Painter, but now lost. See R. F. Sutton, "The Good, the Base and the Ugly: The Drunken Orgy in Attic Vase Painting and the Athenian Self," in *Not the Classical Ideal: Athens and the Construction of the Other in Greek Art*, ed. B. Cohen (Leiden: Brill, 2000), 199 and fig. 7.9.

77. Compare Lissarrague, "The Sexual Life of Satyrs," 55–56, on the frontality of the satyr and C. Benson, "Medusa and the Gorgons," in *Pandora: Women in Classical Greece*, ed. E. D. Reeder (Princeton, NJ: Princeton University Press, 1995), 413, on the frontal face of the Gorgon. Also see T. J. McNiven, "Behaving Like an Other: Telltale Gestures in Athenian Vase Painting," in *Not the Classical Ideal: Athens and the Construction of the Other in Greek Art*, ed. B. Cohen (Leiden: Brill, 2000), 89, on the frontal face of a Persian.

78. McClure, *Courtesans at Table*, 143–49.

79. M. McCoy, "The Politics of Prostitution: Clodia, Cicero, and Social Order in the Late Roman Republic," in *Prostitutes and Courtesans in the Ancient World*, edited by C. A. Faraone and L. K. McClure (Madison: University of Wisconsin Press, 2006).

80. Halperin, *One Hundred Years of Homosexuality*, 97.

81. Compare Ogden in this volume, chapter 3.

82. J. Walters, "Invading the Roman Body: Manliness and Impenetrability in Roman Thought," in *Roman Sexualities*, ed. J. P. Hallett and M. B. Skinner (Princeton, NJ: Princeton University Press, 1997), 34–35.

83. McGinn points out that male prostitutes were more despised than female ones (*Prostitution, Sexuality, and the Law*, 48, 56).

84. Adams argues for a more direct correlation between a term and the named prostitute's practices ("Words for 'Prostitute' in Latin," 321–58).

85. McGinn refers to a stance of "toleration and degradation" (*The Economy of Prostitution*, 9). See also McGinn, *Prostitution, Sexuality, and the Law*, 343–44.

Chapter 9

1. J. Boswell, *Christianity, Social Tolerance, and Homosexuality: Gay People in Western Europe from the Beginning of the Christian Era to the Fourteenth Century* (Chicago: University of Chicago Press, 1980); A. Richlin, "Not before Homosexuality: The Materiality of the *cinaedus* and the Roman Law against Love between Men," *Journal of the History of Sexuality* 3 (1993): 523–73.

2. M. Foucault, *The History of Sexuality: vol. 1, An Introduction*, tr. R. Hurley (London: Allen Lane, 1979).

3. Compare D. M. Halperin, *One Hundred Years of Homosexuality and Other Essays on Greek Love* (New York: Routledge, 1990).

4. D. M. Halperin, J. J. Winkler, and F. I. Zeitlin, eds., *Before Sexuality: The Construction of Erotic Experience in the Ancient Greek World* (Princeton, NJ: Princeton University Press, 1990).

5. W. M. Kendrick, *The Secret Museum: Pornography in Modern Culture* (Berkeley: University of California Press, 1996).

6. P. Carcani, ed., *De' bronzi di Ercolano e contorni, t. 2, Statue,* Le antichità di Ercolano (Naples: Nella Regia Stamperia, 1757–1792).

7. J. R. Clarke, *Roman Sex: 100 B.C. to A.D. 250, with New Photography by Michael Larvey* (New York: Harry N. Abrams, 2003), 26, fig. 8; A. Stähli, *Die Verweigerung der Lüste: erotische Gruppen in der antiken Plastik* (Berlin: Reimer, 1999), 24–30.

8. P. d'Onofri, *Elogio estemporaneo per la gloriosa memoria di Carlo III* (Naples, 1789), CV, note XXX.

9. R. P. Knight, *Discourse on the Worship of Priapus, and its Connection with the Mystic Theology of the Ancients* (London: Privately printed, 1794).

10. M. Arditi, 1825, *Il fascino e l'amuleto contro del fascino presso gli antichi,* 2nd ed., edited by R. De Falco (Capri: La Conchiglia, 1991).

11. L. Barré, *Herculanum et Pompéi : recueil général des peintures, bronzes, mosaïques, etc., découverts jusqu'à ce jour, et reproduits d'après le Antichità di Ercolano, Il Museo borbonico, et tous les ouvrages analogues, augmenté de sujets inédits gravés au trait sur cuivre; par H. Roux Aîné: Vol. 8. Le musée secret* (Paris: Firmin Didot frères, 1839).

12. L. García y García and L. Jacobelli, *Museo segreto: Louis Barré* (Pompei: Marius, 2001).

13. C. Johns, *Sex or Symbol: Erotic Images of Greece and Rome* (Austin: University of Texas Press, 1982), 15–39.

14. G. Fiorelli, *Catalogo del Museo Nazionale di Napoli. Raccolta pornografica* (Naples: Stabilimento Tipografica in S. Teresa, 1866).

15. S. De Caro, *Il gabinetto segreto del Museo Nazionale Archeologico di Napoli* (Naples: Electa, 2000).

16. J. Henderson, "Greek Attitudes toward Sex," in *Civilization of the Ancient Mediterranean: Greece and Rome,* 2, ed. M. Grant and R. Kitzinger (New York: Scribner's, 1988).

17. K. J. Dover, *Greek Homosexuality* (Cambridge, MA: Harvard University Press, 1978).

18. Clarke, *Roman Sex,* 39–40, fig. 15.

19. Dover, *Greek Homosexuality*; J. N. Davidson, *Courtesans and Fishcakes: The Consuming Passions of Classical Athens* (New York: Fontana, 1997).

20. F. Lissarrague, "The Sexual Life of Satyrs," in *Before Sexuality: The Construction of Erotic Experience in the Ancient Greek World,* ed. D. M. Halperin, J. J. Winkler, and F. I. Zeitlin (Princeton, NJ: Princeton University Press, 1990).

21. T. J. McNiven, "The Unheroic Penis: Otherness Exposed," *Source* 15 (1995): 10–16.

22. M.-L. Säflund, *The East Pediment of the Temple of Zeus at Olympia: A Reconstruction and Interpretation of its Composition,* Studies in Mediterranean Archaeology (Göteborg: Lund, 1970).

23. V. Dasen, *Dwarfs in Ancient Egypt and Greece* (Oxford: Oxford University Press, 1993), 169–74.

24. O. J. Brendel, "The Scope and Temperament of Erotic Art in the Greco-Roman World," in *Studies in Erotic Art*, ed. T. Bowie and C. V. Christenson (New York: Basic Books, 1970), 42–46.

25. Clarke, *Roman Sex*, 42–43, fig. 17.

26. Ibid., 42–43, fig. 16.

27. A. F. Stewart, "Reflections," in *Sexuality in Ancient Art*, ed. N. B. Kampen (New York: Cambridge University Press, 1996), 147–49.

28. J. R. Clarke, *Looking at Lovemaking: Constructions of Sexuality in Roman Art 100 B.C.-A.D. 250* (Berkeley: University of California Press, 1998), 30–35, fig. 6.

29. Brendel, "The Scope and Temperament of Erotic Art," 54–57.

30. Clarke, *Looking at Lovemaking*, 30–35, fig. 6.

31. H. N. Parker, "Love's Body Anatomized: The Ancient Erotic Handbooks and the Rhetoric of Sexuality," in *Pornography and Representation in Greece and Rome*, ed. A. Richlin (New York: Oxford University Press, 1992).

32. Clarke, *Looking at Lovemaking*, 35–38, figs. 7–8.

33. Clarke, *Roman Sex*, 92, fig. 62.

34. Clarke, *Looking at Lovemaking*, 38–42.

35. Brendel, "The Scope and Temperament of Erotic Art," 52.

36. See also N. Loraux, *The Experiences of Tiresias: The Feminine and the Greek Man*, trans. P. Wissing (Princeton, NJ: Princeton University Press, 1995).

37. J. J. Pollitt, *Art in the Hellenistic Age* (Cambridge: Cambridge University Press, 1986), 147–49.

38. Clarke, *Looking at Lovemaking*, 51, figs. 11–12.

39. A. Ajootian, "Hermaphroditos," in *Lexicon Iconographicum Mythologiae Classicae 5* (Zürich: Artemis, 1990), 276–77.

40. Clarke, *Looking at Lovemaking*, 50–54, figs. 13–14.

41. Ibid., 53–55, fig. 15; J. R. Clarke, *Looking at Laughter: Humor, Power, and Transgression in Roman Visual Culture, 100 B.C.-A.D. 250* (Berkeley: University of California Press, 2007), 182–84, figs. 90–91.

42. J. R. Clarke, *Houses of Roman Italy, 100 B.C.-A.D. 250: Ritual, Space, and Decoration* (Berkeley: University of California Press, 1991), 98–105; B. Bergmann, "Seeing Women in the Villa of the Mysteries: A Modern Excavation of the Dionysiac Murals," in *Antiquity Recovered: The Legacy of Pompeii and Herculaneum*, ed. V.C.G. Coates and J. L. Seydl (Los Angeles: The J. Paul Getty Museum, 2007).

43. M. Bieber, "Die Mysteriensaal der Villa Item," *Jahrbuch des deutschen archäologischen Instituts* 43 (1928): 298–330.

44. Clarke, *Roman Sex*, 47–56, figs. 20–30.

45. Ibid., 78–83, figs. 54–55.

46. Ibid., 84–86, figs. 57–58.

47. J. R. Clarke, "The Warren Cup and the Contexts for Representations of Male-to-Male Lovemaking in Augustan and Early Julio-Claudian Art," *The Art Bulletin* 75 (1993): 275–94; D. Williams, *The Warren Cup* (London: British Museum Press, 2005).

48. J. Pollini, "The Warren Cup: Homoerotic Love and Symposial Rhetoric in Silver," *The Art Bulletin* 81 (1999): 21–52.

49. Clarke, *Roman Sex,* 153, fig. 52.

50. A. Maiuri, *La Casa del Menandro e il suo tesoro di argenteria* (Rome: Libreria dello Stato, 1933), 1: 321–30, figs. 125–26, 2: pls. 31–36; K. S. Painter, *The Insula of the Menander at Pompeii: The Silver Treasure,* The Insula of the Menander at Pompeii, vol. 4 (Oxford: Clarendon Press, 2001), 56–58, fig. 3, pls. 5–6.

51. I. Bragantini and M. de Vos, *Le decorazioni della villa romana della Farnesina* (Rome: De Luca, 1982); Clarke, *Looking at Lovemaking,* 93–107, figs. 28–35.

52. P. Zanker, *Pompeii: Public and Private Life,* trans. D. L. Schneider (Cambridge, MA: Harvard University Press, 1998), 252–54.

53. Clarke, *Looking at Lovemaking,* 148–53, figs. 49–50.

54. Ibid., 153–56, pl. 6.

55. Ibid., 161–69, figs. 57–58, pl. 7.

56. Ibid., 157–58.

57. A. M. Riggsby, " 'Public' and 'Private' in Roman Culture: The Case of the Cubiculum," *Journal of Roman Archaeology* 10 (1997): 36–56.

58. Clarke, *Roman Sex,* 44–46, figs. 18–19.

59. Clarke, *Looking at Lovemaking,* 196–206, figs. 79–85; Clarke, *Roman Sex,* 60–67, figs. 31–40.

60. Clarke, *Roman Sex,* 106, fig. 35.

61. Ibid., 116–17, fig. 79–80.

62. L. Jacobelli, *Le pitture erotiche delle Terme Suburbane di Pompe* (Rome: 'L'Erma' di Bretschneider, 1995), 92–97; Clarke, *Looking at Laughter,* 194–215.

63. Clarke, *Looking at Lovemaking,* 220–23, nn. 52–58.

64. Clarke, *Roman Sex,* 124, fig. 83.

65. Ibid., 130–31, fig. 90.

66. "69"; ibid., 126, fig. 86.

67. Ibid., 126, fig. 85.

68. Ibid., 127–28, fig. 87.

69. Richlin, "Not before Homosexuality"; H. N. Parker, "The Teratogenic Grid," in *Roman Sexualities,* ed. J. P. Hallett and M. B. Skinner (Princeton, NJ: Princeton University Press, 1998).

70. C. A. Williams, *Roman Homosexuality: Ideologies of Masculinity in Classical Antiquity* (Oxford: Oxford University Press, 1999).

71. Clarke, *Roman Sex,* 128–30, fig. 88.

72. Clarke, *Looking at Lovemaking,* 234, n. 92.

73. Clarke, *Roman Sex,* 130–31, fig. 90.

74. W. A. Krenkel, "Fellatio and irrumatio," *Wissenschaftliche Zeitschrift der Wilhelm-Pieck-Universität Rostock* 29 (1980): 77–78; A. Richlin, "The Meaning of *irrumare* in Catullus and Martial," *Classical Philology* 76 (1981): 40–46.

75. Parker, "The Teratogenic Grid."

76. Clarke, *Roman Sex,* 68–70, fig. 43.

77. G. Siebert, "Hermes," in *Lexicon Iconographicum Mythologiae Classicae* 5 (Zürich: Artemis, 1990).

78. Clarke, *Roman Sex,* 104–5, fig. 71.

79. Ibid., 97, fig. 63.

80. De Caro, *Il gabinetto segreto,* 74–75.

81. Clarke, *Roman Sex,* 98, fig. 65; Clarke, *Looking at Laughter,* 70–71.

82. Clarke, *Looking at Laughter,* 72–74, figs. 28–29.

83. Clarke, *Roman Sex,* 106, fig. 72.

84. A. Richlin, ed., *The Garden of Priapus: Sexuality and Aggression in Roman Humour* (New Haven, CT: Yale University Press, 1983), 116.

85. *Priap.* 25, trans. Richlin, *The Garden of Priapus,* 122.

86. Richlin, *The Garden of Priapus.*

87. F. T. Elworthy, 1895, *The Evil Eye: An Account of this Ancient and Widespread Superstition* (New York: Julian Press, 1958); A. Dundes, ed., *The Evil Eye: A Casebook* (Madison: University of Wisconsin Press, 1981); P. B. Gravel, *The Malevolent Eye: An Essay on the Evil Eye, Fertility and the Concept of Mana* (New York: Peter Lang, 1995); T. Rakoczy, *Böser Blick: Macht des Auges und Neid der Götter: eine Untersuchungen zur Kraft des Blickes in der griechischen Literatur* (Tübingen: Gunter Narr, 1996).

88. D. Levi, "The Evil Eye and the Lucky Hunchback," in *Antioch-on-the-Orontes,* ed. R. Stillwell (Princeton, NJ: Princeton University Press, 1941), 225.

89. A. H. Sommerstein, ed. and trans., *Aristophanes* Clouds (Atlantic Highlands, NJ: Humanities Press, 1982), 107–8.

90. Levi, "The Evil Eye."

91. Clarke, *Looking at Laughter,* 103–4.

92. Ibid., pl. 7.

93. J. R. Clarke, *Art in the Lives of Ordinary Romans: Visual Representation and Non-elite Viewers in Italy, 100 B.C.-A.D. 315* (Berkeley: University of California Press, 2003), 210–15, fig. 122–23.

94. Clarke, *Looking at Laughter,* 87–107; P. G. Meyboom and M. J. Versluys, "The Meaning of Dwarfs in Nilotic Scenes," in *Nile into Tiber: Egypt in the Roman World. Proceedings of the IIIrd International Conference on Isis Studies,* ed. L. Bricault, M. J. Versluys and P. G. Meyboom (Leiden: Brill, 2007).

95. M. J. Versluys, *Aegyptiaca Romana: Nilotic Scenes and the Roman Views of Egypt* (Leiden: Brill, 2002); Clarke, *Looking at Laughter,* 63–107.

96. A. Leibundgut, *Die römischen Lampen in der Schweiz* (Bern: Francke, 1977), 199.

97. D. M. Bailey, *A Catalogue of Lamps in the British Museum, vol. 2. Roman Lamps Made in Italy* (London: British Museum, 1980), 64.

98. P. Wuilleumier and A. Audin, *Les médaillons d'applique gallo-romains de la vallée du Rhône* (Paris: Les Belles Lettres, 1952); A. Desbat, "Vases à médaillons d'applique des fouilles récentes de Lyon," *Figlina* 5–6 (1980–1981): 1–203.

99. Clarke, *Roman Sex,* 140–41, fig. 94.

100. Ibid., 141–42, fig. 95.

101. Clarke, *Looking at Lovemaking,* 260–61, fig. 163.

102. A. E. Todd, "Three Pompeian Wall-inscriptions, and Petronius," *Classical Review* 53 (1939): 7–8.

103. Clarke, *Looking at Lovemaking*, 257–58, fig. 99.

104. Clarke, *Roman Sex*, 154–55, fig. 107; J. L. Butrica, "Review of John R. Clarke, *Roman Sex*," *Bryn Mawr Classical Review*, http://ccat.sas.upenn.edu/bmcr/2004/2004–01–03.html.

105. S. Marquié, "Les médaillons d'applique rhodaniens de la Place des Célestins à Lyon," *Revue archéologique de l'est* 50 (1999–2000): 268–70, figs. 16, 31; Clarke, *Roman Sex*, 142–44 fig. 96.

106. G. Neumann, *Gesten und Gebärden in der griechischen Kunst* (Berlin: de Gruyter, 1965), 67–69; L. Steinberg, *The Sexuality of Christ in Renaissance Art and in Modern Oblivion* (New York: Pantheon Books, 1983), 3.

107. Clarke, *Roman Sex*, 148–51, fig. 103.

108. Wuilleumier and Audin, *Les médaillons d'applique*, 49–58, 125–38.

109. Clarke, *Roman Sex*, 146, fig. 100; Clarke, *Looking at Laughter*, 224–26, fig. 118.

110. Clarke, *Roman Sex*, 151, fig. 104; Clarke, *Looking at Laughter*, 222–24, fig. 116.

111. Johns, *Sex or Symbol*, 110–11, fig. 90; Clarke, *Looking at Laughter*, 226, fig. 119.

112. Clarke, *Looking at Lovemaking*, 265–74, figs. 104–7.

BIBLIOGRAPHY

Accademia Ercolanese di Archeologia, eds. *Le antichità di Ercolano esposte.* 1757–1792.

Adams, J. N. *The Latin Sexual Vocabulary*. Baltimore: Johns Hopkins University Press, 1990.

Adams, J. N. "Words for 'Prostitute' in Latin." *Rheinisches Museum für Philologie* 126 (1983): 321–58.

Ager, S. L. "Familiarity Breeds: Incest and the Ptolemaic Dynasty." *Journal of Hellenic Studies* 125 (2005): 1–34.

Ajootian, A. "Hermaphroditos." In *Lexicon Iconographicum Mythologiae Classicae 5*, 268–85. Zürich: Artemis, 1990.

Ajootian, A. "The Only Happy Couple: Hermaphrodites and Gender." In *Naked Truths: Women, Sexuality, and Gender in Classical Art and Archaeology*, edited by C. Lyons and A. Koloski-Ostrow, 220–42. London: Routledge, 1997.

Akamates, I. M. *Pulíes mêtres aggeíôn apò tên Pélla. Sumbolê stê meletê tês ellênistikés keramikês*. Athens: Greek Ministry of Culture, 1993.

Alexander, R. *The Biology of Moral Systems*. Hawthorne, NY: Aldine de Gruyter, 1987.

Allen, D. *The World of Prometheus: The Politics of Punishing in Democratic Athens*. Princeton, NJ: Princeton University Press, 2000.

D'Ambra, E. "The Calculus of Venus: Nude Portraits of Roman Matrons." In *Sexuality in Ancient Art*, edited by N. B. Kampen, 219–32. Cambridge: Cambridge University Press, 1996.

D'Ambrosio, A., ed. *Women and Beauty in Pompeii*, translated by Graham Sells. Los Angeles: 'L'Erma' di Bretschneider and J. Paul Getty Museum, 2001.

Andreatta, D. "237 Reasons Why We Do the Deed." *The Globe and Mail*, August 1, 2007, p. L1.

Arditi, M. 1825. *Il fascino e l'amuleto contro del fascino presso gli antichi*, 2nd ed., edited by R. De Falco. Capri: La Conchiglia, 1991.

Arieti, J. A. "Rape and Livy's View of Roman History." In *Rape in Antiquity: Sexual Violence in the Greek and Roman Worlds*, edited by S. Deacy and K. F. Pierce, 209–29. London: Duckworth, 2002.

Armini, H. "Ad carminum epigraphicorum tertium uolumen adnotatiunculae." *Eranos* 34 (1936): 104–41.

Arnaoutoglou, I. *Ancient Greek Laws: A Sourcebook*. London: Routledge, 1998.

Astin, A. E. "Regimen morum." *Journal of Roman Studies* 78 (1988): 14–34.

Audollent, A. M. H. *Defixionum tabellae quotquot innotuerunt, tam in Graecis Orientis quam in totius Occidentis partibus praeter Atticas in corpore inscriptionum Atticarum editas*. Paris: A. Fontemoing, 1904.

Ault, B. A. "Housing the Poor and Homeless in Ancient Greece." In *Ancient Greek Houses and Households: Chronological, Regional and Social Diversity*, edited by B. A. Ault and L. C. Nevett, 140–59. Philadelphia: University of Pennsylvania Press, 2005.

Badian, E. "A Phantom Marriage Law." *Philologus* 129 (1985): 82–98.

Bailey, D. M. *A Catalogue of the Lamps in the British Museum, vol. 2: Roman Lamps Made in Italy*. London: British Museum, 1980.

Bailey, D. M. *A Catalogue of the Lamps in the British Museum, vol. 3: Roman Provincial Lamps*. London: British Museum, 1988.

Bain, D. "Six Greek Verbs of Sexual Congress (*binō, kinō, pugizō, lēkō, oiphō, laikazō*)." *Classical Quarterly* 41 (1991): 51–77.

Baltrusch, E. *Regimen Morum: Die Reglementierung des Privatlebens der Senatoren und Ritter in der römischen Republik und frühen Kaiserzeit*. Vestigia, 41. Munich: C. H. Beck, 1989.

Barfield, T. *The Dictionary of Anthropology*. Oxford: Blackwell, 2001.

Barré, L. *Herculanum et Pompéi: recueil général des peintures, bronzes, mosaïques, etc., découverts jusqu'à ce jour, et reproduits d'après le Antichità di Ercolano, Il Museo borbonico, et tous les ouvrages analogues, augmenté de sujets inédits gravés au trait sur cuivre; par H. Roux Aîné: Vol. 8. Le musée secret*. Paris: Firmin Didot frères, 1839.

Barringer, J. M. *The Hunt in Ancient Greece*. Baltimore: Johns Hopkins University Press, 2001.

Barton, C. A. "All Things Beseem the Victor: Paradoxes of Masculinity in Early Imperial Rome." In *Gender Rhetorics: Postures of Dominance and Submission in History*, edited by R. C. Trexler, 83–92. Binghamton: Medieval & Renaissance Texts & Studies, 1994.

Bassi, K. "The Semantics of Manliness in Ancient Greece." In *Andreia: Studies in Manliness and Courage in Classical Antiquity*, edited by R. M. Rosen and I. Sluiter, 25–58. Leiden: Brill Academic Publishers, 2003.

Bauman, R. A. "The Rape of Lucretia." *Latomus* 52 (1993): 550–56.

Bauman, R. A. "Some Remarks on the Structure and Survival of the *quaestio de adulteriis*." *Antichthon* 2 (1968): 68–93.

Baxter, C. *The Feast of Love*. New York: Pantheon, 2000.

Bažant, Jan. "Les vases athéniens et les réformes démocratiques." In *Images et société en Grèce ancienne. L'iconographie comme méthode d'analyse (Actes du Colloque international, Lausanne 8–11 février 1984*), edited by C. Bérard, C. Bron, and A. Pomari, 33–40. Lausanne: Institut d'archéologie et d'histoire ancienne, Université de Lausanne, 1987.

Beacham, R. C. *Spectacle Entertainments of Early Imperial Rome.* New Haven, CT: Yale University Press, 1999.

Beard, M. "Adopting an Approach II." In *Looking at Greek Vases*, edited by T. Rasmussen and N. Spivey, 12–35. Cambridge: Cambridge University Press, 1991.

Beard, M. "The Erotics of Rape: Livy, Ovid and the Sabine Women." In *Female Networks and the Public Sphere in Roman Society*, edited by P. Setälä and L. Savunen, 1–10. Rome: Institutum Romanum Finlandiae, 1999.

Beard, M., and J. Henderson. "With This Body I Thee Worship: Sacred Prostitution in Antiquity." In *Gender and the Body in the Ancient Mediterranean*, edited by M. Wyke, 56–79. Oxford: Blackwell Publishers, 1998.

Beazley, J. D. *Attic Black-Figure Vase-Painters.* Oxford: Clarendon Press, 1956.

Beazley, J. D. *Attic Red-Figure Vase-Painters*, 2nd ed. Oxford: Clarendon Press, 1963.

Beazley, J. D. *Paralipomena: Additions to Attic Black-Figure Vase-Painters and to Attic Red-Figure Vase-Painters, 2nd ed.* Oxford: Clarendon Press, 1971.

Benner, A. R., and F. H. Fobes. *Alciphron, Aelian, Philostratus: The Letters.* Cambridge, MA: Harvard University Press, 1949.

Bennett, Tony. "Popular Culture: A Teaching Object." *Screen Education* 34 (1980): 17–29.

Benson, C. "Medusa and the Gorgons." In *Pandora: Women in Classical Greece*, edited by E. D. Reeder, 410–15. Princeton, NJ: Princeton University Press, 1995.

Bergmann, B. "Seeing Women in the Villa of the Mysteries: A Modern Excavation of the Dionysiac Murals." In *Antiquity Recovered: The Legacy of Pompeii and Herculaneum*, edited by V.C.G. Coates and J. L. Seydl, 231–69. Los Angeles: The J. Paul Getty Museum, 2007.

Bergmann, B. "Varia Topia: Architectural Landscapes in Roman Painting of the Late Republic and Early Empire." PhD dissertation, Columbia University, New York, 1986.

Bernand, A. *Le Delta égyptien d'après les textes grecques, I: Les Confins libyques*, 3 vols., Mémoires 91. Cairo: Institut français d'archéologie orientale du Caire, 1970.

Bernand, A. *De Koptos à Kosseir.* Leiden: Brill, 1972.

Bethe, E. "Die dorische Knabenliebe." *Rheinisches Museum* 62 (1907): 438–75.

Betz, H. D. *The Greek Magical Papyri in Translation, Including the Demotic Spells*, 2nd ed. Chicago: University of Chicago Press, 1992.

Betzig, L. *Despotism and Differential Reproduction: A Darwinian View of History.* New York: Aldine, 1986.

Betzig, L. "Roman Polygyny," *Ethnology and Sociobiology* 13 (1992): 309–49.

Bianchi, R. S. "Tattoo in Ancient Egypt." In *Marks of Civilization*, edited by A. Rubin, 21–28. Los Angeles: University of California, Los Angeles, Museum of Cultural History, 1988.

Bieber, M. "Die Mysteriensaal der Villa Item." *Jahrbuch des deutschen archäologischen Instituts* 43 (1928): 298–330.

Blegen, C. W. "Inscriptions on Geometric Pottery from Hymettos." *American Journal of Archaeology* 38 (1934): 10–28.

Blok, J. "Becoming Citizens: Some Notes on the Semantics of 'citizen' in Archaic Greece and Classical Athens." *Klio* 87 (2005): 7–40.

Boardman, J. *Athenian Red Figure Vases: The Classical Period: A Handbook*. London: Thames and Hudson, 1989.

Boardman, J. *The History of Greek Vases: Potters, Painters, and Pictures*. New York: Thames & Hudson, 2001.

Boardman, J. "Review of Michael J. Vickers, and David Gill, *Artful Crafts: Ancient Greek Silverware and Pottery*." *Classical Review* 46 (1996): 123–26.

Boardman, J. "Review of Richard T. Neer, *Style and Politics in Athenian Vase-Painting: The Craft of Democracy, circa 530–470 B.C.E.*" *Common Knowledge* 10 (2004): 353.

Boardman, J. "Sixth-century Potters and Painters." In *Looking at Greek Vases*, edited by T. Rasmussen and N. Spivey, 79–102. Cambridge: Cambridge University Press, 1991.

Boegehold, A. L. "Perikles' Citizenship Law of 451/0 B.C." In *Athenian Identity and Civic Ideology*, edited by A. L. Boegehold and A. C. Scafuro, 57–66. Baltimore: Johns Hopkins University Press, 1994.

Boehm, C. *Hierarchy in the Forest: The Evolution of Egalitarian Behavior*. Cambridge, MA: Harvard University Press, 1999.

Boehringer, S. "'Ces monstres de femmes.' Topique des thaumata dans les discours sur l'homosexualité féminine aux premiers siècles de notre ère." In *Mirabilia. Conceptions et représentations de l'extraordinaire dans le monde antique. Actes du colloque internationale, Lausanne 20–22 mars 2003*, edited by O. Bianchi and O. Thévenaz, 75–98. Bern: Peter Lang, 2004.

Boswell, J. *Christianity, Social Tolerance, and Homosexuality: Gay People in Western Europe from the Beginning of the Christian Era to the Fourteenth Century*. Chicago: University of Chicago Press, 1980.

Bosworth, A. B. "Vespasian and the Slave Trade." *Classical Quarterly* 52 (2002): 350–57.

Bourdieu, P. "Cultural Reproduction and Social Reproduction," in *Knowledge, Education and Cultural Change*, edited by Richard Brown, 71–112. London: Tavistock, 1973.

Bourdieu, P. "The Forms of Capital." In *Handbook of Theory and Research for the Sociology of Education*, edited by John Richardson, 241–58. New York: Greenwood Press, 1986.

Bourdieu, P. *Outline of a Theory of Practice*. Cambridge: Cambridge University Press, 1977.

Bradley, K. "Prostitution, the Law of Rome, and Social Policy." *Journal of Roman Archaeology* 13 (2000): 468–75.

Bradley, K. *Slaves and Masters in the Roman Empire: A Study in Social Control*. New York: Oxford University Press, 1987.

Bragantini, I., and M. de Vos. *Le decorazioni della villa romana della Farnesina*. Rome: De Luca, 1982.

Brann, E. "Late Geometric Well Groups from the Athenian Agora." *Hesperia* 30 (1961): 93–146.

Bremer, J. M., A. Maria van Erp Taalman Kip, and S. R. Slings. *Some Recently Found Greek Poems: Text and Commentary, Mnemosyne*, Supplementum 99. Leiden: E. J. Brill, 1987.

Bremmer, J. N. "Adolescents, *symposion*, and Pederasty." In *Sympotica: A Symposium on the Symposion*, edited by O. Murray, 135–48. Oxford: Oxford University Press, 1990.

Bremmer, J. N. "An Enigmatic Indo-European Rite: Pederasty." *Arethusa* 13 (1980): 279–98.

Brendel, O. J. "Der Affen-Aeneas." *Mitteilungen des deutschen archäologischen Instituts, Römische Abteilung* 60 (1953): 153–59.

Brendel, O. J. "The Scope and Temperament of Erotic Art in the Greco-Roman World." In *Studies in Erotic Art*, edited by T. Bowie and C. V. Christenson, 3–107. New York: Basic Books, 1970.

Brisson, L. *Sexual Ambivalence: Androgyny and Hermaphroditism in Graeco-Roman Antiquity*, translated by J. Lloyd. Berkeley: University of California Press, 2002.

Broadbent, M. *Studies in Greek Genealogy*. Leiden: E. J. Brill, 1968.

Brommer, F. "Themenwahl aus örtlichen Gründen." In *Ancient Greek and Related Pottery: Proceedings of the International Symposion in Amsterdam 12–15 April 1984*, edited by H.A.G Brijder, 178–84. Amsterdam: Allard Pierson Museum, 1984.

Brooten, B. J. *Love between Women: Early Christian Responses to Female Homoeroticism*. Chicago: University of Chicago Press, 1996.

Brown, P. *The Body and Society: Men, Women, and Sexual Renunciation in Early Christianity*. New York: Columbia University Press, 1988.

Brown, P. G. McC. "Love and Marriage in Greek New Comedy." *Classical Quarterly* 43 (1993): 184–205.

Brown, R. "Livy's Sabine Women and the Ideal of Concordia." *Transactions of the American Philological Association* 125 (1995): 291–319.

Brown, R. D. *Lucretius on Love and Sex: A Commentary on* De rerum natura *IV, 1030–1287 with Prolegomena, Text, and Translation*. Leiden: Brill, 1987.

Brown, S. "Death as Decoration: Scenes from the Arena on Roman Domestic Mosaics." In *Pornography and Representation in Greece and Rome*, edited by A. Richlin, 180–211. New York: Oxford University Press, 1992.

Brunner, H. "Review of R. and J. Janssen, *Growing Up in Ancient Egypt*." *Discussions in Egyptology* 21 (1991): 77–78.

Buchheit, V. *Studien zum Corpus Priapeorum*. Zetemata 28: Munich, 1962.

Budin, S. L. *The Myth of Sacred Prostitution in Antiquity*. Cambridge: Cambridge University Press, 2008.

Budin, S. L. "*Pallakai*, Prostitutes and Prophetesses." *Classical Philology* 98 (2003): 148–59.

Budin, S. L. "Sacred Prostitution in the First Person." In *Prostitutes and Courtesans in the Ancient World*, edited by C. A. Faraone and L. K. McClure, 77–94. Madison: University of Wisconsin Press, 2006.

Buffière, F. *Éros adolescent: la pédérastie dans la Grèce antique*. Paris: Belles Lettres, 1980.

Burguière, P., D. Gourevitch, and Y. Malinas, ed., tr., and comm. *Soranos d'Éphèse, Maladies des Femmes,* 4 vols. Paris: Les Belles Lettres, 1988–2000.

Burke, P. *Popular Culture in Early Modern Europe.* New York: Harper & Row, 1978.

Burn, L. *The Meidias Painter.* Oxford: Clarendon Press, 1987.

Burnett, A. P. *Three Archaic Poets: Archilochus, Alcaeus, Sappho.* London: Duckworth, 1983.

Burstein, S. M., ed. and trans. *Agatharchides of Cnidus: On the Erythraean Sea.* London: Hakluyt Society, 1989.

Butler, J. "Beside Oneself: On the Limits of Sexual Autonomy." In *Undoing Gender,* edited by J. Butler, 17–39. New York: Routledge, 2004.

Butrica, J. L. "Review of John R. Clarke, *Roman Sex." Bryn Mawr Classical Review.* http://ccat.sas.upenn.edu/bmcr/2004/2004–01–03.html.

Butrica, J. L. "Some Myths and Anomalies in the Study of Roman Sexuality." In *Same-Sex Desire and Love in Greco-Roman Antiquity and in the Classical Tradition of the West,* edited by B. C. Verstraete and V. Provencal, 209–70. Binghamton: Haworth Press, 2005.

Cairns, D. L. "Hybris, Dishonour, and Thinking Big." *Journal of Hellenic Studies* 116 (1996): 1–32.

Cairns, D. L. "The Politics of Envy: Envy and Equality in Ancient Greece." In *Envy, Spite, and Jealousy: The Rivalrous Emotions in Ancient Greece,* edited by D. Konstan and K. Rutter, 235–52. Edinburgh: Edinburgh University Press, 2003.

Calame, C. *Choruses of Young Women in Ancient Greece.* Lanham, MD: Rowman and Littlefield, 1997. (Translation of *Les choeurs de jeunes filles en Grèce archaïque,* 2 vols. Rome: Edizioni dell' Ateneo and Bizzarri, 1977.)

Campbell, D. A. *Greek Lyric,* vol. 1. *Sappho and Alcaeus.* Cambridge, MA: Harvard University Press, 1982.

Campbell, D. A. *Greek Lyric,* vol. 2. Cambridge, MA: Harvard University Press, 1988.

Cantarella, E. *Bisexuality in the Ancient World.* New Haven, CT: Yale University Press, 1992. (Translation of *Secondo Natura.* Rome: Editori Riuniti, 1988.)

Cantarella, E. "Gender, Sexuality and Law." In *The Cambridge Companion to Ancient Greek Law,* edited by M. Gagarin and D. Cohen, 236–53. Cambridge: Cambridge University Press, 2005.

Cantarella, E. "Homicides of Honor: The Development of Italian Adultery Law over Two Millennia." In *The Family in Italy from Antiquity to the Present,* edited by D. Kertzer and R. Saller, 229–44. New Haven, CT: Yale University Press, 1991.

Cantarella, E. "Marriage and Sexuality in Republican Rome: A Roman Conjugal Love Story." In *The Sleep of Reason: Erotic Experience and Sexual Ethics in Ancient Greece and Rome,* edited by M. C. Nussbaum and J. Sihvola, 269–82. Chicago: University of Chicago Press, 2002.

Cantarella, E. "Moicheia: Reconsidering a Problem." In *Symposion 1990: Vorträge zur griechischen und hellenistischen Rechtsgeschichte,* edited by M. Gagarin, 289–96. Cologne: Böhlau, 1991.

Carawan, E. *The Rhetoric and Law of Draco*. Oxford: Oxford University Press, 1998.

Carcani, P., ed. *De' bronzi di Ercolano e contorni, t. 2, Statue*. Le antichità di Ercolano. Naples: Nella Regia Stamperia, 1757–1792.

Carey, C. *Apollodoros Against Neaira. [Demosthenes] 59*. Warminster: Aris & Phillips, 1992.

Carey, C. "Rape and Adultery in Athenian Law." *Classical Quarterly* 45 (1995): 407–17.

Carey, C. "The Return of the Radish or Just When You Thought it Was Safe to Go Back into the Kitchen." *Liverpool Classical Monthly* 18 (1993): 53–55.

Carpenter, T. H. *Beazley Addenda: Additional References to ABV, ARV² & Paralipomena*, 2nd ed. Oxford: Published for the British Academy by Oxford University Press, 1989.

Carson, A. "Putting Her in Her Place: Woman, Dirt, and Desire." In *Before Sexuality: The Construction of Erotic Experience in the Ancient Greek World*, edited by D. M. Halperin, J. J. Winkler, and F. I. Zeitlin, 135–69. Princeton, NJ: Princeton University Press, 1990.

Cartledge, P. "Class Struggle." In *The Oxford Classical Dictionary*, 3d ed., edited by Simon Hornblower and Antony Spawforth, 335–36. Oxford: Oxford University Press, 1996.

Cartledge, P. "The Politics of Spartan Pederasty." *Proceedings of the Cambridge Philological Society* 27 (1981): 17–36.

Cartledge, P. *Spartan Reflections*. Berkeley: University of California Press, 2001.

Cartledge, P. "Spartan Wives: Liberation or License?" *Classical Quarterly* 31 (1981): 84–105.

Cartledge, P. "'Trade and Politics' Revisited: Archaic Greece." In *Trade in the Ancient Economy*, edited by P. Garnsey, K. Hopkins, and C. R. Whittaker, 1–15. Berkeley: University of California Press, 1983.

Caston, R. R. "Love as Illness: Poets and Philosophers on Romantic Love." *Classical Journal* 101 (2006): 271–98.

Chantraine, P. *Dictionnaire étymologique de la langue grecque. Histoire des mots*. Paris: Klincksieck, 1984.

Cherry, D. "The Minician Law: Marriage and the Roman Citizenship." *Phoenix* 44 (1990): 244–68.

Claassen, J. "The Familiar Other: The Pivotal Role of Women in Livy's Narrative of Political Development in Early Rome." *Acta Classica* 16 (1998): 71–103.

Clark, E. "Antifamilial Tendencies in Ancient Christianity." *Journal of the History of Sexuality* 5 (1995): 356–80.

Clark, E. "1990 Presidential Address: Sex, Shame, and Rhetoric: En-gendering Early Christian Ethics." *Journal of the American Academy of Religion* 59 (1991): 221–45.

Clark, E. *Reading Renunciation: Asceticism and Scripture in Early Christianity*. Princeton, NJ: Princeton University Press, 1999.

Clarke, J. R. *Art in the Lives of Ordinary Romans: Visual Representation and Non-elite Viewers in Italy, 100 B.C.–A.D. 315*. Berkeley: University of California Press, 2003.

Clarke, J. R. *Houses of Roman Italy, 100 B.C.–A.D. 250: Ritual, Space, and Decoration.* Berkeley: University of California Press, 1991.

Clarke, J. R. *Looking at Laughter: Humor, Power, and Transgression in Roman Visual Culture, 100 B.C.–A.D. 250.* Berkeley: University of California Press, 2007.

Clarke, J. R. *Looking at Lovemaking: Constructions of Sexuality in Roman Art 100 B.C.–A.D. 250.* Berkeley: University of California Press, 1998.

Clarke, J. R. "Look Who's Laughing at Sex: Men and Women Viewers in the Apodyterium of the Suburban Baths at Pompeii." In *The Roman Gaze: Vision, Power, and the Body*, edited by D. Fredrick, 149–81. Baltimore: Johns Hopkins University Press, 2002.

Clarke, J. R. *Roman Sex: 100 B.C. to A.D. 250, with New Photography by Michael Larvey.* New York: Harry N. Abrams, 2003.

Clarke, J. R. "The Warren Cup and the Contexts for Representations of Male-to-Male Lovemaking in Augustan and Early Julio-Claudian Art." *The Art Bulletin* 75 (1993): 275–94.

Cohen, D. "The Augustan Law on Adultery." In *The Family in Italy from Antiquity to the Present*, edited by D. Kertzer and R. Saller, 209–26. New Haven, CT: Yale University Press, 1991.

Cohen, D. "The Athenian Law of Adultery." *Revue internationale des droits de l'antiquité* 31 (1984): 147–65.

Cohen, D. "Consent and Sexual Relations in Classical Athens." In *Consent and Coercion to Sex and Marriage in Ancient and Medieval Societies*, edited by A. E. Laiou, 5–16. Washington, DC: Dumbarton Oaks, 1993.

Cohen, D. *Law, Sexuality, and Society: The Enforcement of Morals in Classical Athens.* Cambridge: Cambridge University Press, 1991.

Cohen, D. *Law, Violence, and Community in Classical Athens.* Cambridge: Cambridge University Press, 1995.

Cohen, D. "Sexuality, Violence, and the Athenian Law of *hybris.*" *Greece and Rome* 38 (1991): 171–88.

Cohen, D. "The Social Context of Adultery at Athens." In *Nomos: Essays in Athenian Law, Politics, and Society*, edited by P. Cartledge, P. Millett, and S. Todd, 147–65. Cambridge: Cambridge University Press, 1990.

Cohen, D., and R. Saller. "Foucault on Sexuality in Greco-Roman Antiquity." In *Foucault and the Writing of History*, edited by J. Goldstein, 35–59. Oxford: Blackwell, 1994.

Cohen, E. E. *The Athenian Nation.* Princeton, NJ: Princeton University Press, 2000.

Cohen, E. E. "Free and Unfree Sexual Work: An Economic Analysis of Athenian Prostitution." In *Prostitutes and Courtesans in the Ancient World*, edited by C. A. Faraone and L. K. McClure, 95–124. Madison: University of Wisconsin Press, 2006.

Cohen, E. E. "'Whoring under Contract': The Legal Context of Prostitution in Fourth-century Athens." In *Law and Social Status in Classical Athens*, edited by V. Hunter and J. Edmondson, 113–48. Oxford: Oxford University Press, 2000.

Cole, S. G. "Greek Sanctions against Sexual Assault." *Classical Philology* 79 (1984): 97–113.

Cole, S. G. *Landscapes, Gender, and Ritual Space.* Berkeley: University of California Press, 2004.

Collier, J. F., and S. J. Yanagisako. "Toward a Unified Analysis of Gender and Kinship." In *Gender and Kinship: Essays toward a Unified Analysis,* edited by J. F. Collier and S. J. Yanagisako, 14–50. Stanford, CA: Stanford University Press, 1987.

Comfort, H. "An Insulting Latin Graffito." *American Journal of Archaeology* 52 (1948): 321–22.

Connor, W. R. "City Dionysia and Athenian Democracy." *Classica & Mediaevalia* 40 (1989): 7–32.

Connor, W. R. "The Problem of Athenian Civic Identity." In *Athenian Identity and Civic Ideology,* edited by A. Boegehold and A. Scafuro, 34–44. Baltimore: Johns Hopkins University Press, 1994.

Corbeill, A. *Controlling Laughter: Political Humor in the Late Roman Republic.* Princeton, NJ: Princeton University Press, 1996.

Corbett, P. E. *The Roman Law of Marriage.* Oxford: Oxford University Press, 1930.

Corbier, M. "Constructing Kinship in Rome: Marriage and Divorce, Filiation and Adoption." In *The Family in Italy from Antiquity to the Present,* edited by D. L. Kertzer and R. P. Saller, 127–44. New Haven, CT: Yale University Press, 1991.

Cordier, P. "Tertium genus hominum. L'étrange sexualité des castrats dans l'Empire romain." In *Corps romains,* edited by P. Moreau, 61–75. Grenoble: Jérome Millon, 2002.

Cornell, T. "Some Observations on the *crimen incesti.*" *Le délit religieux dans la cité antique (Table ronde Rome 6-7 avril 1978), Collection de l'École française de Rome* 48 (1981): 27–31.

Cott, N. "Giving Character to Our Whole Civil Polity: Marriage and the Public Order in the Late Nineteenth Century." In *U.S. History as Women's History,* edited by L. Kerber et al., 107–21. Chapel Hill: University of North Carolina Press, 1995.

Courtney, E. *Musa Lapidaria: A Selection of Latin Verse Inscriptions.* Atlanta, GA: Scholars Press, 1995.

Cox, C. *Household Interests.* Princeton, NJ: Princeton University Press, 1998.

Craik, E. M., ed., tr., and comm. *Hippocrates,* Places in Man. Oxford: Clarendon Press, 1998.

Crawford, K. *European Sexualities, 1400–1800.* New York: Cambridge University Press, 2007.

Crook, J. "*Patria potestas.*" *Classical Quarterly* 17 (1967): 113–22.

Crooke, H. *Microcosmographia: A Description of the Body of Man.* London, 1615.

Crowther, N. B. "Weightlifting in Antiquity: Achievement and Training." *Greece & Rome* 24 (1977): 111–20.

Csapo, E. G., and W. J. Slater. *The Context of Ancient Drama.* Ann Arbor: University of Michigan Press, 1995.

Csillag, P. *The Augustan Laws on Family Relations.* Budapest: Akademiai Kiado, 1976.

Dahl, R. *Democracy and Its Critics.* New Haven, CT: Yale University Press, 1989.

Dalby, A. "Levels of Concealment: The Dress of Hetairai and Pornai in Greek Texts." In *Women's Dress in the Ancient Greek World,* edited by L. Llewellyn-Jones, 111–24. London: Duckworth, 2002.

Daly, M., and M. Wilson. *Sex, Evolution, and Behavior.* Boston: Willard Grant, 1983.

Daniel, R. W., and F. Maltomini. *Supplementum Magicum,* 2 vols. Papyrologica Coloniensia vols. 16.1 and 16.2. Cologne: Westdeutscher Verlag, 1990–1992.

Danto, A. C. "The Artworld." *Journal of Philosophy* 61 (1964): 571–84.

Danto, A. C. *The Transfiguration of the Commonplace.* Cambridge, MA: Harvard University Press, 1981.

Daremberg, C., and C. E. Ruelle. *Oeuvres de Rufus d'Ephèse.* Paris: Baillière, 1879.

Dasen, V. *Dwarfs in Ancient Egypt and Greece.* Oxford: Oxford University Press, 1993.

Davidson, J. N. *Courtesans and Fishcakes: The Consuming Passions of Classical Athens.* New York: Fontana, 1997.

Davidson, J. N. "Dover, Foucault and Greek Homosexuality: Penetration and the Truth of Sex." *Past and Present* 170 (2001): 3–51. (Reprinted in R. Osborne, ed. *Studies in Ancient Greek and Roman Society,* 78–118. Cambridge: Cambridge University Press, 2004.)

Davidson, J. N. *The Greeks and Greek Love.* London: Weidenfeld and Nicolson, 2007.

Davidson, J. N. "Making a Spectacle of Her(self): The Greek Courtesan and the Art of the Present." In *The Courtesan's Arts: Cross-Cultural Perspectives,* edited by M. Feldman and B. Gordon, 29–51. Oxford: Oxford University Press, 2006.

Davies, J. K. "Athenian Citizenship: The Descent Group and the Alternatives." *Classical Journal* 73 (1977/1978): 105–21.

Davies, J. K. "Deconstructing Gortyn: When Is a Code a Code?" In *Greek Law in its Political Setting: Justifications not Justice,* edited by L. Foxhall and A.D.E. Lewis, 33–56. Oxford: Oxford University Press, 1996.

Davies, J. K. "The Gortyn Laws." In *The Cambridge Companion to Ancient Greek Law,* edited by M. Gagarin and D. Cohen, 305–27. Cambridge: Cambridge University Press, 2005.

Dean-Jones, L. "The Politics of Pleasure: Female Sexual Appetite in the Hippocratic Corpus." *Helios* 19 (1992): 72–91.

Dean-Jones, L. *Women's Bodies in Classical Greek Science.* Oxford: Oxford University Press, 1994.

De Caro, S. *Il gabinetto segreto del Museo Nazionale Archeologico di Napoli.* Naples: Electa, 2000.

DeFelice, J. *Roman Hospitality: The Professional Women of Pompeii.* Warren Center, PA: Shangri-La Publications, 2001.

Demand, N. *Birth, Death, and Motherhood in Classical Greece.* Baltimore: Johns Hopkins University Press, 1994.

Demand, N. "Women and Slaves as Hippocratic Patients." In *Women and Slaves in Greco-Roman Culture: Differential Equations,* edited by S. Joshel and S. Murnaghan, 69–84. London: Routledge, 1998.

den Boer, W. *Laconian Studies.* Amsterdam: North-Holland, 1954.

Desbat, A. "Vases à médaillons d'applique des fouilles récentes de Lyon." *Figlina* 5–6 (1980–1981): 1–203.

de Ste. Croix, G.E.M. *The Class Struggle in the Ancient Greek World from the Archaic Age to the Arab Conquests.* London: Duckworth, 1981.

Detienne, M. *Être autochtone: du pur Athénien au Français raciné*. Paris: Seuil, 2003.

Detienne, M. *The Gardens of Adonis: Spices in Greek Mythology,* translated by J. E. Lloyd. Hassocks: Harvester Press, 1977. (First published as *Les Jardins d'Adonis.* Paris: Gallimard, 1972.)

Detienne, M. "The Violence of Well-born Ladies: Women in the Thesmophoria." In *The Cuisine of Sacrifice Among the Greeks,* edited by M. Detienne and J.-P. Vernant, 129–47. Chicago: University of Chicago Press, 1989. (First published as *La Cuisine du sacrifice en pays grec.* Paris: Gallimard, 1979.)

Devereux, G. "Greek 'Pseudo-homosexuality' and the Greek Miracle." *Symbolae Osloenses* 42 (1967): 69–92.

DeVries, K. "The 'Frigid Eromenoi' and Their Wooers Revisited: A Closer Look at Greek Homosexuality in Vase Painting." In *Queer Representations: Reading Lives, Reading Cultures,* edited by M. Duberman, 14–24. New York: New York University Press, 1997.

Dickie, G. *Art and the Aesthetic: An Institutional Analysis.* Ithaca, NY: Cornell University Press, 1974.

Dickie, G. *The Art Circle: A Theory of Art.* New York: Haven, 1984.

Dickie, G. *Art and Value.* Malden, MA: Blackwell Publishers, 2001.

Dickie, G. "What Is Art: An Institutional Analysis." In *Art and Philosophy: Readings in Aesthetics,* edited by W. E. Kennick, 82–95. New York: St. Martin's Press, 1979.

Diehl, E. *Pompeianische Wandinschriften und Verwandtes,* 2nd ed. Berlin: de Gruyter, 1930.

Diggle, J. *Theophrastus: Characters.* Cambridge: Cambridge University Press, 2004.

Diller, A. *Race Mixture Among the Greeks before Alexander.* Urbana: University of Illinois Press, 1937.

Dillon, M. *Girls and Women in Classical Greek Religion.* London: Routledge, 2003.

Dimakis, P. "Orateurs et hetaïres dans l'Athènes classique." In *Éros et droit en Grèce classique,* edited by P. Dimakis. Paris: Les Belles Lettres, 1988.

Dixon, S. *Reading Roman Women: Sources, Genres, and Real Life.* London: Duckworth, 2001.

Dixon, S. "The Sentimental Ideal of the Roman Family." In *Marriage, Divorce, and Children in Ancient Rome,* edited by B. Rawson, 99–113. Oxford: Clarendon Press, 1991.

Dougherty, C. "Democratic Contradictions and the Synoptic Illusions of Euripides' Ion." In *Demokratia: A Conversation on Democracies, Ancient and Modern,* edited by J. Ober and C. Hedrick, 249–70. Princeton, NJ: Princeton University Press, 1996.

Dougherty, C. *The Poetics of Colonization: From City to Text in Archaic Greece.* New York: Oxford University Press, 1993.

Douglas, M. *Purity and Danger: An Analysis of Concepts of Pollution and Taboo.* London: Routledge and K. Paul, 1966.

Dover, K. J. "Classical Greek Attitudes to Sexual Behaviour." *Arethusa* 6 (1973): 59–73.

Dover, K. J. "The Date of Plato's *Symposium.*" *Phronesis* 10 (1965): 2–20.

Dover, K. J. "Eros and nomos." *Bulletin of the Institute of Classical Studies* 11 (1964): 31–42.

Dover, K. J. *Greek Homosexuality.* Cambridge, MA: Harvard University Press, 1978.

Dover, K. J. "Greek Homosexuality and Initiation." In *The Greeks and their Legacy,* edited by K. J. Dover, 115–34. Oxford: Oxford University Press, 1988.

Dover, K. J. *Greek Popular Morality in the Time of Plato and Aristotle.* Oxford: Blackwell, 1974.

Drabkin, I. E., ed. and tr. *Caelius Aurelianus On Acute Diseases and Chronic Diseases.* Chicago: University of Chicago Press, 1950.

Drago, C. *Corpus vasorum antiquorum. Italia. R. Museo nazionale di Taranto.* Fascicolo 18, Rome: Libreria dello Stato, 1942.

duBois, P. *Centaurs and Amazons: Women and the Pre-history of the Great Chain of Being.* Ann Arbor: University of Michigan Press, 1991.

duBois, P. *Sowing the Body: Psychoanalysis and Ancient Representations of Women.* Chicago: University of Chicago Press, 1988.

duBois, P. "The Subject in Antiquity after Foucault." In *Rethinking Sexuality: Foucault and Classical Antiquity,* edited by D.H.J. Larmour, P. A. Miller, and C. Platter, 85–103. Princeton, NJ: Princeton University Press, 1998.

Duchêne, H. *La stèle du port. Fouilles du port 1. Recherches sur une nouvelle inscription thasienne,* Études Thasiennes 14. Paris: de Boccard, 1992.

Dunbar, N. *Aristophanes: Birds.* Oxford: Clarendon Press, 1995.

Dundes, A., ed. *The Evil Eye: A Casebook.* Madison: University of Wisconsin Press, 1981.

Dunkle, R. "The Greek Tyrant and Roman Political Invective of the Late Republic." *Transactions of the American Philological Association* 98 (1967): 151–71.

Dupont, F., and T. Eloi. *L'érotisme masculin dans la Rome antique.* Paris: Belin, 2001.

Earp, F. R. *The Way of the Greeks.* London: Oxford University Press, 1929.

Edmonds, J. M. *The Fragments of Attic Comedy after Meineke, Bergk and Kock.* Leiden: Brill, 1957–1961.

Edwards, C. *The Politics of Immorality in Ancient Rome.* Cambridge: Cambridge University Press, 1993.

Edwards, C. "Unspeakable Professions: Public Performance and Prostitution in Ancient Rome." In *Roman Sexualities,* edited by J. P. Hallett and M. B. Skinner, 66–95. Princeton, NJ: Princeton University Press, 1997.

Ehrenberg, V. *The People of Aristophanes: A Sociology of Old Attic Comedy,* 3rd rev. ed. New York: Schocken Books, 1962.

Elsner, J. *Art and the Roman Viewer: The Transformation of Art from the Pagan World to Christianity.* Cambridge: Cambridge University Press, 1997.

Elsner, J. *Roman Eyes: Visuality and Subjectivity in Art and Text.* Princeton, NJ: Princeton University Press, 2007.

Elworthy, F. T. 1895. *The Evil Eye: An Account of this Ancient and Widespread Superstition.* New York: Julian Press, 1958.

Evans-Grubbs, J. *Law and the Family in Late Antiquity.* Oxford: Blackwell, 1995.

Evans-Grubbs, J. "'Marriage More Shameful Than Adultery': Slave-mistress Relationships, 'Mixed Marriages' and Late Roman Law." *Phoenix* 47 (1993): 125–54.

Fantham, E. "Sex, Status and Survival in Hellenistic Athens, a Study of Women in New Comedy." *Phoenix* 29 (1975): 44–74.

Fantham, E. "*Stuprum*: Public Attitudes and Penalties for Sexual Offenses in Republican Rome." *Echos du monde classique/Classical Views* 10 (1991): 267–91.

Faraone, C. *Ancient Greek Love Magic.* Cambridge, MA: Harvard University Press, 1999.

Faraone, C. "Sex and Power: Male-targeting Aphrodisiacs in the Greek Magical Tradition." *Helios* 19 (1992): 92–103.

Faraone, C. A. "Agents and Victims: Constructions of Gender and Desire in Ancient Greek Love Magic." In *The Sleep of Reason: Erotic Experience and Sexual Ethics in Ancient Greece and Rome*, edited by M. C. Nussbaum and J. Sihvola, 400–26. Chicago: University of Chicago Press, 2002.

Faraone, C. A. "New Light on Ancient Greek Exorcisms of the Wandering Womb." *Zeitschrift für Papyrologie und Epigraphik* 144 (2003): 189–97.

Fellmann, B. "Zur Deutung frühgriechischer Körperornamente." *Jahrbuch des deutschen archäologischen Instituts* 93 (1978): 1–29.

Ferrand, Jacques. *De la maladie d'amour, ou maladie érotique. Discours curieux qui enseigne à cognoistre l'essence, les causes, les signes, et les remèdes de ce mal fantastique.* Paris, 1623. Translated as *Treatise on Lovesickness*, tr. and ed. D. A Beecher and M. Ciavollella. Syracuse, NY: Syracuse University Press, 1990.

Ferrari, G. *Figures of Speech: Men and Maidens in Ancient Greece.* Chicago: University of Chicago Press, 2002.

Ferrari, G. "Myth and Genre on Athenian Vases." *Classical Antiquity* 22 (2003): 37–54.

Finley, M. I. *The Ancient Economy*, 2nd ed. Berkeley: University of California Press, 1985.

Finley, M. I. *Ancient Slavery and Modern Ideology.* New York: Viking, 1980.

Finley, M. I. "Was Greek Civilization Based on Slave Labour?" *Historia* 8 (1959): 145–64.

Fiorelli, G. *Catalogo del Museo Nazionale di Napoli. Raccolta Pornografica.* Naples: Stabilimento Tipografica in S. Teresa, 1866.

Fisher, N.R.E. *Aeschines Against Timarchos.* Oxford: Oxford University Press, 2001.

Fisher, N.R.E. *Hybris.* Warminster: Aris & Phillips, 1992.

Fisher, N.R.E. "Hybris, Revenge and Stasis in the Greek City-states." In *War and Violence in Ancient Greece*, edited by H. van Wees, 83–124. London: Duckworth, 2000.

Fisher, N.R.E. "Hybris, Status, and Slavery." In *The Greek World*, edited by A. Powell, 44–84. London: Routledge, 1995.

Fisher, N.R.E. "Let Envy Be Absent: Envy, Liturgies, and Reciprocity in Athens." In *Envy, Spite, and Jealousy: The Rivalrous Emotions in Ancient Greece*, edited by D. Konstan and K. Rutter, 181–216. Edinburgh: Edinburgh University Press, 2003.

Fisher, N.R.E. "Symposiasts, Fish-eaters and Flatterers: Social Mobility and Moral Concerns." In *The Rivals of Aristophanes: Studies in Athenian Old Comedy*, edited by D. Harvey and J. Wilkins, 355–96. London: Duckworth and the Classical Press of Wales, 2000.

Fisher, N.R.E. "Violence, Masculinity and the Law in Classical Athens." In *When Men Were Men: Masculinity, Power, and Identity in Classical Antiquity*, edited by L. Foxhall and J. Salmon, 68–97. London: Routledge, 1998.

Fiske, J. *Understanding Popular Culture*. Boston: Unwin Hyman, 1989.

Fitzgerald, W. *Slavery and the Roman Literary Imagination*. Cambridge: Cambridge University Press, 2000.

Flemming, R. *Medicine and the Making of Roman Women: Gender, Nature, and Authority from Celsus to Galen*. Oxford: Oxford University Press, 2000.

Flemming, R. "*Quae corpore quaestum fecit*: The Sexual Economy of Female Prostitution in the Roman Empire." *Journal of Roman Studies* 89 (1999): 38–61.

Flory, S. "Dressed to Kill: The Aesthetics of Archaic and Classical Greek Hoplite Warfare." *American Journal of Archaeology* 98 (1994): 333.

Foley, H. P. *Female Acts in Greek Tragedy*. Princeton, NJ: Princeton University Press, 2001.

Föllinger, S. "*Skhetlia drôsi*. 'Hysterie' in den hippokratischen Schriften." In *Hippokratische Medizin und antike Philosophie*, edited by R. Wittern and P. Pellegrin, 437–50. Zürich: Olms Weidmann, 1996.

Foucault, M. *The Care of the Self*, translated by R. Hurley. New York: Vintage Books, 1988.

Foucault, M. *The History of Sexuality: vol. 1, An Introduction*, translated by R. Hurley. London: Allen Lane, 1979.

Foucault, M. *The History of Sexuality: vol. 2, The Use of Pleasure*, translated by R. Hurley. Harmondsworth: Viking, 1985.

Foucault, M. *Society Must be Defended: Lectures at the Collège de France 1975–6*, edited by M. Bertani and A. Fontana. London: Allen Lane, 2003.

Fowler, B. *Iceman: Uncovering the Life and Times of a Prehistoric Man Found in an Alpine Glacier*. New York: Random House, 2000.

Foxhall, L. "Household, Gender and Property in Classical Athens." *Classical Quarterly* 39 (1989): 22–44.

Foxhall, L. "Pandora Unbound: A Feminist Critique of Foucault's *History of Sexuality*." In *Rethinking Sexuality: Foucault and Classical Antiquity*, edited by D.H.J. Larmour, P. A. Miller, and C. Platter, 122–37. Princeton, NJ: Princeton University Press, 1998.

Foxhall, L. "Response to Eva Cantarella." In *Symposion 1990: Vorträge zur griechischen und hellenistischen Rechtsgeschichte*, edited by M. Gagarin, 297–303. Cologne: Böhlau, 1991.

Foxhall, L., and A.D.E. Lewis. "Introduction." In *Greek Law in its Political Setting*, edited by L. Foxhall and A.D.E. Lewis, 1–8. Oxford: Clarendon Press, 1996.

Franklin, J. L., Jr. "Literacy and the Parietal Inscriptions of Pompeii." In *Literacy in the Roman World*, edited by J. H. Humphrey, 77–98. *Journal of Roman Archaeology* Supplementary Series, 3. Ann Arbor: University of Michigan Press, 1991.

Friedl, R. *Der Konkubinat im Kaiserzeitlichen Rom von Augustus bis Septimius*. Stuttgart: Franz Steiner, 1996.

Friedländer, P. *Epigrammata: Greek Inscriptions in Verse from the Beginnings to the Persian Wars*. Berkeley: University of California Press, 1948.

Frontisi-Ducroux, F. "Eros, Desire and the Gaze." In *Sexuality in Ancient Art: Near East, Egypt, Greece, and Italy*, edited by N. B. Kampen, 81–100. Cambridge: Cambridge University Press, 1996.

Gaca, K. L. *The Making of Fornication: Eros, Ethics, and Political Reform in Greek Philosophy and Early Christianity*. Berkeley: University of California Press, 2003.

Gagarin, M. *Drakon and Early Athenian Homicide Law*. New Haven, CT: Yale University Press, 1981.

Gagarin, M. *Early Greek Law*. Berkeley: University of California Press, 1986.

Gagarin, M. "The Organisation of the Gortyn Law Code." *Greek, Roman, and Byzantine Studies* 23 (1982): 129–46.

Gager, J. G. *Curse Tablets and Binding Spells from the Ancient World*. New York: Oxford University Press, 1992.

García y García, L., and L. Jacobelli. *Museo segreto: Louis Barré*. Pompeii: Marius, 2001.

Gardiner, A. *Egyptian Grammar; Being an Introduction to the Study of Hieroglyphs*, 2nd ed. London: Oxford University Press for the Griffith Institute, Ashmolean Museum, Oxford, 1950.

Gardner, J. F. *Being a Roman Citizen*. London: Routledge, 1993.

Gardner, J. F. *Family and Familia in Roman Law and Life*. Oxford: Clarendon Press, 1998.

Gardner, J. F. *Women in Roman Law and Society*. London: Croom Helm, 1986.

Garnsey P. "Adultery Trials and the Survival of the *quaestiones* in the Severan Age." *Journal of Roman Studies* 57 (1967): 56–60.

Garrison, D. H. *Sexual Culture in Ancient Greece*. Norman: University of Oklahoma Press, 2000.

Geffcken, K. A. *Comedy in the Pro Caelio*. Leiden: Brill, 1973.

La Genière, J. de. "Clients, potiers et peintres." In *Les clients de la céramique grecque*, edited by J. de La Genière, 9–15. Paris: Académie des Inscriptions et Belles-lettres, 2006.

Gernet, L. *The Anthropology of Ancient Greece*, translated by J. Hamilton and B. Nagy. Baltimore: Johns Hopkins University Press, 1981.

Giardina, A., ed. *The Romans*, translated by Lydia G. Cochrane. Chicago: University of Chicago Press, 1993.

Giddens, A. *The Class Structure of the Advanced Societies*. New York: Harper & Row, 1973.

Gilfoyle, T. J. "Prostitutes in History: From Parables of Pornography to Metaphors of Modernity." *American Historical Review* 104 (1999): 117–41.

Gilhuly, K. "The Phallic Lesbian: Philosophy, Comedy, and Social Inversion in Lucian's *Dialogues of the Courtesans*." In *Prostitutes and Courtesans in the Ancient World*, edited by C. A. Faraone and L. K. McClure, 274–91. Madison: University of Wisconsin Press, 2006.

Gilman, S., et al. *Hysteria beyond Freud*. Berkeley: University of California Press, 1993.

Gilula, D. "Comic Food and Food for Comedy." In *Food in Antiquity*, edited by J. Wilkins, D. Harvey, and M. Dobson, 386–99. Exeter: Exeter University Press, 1995.

Glazebrook, A. "The Bad Girls of Athens: The Image and Function of Hetairai in Judicial Oratory." In *Prostitutes and Courtesans in the Ancient World,* edited by C. A. Faraone and L. K. McClure, 125–38. Madison: University of Wisconsin Press, 2006.

Glazebrook, A. "The Making of a Prostitute: Apollodoros's Portrait of Neaira." *Arethusa* 38 (2005): 161–88.

Glazebrook, A. "*Porneion*: Prostitution in Athenian Civic Space." In *Greek Prostitutes in the Ancient Mediterranean, 800 B.C.E.–200 C.E.,* edited by A. Glazebrook and M. M. Henry. Madison: University of Wisconsin Press, 2011.

Glazebrook, A. "Prostituting Female Kin (Plut. *Sol.* 23.1–2)." *Dike* 8 (2005): 33–52.

Gleason, M. W. "The Semiotics of Gender: Physiognomy and Self-fashioning in the Second Century C.E." In *Before Sexuality: The Construction of Erotic Experience in the Ancient Greek World,* edited by D. M. Halperin, J. J. Winkler, and F. I. Zeitlin, 389–416. Princeton, NJ: Princeton University Press, 1990.

Gold, B. K. "Dionysus, Greek Festivals and the Treatment of Hysteria." *Laetaberis* 6 (1988): 16–28.

Goldberg, C. *Carmina Priapea: Einleitung, Übersetzung, Interpretation und Kommentar.* Heidelberg: Winter, 1992.

Golden, M. *Children and Childhood in Classical Athens.* Baltimore and London: Johns Hopkins University Press, 1990.

Golden, M. "Slavery and Homosexuality at Athens." *Phoenix* 38 (1984): 308–24.

Golden, M. "Thirteen Years of Homosexuality (and Other Recent Work on Sex, Gender and the Body in Ancient Greece)." *Echos du monde classique/Classical Views* 10 (1991): 327–40.

Golden, M., and P. Toohey, eds. *Sex and Difference in Ancient Greece and Rome.* Edinburgh: Edinburgh University Press, 2003.

Goldhill, S. "The Audience of Athenian Tragedy." In *The Cambridge Companion to Greek Tragedy,* edited by P. E. Easterling, 54–68. Cambridge: Cambridge University Press, 1997.

Goldhill, S. *Foucault's Virginity: Ancient Erotic Fiction and the History of Sexuality (The Stanford Memorial Lectures).* Cambridge: Cambridge University Press, 1995.

Goldhill, S. "Representing Democracy: Women at the Great Dionysia." In *Ritual Finance Politics: Athenian Democratic Accounts Presented to David Lewis,* edited by R. Osborne and S. Hornblower, 347–70. Oxford: Clarendon Press, 1994.

Goldhill, S. "The Seductions of the Gaze: Socrates and His Girlfriends." In *Komos: Essays in Order, Conflict and Community in Classical Athens,* edited by P. Cartledge, P. Millett, and S. von Reden 105–24. Cambridge: Cambridge University Press, 1998.

Gordon, P. "The Lover's Voice in *Heroides* 15: Or, Why Is Sappho a Man?" In *Roman Sexualities,* edited by J. P. Hallett and M. B. Skinner, 274–91. Princeton, NJ: Princeton University Press, 1997.

Gotteland, S. "L'origine des cités grecques dans les discours athéniens." In *Origines Gentium,* edited by V. Fromentin and S. Gotteland. Paris: Diffusion De Boccard, 2001.

Gourevitch, D. "Cherchez la femme." In *Le Traité des Maladies Aiguës et des Maladies Chroniques de Caelius Aurelianus. Nouvelles approches. Actes du colloque de Lausanne, 1996,* edited by P. Mudry, O. Bianchi, and D. Castaldo, 177–205. Université de Nantes: Institut Universitaire de France, 1999.

Gourevitch, D. *Le mal d'être femme. La femme et la médecine dans la Rome antique.* Paris: Les Belles Lettres, 1984.

Gourevitch, D. "Women Who Suffer from a Man's Disease: The Example of Satyriasis and the Debate on Affections Specific to the Sexes." In *Women in Antiquity: New Assessments,* edited by R. Hawley and B. Levick, 149–65. London: Routledge, 1995.

Graham, A. J. "The Woman at the Window: Observations on the 'Stele from the Harbour' of Thasos." *Journal of Hellenic Studies* 118 (1998): 22–40.

Gravel, P. B. *The Malevolent Eye: An Essay on the Evil Eye, Fertility and the Concept of Mana.* New York: Peter Lang, 1995.

Graves, D. "The Institutional Theory of Art: A Survey." *Philosophia* 25 (1997): 51–67.

Gregersen, E. *Sexual Practices: The Story of Human Sexuality.* New York: Franklin Watts, 1983.

Griffin, J. *Latin Poets and Roman Life.* Chapel Hill: University of North Carolina Press, 1986.

Griffith, M. *Sophocles: Antigone.* Cambridge: Cambridge University Press, 1999.

Grmek, M. *Diseases in the Ancient World,* translated by M. Muellner and L. Muellner. Baltimore: Johns Hopkins University Press, 1989.

Guillaud, J., and M. Guillaud. *Frescoes in the Time of Pompeii.* Paris: Guillaud Editions, 1990.

Guillroy, J. *Cultural Capital: The Problem of Literary Canon Formation.* Chicago: University of Chicago Press, 1993.

Gulick, C. B. *Athenaeus, The Deipnosophists,* vol. 6. Cambridge, MA: Harvard University Press, 1937.

Guzzo, P. G., and V. S. Ussani. *Veneris figurae: Immagine di prostituzione e sfruttamento a Pompei.* Naples: Ministero per i Beni e le Attività Culturali, Soprintendenza Archeologica di Napoli e Caserta, 2000.

Habinek, T. "The Invention of Sexuality in the World City of Rome." In *The Roman Cultural Revolution,* edited by T. Habinek and A. Schiesaro, 23–43. Cambridge: Cambridge University Press, 1997.

Haley, S. P. "Lucian's 'Leaena and Clonarium': Voyeurism or a Challenge to Assumptions." In *Among Women: From the Homosocial to the Homoerotic in the Ancient World,* edited by N. S. Rabinowitz and L. Auanger, 286–303. Austin: University of Texas Press, 2002.

Hall, E. *Inventing the Barbarian: Greek Self-definition through Tragedy.* Oxford: Oxford University Press, 1989.

Hall, J. M. *Ethnic Identity in Greek Antiquity.* Cambridge: Cambridge University Press, 1997.

Hall, R. G. "Epispasm: Circumcision in Reverse." *Bible Review* 8, no. 4 (1992): 52–57.

Hallett, J. P. *Fathers and Daughters in Roman Society: Women and the Elite Family.* Princeton, NJ: Princeton University Press, 1984.

Hallett, J. P. "Female Homoeroticism and the Denial of Roman Reality in Latin Literature." In *Roman Sexualities,* edited by J. P. Hallett and M. B. Skinner, 255–73. Princeton, NJ: Princeton University Press, 1997.

Hallett, J. P. "*Perusinae glandes* and the Changing Image of Augustus." *American Journal of Ancient History* 2 (1977): 151–71.

Hallett, J. P., and M. B. Skinner, eds. *Roman Sexualities.* Princeton, NJ: Princeton University Press, 1997.

Halperin, D. M. "Homosexuality." In *The Oxford Classical Dictionary,* 3rd ed., edited by S. Hornblower and A. Spawforth, 720–23. Oxford: Oxford University Press, 1996.

Halperin, D. M. *How to Do the History of Homosexuality.* Chicago: University of Chicago Press, 2002.

Halperin, D. M. *One Hundred Years of Homosexuality and Other Essays on Greek Love.* New York: Routledge, 1990.

Halperin, D. M. "Plato and Erotic Reciprocity." *Classical Antiquity* 5 (1986): 60–80.

Halperin, D. M. "Questions of Evidence: Commentary on Koehl, DeVries, and Williams." In *Queer Representations,* edited by M. Duberman, 39–54. New York: New York University Press, 1997.

Halperin, D. M. *Saint Foucault: Towards a Gay Hagiography.* Oxford: Oxford University Press, 1996.

Halperin, D. M., J. J. Winkler, and F. I. Zeitlin, eds. *Before Sexuality: The Construction of Erotic Experience in the Ancient Greek World.* Princeton, NJ: Princeton University Press, 1990.

Halperin, D. M., J. J. Winkler, and F. I. Zeitlin. "Introduction." In *Before Sexuality: The Construction of Erotic Experience in the Ancient Greek World,* edited by D. M. Halperin, J. J. Winkler, and F. I. Zeitlin, 3–20. Princeton, NJ: Princeton University Press, 1990.

Hansen, M. H., and T. H. Nielsen. *An Inventory of Archaic and Classical Poleis.* Oxford: Oxford University Press, 2004.

Hanson, A. E. "Conception, Gestation, and the Origin of Female Nature in the Corpus Hippocraticum." *Helios* 19 (1992): 31–71

Hanson, A. E. "The Medical Writers' Woman." In *Before Sexuality: The Construction of Erotic Experience in the Ancient Greek World,* edited by D. M. Halperin, J. J. Winkler, and F. I. Zeitlin, 309–38. Princeton, NJ: Princeton University Press, 1990.

Harris, E. "Did the Athenians Regard Seduction as a Worse Crime Than Rape?" *Classical Quarterly* 40 (1990): 370–77.

Harris, E. "Review-discussion of Deacy and Pierce, *Rape in Antiquity: Sexual Violence in the Greek and Roman Worlds.*" *Echos du monde classique/ Classical Views* 40 (1997): 483–96.

Harris, E. M. "Did Rape Exist in Classical Athens? Further Reflections on the Laws about Sexual Violence." *Dike* 7 (2004): 41–83.

Harris, W. *Ancient Literacy.* Cambridge, MA: Harvard University Press, 1989.

Harrison, A.R.W. *The Law of Athens.* Oxford: Clarendon Press, 1968–1971.

Harvey, D. "Lydian Specialities, Croesus' Golden Baking-woman, and Dogs' Dinners." In *Food in Antiquity*, edited by J. Wilkins, D. Harvey, and M. Dobson, 273–85. Exeter: Exeter University Press, 1995.

Hastrup, H. B. "La clientèle étrusque de vases attiques a-t-elle acheté des vases ou des images?" In *Céramique et peinture grecques: Modes d'emploi*, edited by M.-C. Villanueva-Puig, F. Lissarrague, P. Rouillard, and A. Rouveret, 439–44. Paris: Documentation française, 1999.

Heath, M. *Political Comedy in Aristophanes*. Göttingen: Vandenhoeck & Ruprecht, 1987.

Hemker, J. "Rape and the Founding of Rome." *Helios* 12 (1985): 41–47.

Henderson, J. *Aristophanes: Acharnians. Knights*. Cambridge, MA: Harvard University Press, 1998.

Henderson, J. "Greek Attitudes toward Sex." In *Civilization of the Ancient Mediterranean: Greece and Rome*, 2, edited by M. Grant and R. Kitzinger, 1249–64. New York: Scribner's, 1988.

Henderson, J. *The Maculate Muse: Obscene Language in Attic Comedy*, 2nd ed. New York: Oxford University Press, 1991.

Henderson, J. "Women and the Athenian Dramatic Festivals." *Transactions of the American Philological Association* 121 (1991): 133–47.

Hendrix, E. "Some Methods for Revealing Paint on Early Cycladic Figures." In *Metron* (*Aegaeum* 24), edited by K. Foster and R. Laffineur, 139–45. Liège: Université de Liège, 2003.

Hendrix, E. A. "Painted Early Cycladic Figures: An Exploration of Context and Meaning." *Hesperia* 72 (2003): 405–46.

Henrichs, A. "Greek Maenadism from Olympias to Messalina." *Harvard Studies in Classical Philology* 82 (1978): 121–60.

Henry, A. "Hookers and Lookers: Prostitution and Soliciting in Late Archaic Thasos." *Annual of the British School at Athens* 97 (2002): 217–21.

Henry, M. M. "The Edible Woman: Athenaeus's Concept of the Pornographic." In *Pornography and Representation in Greece and Rome*, edited by A. Richlin, 250–68. New York: Oxford University Press, 1992.

Henry, M. M. *Prisoner of History: Aspasia of Miletus and her Biographical Tradition*. Oxford: Oxford University Press, 1995.

Herder, Johann Gottfried. "Auszug aus einem Briefwechsel über Ossian und die Lieder alter Völker." In *Herder. Werke. Band 1. Herder und der Sturm und Drang 1764–1774*, 477–525. Munich: Carl Hanser, 1984 [1773].

Herder, Johann Gottfried. *Outlines of a Philosophy of the History of Man*, translated by T. Churchill. London: Printed for J. Johnson, by Luke Hansard, 1800; reprinted New York: Bergman Publishers, 1966.

Herder, Johann Gottfried. "Über die Wirkung der Dichtkunst auf die Sitten der Völker in alten und neuen Zeiten." In *Herder. Werke, in fünf Bänden* 3, edited by Wilhelm Dobbek, 195–255. Berlin: Aufbau-Verlag, 1964.

Herder, Johann Gottfried. *On World History: An Anthology*, edited by H. Adler and E. A. Menze, translated by E. Menze with M. Palma. Armonk, NY: M. E. Sharpe, 1997.

Herdt, G. H. *Guardians of the Flutes: Images of Masculinity*, 2nd ed. New York: McGraw-Hill, 1987.

Herman, G. "How Violent was Athenian Society." In *Ritual Finance Politics: Athenian Democratic Accounts Presented to David Lewis*, edited by R. Osborne and S. Hornblower, 99–117. Oxford: Oxford University Press, 1994.

Herman, G. *Ritualized Friendship and the Greek City*. Cambridge: Cambridge University Press, 1987.

Herman, J. *Vulgar Latin*, translated by R. Wright. University Park: Pennsylvania State University Press, 2000.

Herrmann, P., and F. Bruckmann. *Denkmäler der Malerei des Altertums*. Munich: F. Bruckmann, 1904–1950.

Herter, H. *De Priapo*. Giessen: A. Töpelmann, 1932.

Herter, H. "The Sociology of Prostitution in Antiquity in the Context of Pagan and Christian Writing," translated by L. DeLong. In *Sex and Difference in Ancient Greece and Rome*, edited by M. Golden and P. Toohey, 57–113. Edinburgh: Edinburgh University Press, 2003.

Heuser, G. *Die Personennamen der Kopten*. Leipzig: Dieterich, 1929.

Hillard, T. "On the Stage, behind the Curtain: Images of Politically Active Women in the Late Roman Republic." In *Stereotypes of Women in Power: Historical Perspectives and Revisionist Views*, edited by B. Garlick, S. Dixon, and P. Allen, 37–64. London: Greenwood Press, 1992.

Hodkinson, S. "Inheritance, Marriage, and Demography: Perspectives upon the Success and Decline of Classical Sparta." In *Classical Sparta: Techniques Behind her Success*, edited by A. Powell, 79–121. London: Routledge, 1989.

Hodkinson, S. "Land Tenure and Inheritance in Classical Sparta." *Classical Quarterly* 36 (1986): 378–406.

Hopkins, K. "Contraception in the Roman Empire." *Comparative Studies in Society and History* 8 (1965): 124–51.

Hopkins, K. *Death and Renewal*. Cambridge: Cambridge University Press, 1983.

Horkheimer, M., and T. W. Adorno. "The Culture Industry: Enlightenment as Mass Deception." In *Dialectic of Enlightenment*, translated by J. Cumming, 120–67. New York: Herder and Herder, 1972; German original 1944.

Horfall, N. *The Culture of the Roman Plebs*. London: Duckworth, 2003.

Hubbard, T. K., ed. *Greek Love Reconsidered*. New York: W. Hamilton, 2000.

Hubbard, T. K., ed. *Homosexuality in Greece and Rome: A Sourcebook of Basic Documents*. Berkeley: University of California Press, 2003.

Hubbard, T. K. "Popular Perceptions of Elite Homosexuality in Classical Athens." *Arion* 6 (1998): 48–78.

Huebner, S. R. "'Brother-sister' Marriage in Roman Egypt: A Curiosity of Mankind or a Widespread Family Strategy?" *Journal of Roman Studies* 97 (2007): 21–49.

Hugo, V. *L'homme qui rit* (trans., *By Order of the King*). New York: The Co-operative Publication Society, 1869 [1920].

Humphreys, S. C. *The Family, Women, and Death*. Ann Arbor: University of Michigan Press, 1993.

Humphreys, S. C. "A Historical Approach to Drakon's Law on Homicide." In *Symposion 1990: Vorträge zur griechischen und hellenistischen Rechtsgeschichte,* edited by M. Gagarin, 17–45. Cologne: Böhlau, 1991.

Humphreys, S. C. "The *nothoi* of Kynosarges." *Journal of Hellenic Studies* 94 (1974): 88–95.

Hunt, A. S., and C. C. Edgar. *Select Papyri,* 4 vols. Cambridge, MA: Harvard University Press, 1970.

Hunter, V. "Gossip and the Politics of Reputation in Classical Athens." *Phoenix* 44 (1990): 299–325.

Hunter, V. *Policing Athens: Social Control in the Attic Lawsuits.* Princeton, NJ: Princeton University Press, 1994.

Hupperts, C. A. "Greek Love: Homosexuality or Pederasty? Greek Love in Black-figure Vase Painting." In *Proceedings of the 3rd Symposium on Ancient Greek and Related Pottery,* edited by J. Christiansen et al., 255–68. Copenhagen: Nationalmuseet, Ny Carlsberg Glyptotek, Thorvaldsens Museum, 1988.

Ingalls, W. "*Paida nean malista*: When Did Athenian Girls Really Marry?" *Mouseion* 1 (2001): 17–29.

Isaac, B. H. *The Invention of Racism in Classical Antiquity.* Princeton, NJ: Princeton University Press, 2004.

Isager, S. "The Marriage Pattern in Classical Athens: Men and Women in Isaios." *Classica & Mediaevalia* 33 (1980–1981): 81–96.

Jacobelli, L. *Le pitture erotiche delle Terme Suburbane di Pompe.* Rome: 'L'Erma' di Bretschneider, 1995.

James, S. "A Courtesan's Choreography: Female Liberty and Male Anxiety at the Roman Dinner Party." In *Prostitutes and Courtesans in the Ancient World,* edited by C. A. Faraone and L. K. McClure, 224–51. Madison: University of Wisconsin Press, 2006.

Jeffery, L. H. *The Local Scripts of Archaic Greece,* rev. ed. with a supplement by A. W. Johnston. Oxford: Clarendon Press, 1990.

Jenkyns, R. *The Victorians and Ancient Greece.* Cambridge, MA: Harvard University Press, 1980.

Jocelyn, H. D. "A Greek Indecency and its Students: *laikazein.*" *Proceedings of the Cambridge Philological Society* 26 (1980): 12–66.

Johns, C. *Sex or Symbol: Erotic Images of Greece and Rome.* Austin: University of Texas Press, 1982.

Johnson, M., and T. Ryan, eds. *Sexuality in Greek and Roman Society and Literature.* London: Routledge, 2005.

Johnston, W. *The Divine Ryans.* Toronto: Vintage, 1990.

Joplin, P. K. "Ritual Work on Human Flesh: Livy's Lucretia and the Rape of the Body Politic." *Helios* 17 (1990): 51–70.

Joshel, S. "The Body Female and the Body Politic: Livia's Lucretia and Verginia." In *Pornography and Representation in Greece and Rome,* edited by A. Richlin, 112–30. New York: Oxford University Press, 1992.

Joshel, S. "Female Desire and the Discourse of Empire: Tacitus' Messalina." *Signs* 21 (1995): 50–82.

Just, R. *Women in Athenian Law and Life*. London: Routledge, 1989.

Kampen, N. B., ed. *Sexuality in Ancient Art*. Cambridge: Cambridge University Press, 1996.

Kampen, N. B. "What Could Hadrian Feel for Antinoos?" In *Geschlechterdefinitionen und Geschlechtergrenzen in der Antike*, edited by E. Hartmann, U. Hartmann and K. Pietzner, 199–207. Stuttgart: Franz Steiner, 2007.

Kapparis. K. *Apollodorus, "Against Neaira" [D. 59]*. Berlin: Walter de Gruyter, 1999.

Kapparis. K. "Humiliating the Adulterer: The Law and the Practice in Classical Athens." *Revue internationale des droits de l'antiquité* 43 (1996): 63–77.

Kapparis. K. "When Were the Athenian Adultery Laws Introduced?" *Revue international des droits de l'antiquité* 42 (1995): 97–122.

Karras, R. M. "Active/passive, Acts/passions: Greek and Roman Sexualities." *American Historical Review* 105 (2000): 1250–65.

Katz, J. N. *The Invention of Heterosexuality*. Chicago: University of Chicago Press, 1995.

Katz, M. A. "Women and Democracy in Ancient Greece." In *Contextualizing Classics: Ideology, Performance, Dialogue, Essays in Honor of John J. Peradotto*, edited by T. M. Falkner, N. Felson and D. Konstan, 41–68. Lanham: Rowman & Littlefield, 1999.

Kendrick, W. M. *The Secret Museum: Pornography in Modern Culture*. Berkeley: University of California Press, 1996.

Keuls, E. "The Hetaera and the Housewife: The Splitting of the Female Psyche in Greek Art." *Mededelingen van het Nederlands Instituut te Rome* 44/45 (1983): 23–40.

Keuls, E. C. *The Reign of the Phallus: Sexual Politics in Ancient Athens*. New York: Harper & Row, 1985.

Kilmer, M. F. "Genital Phobia and Depilation." *Journal of Hellenic Studies* 102 (1982): 104–12.

Kilmer, M. F. *Greek Erotica on Attic Red-Figure Vases*. London: Duckworth, 1993.

Kilmer, M. F. "Painters and Pederasts: Ancient Art, Sexuality, and Social History." In *Inventing Ancient Culture: Historicism, Periodization, and the Ancient World*, edited by M. Golden and P. Toohey, 36–49. London: Routledge, 1997.

Kilmer, M. F. "Sexual Violence: Archaic Athens and the Recent Past." In *Owls to Athens: Essays on Classical Subjects Presented to Sir Kenneth Dover*, edited by E. M. Craik, 261–80. Oxford: Clarendon Press, 1990.

King, H. "Bound to Bleed: Artemis and Greek Women." In *Images of Women in Antiquity*, edited by A. Cameron and A. Kuhrt, 109–27. Detroit: Wayne State University Press, 1983. (Reprinted in L. K. McClure, ed. *Sexuality and Gender in the Classical World: Readings and Sources*. Oxford: Blackwell, 2002, 77–97.)

King, H. *The Disease of Virgins: Green Sickness, Chlorosis, and the Problems of Puberty*. London: Routledge, 2004.

King, H. "Food and Blood in Hippokratic Gynaecology." In *Food in Antiquity*, edited by J. Wilkins, D. Harvey, and M. Dobson, 351–58. Exeter: Exeter University Press, 1995.

King, H. *Hippocrates' Woman: Reading the Female Body in Ancient Greece.* London: Routledge, 1998.

King, H. "The Mathematics of Sex: One to Two, or Two to One?" *Studies in Medieval and Renaissance History: Sexuality and Culture in Medieval and Renaissance Europe* 2 (2005): 47–58.

King, H. "Once upon a Text: The Hippocratic Origins of Hysteria." In *Hysteria Beyond Freud,* edited by S. Gilman, H. King, R. Porter, G. S. Rousseau, and E. Showalter, 3–90. Berkeley: University of California Press, 1993.

King, H. "Women's Health in the Hippocratic Corpus." In *Health in Antiquity,* edited by H. King, 150–61. London: Routledge, 2005.

Kingsolver, B. *The Poisonwood Bible.* New York: Harper, 1998.

Kleiner, D.E.E. *Roman Sculpture.* New Haven, CT: Yale University Press, 1992.

Klinck, A. L. "'Sleeping in the Bosom of a Tender Companion': Homoerotic Attachments in Sappho." In *Same-Sex Desire and Love in Greco-Roman Antiquity and in the Classical Tradition of the West,* edited by B. C. Verstraete and V. Provencal, 193–208. Binghamton: Haworth Press, 2005.

Knigge, U. *The Athenian Kerameikos,* translated by J. Binder. Athens: Krene Editions, 1991.

Knigge, U. *Kerameikos Bd.17: Bau Z.* Munich: Hirmer Verlag, 2005.

Knight, R. P. *Discourse on the Worship of Priapus, and its Connection with the Mystic Theology of the Ancients.* London: Privately printed, 1794.

Koch-Harnack, G. *Knabenliebe und Tiergeschenke: ihre Bedeutung im päderastischen Erziehungssystem Athens.* Berlin: Gebr. Mann, 1983.

Konstan, D. *Greek Comedy and Ideology.* New York: Oxford University Press, 1995.

Konstan, D. "Ideology and Narrative in Livy, Book 1." *Classical Antiquity* 5 (1986): 197–215.

Konstan, D. "Premarital Sex, Illegitimacy, and Male Anxiety in Menander and Athens." In *Athenian Identity and Civic Ideology,* edited by A. Scafuro and A. Boegehold, 217–35. Baltimore: Johns Hopkins University Press, 1994.

Krenkel, W. A. "Fellatio and irrumatio." *Wissenschaftliche Zeitschrift der Wilhelm-Pieck-Universität Rostock* 29 (1980): 77–78.

Krenkel, W. A. "Masturbation in der Antike." *Wissenschaftliche Zeitschrift der Wilhelm-Pieck-Universität Rostock* 28 (1979): 159–78.

Krenkel, W. A. *Naturalia non turpia: Sex and Gender in Ancient Greece and Rome; Schriften zur antiken Kultur- und Sexualwissenschaft,* edited by W. Bernard and C. Reitz. Hildesheim: Olms, 2006.

Krenkel, W. A. "Review of Antonio Varone, *Erotica pompeiana.*" *Gnomon* 69 (1997): 552–54.

Krenkel, W. A. "Tonguing." *Wissenschaftliche Zeitschrift der Wilhelm-Pieck-Universität Rostock* 30 (1981): 37–54.

Krenkel, W. A. "Zur Prosopographie der antike Pornographie." *Wissenschaftliche Zeitschrift der Wilhelm-Pieck-Universität Rostock* 19 (1970): 615–19.

Kroll, W. "Lesbische Liebe." *Real-Encyclopädie der klassischen Altertumswissenschaft* 12.2 (1925): 2100–2102.

Kurke, L. *Coins, Bodies, Games, and Gold: The Politics of Meaning in Archaic Greece.*
Princeton, NJ: Princeton University Press, 1999.

Kurke, L. "Gender, Politics, and Subversion in the *Chreiai* of Machon." *Proceedings of the Cambridge Philological Society* 48 (2002): 20–65.

Kurke, L. "Inventing the Hetaira: Sex, Politics, and Discursive Conflict in Archaic Greece." *Classical Antiquity* 16 (1997): 106–50.

Kurke L. *The Traffic in Praise: Pindar and the Poetics of Social Economy.* Ithaca, NY: Cornell University Press, 1991.

Kytzler, B. *Carmina Priapea: Gedichte an den Gartengott.* Zurich: Artemis, 1978.

Lacey, W. K. "*Patria potestas.*" In *The Family in Ancient Rome,* edited by B. Rawson, 121–45. London: Croom Helm, 1986.

Laes, C. "Desperately Different? *Delicia* Children in the Roman Household." In *Early Christian Families in Context: An Interdisciplinary Dialogue,* edited by D. L. Balch and C. Osiek, 298–323. Grand Rapids, MI: Eerdmans, 2003.

Lang, M. *Graffiti and Dipinti:* The Athenian Agora 21. Princeton, NJ: American School of Classical Studies at Athens, 1976.

Langdon, M. K. *A Sanctuary of Zeus on Mount Hymettos: Hesperia* Supplement 16. Princeton, NJ: American School of Classical Studies at Athens, 1976.

Langlands, R. *Sexual Morality in Ancient Rome.* Cambridge: Cambridge University Press, 2006.

Langner, M. *Antike Graffitizeichnungen: Motive, Gestaltung und Bedeutung.* Wiesbaden: Ludwig Reichert, 2001.

Lapatin, K.D.S. "Review of *Polykleitos, the Doryphoros, and Tradition,* edited by W. G. Moon, *Sculptors and Physicians in Fifth-century Greece: A Preliminary Study,* by G.P.R. Métraux, and *The Aphrodite of Knidos and Her Successors: A Historical Review of the Female Nude in Greek Art,* by C. M. Havelock." *Art Bulletin* 79 (1997): 148–56.

Lape, S. "Democratic Ideology and the Poetics of Rape in Menander's Comedy." *Classical Antiquity* 20 (2001): 79–120.

Lape, S. "The Psychology of Prostitution in Aeschines' Speech against Timarchus." In *Prostitutes and Courtesans in the Ancient World,* edited by C. A. Faraone and L. K. McClure, 139–60. Madison: University of Wisconsin Press, 2006.

Lape, S. "Racializing Democracy: The Politics of Sexual Reproduction in Classical Athens." *Parallax* 9 (2003): 52–63.

Lape, S. *Reproducing Athens: Menander's Comedy, Democratic Culture and the Hellenistic City.* Princeton, NJ: Princeton University Press, 2004.

Lape, S. "Solon and the Institution of the Democratic Family Form." *Classical Journal* 98 (2002/2003): 117–39.

Laqueur, T. *Making Sex: Body and Gender from the Greeks to Freud.* Cambridge, MA: Harvard University Press, 1990.

Laurence, R. *Roman Pompeii: Space and Society.* New York: Routledge, 1994.

Layton, B. *A Coptic Grammar: With Chrestomathy and Glossary: Sahidic Dialect.* Wiesbaden: Harrassowitz, 2000.

Leader, R. E. "In Death not Divided: Gender, Family, and State on Classical Athenian Grave Stelae." *American Journal of Archaeology* 101 (1997): 683–99.

Leduc, C. "Marriage in Ancient Greece." In *A History of Women in the West vol. 1: From Ancient Goddesses to Christian Saints*, edited by P. S. Pantel, 235–95. Cambridge, MA: Belknap Press of Harvard University Press, 1992.

Lee, M. "Review of Sian Lewis, *The Athenian Woman: An Iconographic Handbook*." *Bryn Mawr Classical Review*. http://ccat.sas.upenn.edu/bmcr/2003/2003-09-28.html.

Lefkowitz, M. R. *Heroines and Hysterics*. New York: St. Martin's Press, 1981.

Lefkowitz, M. R. "Predatory Goddesses." *Hesperia* 71 (2002): 325–44.

Lefkowitz, M. R., and M. B. Fant. *Women's Life in Greece and Rome: A Source Book in Translation*, 3rd ed. Baltimore: Johns Hopkins University Press, 2005.

Leibundgut, A. *Die römischen Lampen in der Schweiz*. Bern: Francke, 1977.

Leigh, M. "Introduction." In *The Comedies of Terence*, translated by F. W. Clayton, vii–xxvi. Exeter: University of Exeter Press, 2006.

Leitao, D. "The Legend of the Sacred Band." In *The Sleep of Reason: Erotic Experience and Sexual Ethics in Ancient Greece and Rome*, edited by M. Nussbaum and J. Sihvola, 143–69. Chicago: University of Chicago Press, 2002.

Leitao, D. "The Perils of Leukippos: Initiatory Transvestism and Male Gender Ideology in the Ekdusia at Phaistos." *Classical Antiquity* 14 (1995): 130–63.

Leitao, D. "A Male Pregnancy Ritual from Amathous, Cyprus, and the Strategies of Replacement." *Abstracts of the American Philological Association, 130th Annual Meeting*, 143. New York: American Philological Association, 1998.

Lelis, A. A., W. A. Percy, and B. C. Verstraete. *The Age of Marriage in Ancient Rome*. Lewiston, NY: Edwin Mellen Press, 2003.

Levi, D. "The Evil Eye and the Lucky Hunchback." In *Antioch-on-the-Orontes*, edited by R. Stillwell, 220–32. Princeton, NJ: Princeton University Press, 1941.

Levine, D. "*Eraton bama* ('Her Lovely Feet'): *The Erotics of Feet in Ancient Greece*." In *Body Language in the Greek and Roman Worlds*, edited by D. L. Cairns, 55–72, Swansea: Classical Press of Wales, 2005.

Lewis, D. M. "Keeping Roads Clean in Thasos." *Classical Review* 43 (1993): 402–3.

Lewis, S. *The Athenian Woman: An Iconographic Handbook*. London: Routledge, 2002.

Lewis, S. "Representation and Reception: Athenian Pottery in its Italian Context." In *Inhabiting Symbols: Symbol and Image in the Ancient Mediterranean*, edited by J. Wilkins and E. Herring, 175–92. London: Accordia Research Institute, University of London, 2003.

Lewis, S. "Shifting Images: Athenian Women in Etruria." In *Gender and Ethnicity in Ancient Italy*, edited by T. Cornell and K. Lomas, 141–54. London: Accordia Research Institute, University of London, 1997.

Licht, H. *Sexual Life in Ancient Greece*, translated by J. H. Freese. London: Routledge, 1932.

Lilja, S. *Homosexuality in Republican and Augustan Rome*. Helsinki: Societas Scientiarum Fennica, 1983.

Lind, H. "Ein Hetärenhaus am Heiligen Tor? Der Athener Bau Z und die bei Isaios (6, 20f.) erwähnte Synoikia Euktemons." *Museum Helveticum* 45 (1988): 158–69.

Lindsay, J. *The Writing on the Wall: An Account of Pompeii in Its Last Days*. London: Frederick Muller, 1960.

Lissarrague, F. *The Aesthetics of the Greek Banquet: Images of Wine and Ritual*. Princeton, NJ: Princeton University Press, 1990.

Lissarrague, F. "The Sexual Life of Satyrs." In *Before Sexuality: The Construction of Erotic Experience in the Ancient Greek World*, edited by D. M. Halperin, J. J. Winkler, and F. I. Zeitlin, 53–81. Princeton, NJ: Princeton University Press, 1990.

Lissarrague, F. "Voyages d'images: iconographie et aires culturelles." *Revue des études anciennes* 89 (1987): 261–70.

Livrea, E. "La morte di Clitorio (SH 975)." *Zeitschrift für Papyrologie und Epigraphik* 68 (1987): 21–28.

Lloyd, G.E.R. *Science, Folklore, and Ideology: Studies in the Life Sciences in Ancient Greece*. Cambridge: Cambridge University Press, 1983.

Lobel, E., and D. L. Page. *Poetarum Lesbiorum Fragmenta*. Oxford: Oxford University Press, 1955.

Lonie, I. M. *The Hippocratic Treatises "On Generation," "On the Nature of the Child," "Diseases IV."* Berlin: de Gruyter, 1981.

Loomis, W. T. *Wages, Welfare Costs, and Inflation in Classical Athens*. Ann Arbor: University of Michigan Press, 1998.

Loprieno, A. *Ancient Egyptian: A Linguistic Introduction*. Cambridge: Cambridge University Press, 1995.

Loraux, N. *Born of the Earth: Myth and Politics in Athens*, translated by S. Stewart. Ithaca, NY: Cornell University Press, 2000.

Loraux, N. *The Children of Athena: Athenian Ideas about Citizenship and the Division between the Sexes*, translated by C. Levine. Princeton, NJ: Princeton University Press, 1993.

Loraux, N. *The Experiences of Tiresias: The Feminine and the Greek Man*, translated by P. Wissing. Princeton, NJ: Princeton University Press, 1995.

Loraux, N. *The Invention of Athens: The Funeral Oration in the Classical City*, translated by A. Sheridan. Cambridge, MA: Harvard University Press, 1986.

Lupu, E. *Greek Sacred Law: A Collection of New Documents* (NGSL). Leiden: Brill, 2005.

Lutz, C. "Musonius Rufus: The Roman Socrates." *Yale Classical Studies* 10 (1947): 3–147.

Lyne, R.O.A.M. *Horace: Behind the Public Poetry*. New Haven, CT: Yale University Press, 1995.

Maas, M., and J. Snyder. *Stringed Instruments in Ancient Greece*. New Haven, CT: Yale University Press, 1989.

MacDowell, D. M. *Demosthenes, Against Meidias (Oration 21)*. Oxford: Oxford University Press, 1990.

MacKinnon, C. A. *Toward a Feminist Theory of the State*. Cambridge, MA: Harvard University Press, 1989.

MacLachlan, B. "Sacred Prostitution and Aphrodite." *Studies in Religion* 21 (1992): 145–62.

MacMullen, R. "Roman Attitudes to Greek Love." *Historia* 31 (1982): 484–502.

MacMullen, R. *Roman Social Relations, 50 B.C. to A.D. 284*. New Haven, CT: Yale University Press, 1974.

Maffi, A. "Matrimonio, concubinato e filiazione illegitima nell'Atene degli oratori." In *Symposion 1985: Vorträge zur griechischen und hellenistischen Rechtsgeschichte*, edited by G. Thür, 177–214. Cologne: Böhlau, 1989.

Maire, B. "L'imprégnation par le regard ou l'influence des 'simulacres' sur l'embryon." In *Mirabilia. Conceptions et représentations de l'extraordinaire dans le monde antique. Actes du colloque international, Lausanne 20–22 mars 2003*, edited by O. Bianchi and O. Thévenaz, 279–94. Bern: Peter Lang, 2004.

Maiuri, A. *La Casa del Menandro e il suo tesoro di argenteria*. Rome: Libreria dello Stato, 1933.

Manuli, P. "Donne mascoline, femmine sterili, vergini perpetue: la ginecologia greca tra Ippocrate e Sorano." In *Madre materia: sociologia e biologia della donna greca*, edited by S. Campese, 149–92. Turin: Boringhieri, 1983.

Manville, P. B. *The Origins of Citizenship in Ancient Athens*. Princeton, NJ: Princeton University Press, 1990.

Marcadé, J. *Eros Kalos: Essay on Erotic Elements in Greek Art*. Geneva: Nagel, 1962.

Marcadé, J. *Roma Amor: Essay on Erotic Elements in Etruscan and Roman Art*. Geneva: Nagel, 1965.

Marks, M. "Heterosexual Coital Position as a Reflection of Ancient and Modern Cultural Attitudes." PhD dissertation, SUNY-Buffalo, 1978.

Marquié, S. "Les médaillons d'applique rhodaniens de la Place des Célestins à Lyon." *Revue archéologique de l'est* 50 (1999–2000): 239–92.

Mau, A. *Pompeii, Its Life and Art*, translated by F. W. Kelsey. New York: Macmillan, 1902.

McClure, L. *Courtesans at Table: Gender and Greek Literary Culture in Athenaeus*. New York: Routledge, 2003.

McCoy, M. "The Politics of Prostitution: Clodia, Cicero, and Social Order in the Late Roman Republic." In *Prostitutes and Courtesans in the Ancient World*, edited by C. A. Faraone and L. K. McClure, 177–85. Madison: University of Wisconsin Press, 2006.

McGinn, T.A.J. "The Augustan Marriage Legislation and Social Practice: Elite Endogamy versus Male 'marrying down.'" In *Speculum Iuris: Roman Law as a Reflection of Social and Economic Life in Antiquity*, edited by J. J. Aubert and B. Sirks, 46–93. Ann Arbor: University of Michigan Press, 2002.

McGinn, T.A.J. "Concubinage and the *Lex Iulia* on Adultery." *Transactions of the American Philological Association* 121 (1991): 335–75.

McGinn, T.A.J. *The Economy of Prostitution in the Roman World: A Study of Social History and the Brothel*. Ann Arbor: University of Michigan Press, 2004.

McGinn, T.A.J. "Pompeian Brothels and Social History." In *Pompeian Brothels, Pompeii's Ancient History, Mirrors And Mysteries, Art and Nature at Oplontis, and the Herculaneum "Basilica,"* T. A. J. McGinn, P. Carafa, N. de Grummond, B. Bergmann, and T. Najbjerg. *Journal of Roman Archaeology* Supplement 47 (2002): 7–46.

McGinn, T.A.J. *Prostitution, Sexuality, and the Law in Ancient Rome*. New York: Oxford University Press, 1998.

McGinn, T.A.J. "Zoning Shame in the Roman City." In *Prostitutes and Courtesans in the Ancient World*, edited by C. A. Faraone and L. K. McClure, 161–76. Madison: University of Wisconsin Press, 2006.

McNiven, T. J. "Behaving Like an Other: Telltale Gestures in Athenian Vase Painting." In *Not the Classical Ideal: Athens and the Construction of the Other in Greek Art*, edited by B. Cohen, 71–97. Leiden: Brill, 2000.

McNiven, T. J. "The Unheroic Penis: Otherness Exposed." *Source* 15 (1995): 10–16.

Meinardus, O. "Mythological, Historical, and Sociological Aspects of the Practice of Female Circumcision among the Egyptians." *Acta Ethnographica Academiae Scientiarum Hungaricae* ser. 9, 16 (1967): 387–97.

Mencacci, F. "Päderastie und lesbische Liebe: die Ursprünge zweier sexueller Verhaltensweisen und der Unterschied der Geschlechter in Rom." In *Rezeption und Identität: die kulturelle Auseinandersetzung Roms mit Griechenland als europäisches Paradigm*, edited by G. Vogt-Spira and B. Rommel, 60–80. Stuttgart: F. Steiner, 1999.

Meyboom, P. G., and M. J. Versluys. "The Meaning of Dwarfs in Nilotic Scenes." In *Nile into Tiber: Egypt in the Roman World. Proceedings of the IIIrd International Conference on Isis Studies*, edited by L. Bricault, M. J. Versluys and P. G. Meyboom, 170–208. Leiden: Brill, 2007.

Micale, M. S. *Approaching Hysteria: Disease and Its Interpretations*. Princeton, NJ: Princeton University Press, 1995.

Miles, G. B. "The First Roman Marriage and the Theft of the Sabine Women." In *Innovations of Antiquity*, edited by R. Hexter and D. Selden, 161–96. New York: Routledge, 1992.

Miller, R. A. *The Limits of Bodily Integrity: Abortion, Adultery and Rape Legislation in Comparative Perspective*. Aldershot: Ashgate, 2007.

Mills, H. "Greek Clothing Regulations: Sacred and Profane?" *Zeitschrift für Papyrologie und Epigraphik* 55 (1984): 255–65.

Milne, M. J., and D. von Bothmer. "Katapugôn, katapugaina." *Hesperia* 22 (1953): 215–24.

Milner, K. *Gender, Domesticity and the Age of Augustus: Inventing Private Life*. Oxford: Oxford University Press, 2005.

Mirabeau, H.-G. *Errotika biblion*. Rome: De l'Imprimerie du Vatican, 1783.

Mommsen, H. *Der Affecter*. Mainz: P. von Zabern, 1975.

Mommsen, T. *Corpus Iuris Civilis*, vols. 1–3. Berlin: Wiedmann, 1911–1928.

Montanari, E. *Il mito dell'autoctonia: linee di una dinamica mitico-politica ateniese*. Rome: Bulzoni, 1981.

Montserrat, D. *Sex and Society in Graeco-Roman Egypt*. London: Kegan Paul International, 1996.

Moore, T. J. "Morality as History and Livy's Wronged Women." *Eranos* 91 (1993): 38–73.

Moreau, P. "Review of Antonio Varone, *Erotica pompeiana*." *Antiquité classique* 64 (1995): 434–45.

Morris, C. "From Ideologies of Motherhood to 'Collecting Mother Goddesses.'" In *Archaeology and European Modernity: Producing and Consuming the "Minoans"*

(Atti del convegno, Venezia, 25–27 novembre 2005), edited by Y. Hamilakis and N. Momigliano, 69–78. Padua: Bottega d'Erasmo, 2006.

Morris, I. *Archaeology as Cultural History: Words and Things in Iron Age Greece* Malden, MA: Blackwell, 1999.

Morris, I. "The Strong Principle of Equality and the Archaic Origins of Greek Democracy." In *Dêmokratia: A Conversation on Democracies, Ancient and Modern,* edited by J. Ober and C. Hedrick, 19–48. Princeton, NJ: Princeton University Press, 1996.

Moses, D. C. "Livy's Lucretia and the Validity of Coerced Consent in Roman Law." In *Consent and Coercion to Sex and Marriage in Ancient and Medieval Societies,* edited by A. E. Laiou, 39–81. Washington, DC: Dumbarton Oaks, 1993.

Mossé, C. "La place de la *pallaké* dans la famille athénienne." In *Symposion 1990: Vorträge zur griechischen und hellenistischen Rechtsgeschichte,* edited by M. Gagarin, 273–79. Cologne: Böhlau, 1991.

Mossé, C. "Quelques remarques sur la famille à Athènes à la fin du IVème siècle: Le témoignage du théâtre de Ménandre." In *Symposion 1982: Vorträge zur griechischen und hellenistischen Rechtsgeschichte,* edited by F. J. Fernández Nieto, 129–34. Cologne: Böhlau, 1989.

Mudry, P., O. Bianchi and D. Castaldo, eds. *Le Traité des Maladies Aiguës et des Maladies Chroniques de Caelius Aurelianus. Nouvelles approches. Actes du colloque de Lausanne, 1996.* Université de Nantes: Institut Universitaire de France, 1999.

Müller, O. "Untersuchungen zur Geschichte des attischen Bürger- und Eherechts." *Jahrbuch für Classischen Philologie* 25 (1899): 710–32.

Murnaghan. S. "How a Woman Can Be More Like a Man: The Dialogue between Ischomachus and His Wife in Xenophon's *Oeconomicus.*" *Helios* 15 (1988): 9–22.

Myerowitz, M. "The Domestication of Desire: Ovid's *Parva Tabella* and the Theater of Love." In *Pornography and Representation in Greece and Rome,* edited by A. Richlin, 131–57. New York: Oxford University Press, 1992.

Myers, K. S. "The Poet and the Procuress: The *lena* in Latin Love Elegy." *Journal of Roman Studies* 86 (1996): 1–21.

Neer, R. T. *Style and Politics in Athenian Vase-Painting: The Craft of Democracy, ca. 530–460 B.C.E.* Cambridge: Cambridge University Press, 2002.

Neils, J. "Others within the Other: An Intimate Look at Hetairai and Maenads." In *Not the Classical Ideal: Athens and the Construction of the Other in Greek Art,* edited by B. Cohen, 203–26. Leiden: Brill, 2000.

Nelson, M. "A Note on the Olisbos." *Glotta* 76 (2000): 75–82.

Neumann, G. *Gesten und Gebärden in der griechischen Kunst.* Berlin: de Gruyter, 1965.

Nicolet, C. "Les ordres romains: définition, recrutement et fonctionnement." In *Des ordres à Rome,* edited by C. Nicolet, 7–21. Paris: Publications de la Sorbonne, 1984.

Nicolet, C. *The World of the Citizen in Republican Rome,* translated by P. S. Falla. Berkeley: University of California Press, 1980.

Nicolson, D., and L. Bibbings. *Feminist Perspectives on Criminal Law.* London: Cavendish, 2000.

Nussbaum, M. C. *The Fragility of Goodness: Luck and Ethics in Greek Tragedy and Philosophy*. Cambridge: Cambridge University Press, 1986.

Nussbaum, M. C. *The Therapy of Desire: Theory and Practice in Hellenistic Ethics*. Princeton, NJ: Princeton University Press, 1994.

Nussbaum, M. C., and J. Sihvola. "Introduction." In *The Sleep of Reason: Erotic Experience and Sexual Ethics in Ancient Greece and Rome*, edited by M. C. Nussbaum and J. Sihvola, 1–20. Chicago: University of Chicago Press, 2002.

Nutton, V., ed., tr., and comm. *Galen, On Prognosis* (CMG V.8, 1). Berlin: Akademie-Verlag, 1979.

Oakley, J. H. "Review of Richard T. Neer, *Style and Politics in Athenian Vase-Painting: The Craft of Democracy, ca. 530–460 B.C.E.*" *American Journal of Archaeology* 107 (2003): 509–10.

Ober, J. *The Athenian Revolution: Essays on Ancient Greek Democracy and Political Theory*. Princeton, NJ: Princeton University Press, 1996.

Ober, J. *Mass and Elite in Democratic Athens: Rhetoric, Ideology, and the Power of the People*. Princeton, NJ: Princeton University Press, 1989.

Obermayer, H. P. *Martial und der Diskurs über männliche Homosexualität in der Literatur der frühen Kaiserzeit*. Tübingen: G. Narr Verlag, 1998.

O'Connor, E. M. *Symbolum Salacitatis: A Study of the God Priapus as a Literary Character*. Studien zur klassischen Philologie, Band 40. Frankfurt am Main: Lang, 1989.

Ogden, D. "Binding Spells: Curse Tablets and Voodoo Dolls in the Greek and Roman Worlds." In V. Flint, R. Gordon, G. Luck, and D. Ogden, *The Athlone History of Witchcraft and Magic in Europe: Vol. 2. Ancient Greece and Rome*, 1–90. London: Athlone, 1999.

Ogden, D. "Controlling Women's Dress: Gynaikonomoi." In *Women's Dress in the Ancient Greek World*, edited by L. Llewellyn-Jones, 203–25. London: Duckworth, 2002.

Ogden, D. *Greek Bastardy in the Classical and Hellenistic Periods*. Oxford: Oxford University Press, 1996.

Ogden, D. "Homosexuality and Warfare in Ancient Greece." In *Battle in Antiquity*, edited by A. B. Lloyd, 107–68. London: Classical Press of Wales and Duckworth, 1996.

Ogden, D. *Polygamy, Prostitutes and Death*. London: Duckworth, 1997.

Ogden, D. "Rape, Adultery and Protection of Bloodlines in Classical Athens." In *Rape in Antiquity: Sexual Violence in the Greek and Roman Worlds,* edited by S. Deacy and K. F. Pierce, 25–41. London: Duckworth, 2002.

Ogden, D. "Women and Bastardy in Ancient Greece and the Hellenistic World." In *The Greek World*, edited by A. Powell, 219–44. London: Routledge, 1995.

Olsen, B. A. "Women, Children and the Family in the Late Aegean Bronze Age: Differences in Minoan and Mycenaean Constructions of Gender." *World Archaeology* 2 (1998): 380–92.

Olson, K. "*Matrona* and Whore: Clothing and Definition in Roman Antiquity." In *Prostitutes and Courtesans in the Ancient World,* edited by C. A. Faraone and L. K. McClure, 186–206. Madison: University of Wisconsin Press, 2006.

Omitowoju, R. *Rape and the Politics of Consent in Classical Athens*. Cambridge: Cambridge University Press, 2002.

Omitowoju, R. "Regulating Rape: Soap Operas and Self-interest in the Athenian Courts." In *Rape in Antiquity: Sexual Violence in the Greek and Roman Worlds*, edited by S. Deacy and K. F. Pierce, 1–24. London: Duckworth, 2002.

d'Onofri, P. *Elogio estemporaneo per la gloriosa memoria di Carlo III*. Naples, 1789.

Osborne, R. "Desiring Women on Athenian Pottery." In *Sexuality in Ancient Art*, edited by N. B. Kampen, 65–80. Cambridge: Cambridge University Press, 1996.

Osborne, R. "Law in Action in Classical Athens." *Journal of Hellenic Studies* 105 (1985): 40–58.

Osborne, R. "Law and the Representation of Women in Athens." *Past & Present* 155 (1997): 3–33.

Osborne, R. "Why Did Athenian Pots Appeal to the Etruscans?" *World Archaeology* 33 (2001): 277–95.

Ostwald, M. "Was There a Concept *agraphos nomos* in Classical Greece?" In *Exegesis and Argument: Studies in Greek Philosophy Presented to G. Vlastos, Phronesis* suppl.1, edited by E. N. Lee, A.P.D. Mourelatos and R. M. Rorty, 70–104. Assen: Van Gorcum, 1973.

Page, D. L. *Supplementum Lyricis Graecis*. Oxford: Oxford University Press, 1974.

Painter, K. S. *The Insula of the Menander at Pompeii: The Silver Treasure*, The Insula of the Menander at Pompeii, vol. 4. Oxford: Clarendon Press, 2001.

Panciera, M. "Alicaria in Plautus, Festus and Pompeii." *Classical Quarterly* 57 (2007): 303–6.

Paradiso, A. "Gli Iloti e l' 'oikos.'" In *Schiavi e dipendenti nell'ambito dell' "oikos" e della "familia,"* edited by M. Moggi and G. Cordiano, 73–90. Pisa: Edizioni ETS, 1997.

Paradiso, A. "Schiavitù femminile e violenza carnale: stupro e coscienza dello stupro sulle schiave in Grecia." In *Femmes-Esclaves. Modèles d'interprétation anthropologique, économique, juridique. Atti del XXI colloquio internazionale GIREA (Lacco Ameno-Ischia, 27–29 ottobre 1994)*, edited by F. Reduzzi Merola and A. Storchi Marino, 145–62. Naples: Jovene, 1999.

Park, K. *Secrets of Women. Gender, Generation and the Origins of Human Dissection*. New York: Zone Books, 2006.

Park, K., and R. A. Nye. "Destiny Is Anatomy." *New Republic* 18 (1991): 53–57.

Parker, H. N. "Heterosexuality." In *The Oxford Classical Dictionary*, 3rd ed., edited by S. Hornblower and A. Spawforth, 702–3. Oxford: Oxford University Press, 1996.

Parker, H. N. "Love's Body Anatomized: The Ancient Erotic Handbooks and the Rhetoric of Sexuality." In *Pornography and Representation in Greece and Rome*, edited by A. Richlin, 90–107. New York: Oxford University Press, 1992.

Parker, H. N. "The Myth of the Heterosexual or the Anthropology of Sexuality for Classicists." *Arethusa* 34 (2001): 313–62.

Parker, H. N. "The Observed of All Observers: Spectacle, Applause, and Cultural Poetics in the Roman Audience." In *The Art of Ancient Spectacle*, edited by B. Bergmann and C. Kondoleon, 163–79. Washington, DC: National Gallery of Art, 1999.

Parker, H. N. "Sappho Schoolmistress." *Transactions of the American Philological Association* 123 (1993): 309–51.

Parker, H. N. "The Teratogenic Grid." In *Roman Sexualities*, edited by J. P. Hallett and M. B. Skinner, 47–65. Princeton, NJ: Princeton University Press, 1997.

Parker, H. N. "Why Were the Vestals Virgins? Or the Chastity of Women and the Safety of the Roman State." *American Journal of Philology* 125 (2004): 563–601.

Parker, R. *Athenian Religion: A History.* Oxford: Oxford University Press, 1996.

Parker, R. "Law and Religion." In *The Cambridge Companion to Ancient Greek Law*, edited by M. Gagarin and D. Cohen, 61–81. Cambridge: Cambridge University Press, 2005.

Parker, R. *Miasma: Pollution and Purification in Early Greek Religion.* Oxford: Clarendon Press, 1983.

Parker, R. *Polytheism and Society at Athens.* Oxford: Oxford University Press, 2005.

Parker, R. "What Are Sacred Laws?" In *The Law and the Courts in Ancient Greece*, edited by E. Harris and L. Rubinstein, 57–70. London: Duckworth, 2004.

Parker, W. H. *Priapea: Poems for a Phallic God.* London: Croom Helm, 1988.

Patterson, C. "Athenian Citizenship Law." In *The Cambridge Companion to Ancient Greek Law*, edited by M. Gagarin and D. Cohen, 267–89. Cambridge: Cambridge University Press, 2005.

Patterson, C. "The Case against Neaira and the Public Ideology of the Athenian Family." In *Athenian Identity and Civic Ideology*, edited by A. Scafuro and A. L. Boegehold, 199–216. Baltimore: Johns Hopkins University Press, 1994.

Patterson, C. *The Family in Greek History.* Cambridge, MA: Harvard University Press, 1998.

Patterson, C. "Marriage and Married Women in Athenian Law." In *Women's History and Ancient History*, edited by S. Pomeroy, 48–72. Chapel Hill: University of North Carolina Press, 1991.

Patterson, C. *Pericles' Citizenship Law of 451–450 B.C.* Salem, NH: Arno Press, 1981.

Patterson, C. "Those Athenian Bastards." *Classical Antiquity* 9 (1990): 39–73.

Patzer, H. *Die griechische Knabenliebe.* Wiesbaden: F. Steiner, 1982.

Pembroke, S. "Women in Charge: The Function of Alternatives in Early Greek Tradition and the Ancient Idea of Matriarchy." *Journal of the Warburg and Courtauld Institutes* 30 (1967): 1–35.

Pépin, R., ed. and trans. *Quintus Serenus (Serenus Sammonicus) Liber Medicinalis.* Paris: Presses Universitaires de France, 1950.

Percy, W. A. III. *Pederasty and Pedagogy in Archaic Greece.* Urbana: University of Illinois Press, 1996.

Peschel, I. *Die Hetäre bei Symposion und Komos in der attisch-rotfigurigen Vasenmalerei des 6.-4. Jahrhunderts v. Christus.* Frankfurt am Main: P. Lang, 1987.

Petersen, L. H. "Divided Consciousness and Female Companionship: Reconstructing Female Subjectivity on Greek Vases." *Arethusa* 30 (1997): 35–74.

Phillipides, S. N. "Narrative Strategies and Ideology in Livy's 'Rape of Lucretia.'" *Helios* 10 (1983): 113–19.

Pickard-Cambridge, A. W. *The Dramatic Festivals of Athens*, 2nd ed., edited by J. Gould and D. M. Lewis. Oxford: Oxford University Press, 1988.

Pierce, C. "Equality: Republic V." *The Monist* 57 (1973): 1–11.

Pinault, J. R. *Hippocratic Lives and Legends.* Studies in Ancient Medicine 4. Leiden: Brill, 1992.

Pinault, J. R. "The Medical Case for Virginity." *Helios* 19 (1992): 123–39.

Pinney, G. F. "For the Heroes Are at Hand." *Journal of Hellenic Studies* 104 (1984): 181–83.

Pintabone, D. T. "Ovid's Iphis and Ianthe: When Girls Won't Be Girls." In *Among Women: From the Homosocial to the Homoerotic in the Ancient World,* edited by N. S. Rabinowitz and L. Auanger, 256–85. Austin: University of Texas Press, 2002.

Plassard, J. *Le concubinat romain sous le haut empire.* Paris: Tenin, 1921.

Podlecki, A. J. "Could Women Attend the Theater in Ancient Athens? A Collection of Testimonia." *Ancient World* 21 (1990): 27–43.

Pólay, E. "Das *Regimen Morum* des Zensors und die sogenannte Hausgerichtsbarkeit." In *Studi in onore di Edoardo Volterra,* Vol. 3, 263–317. Milan: A. Giuffrè, 1971.

Pollini, J. "The Warren Cup: Homoerotic Love and Symposial Rhetoric in Silver." *The Art Bulletin* 81 (1999): 21–52.

Pollitt, J. J. *Art in the Hellenistic Age.* Cambridge: Cambridge University Press, 1986.

Pomeroy, S. B. *Families in Classical and Hellenistic Greece: Representations and Realities.* Oxford: Oxford University Press, 1997.

Pomeroy, S. B. *Goddesses, Whores, Wives, and Slaves: Women in Classical Antiquity.* New York: Schocken Books, 1975.

Pomeroy, S. B. *Plutarch's* Advice to the Bride and Groom, *and* A Consolation to His Wife: *English Translations, Commentary, Interpretive Essays, and Bibliography.* New York: Oxford University Press, 1999.

Pomeroy, S. B. *Spartan Women.* Oxford: Oxford University Press, 2002.

Pontrandolfo, A. "Dionisio e personaggi fliaciei nelle immagine pertane." *Ostraca* 9 (2000): 117–34.

Pouilloux, J. *Recherches sur l'histoire et les cultes de Thasos.* Paris: De Boccard, 1954.

Preisendanz, K. *Papyri graecae magicae: die griechischen Zauberpapyri,* 2 vols. Leipzig: Teubner, 1928–1931.

Preisigke, F., et al., eds. *Sammelbuch griechischer Urkunden aus Ägypten.* Strassburg: K. J. Trübner, 1915–1993.

Preziosi, P. G., and S. S. Weinberg. "Evidence for Painted Details in Early Cycladic Sculpture." *Antike Kunst* 13 (1970): 4–12.

Pritchett, W. K. "Observations on Chaeronea." *American Journal of Archaeology* 62 (1958): 307–11.

Puccini-Delbey, G. *La vie sexuelle à Rome.* Paris: Tallandier, 2007.

Pütz, B. *The Symposium and Komos in Aristophanes.* Stuttgart: M & P Verlag für Wissenschaft und Forschung, 2003.

Rabinowitz, N. S. "The Erotics of Greek Drama: The Contribution of the Cross-dressed Actor." *Abstracts of One Hundred Twenty-Seventh Meeting, American Philological Association,* 132. Worcester: American Philological Association, 1995.

Rabinowitz, N. S. "Excavating Women's Homoeroticism in Ancient Greece." In *Among Women: From the Homosocial to the Homoerotic in the Ancient World,* edited by N. S. Rabinowitz and L. Auanger, 106–66. Austin: University of Texas Press, 2002.

Rabinowitz, N. S., and L. Auanger, eds. *Among Women: From the Homosocial to the Homoerotic in the Ancient World.* Austin: University of Texas Press, 2002.

Rakoczy, T. *Böser Blick: Macht des Auges und Neid der Götter: eine Untersuchungen zur Kraft des Blickes in der griechischen Literatur.* Tübingen: Gunter Narr, 1996.

Rawson, B. "Roman Concubinage and Other *de facto* Marriages." *Transactions of the American Philological Association* 104 (1974): 279–305.

Rawson, B. "The Roman Family." In *The Family in Ancient Rome*, edited by B. Rawson, 1–57. London: Croom Helm, 1986.

Reeder, E. D. "Representing Women." In *Pandora: Women in Classical Greece*, edited by E. D. Reeder, 123–93. Princeton, NJ: Princeton University Press, 1995.

Reinsberg, C. *Ehe, Hetärentum und Knabenliebe im antiken Griechenland.* Munich: C. H. Beck, 1989.

Reusser, C. *Vasen für Etrurien: Verbreitung und Funktionen attischer Keramik im Etrurien des 6. und 5. Jahrhunderts vor Christus.* Zürich: Akanthus, 2002.

Rhodes, P. J. *A Commentary on the Aristotelian* Athenaion Politeia. Oxford: Oxford University Press, 1981.

Riccobono, S., et al. *Fontes juris romani antejustiniani.* Florence: G. Barbera, 1940–1943 (1992, translated by E. Cantarella).

Richlin, A. "Approaches to the Sources on Adultery at Rome." *Women's Studies* 8 (1981): 225–50.

Richlin, A. "Foucault's History of Sexuality: A Useful Theory for Women?" In *Rethinking Sexuality: Foucault and Classical Antiquity*, edited by D.H.J. Larmour, P. A. Miller, and C. Platter, 138–70. Princeton, NJ: Princeton University Press, 1998.

Richlin, A. *The Garden of Priapus: Sexuality and Aggression in Roman Humor.* New Haven, CT: Yale University Press, 1983.

Richlin, A. "The Meaning of *irrumare* in Catullus and Martial." *Classical Philology* 76 (1981): 40–46.

Richlin, A. "Not before Homosexuality: The Materiality of the *cinaedus* and the Roman Law against Love between Men." *Journal of the History of Sexuality* 3 (1993): 523–73.

Richlin, A. "Pliny's Brassiere." In *Roman Sexualities*, edited by J. P. Hallett and M. B. Skinner, 197–220. Princeton, NJ: Princeton University Press, 1997.

Richlin, A., ed. *Pornography and Representation in Greece and Rome.* New York: Oxford University Press, 1992.

Richlin, A. "Reading Ovid's Rapes." In *Pornography and Representation in Greece and Rome,* edited by A. Richlin, 158–79. New York: Oxford University Press, 1992.

Richlin, A. "Sexuality in the Roman Empire." In *A Companion to the Roman Empire*, edited by D. S. Potter, 327–53. Malden, MA: Blackwell, 2006.

Riddle, J. *Contraception and Abortion from the Ancient World to the Renaissance.* Cambridge, MA: Harvard University Press, 1992.

Riddle, J. *Eve's Herbs: A History of Contraception and Abortion in the West.* Cambridge, MA: Harvard University Press, 1997.

Ridgway, B. S. *Hellenistic Sculpture 2: The Styles of ca. 200–100 B.C.* Madison: University of Wisconsin Press, 2000.

Riggsby, A. M. " 'Public' and 'Private' in Roman Culture: The Case of the Cubiculum." *Journal of Roman Archaeology* 10 (1997): 36–56.

Robertson, M. *Art of Vase Painting in Classical Athens.* Cambridge: Cambridge University Press, 1992.

Robinson, E. W. *The First Democracies: Early Popular Government Outside Athens.* Stuttgart: Franz Steiner Verlag, 1997.

Robinson, O. F. *The Criminal Law of Ancient Rome.* London: Duckworth, 1995.

Roller, M. "Horizontal Women: Posture and Sex in the Roman Convivium." *American Journal of Philology* 124 (2003): 377–422.

Rosivach, V. "Autochthony and the Athenians." *Classical Quarterly* 37 (1987): 294–306.

Rosivach, V. *When a Young Man Falls in Love: The Sexual Exploitation of Women in New Comedy.* London: Routledge, 1998.

Rousselle, A. *Porneia. On Desire and the Body in Antiquity,* translated by F. Pheasant. Oxford: Blackwell, 1988.

Rowlandson, J., and R. Takahashi. "Brother-Sister Marriage and Inheritance Strategies in Greco-Roman Egypt." *Journal of Roman Studies* 109 (2009): 104–39.

Roy, J. "An Alternative Sexual Morality for Classical Athens." *Greece and Rome* 44 (1997): 11–22.

Ruggini, L. C. "Juridical Status and the Historical Role of Women in Roman Patriarchal Society." *Klio* 71 (1989): 604–19.

Säflund, M.-L. *The East Pediment of the Temple of Zeus at Olympia: A Reconstruction and Interpretation of its Composition.* Studies in Mediterranean Archaeology. Göteborg: Lund, 1970.

Saller, R. P. "The Social Dynamics of Consent to Marriage and Sexual Relations: The Evidence of Roman Comedy." In *Consent and Coercion to Sex and Marriage in Ancient and Medieval Societies,* edited by A. E. Laiou, 83–104. Washington, DC: Dumbarton Oaks, 1993.

Saller, R. P. "Corporal Punishment, Authority, and Obedience in the Roman Household." In *Marriage, Divorce, and Children in Ancient Rome,* edited by B. Rawson, 144–65. Oxford: Oxford University Press, 1991.

Saller, R. P. "Men's Age at Marriage and its Consequences in the Roman Family." *Classical Philology* 82 (1987): 21–34.

Saller, R. P. "*Pater Familias, Mater Familias* and the Gendered Semantics of the Roman Household." *Classical Philology* 94 (1999): 182–97.

Saller, R. P. "*Patria Potestas* and the Stereotype of the Roman Family." *Continuity and Change* 1 (1986): 7–22.

Saller, R. P. *Patriarchy, Property, and Death in the Roman Family.* Cambridge: Cambridge University Press, 1994.

Saller, R. P. "Slavery and the Roman Family." In *Classical Slavery,* edited by M. I. Finley, 65–87. London: F. Cass, 1987.

Salviat, F., and C. Vatin. "La répression des violences sexuelles dans la convention entre Delphes et Pellana, le droit d'Athènes et les lois de Platon." In *Inscriptions de Grèce Centrale,* 63–75. Paris: Editions de Boccard, 1971.

Sanders, S. A., and J. M. Reinisch. "Would You Say You 'Had Sex' If ... ?" *Journal of the American Medical Association* 281 (1999): 275–77.

Sansone, D. *Greek Athletics and the Genesis of Sport*. Berkeley: University of California Press, 1988.

Scanlon, T. F. "The Dispersion of Pederasty and the Athletic Revolution in Sixth-century B.C. Greece." In *Same-Sex Desire and Love in Greco-Roman Antiquity and in the Classical Tradition of the West*, edited by B. C. Verstraete and V. Provencal, 63–85. Binghamton: Haworth Press, 2005.

Scanlon, T. F. *Eros and Greek Athletics*. Oxford: Oxford University Press, 2002.

Schaff, P. *The Twelve Patriarchs, Excerpts and Epistles, The Clementina, Apocrypha, Decretals, Memoirs of Edessa and Syriac Documents, Remains of the First Ages*. Vol. 8 of *The Ante-Nicene Fathers: Translations of the Writings of the Fathers down to A.D. 325*. New York: Charles Scribner's Sons, 1899.

Scheidel, W. *Measuring Sex, Age and Death in the Roman Empire: Explorations in Ancient Demography. Journal of Roman Archaeology* Supplement 21. Portsmouth, RI: Journal of Roman Archaeology, 1996.

Schleiner, W. *Medical Ethics in the Renaissance*. Washington, DC: Georgetown University Press, 1995.

Schmitz, W. "Der nomos moicheias—Das athenische Gesetz über den Ehebruch." *Zeitschrift der Savigny-Stiftung für Rechtsgeschichte. Romanistische Abteilung* 114 (1997): 45–140.

Schnapp, A. "Eros the Hunter." In *A City of Images: Iconography and Society in Ancient Greece*, edited by C. Bérard et al., translated by D. Lyons, 71–88. Princeton, NJ: Princeton University Press, 1989.

Scott S. P. *Corpus Iuris Civilis*, vols. I–17. New York: AMS Press, 1973.

Sergent, B. *Homosexuality in Greek Myth*, translated by A. Goldhammer. London: Athlone, 1987.

Severy, B. *Augustus and the Family at the Birth of the Roman Empire*. New York: Routledge, 2003.

Shackleton Bailey, D. R. "Notes on Minor Latin Poetry." *Phoenix* 32 (1978): 305–25.

Shapiro, H. A. *Art, Myth, and Culture: Greek Vases from Southern Collections*. New Orleans: New Orleans Museum of Art, Tulane University, 1981.

Shapiro, H. A. "Autochthony and the Visual Arts in Fifth-century Athens." In *Democracy, Empire, and the Arts in Fifth-century Athens*, edited by D. Boedeker and K. Raaflaub, 127–51. Cambridge, MA: Harvard University Press, 1998.

Shapiro, H. A. "Courtship Scenes in Attic Vase-Painting." *American Journal of Archaeology* 85 (1981): 133–43.

Shapiro, H. A. "Eros in Love: Pederasty and Pornography in Greece." In *Pornography and Representation in Greece and Rome*, edited by A. Richlin, 53–72. New York: Oxford University Press, 1992.

Shapiro, H. A. "Leagros and Euphronios: Painting Pederasty in Athens." In *Greek Love Reconsidered*, edited by T. K. Hubbard, 12–32. New York: W. Hamilton Press, 2000.

Sharp, J. *The Midwives Book*, edited by E. Hobby, *The Midwives Book, Or, the Whole Art of Midwifry Discovered*. 1671. New York: Oxford University Press, 1999.

Shaw, B. "The Age of Roman Girls at Marriage: Some Reconsiderations." *Journal of Roman Studies* 77 (1987): 30–46.

Shaw, B. "Review of Thomas A. J. McGinn, *Prostitution, Sexuality and the Law in Ancient Rome.*" *Bryn Mawr Classical Review.* http://ccat.sas.upenn.edu/bmcr/1999/1999-09-22.html.

Shaw, B., and R. Saller. "Tombstones and Family Relations in the Principate: Civilians, Soldiers, and Slaves." *Journal of Roman Studies* 74 (1984): 124–56.

Shiach, Morag. *Discourse on Popular Culture.* Cambridge: Polity Press, 1989.

Shrimpton, G. S. *Theopompus the Historian.* Montreal: McGill-Queen's University Press, 1991.

Siebert, G. "Un bol à reliefs inscrit à représentations érotiques." *Antike Kunst* 27 (1984): 14–20.

Siebert, G. "Hermes." In *Lexicon Iconographicum Mythologiae Classicae* 5, 285–387. Zürich: Artemis, 1990.

Simon, B. *Mind and Madness in Ancient Greece: The Classical Roots of Modern Psychiatry.* Ithaca, NY: Cornell University Press, 1978.

Simon, E. *Festivals of Attica: An Archaeological Commentary.* Madison: University of Wisconsin Press, 1983.

Sinos, R., and J. Oakley. *The Wedding in Ancient Athens.* Madison: University of Wisconsin Press, 1993.

Sissa, G. "Maidenhood without Maidenhead: The Female Body in Ancient Greece," translated by R. Lamberton. In *Before Sexuality: The Construction of Erotic Experience in the Ancient Greek World*, edited by D. M. Halperin, J. J. Winkler, and F. I. Zeitlin, 339–64. Princeton, NJ: Princeton University Press, 1990.

Skinner, M. "Clodia Metelli." *Transactions of the American Philological Association* 113 (1983): 273–87.

Skinner, M. *Sexuality in Greek and Roman Culture.* Oxford: Blackwell, 2005.

Skoda, F. *Médecine ancienne et métaphore: Le vocabulaire de l'anatomie et de la pathologie en grec ancien.* Paris: Peeters/Selaf, 1988.

Small, J. "Scholars, Etruscans, and Attic Painted Vases." *Journal of Roman Archaeology* 7 (1994): 34–58.

Smallwood, E. M. "The Legislation of Hadrian and Antoninus Pius against Circumcision." *Latomus* 18 (1959): 334–47.

Snodgrass, A. M. *Archaic Greece: The Age of Experiment.* Berkeley: University of California Press, 1980.

Snyder, J. M. *Lesbian Desire in the Lyrics of Sappho.* New York: Columbia University Press, 1997.

Solin, H. "Un epigramma della Domus Aurea." *Rivista di filologia e di istruzione classica* 109 (1981): 268–71.

Solin, H. "Griechische Graffiti aus Ostia." *Arctos* 7 (1972): 190–99.

Solin, H. "Pompeiana." *Epigraphica* 30 (1968): 105–25.

Solin, H. "Die Wandinschriften im sog. Haus des M. Fabius Rufus." In *Neue Forschungen in Pompeji und den anderen vom Vesuvausbruch 79 nach Christus verschütteten Städten*, 243–66. Recklinghausen: Bongers, 1975.

Sommerstein, A. H., ed. and trans. *Aristophanes* Clouds. Atlantic Highlands, NJ: Humanities Press, 1982.

Sommerstein, A. H. "Rape and Consent in Athenian Tragedy." In *Dionysalexandros: Essays on Aeschylus and His Fellow Tragedians in Honour of Alexander F. Garvie*, edited by D. L. Cairns and V. Liapis, 233–51. Swansea: Classical Press of Wales, 2006.

Sourvinou-Inwood, C. "Something to Do with Athens: Tragedy and Ritual." In *Ritual Finance Politics: Athenian Democratic Accounts Presented to David Lewis*, edited by R. Osborne and S. Hornblower, 269–90. Oxford: Oxford University Press, 1994.

Sparkes, B. A. *The Red and the Black: Studies in Greek Pottery*. London: Routledge, 1996.

Sparkes, B. A. "Sex in Classical Athens." In *Greek Civilisation: An Introduction*, edited by B. A. Sparkes, 216–31. Oxford: Blackwell, 1998.

Spivey, N. "Greek Vases in Etruria." In *Looking at Greek Vases*, edited by T. Rasmussen and N. Spivey, 131–50. Cambridge: Cambridge University Press, 1991.

Stähli, A. *Die Verweigerung der Lüste: erotische Gruppen in der antiken Plastik*. Berlin: Reimer, 1999.

Stansbury-O'Donnell, M. *Vase Painting, Gender, and Social Identity in Archaic Athens*. New York: Cambridge University Press, 2006.

Starr, C. "An Evening with the Flute-girls." *La Parola del Passato* 33 (1978): 401–10.

Stears, K. "Dead Women's Society: Constructing Female Gender in Classical Athenian Funerary Sculpture." In *Time, Tradition, and Society in Greek Archaeology: Bridging the "Great Divide,"* edited by N. Spencer, 109–31. London: Routledge, 1995.

Stehle, E. "Venus, Cybele, and the Sabine Women: The Roman Construction of Female Sexuality." *Helios* 16 (1989): 143–64.

Steinberg, L. *The Sexuality of Christ in Renaissance Art and in Modern Oblivion*. New York: Pantheon Books, 1983.

Steiner, A. *Reading Greek Vases*. Cambridge: Cambridge University Press, 2007.

Steingräber, S., ed. *Etruscan Painting: Catalogue Raisonné of Etruscan Wall Paintings*. New York: Harcourt Brace Jovanovich, 1985.

Stevens, J. *Reproducing the State*. Princeton, NJ: Princeton University Press, 1999.

Stewart, A. F. *Art, Desire, and the Body in Ancient Greece*. Cambridge: Cambridge University Press, 1997.

Stewart, A. F. "Reflections." In *Sexuality in Ancient Art*, edited by N. B. Kampen, 136–54. New York: Cambridge University Press, 1996.

Stissi, V. "Production, Circulation, and Consumption of Archaic Greek Pottery (Sixth and Early Fifth Centuries B.C.)." In *The Complex Past of Pottery: Production, Circulation and Consumption of Mycenaean and Greek Pottery (16th to Early 5th Centuries B.C.)*, edited by J. P. Crielaard, V. Stissi, and G. J. van Wijngaarden, 83–113. Amsterdam: J. C. Gieben, 1999.

Stol, M. *Birth in Babylonia and the Bible: Its Mediterranean Setting*. Groningen: Styx/Brill, 2000.

Storey, J. *Cultural Theory and Popular Culture: An Introduction*, 4th ed. Athens, GA: University of Georgia Press, 2006.

Storey, J. *Inventing Popular Culture: From Folklore to Globalization*. Malden, MA: Blackwell, 2003.

Storey, J. "The Popular." In *New Keywords: A Revised Vocabulary of Culture and Society,* edited by T. Bennett, L. Grossberg, and M. Morris. Malden, MA: Blackwell, 2005.

Strauss, B. *Fathers and Sons in Athens: Ideology and Society in the Era of the Peloponnesian War.* Princeton, NJ: Princeton University Press, 1994.

Strauss, L. *The Argument and the Action of Plato's Laws.* Chicago: University of Chicago Press, 1975.

Strong, R. A. "The Most Shameful Practice: Temple Prostitution in the Ancient Greek World." PhD dissertation, University of California, Los Angeles, 1997.

Stroud, R. S. *Drakon's Law on Homicide.* Berkeley: University of California Press, 1968.

Sutton, R. F. "The Good, the Base and the Ugly: The Drunken Orgy in Attic Vase Painting and the Athenian Self." In *Not the Classical Ideal: Athens and the Construction of the Other in Greek Art,* edited by B. Cohen, 180–202. Leiden: Brill, 2000.

Sutton, R. F. "Pornography and Persuasion on Attic Pottery." In *Pornography and Representation in Greece and Rome,* edited by A. Richlin, 3–35. New York: Oxford University Press, 1992.

Sweet, W. "Protection of the Genitals in Greek Athletics." *Ancient World* 11 (1985): 43–52.

Syme, R. "Bastards in the Roman Aristocracy." *Proceedings of the American Philosophical Society* 104 (1960): 323–27.

Syme, R. "Livy and Augustus." *Harvard Studies in Classical Philology* 64 (1959): 27–87.

Talalay, L. E. "Body Imagery of the Ancient Aegean." *Archaeology* 44 (1991): 46–49.

Talalay, L. E. *Deities, Dolls, and Devices: Neolithic Figurines from Franchthi Cave, Greece.* Bloomington: Indiana University Press, 1993.

Talalay, L. E. "A Feminist Boomerang: The Great Goddess of Greek Prehistory." *Gender and History* 6 (1994): 165–83.

Tamanaha, B. Z. *Realistic Socio-Legal Theory: Pragmatism and a Social Theory of Law.* Oxford: Clarendon Press, 1997.

Tanzer, H. H. *The Common People of Pompeii: A Study of the Graffiti.* Baltimore: Johns Hopkins University Press, 1939.

Taplin, O. "Phallology, *phlyakes,* Iconography and Aristophanes." *Proceedings of the Cambridge Philological Society* 33 (1987): 92–104.

Temkin, J. "Rape and Criminal Justice at the Millennium." In *Feminist Perspectives on Criminal Law,* edited by D. Nicholson and L. Biddings, 183–203. London: Cavendish, 2000.

Temkin, O. *Galenism: Rise and Decline of a Medical Philosophy.* Ithaca, NY: Cornell University Press, 1973.

Temkin, O. *Soranus' Gynecology.* Baltimore: Johns Hopkins University Press, 1956.

Thompson, D. J. *Memphis under the Ptolemies.* Princeton, NJ: Princeton University Press, 1988.

Thornton, B. S. *Eros: The Myth of Ancient Greek Sexuality.* Boulder, CO: Westview Press, 1997.

Todd, A. E. "Three Pompeian Wall-inscriptions, and Petronius." *Classical Review* 53 (1939): 5–9.

Todd, S. "Lady Chatterley's Lover and the Attic Orators: The Social Composition of the Athenian Jury." *Journal of Hellenic Studies* 110 (1990): 146–73.

Todd, S. *The Shape of Athenian Law.* Oxford: Oxford University Press, 1993.

Todd, S. "Some Notes on the Regulation of Sexuality in Athenian Law." In *Symposion 2003: Vorträge zur griechischen und hellenistischen Rechtsgeschichte,* edited by H. A. Rupprecht, 93–111. Vienna: Verlag der Österreichischen Akademie der Wissenschaften, 2006.

Toner, J. *Popular Culture in Ancient Rome.* Cambridge: Polity, 2009.

Toohey, P. *Melancholy, Love and Time: Boundaries of the Self in Ancient Literature.* Ann Arbor: University of Michigan Press, 2004.

Totelin, L. "Sex and Vegetables in the Hippocratic Gynaecological Treatises." *Studies in History and Philosophy of Biological and Medical Sciences* 38 (2007): 531–40.

Tracy, V. "The *Leno-Maritus.*" *Classical Journal* 72 (1976): 62–64.

Treggiari, S. "*Concubinae.*" *Papers of the British School at Rome* 49 (1981): 59–81.

Treggiari, S. "Libertine Ladies." *Classical World* 64 (1971): 196–98.

Treggiari S. *Roman Marriage: Iusti Coniuges from the Time of Cicero to the Time of Ulpian.* Oxford: Clarendon Press, 1991.

Tsakirgis, B. "Living and Working around the Athenian Agora: A Preliminary Case Study of Three Houses." In *Ancient Greek Houses and Households: Chronological, Regional, and Social Diversity,* edited by B. A. Ault and L. C. Nevett. Philadelphia: University of Pennsylvania Press, 2005.

Uden, J. "Impersonating Priapus." *American Journal of Philology* 128 (2007): 1–26.

Väänänen, V. *Graffiti del Palatino,* 2 vols. Helsinki: Institutum Romanum Finlandiae, *Acta,* vol. 3, 4, 1966.

Väänänen, V. *Le latin vulgaire des inscriptions pompéiennes,* 3rd ed. Berlin: Akademie Verlag, 1966.

van Bremen, R. "Women and Wealth." In *Images of Women in Antiquity,* edited by A. Kuhrt and A. Cameron, 223–42. London: Croom Helm, 1983.

van Wees, H. "The Seleucid Army." *Classical Review* 47 (1997): 356–57.

Varone, A. *Erotica Pompeiana: Love Inscriptions on the Walls of Pompeii,* translated by R. P. Berg. Rome: 'L'Erma' di Bretschneider, 2001.

Varone, A. *Erotica Pompeiana: Love Inscriptions on the Walls of Pompeii,* translated by R. P. Berg, with revisions by David Harwood and Roger Ling. Rome: 'L'Erma' di Bretschneider, 2002.

Varone, A. *Eroticism in Pompeii,* translated by M. Fant. Los Angeles: 'L'Erma' di Bretschneider and J. Paul Getty Museum, 2001.

Vassileiou, A. "Un graffito métrique érotique de Villards d'Héria." In *Mélanges É. Bernand,* edited by N. Fick and J. C. Carrière, 369–86. Paris: Les Belles Lettres, 1991.

Vatin, C. *Recherches sur le mariage et la condition de la femme mariée à l' époque hellénistique.* Paris: E. de Boccard, 1970.

Vattuone, R. *Il mostro e il sapiente: Studi sull'erotica greca.* Bologna: Pàtron, 2004.

Veith, I. *Hysteria: The History of a Disease.* Chicago: University of Chicago Press, 1965.

Vérilhac, A.-M., and C. Vial. *Le mariage grec du vi*ᵉ *siècle av. J.-C. à l'époque d'Auguste.* Paris: Dépositaire, 1998.

Versluys, M. J. *Aegyptiaca Romana: Nilotic Scenes and the Roman Views of Egypt.* Leiden: Brill, 2002.

Verstraete, B. C., and V. Provencal, eds. *Same-Sex Desire and Love in Greco-Roman Antiquity and in the Classical Tradition of the West.* Binghamton: Haworth Press, 2005.

Veyne, P. "La famille et l'amour sous le haut-empire romain." *Annales (ESC)* 33 (1978): 35–63.

Vickers, M. J. "Artful Crafts: The Influence of Metal Work on Athenian Painted Pottery." *Journal of Hellenic Studies* 105 (1985): 108–28.

Vickers, M. J., and D. Gill. *Artful Crafts: Ancient Greek Silverware and Pottery.* Oxford: Clarendon Press, 1994.

Vidal-Naquet, P. *The Black Hunter: Forms of Thought and Forms of Society in the Greek World,* translated by A. Szegedy-Maszak. Baltimore: Johns Hopkins University Press, 1986.

Vlastos, G. "Socratic Irony." *Classical Quarterly* 37 (1987): 79–96.

Vogt, J. *Ancient Slavery and the Ideal of Man,* translated by T. Wiedemann. Cambridge, MA: Harvard University Press, 1975.

Voigt, E.-M. *Sappho et Alcaeus.* Amsterdam: Athenaeum-Polak and Van Gennep, 1971.

von Staden, H., ed., tr., and comm. *Herophilus: The Art of Medicine in Alexandria.* Cambridge: Cambridge University Press, 1989.

Vorberg, G. *Glossarium eroticum.* Hanau am Main: Müller & Kiepenheuer, 1965. (Reprint of original ed. Stuttgart, 1928–32.)

Vout, C. *Power and Eroticism in Imperial Rome.* Cambridge: Cambridge University Press, 2007.

Wack, M. F. *Lovesickness in the Middle Ages: The Viaticum and its Commentaries.* Philadelphia: University of Pennsylvania Press, 1990.

Walcot, P. "Romantic Love and True Love: Greek Attitudes to Marriage." *Ancient Society* 18 (1987): 5–33.

Wallace-Hadrill, A. "Family and Inheritance in the Augustan Marriage Laws." *Proceedings of the Cambridge Philological Society* 27 (1981): 58–80.

Wallace-Hadrill, A. "Public Honour and Private Shame: The Urban Texture of Pompeii." In *Urban Society in Roman Italy,* edited by T. Cornell and K. Lomas, 39–62. New York: St. Martin's Press, 1995.

Walsh, G. B. "The Rhetoric of Birthright and Race in Euripides' Ion." *Hermes* 106 (1978): 301–15.

Walsh, J. J. *Aristotle's Concept of Moral Weakness.* New York: Columbia University Press, 1964.

Walters, J. "Invading the Roman Body: Manliness and Impenetrability in Roman Thought." In *Roman Sexualities,* edited by J. P. Hallett and M. B. Skinner, 29–43. Princeton, NJ: Princeton University Press, 1997.

Ward, R. B. "Women in Roman Baths." *Harvard Theological Review* 85 (1992): 125–47.

Watson, L. "Catullus and the Poetics of Incest." *Antichthon* 40 (2006): 35–48.

Watson, P. A. "*Non tristis torus et tamen pudicus*: The Sexuality of the *matrona* in Martial." *Mnemosyne* 58 (2005): 62–87.

Weaver, P.R.C. "The Status of Children in Mixed Marriages." In *The Family in Ancient Rome: New Perspectives*, edited by B. Rawson, 145–69. Sydney: Croom Helm, 1986.

Weber, Max. *Economy and Society: An Outline of Interpretive Sociology*, 2 vols. Berkeley: University of California Press, 1978.

Wertheimer, A. *Consent to Sexual Relations*. Cambridge: Cambridge University Press, 2003.

West, M. L. *Studies in Greek Elegy and Iambus*. Berlin: de Gruyter, 1974.

White, R. J., tr. and comm. *The Interpretation of Dreams:* Oneirocritica *by Artemidorus*. Park Ridge, NJ: Noyes Classical Studies, 1975.

Whitehead, D. "Norms of Citizenship in Ancient Greece." In *City States in Classical Antiquity and Medieval Italy: Athens and Rome, Florence and Venice,* edited by A. Molho, K. A. Raaflaub, and J. Emlen, 135–54. Ann Arbor: University of Michigan Press, 1991.

Wilcken, U. *Urkunden der Ptolemäerzeit*. Berlin: Walter de Gruyter, 1978.

Wiles, D. "Marriage and Prostitution in Classical New Comedy." *Themes in Drama* 11 (1989): 31–48.

Wilkins, J. *The Boastful Chef: The Discourse of Food in Ancient Greek Comedy*. Oxford: Oxford University Press, 2000.

Wilkins, J., D. Harvey, and M. Dobson, eds. *Food in Antiquity*. Exeter: Exeter University Press, 1995.

Williams, C. A. *Roman Homosexuality: Ideologies of Masculinity in Classical Antiquity*. Oxford: Oxford University Press, 1999.

Williams, D. *The Warren Cup*. London: British Museum Press, 2006.

Williams, G. "*Libertino patre natus*: True or False?" In *Homage to Horace: A Bimillenary Celebration*, edited by S. J. Harrison, 296–313. Oxford: Clarendon Press, 1995.

Williams, R. *Culture and Society 1780–1950*, 2nd ed. Harmondsworth: Penguin, 1971.

Winkler, J. J. *The Constraints of Desire*. London: Routledge, 1990.

Winkler, J. J., and F. I. Zeitlin, eds. *Nothing to Do With Dionysos? Athenian Drama in its Social Context*. Princeton, NJ: Princeton University Press, 1989.

de Wit, C. "La circoncision chez les anciens Egyptiens." *Zeitschrift für Ägyptische Sprache und Altertumskunde* 99 (1972): 41–48.

Wohl, V. *Love among the Ruins: The Erotics of Democracy in Classical Athens*. Princeton, NJ: Princeton University Press, 2002.

Wohl, V. "Scenes from a Marriage: Love and Logos in Plutarch's *Coniugalia Praecepta*." *Helios* 24 (1997): 170–92.

Wolff, H. J. "Marriage Law and Family Organization in Ancient Athens: A Study of the Interrelation of Public and Private Law in the Greek City." *Traditio* 2 (1944): 43–95.

Wright, R. *The Moral Animal: Why We Are, the Way We Are: The New Science of Evolutionary Psychology*. New York: Pantheon, 1994.

Wuilleumier, P., and A. Audin. *Les médaillons d'applique gallo-romains de la vallée du Rhône*. Paris: Les Belles Lettres, 1952.

Wyse, W. *The Speeches of Isaeus*. Cambridge: Cambridge University Press, 1904.

Yanal, R. J. "The Institutional Theory of Art." In *The Encyclopedia of Aesthetics*, edited by M. Kelly. Oxford: Oxford University Press, 1998.

Yates, V. "*Anterastai:* Competition in *eros* and Politics in Classical Athens." *Arethusa* 38 (2005): 33–47.

Yatromanolakis, Y. "Poleos erastes: The Greek City as the Beloved." In *Personification in the Greek World: From Antiquity to Byzantium*, edited by E. Stafford and J. Herrin, 267–83. Aldershot: Ashgate, 2005.

Young, R. S. "Graves from the Phaleron Cemetery." *American Journal of Archaeology* 46 (1942): 23–57.

Younger, J. G. "Bronze Age Representations of Aegean Bull-games, III." In *Politeia* (*Aegaeum* 12), edited by R. Laffineur and P. B. Betancourt, 507–45. Liège: Université de Liège, 1995.

Younger, J. G. *Sex in the Ancient World From A to Z*. New York: Routledge, 2005.

Younger, J. G. "Waist Compression in the Aegean Late Bronze Age." *Archaeological News* 23 (1998–2000): 1–9.

Yuval-Davis, N., and F. Anthias. *Woman-Nation-State*. New York: St. Martin's Press, 1989.

Zacharia, K. *Converging Truths: Euripides' Ion and the Athenian Quest for Self-Definition*. Leiden: Brill, 2003.

Zanker, P. *Pompeii: Public and Private Life*, translated by D. L. Schneider. Cambridge, MA: Harvard University Press, 1998.

Zeitlin, F. I. *Playing the Other: Gender and Society in Classical Greek Literature*. Chicago: University of Chicago Press, 1996.

Ziebarth, E. "Neue Verfluchungstafeln aus Attika, Boiotien und Euboia," Preussische [Deutsche] Akademie der Wissenschaften. *Sitzungsberichte* (1934): 1022–50.

Zimmermann, K. "Tätowierte Thrakerinnen auf griechischen Vasenbildern." *Jahrbuch des deutschen archäologischen Instituts* 95 (1980): 163–96.

CONTRIBUTORS

John R. Clarke is Annie Laurie Howard Regents Professor of Fine Arts in the Department of Art and Art History at the University of Texas at Austin. He is the author of seven books and seventy-eight essays, articles, and reviews, including *Roman Black-and-White Figural Mosaics; The Houses of Roman Italy, 100 B.C.–A.D. 250: Ritual, Space, and Decoration; Looking at Lovemaking: Constructions of Sexuality in Roman Art, 100 B.C.–A.D. 250; Art in the Lives of Ordinary Romans: Visual Representation and Non-elite Viewers in Italy, 100 B.C.–A.D. 315; Roman Sex, 100 B.C.–A.D. 250; Looking at Laughter: Humor, Power, and Transgression in Roman Visual Culture, 100 B.C.–A.D. 250;* and *Roman Life, 100 B.C.–A.D. 200.*

Esther Eidinow teaches at Newman University College, Birmingham. Among her publications are *Oracles, Curses, and Risk Among the Ancient Greeks* (Oxford University Press, 2007), and *Luck, Fate and Fortune: Antiquity and Its Legacy* (I.B. Tauris, forthcoming).

Allison Glazebrook is an associate professor in the Department of Classics at Brock University. Her research relates to the social and cultural history of ancient Greece, focusing on gender and sexuality and ancient rhetoric. Professor Glazebrook's current work focuses on images of women in public male discourse. She is the author of a number of articles on Greek social and cultural history. Allison Glazebrook has edited (with M. M. Henry) *The Greek Prostitute in Context* (University of Wisconsin Press).

Mark Golden is Professor of Classics at the University of Winnipeg and author of, among other books, *Children and Childhood in Classical Athens; Sport and*

Society in Ancient Greece; Sport in the Ancient World from A to Z; and *Greek Sport and Social Status.*

Helen King is Professor of the History of Classical Medicine in the Department of Classics at the University of Reading. A specialist in ancient medicine, she is the author of many books, including *Hippocrates' Woman: Reading the Female Body in Ancient Greece; Greek and Roman Medicine; The Disease of Virgins: Green-Sickness, Chlorosis and the Problems of Puberty; Midwifery, Obstetrics and the Rise of Gynaecology;* and *La Médecine dans l'Antiquité grecque et romaine.*

Susan Lape is Associate Professor of Classics in the Department of Classics at the University of Southern California. She is the author of *Reproducing Athens: Menander's Comedy, Democratic Culture, and the Hellenistic City.* She is currently working on *Demosthenes: Democracy in Difficult Times* under contract with Longman.

Daniel Ogden is Professor of Ancient History in the Department of Classics and Ancient History at the University of Exeter and Academic Associate, UNISA. He is the author of many books. A few of his most recent are *Greek Bastardy in the Classical and Hellenistic Periods; The Crooked Kings of Ancient Greece; Polygamy, Prostitutes and Death: The Hellenistic Dynasties; Greek and Roman Necromancy; Magic, Witchcraft and Ghosts in the Greek and Roman Worlds: A Sourcebook;* and *Night's Black Agents: Witches, Wizards and Ghosts in the Ancient World.*

Holt Parker is Professor of Classics in the Department of Classics at the University of Cincinnati. He has been awarded the Rome Prize, the Women's Classical Caucus Prize for Scholarship, a Loeb Library Foundation grant, and a fellowship from the National Endowment for the Humanities. He also won first prize for shaped yeast bread at the Hamilton County (Ohio) Fair. Among his books are *Olympia Morata: The Complete Writings of an Italian Heretic* and an edition of the *Gynecology* by Metrodora, the oldest surviving work by a woman doctor (forthcoming in *Brill's Studies in Ancient Medicine*). His translation (the first in English) of Censorinus's curious work, *The Birthday Book,* is forthcoming from Chicago.

Peter Toohey is a professor in the Department of Greek and Roman Studies at the University of Calgary and is author of, among other books, *Reading Epic; Epic Lessons;* and *Melancholy, Love, and Time.*

John Younger is Professor of Classics and of Humanities and Western Civilization in the Department of Classics at the University of Kansas. His research focuses on the Bronze Age Aegean and on Greek art, especially sculpture. He has written two books on Minoan-Mycenaean sealstones, as well as one on *Music in the Aegean Bronze Age*. He has also written numerous articles and reviews on various Bronze Age and classical topics. His most recent work has centered on gender and sexuality: *Sex in the Ancient World from A to Z*. Works in progress include a holistic analysis of Cretan hieroglyphic, and *Greek Art & Archaeology, a Social History* (Blackwell).

INDEX OF ANCIENT SOURCES

Compiled by John Tamm

SUBJECT INDEX

Compiled by John Tamm

Italic numbers denote reference to illustrations.